Christianity
and Monasticism
in Upper Egypt

Christianity and Monasticism in Upper Egypt

Volume I
Akhmim and Sohag

Edited by
Gawdat Gabra
Hany N. Takla

A Saint Mark Foundation Book
The American University in Cairo Press
Cairo New York

Copyright © 2008 by
The American University in Cairo Press
113 Sharia Kasr el Aini, Cairo, Egypt
420 Fifth Avenue, New York, NY 10018
www.aucpress.com

Dar el Kutub No. 13710/07
ISBN 978 977 416 122 3

Dar el Kutub Cataloging-in-Publication Data

Gabra, Gawdat
        Christianity and Monasticism in Upper Egypt: Volume 1:
    Akhmim and Sohag / edited by Gawdat Gabra and Hany Takla.—Cairo:
    The American University in Cairo Press, 2007
            p.   cm.
        ISBN 977 416 122 X
        1. Christianity—Egypt—Sohag   I. Gabra, Gawdat (ed.)
        II. Takla, Hany (Jt. ed.)
        270.96231

 1 2 3 4 5 6 7 8   12 11 10 09 08

Designed by Fatiha Bouzidi / AUC Press Design Center
Printed in Egypt

This volume is dedicated to
His Holiness Pope Shenouda III

Contents

Preservation

Illustrations

Figures

Contributors

Heike Behlmer teaches Coptic studies in the department of ancient history, Macquarie University, Sydney, where she has developed the online M.A. program in Coptic studies. Her research interests include Egyptian monasticism, Coptic literature, and gender studies.

Elizabeth S. Bolman is associate professor of medieval art history at Temple University, Philadelphia. She specializes in Coptic and Byzantine art, and is currently directing conservation and archaeology at the Red and White Monasteries in Sohag.

Anne Boud'hors is a CNRS researcher at the Institut de Recherche et d'Histoire des Textes, Paris. Her specialties are Coptic language, literature, and manuscripts and she has edited several catalogues of biblical fragments. She is currently working on Shenoute's *Canons* 8 and on documentary ostraca from the Theban era.

Andrew Crislip is associate professor of religion at the University of Hawaii. He is the author of *From Monastery to Hospital: Christian Monasticism and the Transformation of Health Care in Late Antiquity* (2005), as well as numerous articles on health and illness in early Christianity and Coptic papyrology.

Stephen Emmel is professor of Coptology at the University of Münster, Germany, and former president and now secretary of the International Association for Coptic Studies. He is the author of *Shenoute's Literary Corpus* (2004) and the director of an international project to edit and translate the complete works of Shenoute.

Cäcilia Fluck is a freelance consultant for the Museum of Byzantine Art in Berlin and the University of Münster. She has published books and articles on Egyptian epigraphy and archaeology, particularly textiles, of the late antique and early Christian periods.

James E. Goehring is professor of religion at the University of Mary Washington in Fredericksburg, Virginia. He is author of *Ascetics, Society, and the Desert: Studies in Early Egyptian Monasticism* (1999) and co-editor of *The World of Early Egyptian Christianity* (2007).

Suzana Hodak is a teaching fellow at the Institute for Egyptology and Coptology, Münster. She has worked on several aspects of Coptic art, especially on textiles, and is responsible for the publication of the written documents found in the current excavation of the Dayr al-Bakhit. She is currently working on a project on Coptic ostraca from the Theban area.

Dale Kinney is Eugenia Chase Guild Professor in the Humanities at Bryn Mawr College. She is a specialist in late antique and medieval art and architecture.

Rebecca Krawiec is assistant professor of religious studies and theology at Canisius College in Buffalo, New York. She is the author of *Shenoute and the Women of the White Monastery: Female Monasticism in Late Antiquity* (2002).

Bentley Layton is professor of religious studies and of near eastern languages and civilizations at Yale University. He is currently editing two books of Shenoute's *Canons*, and is author of a Coptic reference grammar, a catalogue of Coptic manuscripts in the British Library, and gnostic text editions.

Catherine Louis is a CNRS researcher at the UMR 7044 (Étude des civilisations de l'antiquité), Strasbourg. Her specialties are Coptic literature and manuscripts. She is preparing several catalogues of literary fragments, and editions of Coptic texts.

Nina Lubomierski studied theology and Coptology in Tübingen, Heidelberg, and Münster and is ordained minister of the Evangelisch-Lutherische Landeskirche in Bayern. She is author of *Die Vita Sinuthii* (2007) and several articles on related subjects.

Nashaat Mekhaiel is doctoral candidate at the University of Münster. His field of research is the Difnar. He is the author of a number of articles on this theme.

Samuel Moawad is a researcher at the University of Leiden. He is also a member of the international project to edit and translate the complete works of Shenoute. He has published articles on Coptic monasticism, Coptic history, and Copto-Arabic literature.

Siegfried G. Richter is a member of the Academy Project Editio Critica Maior of the North Rhine-Westphalian Academy of Science and Humanities at the University of Münster Institute for New Testament Textual Research. He has taught Coptic and Oriental studies in Münster, Bonn, and Munich and is the author of several books and articles on history, culture, and religion in late antique Egypt and Nubia.

Ashraf Alexandre Sadek teaches Egyptology and biblical archaeology at the University of Limoges in France. A one-time inspector for Egypt's Department of Antiquities, he is the author of books on Egyptian philology, including the first Hieroglyphics-French dictionary, and on the history of religion. For thirty years he has been the editor of the journal, *Le Monde Copte*, which has published thirty-three volumes dedicated to Coptic culture.

Sofia Schaten studied Coptology at the University of Münster. She is a member of the German/Swiss archaeological mission in Elephantine and is currently working on a publication of the Coptic ostraca found since 1969 in Elephantine.

Zuzana Skálová is a freelance specialist in the conservation of icons and their technical art history. In 1993 she established the Foundation for the Conservation of Icons in the Middle East. She is co-author of *Icons of the Nile Valley* (2003 and 2006). In 2007 she created the Mobile Icon Restoration Unit—a portable workshop that can travel to the sites of icons within Egypt—in cooperation with the Prince Claus Fund for Culture and Development (sponsor) and the Netherlands–Flemish Institute in Cairo.

Father Bigoul al-Suriany is a Coptic monk and scholar, and curator of manuscripts at the library of the Syrian Monastery in Wadi al-Natrun, responsible for the monastery's conservation, restoration, and excavation projects. He is the author of several books on Coptic history.

Mark N. Swanson is professor of Christian-Muslim studies and church history at the Lutheran School of Theology at Chicago. He co-edited *The Encounter of Eastern Christianity with Early Islam* (2006) and is completing *The Coptic Papacy in Islamic Egypt* (forthcoming from AUC Press).

Hany N. Takla is founding president of the St. Shenouda the Archimandrite Coptic Society, director of the St. Shenouda Center for Coptic Studies, Coptic language instructor at the Pope Shenouda III Theological College in Los Angeles, and a member of the board of trustees for the St. Mark Coptic Cultural Center in Cairo. He is currently a Coptic language lecturer at the University of California Los Angeles (UCLA).

Janet Timbie teaches Coptic language and literature, as well as courses on the history of the Christian Near East, in the Department of Semitic and Egyptian Languages and Literatures at the Catholic University of America. She has recently published articles on the works of Shenoute, the letters of Antony, and Gnostic literature.

Jacques van der Vliet is senior lecturer of Coptology at Leiden University, and extraordinary professor of Egyptology and Coptology at Radboud University, Nijmegen, the Netherlands. He is a member of the Polish archaeological mission in Naqlun, and participates in various epigraphical and papyrological projects.

Youhanna Nessim Youssef is senior research associate at the Centre for Early Christian Studies, Australian Catholic University. He is currently editing the Coptic and Copto-Arabic corpus of Severus of Antioch, and is the author of several books and articles on Coptic literature, history, liturgy, art, and Christian Arabic studies.

Fr. Ugo Zanetti is a monk in the Chevetogne Benedictine Monastery, Belgium. A former professor at the Université catholique de Louvain and a former Bollandist, he has published various books and articles, mainly about Copto-Arabic manuscripts and Coptic liturgy.

Foreword

Fawzy Estafanous

WHEN IN 2002 the St. Mark Foundation for Coptic History Studies began its series of symposia on Christianity and Monasticism in Egypt, I did not expect that so many competent scholars from all over the world would accept our new foundation's invitation to participate. Several factors have contributed to the success of the symposia to date. First, the invaluable support of His Holiness Pope Shenouda III. He not only hosted the first symposium, "Christianity and Monasticism in Wadi al-Natrun" in his residence at the Monastery of St. Bishoi; he inaugurated it and participated in the discussions. There is no doubt that the support of His Holiness—for the St. Mark Foundation in general and for these symposia in particular—has encouraged scholars to devote more research to Coptic monasticism. Moreover, the bishops, who, like His Holiness, were once monks, have shown great interest in welcoming scholars to speak and write about Christianity and monasticism in their dioceses. The St. Mark Foundation has received invitations from a number of bishops to host future symposia. Indeed, I am deeply indebted to His Holiness Pope Shenouda III, and I am very pleased that this volume is dedicated to him. I would also like to express my gratitude to His Grace Bishop Bisadah and His Grace Bishop Bakhoum for their great interest in the Akhmim and Sohag symposium, and to His Grace Bishop Youannes for hosting the symposium in the Monastery of St. Shenouda, Sohag.

Second, the unparalleled dedication of many great scholars to Coptic heritage and their participation in such symposia, which represent a significant contribution to the growing corpus of studies on Coptic history and culture. They willingly interrupt their routines, often traveling great distances, to enrich our symposia with their insights. I would like to thank all the scholars for their important contributions to this volume.

Third, the love and devotion of the organizers of the symposia to the Coptic Church. Their efforts continue to insure a pleasant atmosphere in the Foundation, helping in every way to achieving the aims of the symposia.

Finally, the dedication and professionalism of the staff of the American University in Cairo Press in publishing the proceedings of the symposia. I extend my thanks to them, especially to Mark Linz, director, Neil Hewison, associate director for editorial programs, and Nadia Naqib, managing editor.

Fawzy Estafanous, President
The St. Mark Foundation for Coptic History Studies

Introduction

Gawdat Gabra and Hany N. Takla

CHRISTIANITY AND MONASTICISM *in Upper Egypt, Volume I: Akhmim and Sohag*
brings together the proceedings of the third international symposium of the
St. Mark Foundation for Coptic History Studies and the St. Shenouda the
Archimandrite Coptic Society. These two institutions have decided to dedi-
cate this volume to His Holiness Pope Shenouda III in recognition of his
diligent efforts to revive ancient monastic settlements throughout Egypt and
in the Akhmim and Sohag region in particular. Such efforts are evident in
the renewed monastic life seen in the region. This has in turn facilitated
increased scholarly interest in studying and preserving these monumental
edifices of Coptic Christianity.

The majority of the papers in this volume are related to the legacy of
H.H.'s namesake, St. Shenoute the Archimandrite, who was one of the
great figures of Coptic Christianity during its golden age in the fourth and
fifth centuries. St. Shenoute began his monastic career at an early age under
the guidance of his maternal uncle Apa Bigoul (or Pjol), the founder of the
Pachomian-style White Monastery in Sohag. His asceticism and zeal for
the monastic life made the monks of his monastery choose him as their
abbot in about 385. During his eighty-year career as abbot he transformed
the monastery from a group of thirty monks to one of about four thousand monks and nuns in three different monasteries, now known as the

White Monastery Federation. His sanctity brought multitudes of visitors to his monastery, from ecclesiastical personalities to government officials and ordinary peasants. They all came to benefit from his teachings, to seek advice, and to air their grievances against the oppression of the society they were living in. His zeal for orthodox Christianity made him very effective in eradicating paganism and heterodox teachings from his geographic sphere of influence, which extended from Antinoonpolis in the north to Aswan in the south.

St. Shenoute is considered by Coptologists as the greatest known writer in the Coptic language. His writings are the most advanced texts given to students studying the language. Since 1810, when the Danish scholar, Georg Zoega, published his monumental catalogue of the Coptic manuscripts in the Vatican's Borgia collection, scholars from all over the world have studied or edited his extant writings. In the 1880s Émile Clement Amélineau identified hundreds of folios of his writings among the treasure trove that the Bibliothèque nationale of Paris (BN) acquired at the time, which represented the last remains *in situ* of the ancient library from the saint's monastery in Sohag. Amélineau also published a two-volume edition of these writings based primarily on the Borgia manuscripts. Johannes Leipoldt and Walter Ewing Crum collaborated in the early twentieth century to publish a better-edited two-volume set of the saint's writings, based primarily on the newly acquired BN collection. In 1993, Stephen Emmel revolutionized the field by identifying the surviving scattered remains of these writings as parts of a seventeen-volume corpus that was transmitted over the centuries. This monumental Yale University dissertation helped to rectify the lamentable history of the dismemberment of these writings over the centuries.

The saint's legacy was visibly preserved in the two great structures that he left us from the fifth century, known as the White and Red Monasteries. These great Christian edifices defied the test of time and continued to function as houses of worship long after the vibrant monastic life had left them. They now play a primary role in the resurgent monastic life that H.H. Pope Shenouda III has championed. Their magnificent art and architecture have intrigued travelers to Egypt for centuries and have been the subject of much scholarly writing. For the past quarter century the Egyptian government through the Supreme Council of Antiquities (SCA) has coordinated the repair and restoration of these monuments. In the past few years a new program funded by the American Research Center in Egypt (ARCE), using a team of preservationists and scholars headed by Dr. Elizabeth Bolman, has brought back to life the magnificent iconographic wall paintings of the Red Monastery church. The SCA also permitted and even conducted its own excavations of the area surrounding these two monasteries to uncover the scope of the original monastic settlements that the saint put in place during his lifetime. Visitors can clearly see evidence of these excavations and the rich history of these places.

The present volume contains contributions on the various aspects of the legacy of St. Shenoute the Archimandrite as well as the history, art, and architecture of the greater Sohag–Akhmim area that he made famous. These studies are grouped under three different categories: Language and Literature; Art, Archeology, and Material Culture; and Preservation. The majority of the studies are included in the first category, which is a testimony to the rich literary heritage that St. Shenoute has left us. They deal with his monasticism, rules, and the literary canons that he composed, as well as addressing his other writings in Coptic or attributed to him in Arabic. Others deal with the literary and liturgical sources about his life, his relationships with the patriarchs in Alexandria, and his relations to Pachomian monasticism. There are also studies dealing with the liturgical life, health services, and the famous library of the monastery, as well as with the role of the female elder of the women's monastery. Also in this category are studies dealing with the heterodox landscape of his time and the writing inscriptions found within his area of Akhmim. In the chapters discussing art and related fields, there are studies dealing with the art and architecture of the Red and White Monasteries, the famous textiles of Akhmim, the eighteenth-century style of art found in late Akhmim iconography, and descriptions of some of the older churches in the neighboring area of al-Balyana. The final section of this volume includes a study of the great conservation work carried out on the ancient church of the Red Monastery, which members of the Sohag Consortium have conducted there in 2006 and 2007 as mentioned above.

We would like to express our special thanks to His Holiness Pope Shenouda III for his continued support for the St. Mark Foundation, and to his personal secretary His Grace Bishop Youannes for hosting the symposium at the site of the St. Shenoute monastery in Sohag. Our thanks go also to His Grace Bishop Bisadah and His Grace Bishop Bakhoum for their encouragement and interest in the symposium. We would like to thank Dr. Fawzy Estafanous, President of the St. Mark Foundation, for his continued efforts in encouraging research on Coptic monasticism. Heartfelt thanks are due for the financial support received from all the supporters of the symposium, especially to Sherif Doss and Shahira Loza. Thanks are also due to the organizing committee: Fawzy Estafanous, Fahim Wassef, and Niveen Ramzy, and we would like to thank Hoda Garas, who finalized all the contracts with the contributors.

Finally, we are much obliged to the American University in Cairo Press, and especially to Mark Linz, director, Neil Hewison, associate director for editorial programs, and Nadia Naqib, managing editor, for their interest and care in publishing this volume.

1 "Do Not Believe Every Word Like the Fool . . . !"
Rhetorical Strategies in Shenoute, *Canon* 6

Heike Behlmer

ST. SHENOUTE (*floruit* ~A.D. 385–465) is the major Coptic writer of the late fourth and fifth centuries. The idea of producing texts in Coptic was not his invention, but he brought the language to a peak of literary quality which subsequent writers would struggle to attain. Characteristic of Shenoute's works is a strongly developed, Bible-based rhetoric which he uses to establish his authority as leader of his monastic congregation in Upper Egypt, which consisted of two male and one female monasteries, and to preserve it in conflict situations.[1] Shenoute speaks to his monks and nuns in the voice of biblical figures whose leadership on the path to salvation was universally acknowledged: the Old Testament Prophets and the Apostle Paul.[2] The centrality of Scripture for Shenoute's language, style, and argumentation cannot be overestimated, and in particular the creative appropriation of the biblical text shows the consummate rhetorical skill of this monastic writer. In the following I will undertake to give a demonstration of this skill, examining two passages from one of Shenoute's collections of works on monastic life. Specifically, I hope to achieve three goals:

- To show how Shenoute skillfully uses biblical quotations not only to support his own arguments, but also to deflect attacks by opponents.
- To present an instance where we can grasp a struggle within the monastic community about the correct interpretation of Scripture in the framework of a disagreement about a point of monastic discipline.

1

- To show how the careful examination of rhetorical strategies can complement codicological and philological strategies aimed at the reconstruction of the original sequence of works in a codex and the restitution of the argument.

As identified by Stephen Emmel,[3] Shenoute's works were transmitted in two major collections, nine volumes of *Canons* (mainly on monastic life) and eight volumes of *Discourses* (of various homiletic and pastoral interests). In addition to the *Canons* and *Discourses*, there are a number of letters and unclassified works. The present chapter will focus on two passages from one of the volumes of *Canons*, *Canon* 6.

Shenoute, *Canon* 6

Before I discuss these passages in detail, I will present a short overview of the structure of *Canon* 6, which is based on Stephen Emmel's reconstruction.[4] *Canon* 6 is extant in at least four copies from the library of Shenoute's monastery,[5] Codices XF, XM, XV, and YJ. Codex YK, which includes at least two works from *Canon* 6 in the same order as the other witnesses, may possibly constitute another copy of this *Canon*. *Canon* 6 originally contained at least five separate works, most probably more, since there are numerous extensive lacunae. The following five incipits are preserved: "He Who Sits Upon His Throne," "Remember O Brethren," "Is It Not Written," "Then I Am Not Obliged," and "People Have Not Understood."

Canon 6 has four main topics, several of which are present in more than one of the individual works. These topics are:
- Accusations against Shenoute of excessive force (and his defense): ("He Who Sits upon His Throne;" "Remember, O Brethren;" "Is It Not Written")
- Shenoute's illness ("Remember, O Brethren;" "Is It Not Written;" "Then I Am Not Obliged")
- Affairs of the female community ("He Who Sits upon His Throne;" "Then I Am Not Obliged;" "People Have Not Understood")
- Monastic rules

A more detailed look at the structure of *Canon* 6 will give the necessary background for the discussion of Shenoute's rhetorical strategies.

"He Who Sits Upon His Throne" is a letter addressed to the community. Shenoute defends his use of corporal punishment, especially of an elderly priest among the monks, against accusations of excessive force. Shenoute presents his disciplining the monk as divinely ordained and necessary in order to keep intact the unity of the community as the only path toward salvation.[6] A lacuna (XF 29–YJ 32) in the work before the next incipit may leave room for a new work to begin.[7] The end of the part after the lacuna belongs to a letter to a nun accused of insubordination (an offense which might have resulted in her being expelled from the community, but which is ultimately forgiven).

"Remember O Brethren" again concerns the priest's expulsion at the basis of "He Who Sits upon His Throne." It is also mentioned that Shenoute is ill.

"Is It Not Written" contains about ninety pages of preserved text (the majority of which from Codex XF), interrupted by several larger and smaller lacunae. Most probably it has to be subdivided into several works. The theme of corporal punishment also reappears. The topics of "Is It Not Written" are transgressions of the rule (stealing and hoarding of food; favoritism);[8] corporal punishment (including reference to a member who died after being beaten, possibly the same), and Shenoute's illness. Large parts of "Is It Not Written" are addressed to the monastic community (ⲦⲤⲨⲚⲀⲄⲰⲦⲎ in Coptic) in the second person singular feminine, a form of personification very frequent in both Shenoute and his successor, Besa.

"Then I Am Not Obliged" once more refers to illness. A large part of the text contains monastic rules. A long lacuna of almost fifty pages may again leave room for a new work to begin. The last part concludes with greetings to the superiors of the female community and is concerned with garments that have been sent to Shenoute by the women. Stephen Emmel[9] argues that a reference to unrest before "our old father died" cannot be used for dating. According to Emmel the only information we can glean from this reference is that *Canon* 6 must have been written after the events of *Canon* 1, which took place during Shenoute's initial career.

Finally, "People Have Not Understood" is a response to a request for a transfer by a nun from one house to another house inside the monastery because she does not get along with her superior. Both "I Am Not Obliged" and "People Have Not Understood" have been extensively analyzed by Rebecca Krawiec under the aspect of gender relations in the monastery.[10]

Shenoute's Rhetorical Strategies

In this chapter I cannot discuss the entirety of *Canon* 6, but I wish to draw attention to some interesting parts in Shenoute's rhetorical strategies. A superficial reading of *Canon* 6 may leave the reader slightly wearied owing to the relative uniformity of the predominant topic—obedience and discipline, disobedience and punishment—and the apparently repetitive attempts by Shenoute to justify himself vis-à-vis accusations of excessive severity. However, a detailed analysis of the smaller components of the texts, the individual paragraphs, sentences and phrases, allows us to capture the skill of Shenoute's phrase-turning and construction of argument. This is what the present paper aims to achieve, using examples in which Shenoute applies and adapts Scripture to make his case against his opponents.

Example 1: XM 181–185 ("De iudicio Dei")

The first example is part of a stretch of text from Codex XM following the incipit "Is It Not Written" (after four smaller and one large lacunae, which in Emmel's view could have contained a change of work).[11] Leipoldt has published this passage under the title De iudicio Dei "On the Judgment of God" (XM 175–190).[12] The entire text preserved is concerned with sinners inside the community. Shenoute introduces the particular passage I wish to discuss (XM 181-185) with, "I do not wish that some within you (scil. the community) say a word instead of another word" (XM 181).[13] Allusions about the nature of something hidden follow. Within these he gives an apparently explicit exegesis of his own words by yet another metaphor or parable. He continues, "Do not say to this book: 'law' or 'instruction' or 'commandment.' Instead, name it 'enmity' or 'sighing' or 'reproof' (XM 183)."[14] In the following Shenoute calls his writing "letter" and tells the monks explicitly how to read and interpret it. He does this by juxtaposing biblical quotations. He tells his audience expressly not to apply particular biblical quotations to his letter, but others, quotations that better convey his purpose. He instructs them, at the same time skillfully adapting the biblical text through intertextual strategies of appropriation such as additions or the substitution of the original with a new wording.

In my analysis of Shenoute's rhetorical strategies I subscribe to a functional, reception-oriented concept of literary 'intertextuality,' which analyzes the relations between individual texts, a source text (here the biblical text) and a target text (here Shenoute's quotation in its new context), and tries to classify them.[15] It aims at finding the source(s) of a quotation, analyzing the position and the function of the quotation in the target text, and noting the modifications to which the quotation can be exposed in the process of transposition. It is aware of the intentions of the text producer/author in using and modifying a quotation, but it is also aware of the necessity for the text recipient/reader to recognize, acknowledge, and possibly reinterpret a quotation. Therefore, although this concept is in contrast to the poststructuralist concept of 'intertextuality' which signifies the inescapable, unintentional, unconscious interconnectedness of all cultural phenomena, it does not intend, to use Udo Hebel's words, "to limit a text's semantic openness or to curb the theoretically unlimited and uncontrollable range of associations."[16] "Intertextuality" is defined as a specific characteristic of texts and a specific strategy of texts,[17] but the success of the strategy ultimately depends on the reader.

My analysis has also profited from Elizabeth Clark's important study "Reading Renunciation," in which she analyzes those of the late antique fathers who wish to find a biblical foundation for their propagating sexual continence. She identifies eleven rhetorical strategies by which the sometimes reluctant scriptural text is pressed into service to support the ascetical agenda, usually by skillful strategies of decontextualization and recontextualization. Clark calls one of these strategies "Talking Back."[18] Within "Talking Back" Clark actually describes two quite different strategies: on the one hand the throwing of biblical passages into the face of an opponent in a dispute, on the other the confrontation of passages by the same (biblical) author or other authoritative texts which show conflicting standpoints.

Shenoute uses the latter of these two strategies in the passage in question, when he gives explicit instructions to the audience for the interpretation of his own words. At first he tells the audience which biblical teaching not to apply to the situation, namely the ones advocating patience and gentle reproof for those erring:[19]

> Do not say of this letter, "do not count them as enemies (biblical text: count him as an enemy)[20] or teach them (biblical text: him) as a brother" (II Thessalonians 3:15) and, "bear with the weak, be patient with everyone" (I Thessalonians 5:14). This is not how it is. "Do not turn (biblical text: for you have turned) the law into bile and the fruit of righteousness into bitterness (Amos 6:12)!"

Shenoute's change to the quotation from II Thessalonians 3:15 applies it to a group instead of the individual who is the object of the biblical admonition. His substitution of a negative imperative in Amos 6:12[21] aligns the quotation with the two previous ones, which both start with an imperative, and also with the negative imperative ⲘⲠⲢ︤ⲬⲞⲞⲤ (do not say). Shenoute then proposes an alternative reading, citing biblical passages that in his

interpretation privilege the exclusion of sinners from the group. He again
adapts the biblical text to the situation at hand by continuing:

> Instead read it this way: "do not mix with one or more people who are called
> 'brother' *or 'brothers'*, if he is a fornicator *or they are fornicators* or worshippers
> of idols, greedy, reviling, robbing. Such a person *or persons*, do not eat with
> him *or them*" (I Corinthians 5:11).

The words marked in italics are additions by Shenoute and once more
apply the biblical text, which in the original is directed at an individual, to
a group of persons. The next passage is in my view a fascinating example
of Shenoute's reinterpreting Scripture even as he is quoting it, with his skill
showing clearly in the minimal invasiveness of his intervention in the text:

> Read this letter as follows: "As the violent man, the fornicator, the worship-
> per of idols, the adulterer, the effeminate,[22] the man who has intercourse
> with men, the drunkard or the reviler will not inherit the kingdom of God,
> in the same way the greedy or the robber will not inherit the kingdom of
> God" (I Corinthians 6:9b–10).

The New Testament source text lists ten categories of persons excluded
from the kingdom of God linked by OYΔE "and not." "Greedy" (MΔITO
N2OYO) and "robber" (PEЧTⲰPⲠ) are the seventh and tenth items on this
list of equal members. The structure of Shenoute's quotation is different.
He uses a comparison "as . . . will not inherit the kingdom of God (NϴE
ETEMN . . . [eight members of the original list] . . . NΔKΔHPONOMEI NTMN̄
TEPO MⲠNOYTE), in the same way (TΔI ON TE ϴE) the greedy or the robber
will not inherit the kingdom of God." Shenoute thus skillfully rearranges
the original biblical list to throw the emphasis on "greedy" and "robber."

The following passages do not show any major modifications of the biblical text, except for some minor grammatical changes aimed at seamlessly
inserting the quotations into the grammatical structure of their new co-text.
Their argumentative value lies in the careful choice Shenoute makes of biblical verses to then be put in opposition to one another:

> Do not interpret this letter as follows: "Search for peace, pursue it" (Psalms
> 33:15) or: "make peace with one another" (Mark 9:50), or: "pursue peace"
> (Hebrews 12:14), but read it as follows: "if your eye or your hand or your

feet are a scandal to you, pluck them out or cut them off and throw them away from you" (conflation of Matthew 18:8f; Mark 9:43ff). Do not interpret this letter as: "who hates his brother is a murderer" (1 John 3:15), but call it: "I hate the one who transgresses" (Psalms 100:3). About whom should you sigh or whose enemy should you become? This is no one but those who are doing or will do deceitful deeds and every transgression among you.

In summary, the passage XM 181–185 presents the following picture: community members have sinned. Their sin can be identified as the secret appropriation of food, which explains the skillful rearrangement of the argument in I Corinthians 6:9b–10 to throw a particular emphasis on the words "greedy" and "robbers." Shenoute lines up numerous biblical quotations that could be interpreted as favoring mildness and leniency, and puts them in opposition to other quotations in favor of the expulsion of sinners from a group and the redrawing of group boundaries. Shenoute also assumes the authority to decide the contest in favor of the latter. The refutation by "Talking Back" of numerous biblical admonitions to leniency and brotherly forgiveness are a strong indication, in my view, of the presence of an oppositional position. The sheer accumulation of passages makes it plausible that this oppositional position has in fact been voiced by a party in the monastery advocating a more lenient treatment of the transgressors. The passage under examination here is particularly interesting, because while the skillful adaptation of the biblical text is very frequent in both Shenoute and his successor, Besa,[23] the juxtaposition and the weighing of quotations against one another is a rare rhetorical strategy in Shenoute's works. This raises the question why Shenoute would choose this particular strategy in this situation. I believe that we can find the answer to this question if we examine the continuation of *Canon* 6 following XM 190.

Example 2: XF 241–243
After XM 190 we find two shorter lacunae and then the lengthy continuous passage XF 203–XF 255.[24] The main topics of this passage are as in the previous example the theft of food, favoritism, and criticism of the punishments Shenoute has ordered. Within the text preserved here we can find one of the rare instances in which we can directly grasp an active internal opposition within Shenoute's monastery (XF 241–243). The problem addressed by Shenoute in this passage is not an unusual one: community members have given food to relatives in secret, which transgresses one of the basic tenets

of Shenoute's monastic system, the replacement of the biological family by the monastic family and the equality of all members of the community.[25] However, we rarely have the opportunity to glimpse alternative positions within the monastery, filtered as our perception is by Shenoute's monopoly on the presentation of the issues involved. In this particular case, though, and the filter notwithstanding, I believe that we may get closer than anywhere else to individuating an oppositional current and the arguments used in the dispute.

It becomes quite clear that some of the community members disagree with Shenoute's hard-line approach to those transgressing the rules by stealing, appropriating and illegally distributing food. They argue that a hard-line approach might cause others to lose the fruit of their labors, and they defend their opposition on biblical grounds, basing their argumentation on the Gospel of Matthew (Matthew 22:11–14):

> As those who were reclining at the wedding knew the one who did not have a nuptial garment and did not say anything to him or do anything to him until the Lord came, this is also, they (scil. the opposition) say, how those who know those who do evil in the communities or churches should not expel them until they come before the Lord Jesus or until he comes.

Shenoute harshly disputes the validity of this argument:

> This talk is a scandal. This is not how it is. Do not believe every word like the fool, but become the more wise, and examine every word, every spirit at every time, so that you will not sadden the one who has said through Solomon, "the fool believes every word, what is sound and what is not, the wise man however, pays attention to what is inappropriate and what is appropriate to say" (Proverbs 14:15).

Proverbs 14: 15 is preserved in Sahidic as: [26] ϢⲀⲢⲈⲠⲂⲀⲀϨⲎⲦ ⲦⲀⲚϨⲈⲦϢⲀⲬⲈ ⲚⲒⲘ ϢⲀⲢⲈⲠⲤⲀⲂⲈ ⲆⲈ ⲢϨⲦⲎϤ "The fool believes every word, the wise man, however, pays attention." "What is sound and what is not" and "to what is inappropriate and what is appropriate to say" are seamless insertions of the interpretation directly into the wording of Scripture. They expertly adapt the general wisdom of the biblical text to the particular problem of Shenoute's being confronted with an exegesis of the Bible that advocates a policy diametrically opposed to his own. Shenoute's opponents, the quotation is intended to say, lack discernment in judgment and discernment in speech—the text of Proverbs disqualifies them and their dissenting opinion. Shenoute then directly addresses the rather delicate problem of the dissenters basing their argument on biblical authority:

> Or don't you know that those who stretch these words, bringing them to this meaning, are fighting against the Scriptures or forgetting them? Aren't those (scil. the Scriptures) the ones which say, "Throw out (ⲚⲞⲨⳊⲈ ⲈⲂⲞⲖ) an evil man from a crowd and strife will go together with him. For if he stays in the crowd, they will all be despised" (Proverbs 22:10). And again, "You, you have rejected (ⲚⲞⲨⳊⲈ ⲈⲂⲞⲖ) knowledge, I for my part I will throw you out of the holy place[27] so that you cannot serve me" (Hosea 4:6). And, "I will throw you out (again, the verb is ⲚⲞⲨⳊⲈ ⲈⲂⲞⲖ) of this holy place so that you cannot serve me, as I have expelled your brothers" (Jeremiah 7:15). Again, "I will take away (ϤⲒ ⲈⲂⲞⲖ) all the godless away from you, all the arrogant" (Zephaniah 3:11). In many passages of the Scriptures it is said thus.

The barrage of quotations with which Shenoute tries to silence his opponents is linked by the semantic field of "expulsion," either by the verb ⲚⲞⲨⳊⲈ ⲈⲂⲞⲖ "to throw out" (three cases) or the verb ϤⲒ ⲈⲂⲞⲖ "to take away" (one case). The quotation of Proverbs 22:10 corresponds to the original,[28] its value for the argumentation again lies in its selection. The quotations of Hosea 4:6 and Jeremiah 7:15 show an addition and a substitution respectively. In Hosea 4:6 "out of the holy place" is inserted into the biblical text,[29] in Jeremiah 7:15, although the text is not preserved in Coptic, "out of this holy place" can realistically be assumed to be a substitution for the Greek ἀπὸ προσώπου μου "out of my sight."[30] Both the addition and the substitution redirect the focus of the quotations away from the Old Testament context to the setting of the monastery, Shenoute's "holy place." The disobedient of the biblical text, those who have rejected God's will out of arrogance, become the disobedient of the present situation, those who have rejected Shenoute's interpretation of the holy texts. The fate of the disobedient in the prophetical books, experiencing the wrath of God, being denied access to his presence and thereby losing their own salvation, will also be the fate of Shenoute's opposition and the punishment for their wrong interpretation of Scripture.

I would like to draw three conclusions from this brief discussion of the passages from *Canon* 6. First, there seems to be a continuation of the subject matter from XM 175–190 to XF 241–243, which bridges the two shorter lacunae between the two portions of preserved text. The subject is the secret appropriation of food and the question of how to punish the transgressors— severely, including expulsion, or leniently, with an emphasis on brotherly forgiveness. This continuation raises the suspicion that "Is It Not Written" (or the acephalous work starting in one of the lacunae before XM 175) may continue across the two lacunae we find following XM 190. Second, we gain new information about oppositional movements in the monas- tery. The group that Shenoute is addressing in XF 241f openly contests his authority and questions his monopoly on scriptural interpretation, offering an independent exegesis of Scripture, in this case of Matthew 22:11–14. I suspect that it is both the constant exposure to the biblical and other author- itative texts through Shenoute's works and the unfiltered access to these texts that allows competing interpretations to surface in the monastery. The simple act of quoting a sacred or venerated text is fraught with dangers. A gap opens up between the authoritative source text and the authority the act of quoting wants to monopolize. The recipient/reader of the quotation may refuse to see an identity between the authority of the source text and the authority of the person citing it and apply his or her own interpretation to the text quoted. Shenoute shares this problem with any author quoting an authoritative text, as Simon Goldhill describes:

> In particular, citation, quotation and even the self-reflexive awareness of the texts of the past, become an especially problematic site for the authorized voice: inverted commas open the possibility of comic inversion, or ironic interplay between authorities, or to a display of the contests of voices in and against which an authoritative position is formulated. There is an inevitable gap between the author's voice and the voice of authority.[31]

In Shenoute's case, the problem is intensified by the alphabetization of the community, which was encouraged to learn to read and recite Scripture, and the physical access to the books containing the authoritative texts, which inevitably open up the space for an independent exegesis. Shenoute therefore needs to find strategies to control the competing interpretations arising from the gap described. If the oppositional group of XF 241–243, which offers a competing biblical exegesis, is in fact the same group against which Shenoute justifies his actions in XM 175–190, his strategy of "Talking Back" in XM 183–185 makes perfect sense. He counteracts their alternative, Gospel-based exegesis, with an equally Bible-based argumentation, but with an emphasis on the Old Testament, choosing quotations (or quotation clusters) from the prophetical and wisdom books that support his agenda. Shenoute thus, and this is my final point, not only quotes extensively from the Bible, he carefully chooses the quotations and makes skillful changes to the biblical text to adapt and recontextualize it. In the course of this recontextualization he may even establish a hierarchy of scriptural quotations, privileging the dire threats and severe admonitions of Proverbs and the prophetical books over the exhortations to peace and brotherly love taken chiefly from the New Testament, those quotations which may have been favored by his opponents. It cannot be shown more clearly that Shenoute sees himself as an inspired vessel of God's word, a modern-day prophet whose mission complements that of the prophets of old.

Notes

1. For the structure of the monastic federation which Shenoute led see Emmel 2004b and Krawiec 2002, especially ch. 1.
2. Krawiec 2002: ch. 3.
3. Emmel 2004b.
4. Emmel 2004b: 576–582; 731–44.
5. For the library of Shenoute's monastery see Orlandi 2002.
6. Shenoute's presentation of the monastic community as a privileged path toward salvation is one of the mainstays of his system: see, for example, Krawiec 2002: ch. 3.
7. Emmel 2004b: 577.
8. Layton 2002 discusses the social aspects of food consumption within the monastery.
9. Emmel 2004b: 578.
10. Krawiec 2002: ch. 2.
11. Emmel 2004b: 577; 734f.
12. Leipoldt 1906–13, vol. 3: 188–95.
13. Ibid.: 191.
14. Ibid.: 192.
15. Hebel 1991; Plett 1991.
16. Hebel 1991: 140.
17. Holthuis 1993: 16.
18. Clark 1999: 104–52, esp. pp. 128–32.
19. The quotations discussed in the following are quoted from Leipoldt 1906–13, vol. 3: 192f.

20. The New Testament text used for comparison here is the main text from Horner 1911–1924. The variants given by Horner and most of the texts published since Horner's edition have been checked to make sure that Shenoute's deviations from the biblical text are not due to textual variation within the manuscript tradition itself. If the Coptic text is quoted, the spelling is slightly standardized, with the supralinear stroke being omitted in all cases. The same applies *mutatis mutandis* to the other quotations discussed here. Every quotation has been checked against the Sahidic tradition, and each of Shenoute's deviations from the biblical text has been evaluated individually. Only those deviations have been taken into consideration which not only are so significant and striking as to exclude mere textual variants but which also no longer make sense within the original context, whereas, as will be argued here, they make perfect sense in the new context of Shenoute's argument.

21. Amos 6:12 is not preserved in Sahidic Coptic. The Septuagint Greek translates to "for you have turned judgment into gall, and the fruit of righteousness into bitterness." It is very unlikely that the Coptic imperative ⲘⲠⲢ̄ⲔⲦⲈ ('do not turn') would be a transmission variant for the Greek aorist 2nd pers. pl.

22. For a discussion of the Greek loan-word μαλακός see Behlmer 2000.

23. This strategy firmly anchors both in the late antique tradition of biblical interpretation. I discuss this in detail in Behlmer (forthcoming).

24. Emmel 2004b: 736–38.

25. Krawiec 2002: chs. 7 and 8. For a comprehensive evaluation of the late antique Christian and especially the monastic concept of 'family' see Krawiec 2003.

26. Worrell 1931: 44.

27. XF 243 (Amélineau 1907–1909: 64) has ⲦⲚⲀⲚⲞⲨϪⲔ ⲈⲂⲞⲖ 2ⲘⲠⲘⲀ ⲈⲦⲞⲨⲀⲀⲂ. A control of the original would be necessary to check whether it shows the correct reading ⲦⲚⲀⲚⲞϪⲔ ⲈⲂⲞⲖ (see Ciasca 1885: 325 for the Sahidic version of Hosea 4: 6). It would also be useful to check whether the original reads, parallel to the following quotation, ⲈⲂⲞⲖ 2ⲘⲠⲒⲘⲀ ⲈⲦⲞⲨⲀⲀⲂ ('out of *this* holy place').

28. Worrell 1931: 71.

29. Or: "out of this holy place," see note 24.

30. The Sahidic text of Jeremiah, as far as it is preserved, is now readily accessible in Feder 2002.

31. Goldhill 1993: 151.

2 Some Aspects of Volume 8 of Shenoute's *Canons**

Anne Boud'hors

As a member of the international project to edit the works of Shenoute, directed by Professor Stephen Emmel, I am responsible for editing and translating volume 8 of Shenoute's *Canons*. From a certain point of view this is a real opportunity, because the amount of surviving text is very large. But from another point of view it is a mixed blessing, because the texts of *Canon* 8 are very hard to understand and often seem to be at the very limit of comprehension. In this chapter I would like to touch on two aspects of *Canon* 8: first, the manuscript witnesses and their codicological and textual relevance; and second, I will analyze a few of Shenoute's themes, which can serve to guide us through the meanderings of his discourse.

The Textual Attestation of *Canon* 8

Canon 8 is by far the best attested of the nine books of the *Canons*. The main witness to *Canon* 8 is a manuscript the bulk of which is held by the Institut français d'archéologie orientale du Caire (IFAO) under the designation of IFAO Copte 2. Some 127 leaves are present in this manuscript, and to them can be added a few leaves in London (British Library), Naples (Biblioteca nazionale), and Paris (Bibliothèque nationale), arriving at a total of 141 surviving leaves out of the 161 that must have made up the original

---

* I am deeply grateful to Bentley Layton for translating this paper into English.

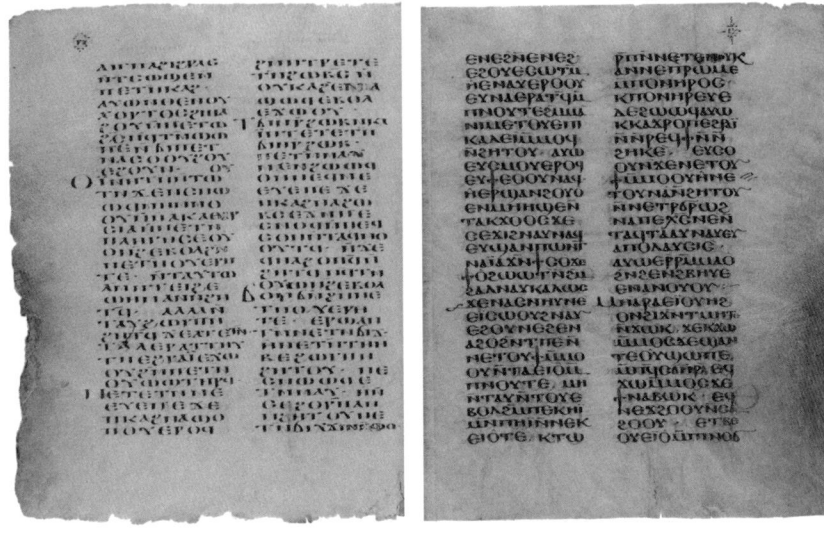

Fig. 2.1: IFAO Copte 2, Codex XO,   Fig. 2.2: IFAO Copte 1, Codex XH,
p. 160. Photograph © IFAO.   p. 207. Photograph © IFAO.

codex. No other manuscript from the White Monastery has survived so completely. (Indeed, in the average Shenoute manuscript, only 10 percent of the leaves survive.) There are six additional witnesses to volume 8, all much more fragmentary, and including the *Florilegium Sinuthianum*, and these allow us to verify that the same sermons were copied there in the same order, and that the transmission of these texts, as a whole, was very stable, to a degree that is otherwise found only with biblical texts. Volume 8 of the *Canons* is thus a very important textual source. The main textual witness, that is, the French Institute manuscript and its related leaves, is designated by the siglum XO in Professor Orlandi's *Corpus dei manoscritti letterari*, and has been described in detail in Stephen Emmel's *Shenoute's Literary Corpus*.[1] The accompanying photograph (Fig. 2.1) will give an idea of this codex. The manuscript is written in biblical uncial in two columns, like the majority of the manuscripts of the works of Shenoute. The regularity of the script contrasts with the vast number of corrections found in the manuscript: omission of letters; repetition of letters—which has generally been corrected by erasure of the parchment; and the dropping of multiple words or phrases through *homoeoteleuton*—such passages have been marked by the ancient corrector with an asterisk and then the missing words have been written into the margin (in one case the omission was so large that the missing passage had to be copied on to supplementary leaves, thus modifying the structure of quire 16).

The script of this manuscript seems to be of a more ancient type than that of the French Institute manuscript IFAO 1, for example. This manuscript is illustrated in Fig. 2.2; it can be dated to about A.D. 930. What is more, the format of Codex XO is not very large, only 24 x 18 cm per leaf. These two facts argue for a relatively ancient date, perhaps the eighth century. On the last page there is a subscription giving the title of the volume: "This is the *Canon* of our holy, prophetic father, Apa Shenoute. The eighth (book). O Jesus Christ, amen." Unfortunately, there is no colophon giving the name of the copyist or the date. This may be an additional argument in favor of a date before the ninth century, a time before the usage of colophons had been established.

It would obviously be tempting, in view of such an early dating, to deem that codex XO is the earliest of the surviving witnesses, and that the others are subsequent copies. However, up to the present time I have not succeeded in establishing a relative chronology of the witnesses.

Biblical Citations

Before passing to the actual content of *Canon* 8, I would like to note the importance of the works of Shenoute for the domain of Coptic Bible versions. Volume 8 of the *Canons*, for example, cites a very long passage from Leviticus, which is not otherwise known in Sahidic because of the fragmentary manuscript situation. The books of the Prophets are frequently cited, above all the book of Jeremiah. Jeremiah is without any doubt the Prophet with whom Shenoute identified himself most frequently. Shenoute, of course, often has the epithet of Prophet in texts that mention him or his works; for example, in the subscription of *Canon* 8 that I mentioned above. The Sahidic text of the book of Jeremiah has not survived complete in any manuscript, and for many passages Shenoute's quotations of Jeremiah are the only surviving attestation. One example will suffice to demonstrate the value of these biblical citations.

Shenoute's sermon entitled *My Heart Is Crushed* begins with a citation of Jeremiah 23:9–10, a passage that is quoted even more extensively later in the sermon. In fact, the only attestation of this passage of Jeremiah in Sahidic is in volume 8 of the *Canons*, attested by Codex XO and Codex FL: "My heart is crushed within me, all my bones have shaken, I have become like a broken man, like a man who is drunk on wine, in the presence of the Lord, and in the presence of the greatness of the beauty of his glory. For the land is filled with adulterers, the country is stricken with grief in the presence of these." Given the faithfulness with which Shenoute usually cites biblical texts, one can consider this quotation to be a good attestation of the Coptic version. In fact, the Coptic text here has an addition not found in the Septuagint, namely, "the land is filled with adulterers." This addition is found in the Masoretic text, and is typical of the Hexapla, but is not from the Septuagint. Additions of this type are rather numerous in the book of Jeremiah, and so this new variant confirms a tendency of the Coptic version.

The Composition and Coherence of *Canon* 8

Volume 8 of the *Canons* comprises seven works. The first two sermons each occupy 62 pages. Then comes a long sermon of 110 pages, which is the central work in the codex, followed by two others, which are shorter (59 and 22 pages respectively). The volume concludes with two very brief texts, two or three pages in length, which have the appearance of letters addressed to precise circumstances. Up to now, it has not been possible to find any overarching theme in the codex. However, a certain number of specific themes seem to be present in one text or another, notably the themes of garments and sickness. These themes often have a metaphorical function and are part of the author's rhetoric. Probably they also contain allusions to precise situations and inform us more or less directly about the structure and organization of the monastic establishment. We should remember that Shenoute was in charge of a federation of three monastic establishments, including a nunnery for women. The job cannot have been easy, to judge from the predominant tone of the most of the sermons, which is that of reproach, accusation, and threat. As I stated at the beginning of this chapter, there are major difficulties in understanding these texts. Of course that could be owing to my insufficient knowledge of Shenoute's language. It can also be explained, I think, from the fact that Shenoute refers to facts and customs that were well known to his audience, so that he is able to make very vague allusions to them. Finally, the repetition of the same phrases and citations from one text to another, the absence of any obvious progression of thought, and the exaggeration of certain images, often give the impression that one is dealing with works written in Shenoute's extreme old age or works that belong to a period of deep depression. I will now try, with a few examples, to give some possible ideas of how to read these texts.

Some Extracts from *Canon* 8

First, let us look at an extract from the beginning of the first sermon: "So listen, O you who have friendship for the man who is discouraged, and look at his affliction when he says, 'Behold, Lord, I am tormented, my heart has been become disturbed, and my heart has turned within me because I am in anger, yes, in anger.' Indeed, this sickness has robbed me of my strength and subjected me to an increase of suffering so that I do not wish my garment, and my garments, to touch . . . . If it were possible, I would throw them away so as not to wear them."

Shenoute often speaks of himself in the third person, referring to himself as "the man" or "this man." This procedure enables him to introduce smoothly a citation of Lamentations 1:20, where he substitutes himself for Jerusalem in the first person pronoun "I." Like many texts of Christian literature, the sermons of Shenoute are literally stuffed with biblical citations and allusions, though few authors make such extensive use of the Prophets. From the very beginning of this sermon, the two dominant themes of Volume 8 are clearly in view. The theme of sickness is susceptible to two readings. On the one hand, it is possible that Shenoute was actually ill with a chronic disease, probably a skin disease that made him subject to unbearable itching, which he sometimes describes with realistic exactitude. On the other hand, the human body was a commonplace metaphor for the Christian community, mainly inspired by the epistles of Paul, and particularly apt for describing a monastic community. As head of the body, the leader of the federation feels the effects of all weaknesses and suffering. Associated with this image of the body is the image of the garment. Just as the monastic habit is the outward sign of a monk, the monks are the finest visible expression of the community, that is, the garment of the monastic body. If this body is ill, it can no longer endure contact with garments. Here too the image is coupled with an allusion to reality: Shenoute's garments are obviously a sensitive issue in the life of the congregation.

Next, an extract from the beginning of the second sermon: "My heart is crushed, and it has become crushed within me because of our affliction that is shown in your faces like a sore—you, O mother superior, and you, O (sister) Tapollé. For you are, and you have been, distraught with much grief; you are, and you have been, saddened; your heart is overturned within you, because of what has been revealed to you and what has been hidden from you. I am talking about the excellent cloak that I requested from you so I could wrap myself in it. And I covered myself whenever I had need. I was very happy with it, and I was satisfied with its color and its style, and with the fact that others admired its beauty, too. And thus, I was all the more filled with grief . . . when the moth ate it, explored it, completely filled it with holes."

Here too the sermon begins with a citation from one of the Prophets (Jeremiah 23:9), which sets the tone of reproach and bitterness. The importance of this rhetorical apostrophe in terms of how the monastic organization worked, is to demonstrate that the manufacture of garments—at least those of the head of the federation—was in the hands of the nuns, who were themselves subject to the authority of a mother superior. The other female personage, named Tapollé, seems to have been at the center of many conflicts, which are mentioned in other books of the *Canons*. On the question of Shenoute's relationships with the congregation of monastic women, I would refer to Rebecca Krawiec's book.[2] It seems possible that all the sermons of *Canon* 8 were addressed to the congregation of women and that the occasion for most of them had to do with the manufacture of these garments. It is difficult to be absolutely sure, inasmuch as the second person plural in Coptic does not make a distinction between masculine and feminine. It is very likely that starting from a particular problem, Shenoute extended his subject matter to larger questions of authority and responsibility concerning the entire monastic federation, which is indicated by his frequent repetition of the expression "both males and females." On the other hand, reference to moths is found in many biblical references, for example, Proverbs 25:20a: "Like a moth in a garment and a worm in a piece of wood, so has sadness afflicted the heart of a man." This clearly indicates that the garment also has a metaphorical reference to monastic behavior. Shenoute is not only upset at the bad condition of his garments; he is also sickened by the disorder of the conduct of his communities.

The continuation of the passage that I cited just above seems to indicate that the nuns made him another cloak, which he did not want to wear: "But you say to me, Why? What is wrong with it? First of all, it hangs heavily on me. For, you should have put fringes and tassels on it, so that if they opened out or parted after a certain time they would still remain intertwined; but instead, you have trimmed it with braid like a tunic or a curtain. You have deliberately constructed it for me as though it were a veil, and I remember the contempt and criticism of this object called 'veil'—and how the prophet fights all the time against the woman whose identity he, for his part, knows well: 'Undo your veil, reveal your gray hairs, uncover your legs'" (Isaiah 47:2). It is difficult to imagine the kind of garment that Shenoute is describing and the defects that he sees in it. On the metaphorical level, however, the notion of hanging heavily probably represents the burden of responsibility felt by the head of the federation; while the comparison with a veil or a drapery—which are broad and billowing pieces of textile—could serve on the one hand to criticize a lack of cohesion and discipline, and on the other hand to denounce the 'perversions' that such a garment would scarcely be able to conceal. At the end of this rhetorical period, Shenoute declares that he will not wear the garments in question. At best, he will ignore them, and at worst, he will tear them to pieces. The threat is fairly clear, and the choice imposed upon the monastic leader is the following: either he withdraws from his communities and hands them over to divine justice, or he punishes the guilty. A third solution, to which Shenoute makes frequent reference, is to throw these spoiled garments onto the scrap heap, that is to say, to expel the trouble makers. This idea is expressed many times in the second sermon, and it is implicit at the beginning of the third.

Finally, an extract from the beginning of sermon three: "Who but God is the witness to that which he said to another: 'Have you seen that once again the moth has entered into the textile products, in the place where they are stored, and it has destroyed not only their borders, but also their center? Can someone bring them back out into the light? Can someone unfold them again and take them out?' That is why I am telling you, who concern yourselves with my garments: it is better for me to have just one, two, or three of these garments that you are making for me and to have them well made, than for me to have this heap, which is a matter of shame for the one who is supposed to wear them." This is the longest and most turbulent sermon, and it picks up and deepens the themes that were already tackled in the second sermon. In sermon three, we can see the dilemma that must have haunted Shenoute during all of his long career as head of the monastic federation: on the one hand, to bring into his congregations the largest possible number of members in order to enlarge the flock of God; but on the other hand, to expel, without any hesitation, those who took advantage of the large monastic population to compromise the salvation of the whole congregation by their abuses—above all, by theft and fornication.

The actual number of monks living in these establishments—and our literary sources speak of several thousand—cannot be verified until the archaeological site has been excavated. But whatever the actual number may have been, questions of discipline seem to be central in volume 8 of the *Canons*, leaving not much room for questions of spirituality. Seen from this point of view, the difference between volume 8 of the *Canons* and the Pachomian corpus is very striking. In order to understand exactly why, we must wait until all of Shenoute's *Canons* has been published.

Notes
1. Emmel 2004.
2. Krawiec 2002.

3 Care for the Sick in Shenoute's Monasteries

Andrew Crislip

SHENOUTE'S WRITINGS PROVIDE a rich store of evidence for the various ways in which the sick were cared for in his monasteries. Care for the sick was a shared value at the heart of the early monastic movement, and certainly this was the case in Shenoute's monasteries. The theological, social, and ideological reasons for the noteworthy monastic interest in care for the sick are all rich areas for investigation, which I have had opportunity to explore elsewhere.[1] In this chapter, however, I will limit myself to the medical and institutional aspects of care for the sick by outlining the basic contours of this important component of monastic life in Shenoute's monasteries.

In Shenoute's monasteries, the infirmary (ⲠⲘⲀ ⲚⲚⲢⲰⲘⲈ ⲈⲦⲰⲰⲚⲈ) served the acutely ill. Coenobitic literature from Egypt in general indicates that the infirmary formed an expected and functionally vital component of the coenobitic life. Unlike virtually every other type of ancient medical care, including that provided in many fourth- and fifth-century semi-eremitical monasteries in Egypt and elsewhere, coenobitic monasteries offered inpatient care under the supervision of trained healers, including a nursing staff and doctors. The writings of Shenoute and Besa are important witnesses to this tradition of monastic healing. It is to be noted that while the monasteries of Shenoute provided a range of charitable services for non-monks, use of the infirmary was restricted to the monastic sick.

As it stands, only one early monastic infirmary in Egypt has been identified as such through excavation: that in the monastery of Apa Jeremias at Saqqara, although the identification of the structure as an infirmary has been treated with some skepticism.[2] Nevertheless, for Shenoute's monasteries we must make do with the literary record for the time being.

Passing comments in Shenoute's *Canons* indicate that the infirmary was architecturally distinct and spatially removed from the rest of the monastic buildings.[3] The reason for the separation was not a need for medical quarantine, since the ancient world lacked modern notions of contagion. Rather, the spatial separation enforced a social quarantine: whatever activities occurred within the infirmary were to be out of sight of healthy monks. We know also from Shenoute's own writings that the infirmary had its own storeroom, refectory, and kitchen.[4]

Within the infirmary's walls several types of monastic healers cared for the sick monks. These included doctors, nurses, and elders.

Shenoute refers to doctors in the monastery on a number of occasions, and doctors are frequently mentioned in other contemporaneous monastic sources. In Shenoute's congregations both male and female doctors joined the monastery and continued to practice medicine for the residents therein.[5] Doctors could also be brought in from outside the community, in which case Shenoute orders that they be paid their customary wages.[6]

In Shenoute's monasteries, as in other coenobitic monasteries in the Pachomian tradition, another class of healers cared for sick monks within the infirmaries. These were "nurses," or rendered literally, "the servers of the sick" (ΝΕΤΔΙΔΚΟΝΕΙ ΕΝΕΤϢϢΝΕ) in Shenoute. Shenoute classifies these "nurses" as among the various professions within his monasteries: bakers, builders, agricultural workers, and so on.[7] As I have argued elsewhere, this occupation, as a defined and distinct specialization, is without precedent in the ancient world; nursing the sick was a duty normally imposed upon lay caregivers and, to the extent that they were present, physicians themselves.[8] In the coenobitic monasteries of Shenoute and his contemporaries we see the emergence of nurses as a profession distinct from both physicians and lay caregivers.

From Shenoute's writings we know that the job of nurse could be an extremely taxing one: he refers rather graphically to his monks' hesitancy to care for the sometimes noxious ailments that the sick suffered.[9] Nonetheless, we know from Shenoute that the nurses served the sick according to the individual prescriptions (often dietary) determined by the elder in charge of the infirmary.[10] We may also presume that they performed hygienic duties such as bathing and comforting the sick, tasks that the sick and infirm normally performed for themselves when not confined to the infirmary.[11] Actual numbers of nurses are not reflected in Shenoute's writings or in other writings of contemporary monasticism, but the nurses must have formed an important part in caring for the sick among the thousands of monks in Shenoute's monastic federation.

Another role in the health care system, specifically in fourth-century coenobitic monasteries, was that of overseer. In Shenoute's monasteries much of this practical administration was performed by so-called 'elders.' For example, an elder was charged with determining the gravity of illness and whether indeed the monk was 'truly' sick, and not just malingering, and then determining whether his or her illness was severe enough to necessitate infirmary care.[12] Then he or she would either give or deny permission to go to the infirmary. They might also allow the monk some special dietary dispensation within the refectory, but of course to be eaten under the elder's watchful eye.[13] Monks who were ill with more specific medical indications, such as a wound, fever, or pain, also had to apply for medical service through the elder in order to receive treatment at the hands of a doctor.[14] In the infirmary, an elder was also responsible for determining the right therapeutic diet for each of the sick monks, to be then administered by nurses.[15] Additionally, the elders were responsible for providing special clothing, medical instruments, and food for monks who were not sick enough to warrant inpatient care. As in all other areas of monastic life, from worship to work to spiritual direction, care for the sick in Shenoute's monasteries depended upon the system of elders and housemasters to aid monks in distress as well as to regulate access to health care and the special benefits (food, rest, and comfort, for example) provided for the sick.

I should also point out that most care for the sick was provided not through the infirmary, or even by the three classes of healers I have just described, but by lay caregivers, that is to say, the sick's fellow monks. Monks were expected to provide basic care for their sick brethren in coenobitic monasteries.[16] Such lay care comprised typical elements of comfort care, but also allowed for minor surgical procedures to be performed on oneself or on fellow monks. Jerome, writing in his introduction to his translation of the Pachomian *Rules*, describes the compassion that monks showed toward their sick brethren as among the most remarkable features of coenobitic monasticism. The case was no different in Shenoute's monasteries, as Shenoute frequently exhort his monks to care for the sick among them.[17]

I will now return to the care for the sick as provided by doctors, nurses, and elders through the infirmary. I will focus on three types of care in the present chapter: dietary care, surgery, and pharmacology, with a special focus on pharmacology.

Dietary care in antiquity was not only a source of comfort, but was also the first line of treatment for most internal ailments. This was certainly no less the case in Shenoute's monasteries. While the standard monastic diet in Shenoute's monastery was decidedly ascetic, it is clear from Shenoute's own writings, as well as those of his contemporaries, that sick monks were held to a distinctly different standard of asceticism and were given access to a whole range of food normally forbidden or at the very least severely restricted for reasons of health, including vinegar, fish, eggs, oil, wine, and perhaps meat.[18] Regulation of access to such foods was of utmost importance in coenobitic health care, particularly with regard to wine. So Shenoute writes:

> And those who serve in that place (the infirmary) shall act in accordance with what is appropriate in the measure that the eldest commands them to give, each one according to each type of illness. But neither the housemaster nor anyone at all, whether male or female, shall say to anyone in his sickness, as to persuade him, "Wouldn't you like some wine to drink?"[19]

To avoid the unnecessary use of wine, requests for it, as for other normally forbidden foodstuffs, had to come from the monks themselves. This safeguard, of course, could not entirely prevent abuse of the special privileges afforded the sick, and Shenoute condemns malingering on a number of occasions.[20]

Beyond the typical provision of special foods to the sick, dietary therapy was also determined by the elder in charge of the infirmary, and served by the nurses, as mentioned previously. The diet for the sick was not uniform, as was the diet for the healthy, but was 'prescribed' by the elder according to the type of illness.[21] Shenoute's writings do not specify what sort of medical training this elder in charge possessed in order to make such determinations, or how treatments were codified, if at all. But in a community in which doctors were a regular feature, both as monks and as visitors from outside, it is more than reasonable to suppose that the elder in charge of the infirmary had some medical training or knowledge, or at the very least had access to it. Monastic sources, furthermore, do not give any indication of how the particular diet was determined for each monk, that is to say, which symptoms called for which types of food—heating or cooling foods, for instance.

Monastic medicine, as attested in Shenoute's writings and elsewhere, also drew on the range of surgical skills available at the time, techniques that are well attested in other monastic sources from late antiquity.[22] As mentioned previously, minor surgery was regularly performed, often by the monks themselves: thorns were removed, wounds cauterized, and bleedings performed.[23] Furthermore, doctors treated pustules and wounds, pulled teeth, and treated eye disorders.[24]

Coptic monasteries also drew on and transmitted the important pharmacological heritage of Egypt. Coptic pharmacy is documented by at least twenty-seven published Coptic medical manuscripts, most of which are regrettably fragmentary.[25] The Coptic corpus of medical literature provides valuable evidence for the care of the sick in Egyptian monasteries, including Shenoute's monastery.[26] While Coptic manuscripts of medical content postdate the life of Shenoute by several centuries, late ancient medicine maintained considerable continuity over time, being a highly conservative rather than an innovative tradition.[27] So it is likely that the sorts of treatments preserved therein reflect manuscript exemplars from earlier centuries.

Three folios from a medical codex probably from the library of the monastery of Shenoute (parts of which were published separately by Georg Zoega and Urbain Bouriant) provide a valuable complement to literary evidence for medical care in Shenoute's monasteries.[28] The Coptic medical manuscript enhances and, in fact, complicates our picture of monastic healing that Shenoute himself presents in his disciplinary literature. For example, pages 214 and 215 of this once very large manuscript preserve a variety of prescriptions for ailments that one might not associate with monastic medicine, venereal ailments, and ailments of the breasts.

For breasts that hurt. It is also useful for the man's "male flesh" (epsoma [for ЄⲠⲤⲰⲘⲀ] Ⲛ2ⲞⲞⲨⲦ ⲘⲠⲢⲰⲘЄ]). Take the plant called cat's eye, with white lead (ⲚⲞⲨⲠⲮⲒⲘⲒⲐⲒⲞⲚ [sic]), litharge, lead, and opium, of equal proportions. Pound them well. Take a little vinegar for them. Mix them up with juice of female grape. Leave them in a lead vessel, and take them (ⲚⲄⳠⲞⲨ, perhaps for ⲚⲄⲬⲒⲦⲞⲨ?) and smear them on them until they heal. . . .

For a breast that is painful. Take mother's milk. Smear on it. It is also useful for testicles (ⲚⲬⲞЄⲒⲦ) and penises (ⲚⲂⲀ2, see Crum, 1939, 47b) that are painful.[29]

The prominent preservation of such remedies in the White Monastery medical manuscript is interesting, especially considering that the treatment of specifically female and male ailments was a topic of some concern for Shenoute himself, who forbade his monks from treating women outsiders and such complaints of men: "All the more, cursed is anyone who treats a woman outsider, or treats the shameful members of a man in the area of the congregation, or anywhere else."[30]

Other recipes in the White Monastery medical codex are lactagogues, to induce lactation, another area of medical treatment that might be surprising to find in a monastic library. So,

> For a woman's breasts, so that they produce milk. Take some dried garlic. Boil them in unmixed wine. Let them drink . . . .
>
> For breasts, so that they produce milk. Take some fava beans. Boil them and have them drink their water (ΠЄΥΜΟΟΥ) first thing after eating . . . .
>
> Another [for breasts, so that they produce milk]. Take some leaf of cucumber. Soak them with salt. Put them on [the breasts,] and they will become full of milk.[31]

These are but a few of the lactagogic recipes in the White Monastery codex. What could such recipes be doing in a monastery? We could argue that they are part of a standard formulary, produced or purchased outside the monastery, and thus they do not necessarily reflect the medical needs or practices of the community in which they were preserved and used. This is possible. But by placing the Coptic medical papyri within the context of both the literary remains of Shenoute's life and of other monastic documents, the prominent presence of lactagogic prescriptions within a monastic codex makes a certain sense. We know from Shenoute's own writings, as well as those of other early coenobitic writers, that orphans were a standard component of the monastic population.[32] Young children were abandoned at the gatehouse or 'donated' to the cloister as a thanksgiving for miraculous services provided by the monks, as the famous child donation contracts from Thebes attest.[33] How then is a group of ostensibly celibate nuns to properly care for orphaned infants? Whether or not such recipes as these were efficacious, in the sense defined by western biomedicine is beside the point,[34] but, the likely and persistent presence of orphaned infants within the monastery does at least provide a plausible pretext for the preservation of such recipes within the monastic codex, even if they were not actually used.

The remainder of the White Monastery medical manuscript (last edited by Zoega in 1810, although translated into German by Till in 1951) is dominated by prescriptions for dermatological ailments. So it begins, "Chapter 136. For mange [ⲦϤⲰⲣⲀ] and conditions that itch."[35] Included in the two folios of Chapter 136 are remedies for mange, scabies, leprosy, running sores, itching over the whole body, lice, and canker sores. The recipes provide a detailed portrait of the types of medicine used in late antique or medieval monasteries. Interestingly, we know from Shenoute's own writings that Shenoute suffered from a chronic, disfiguring skin condition for a number of years. During his illness and convalescence he quarantined himself from the community in a hermit's cell. He continued to write however, and during this extended period he probably penned many of the works that now make up his *Canons* 6 and 8, although chronological ordering of Shenoute's works remains tentative. I would like to draw attention to a passage from *Who But God Is The Witness*, in Shenoute's *Canon* 8, that may shed some light on the care for the sick in Shenoute's monasteries. Speaking about a custom-made garment that had become befouled by his running sores and subsequently eaten by moths, he writes that he is "testing" his illness with "all the medicines appropriate to it."[36] The language Shenoute uses to describe treating his condition, "testing" (ⲬⲰⲚⲦ, per the Greek δοκιμάζειν, Crum, *Coptic Dictionary*, 775b), and "medicine" (Coptic ⲠⲀ2ⲣⲈ), is the typical terminology of Coptic medical literature. Such terminology is used throughout, for example, the Chassinat papyrus roll: "this is tested," "I have tested this medicine myself," and so on.[37] Does Shenoute betray here a familiarity with Coptic medicine? Or perhaps does his rhetoric simply reflect certain shared cultural models about suffering?[38] In fact, Shenoute elsewhere displays some considerable familiarity the traditions of Coptic medicine. So from *Canon* 6:

> Observe: when the doctor applies a cooling or cool medicament to the wou[nd at] the moment [or hour] that it nee[ds] it, it [d]estroys (ⲦⲀⲔⲞ) it (the wound) and gathers together a multitude of worms. But if he applies a medicament that penetrates (ⲠⲈⲦ2ⲞⲦ2Ⲧ) and a solvent (ⲠⲈⲦⲞⲨⲰⲘ) on it at the moment and hour that it needs, and then applies that which cools at the moment and hour that it needs, then the growth (ⲠⲣⲰⲦ) becomes visible, and the one who sees it rejoices because the wound has come out bit by bit.[39]

These are the words of someone with more than a passing familiarity with medicine, of someone who knows a variety of medical treatments for an ailment, classifications of drug types, and perhaps something of the humoral theory underlying the treatments. So when Shenoute draws on the specialized terminology of Coptic medicine, and speaks of "testing this illness with all the medicines that are appropriate to it," we should take this seriously. Where, for instance, is Shenoute finding "all the medicines appropriate to it"? It is possible that Shenoute had with him in his desert retreat a medical manuscript, perhaps like the one preserved in his monastic library from several centuries later. Or more likely he had with him some ostraca or a few slips of papyrus bearing the relevant medicines copied from the master text in the library. We find such medical ostraca in a hermit's cell elsewhere, at the Monastery of Epiphanius in Thebes.[40] As for medicaments, did Shenoute have with him a small collection of *materia medica* to treat his skin condition? From my reading of Shenoute's *Canons* such an arrangement would not have been allowed for regular monks in Shenoute's monasteries, who would have been required to receive treatment through the official channels I have just outlined. But perhaps in this case, as in others, Shenoute was a living exception to his own rules.

Shenoute's own illness experience, and the effect that this had on his administration of the monasteries, his theology, and indeed on the care for the sick in his monasteries is a rich area for future study. For now I would like to conclude by noting that the care for the sick was an essential and distinctive aspect of monastic life in Shenoute's monastery. It is an aspect of life that we will continue to learn more about as Shenoute's *Canons* and *Discourses* are published in the coming decade, and one hopes also as Shenoute's monastery is scientifically excavated.

Notes

1. For more details see: Crislip 2005; Crislip 2006a: 179–209.
2. For example Peter Grossmann's comments that monasteries should not have infirmaries, in Atiya 1991b: 773–74. His skepticism is accepted by Cäcilia Wietheger, *Das Jeremias-Kloster zu Saqqara unter* (1992: 21–22). Abundant literary sources show that the situation is more complicated, as I have discussed in more detail than is possible here: Crislip 2005: 9–14.
3. Shenoute, *Canon* 9, DF 16=Vienna K9345 verso; *Canon* 5, XS 275–6=Mich. 158: 19B. Citations of works of Shenoute are according to bibliographical sigla established by Stephen Emmel (2004b).
4. Shenoute, *Canon* 5, XS 276=Mich. 158.19B; *Canon* 5, XS 325–6=Leipoldt (L.) IV: 55. Cf. the Pachomian evidence in Pachomius's rules, for example, *Praecepta* 105, 44.

5. Shenoute, *Canon* 9, FM 186=L.IV: 160–61, "No physician (ⲥⲁⲉⲓⲛ) among us shall heal an outsider, not only not for wages, but not even free of charge . . . ." And *Canon* 9, FM 186=L. IV: 161, "Female doctors (ⲥ2ⲓⲙⲉ ⲛⲥⲁⲉⲓⲛ) in these communities also shall not behave in this way at any time."

6. *Canon* 5, XS 386–72bis=L.IV: 56.

7. Shenoute, *Canon* 5, XS 326=L.IV: 56.

8. Crislip 2005: 15–17.

9. Ibid.: 86–90.

10. Shenoute, *Canon* 5, XS 326=L.IV: 56. On diet, see Shenoute, *Canon* 5, XS 325–6=L.IV: 55, "And those who serve in that place (the infirmary) shall act according to what is fitting, in the measure that the elder commands unto them, so that they may give to each one according to the type of illness;" also *Canon* 5, XS 319=L.IV: 53–54, "When people are sick, their allotment shall be determined for them [by the elder 2ⲓⲧⲙⲡ2ⲁⲗⲟ, (supplied from previous paragraph)]."

11. Chamber pots, "[No one] shall urinate in a ⲃⲁⲩⲕⲁⲗⲓⲟⲛ or a ⲱⲟⲱⲟⲩ or in any other similar vessel before having been given permission (ⲉⲙⲡⲟⲩⲟⲩⲉ2ⲥⲁ2ⲛⲉ ⲛⲁϥ) by the elder, except for the infirmary only and the elderly (ⲛ2ⲁⲗⲟ ⲉⲁⲩⲣ2ⲁ2 ⲛⲣⲟⲙⲡⲉ). And as for these others, let them seek permission from the elder (ⲉⲧⲣⲉⲩϣⲓⲛⲉ ⲛⲧⲟⲟⲧϥ ⲙⲡ2ⲁⲗⲟ)," Shenoute, *Canon* 3, YA 421=L.IV: 124.

12. The administrative structure is not entirely transparent in the White Monastery, especially due to the imprecision in terminology, Crislip 2005: 153–54; and compare the learned discussions of Shenoute's administration in the contributions by Bentley Layton and Rebecca Krawiec in this volume.

13. *Canon* 5, XS 61–61=L.IV: 78; Shenoute, Canon 5, XS 275–6=Mich.158: 19B.

14. Shenoute, *Canon* 5, XS 372bis=L.IV: 73.

15. Shenoute, *Canon* 5, XS 319=L.IV: 53–54; Canon 5, XS 326=L.IV: 56.

16. "The sick are sustained with wonderful care (*miris obsequiis*) and a great abundance of food (*copia cibis*)," Jerome, *Preface* 5, tr. Veilleux 1980–1982, vol. 2.

17. Shenoute, *Canon* 3, YA 538–9=L.IV: 33–34; *Canon* 4, BZ 26–27=L.III: 127; *Canon* 3, YB 108=BnF ms.copte 130.2 folio 42 verso; *Canon* 3, YB 72=BnF ms.copte 130.2 folio 60 verso; *Canon* 3, YB 73=BnF ms.copte 130.2 folio 61 recto; *Canon* 9, DF 178=BL Or. 3581A(28).

18. For more details see Crislip 2005: 28–30; and Layton 2002: 25–55.

19. Shenoute, *Canon* 5, XS 326=L.IV: 56. The manuscript breaks off, but we can presume that Shenoute went on to order that the sick must request the wine themselves.

20. E.g., "Let us not ask for anything we don't need, lest the Lord condemn us as sinners," Shenoute, *Canon* 3, YB 73=BN ms.copte 130.2 folio 61 recto; "Every one of us, whether man or woman, is despised in the presence of Jesus if they ask for any

dishes deceitfully as if they were sick when they are not sick," Shenoute, *Canon* 5, 537 XS 61–62=L.IV: 78; "Those who ask naively to eat, when they are not sick, are acceptable in the presence of our savior Jesus," *Canon* 5, XS 62=L.IV: 79; "As for the truly ill, who doesn't know that his stomach rejects all dishes? People are not neglected (ΝϹΕϢΛΛΤ ΛΝ) in eating what they need just because they think (ΕΥΜΕΛ-ΗΤΛ ΜΠΛΙ), 'My stomach did not receive it,' or 'I did not want to eat it,' or 'When I ate them, what did I do (ΛΙΡΟΥ)?' The things you ate, they pleased you. They are your portion (ϢΙ). But your stomach did not receive any, because it is diseased," *Canon* 9, DF 49–50=L.IV: 85–86. For more on the regulation of the behavior of the sick, see Crislip 2005: 68–99.

21. Shenoute, *Canon* 5, XS 326=L.IV: 56.
22. Crislip 2005: 36–38.
23. Shenoute, *Canon* 5, XS 372bis=L.IV: 73.
24. Shenoute, *Canon* 5, XS 386–372bis=L.IV: 72–73; on the prevalence of eye problems in Egyptian medicine, see Nunn 1996: 197–202.
25. On the Coptic medical tradition in general, see Krause 1991b: 1886–88; Kolta 1991: 1578–82; Westendorf 1999: 146–56; and Till 1951.
26. See Crislip 2006b: 165–68, at 166.
27. See in particular Nutton 1984: 1–14.
28. Zoega 1973: 626–30; Bouriant 1887: 319–20.
29. Bouriant 1887: 376. Orthography in the manuscript is erratic and nonclassical, a typical feature of Coptic medical manuscripts.
30. *Canon* 9, FM 186=L.IV: 160–61.
31. Bouriant 1887: 376. Other lactagogic recipes are preserved on page 215 of the manuscript, but have been omitted here due to difficulties or obscurities in the text.
32. Crislip 2005: 232.
33. See Wilfong 2002: 99–104.
34. Yet the complexity of the issue of pharmacological efficacy should be recognized. Chemical efficacy is by no means the only, or even the most important, factor in drug effectiveness. See the overview in Helman 1994: 194–223.
35. Zoega 1810: 627.
36. *Canon* 8, XO 126=IFAO Copte 2, unpublished.
37. Chassinat 1921: nos. 26, 56, 80, 109, 123, although in these cases the physician tests the medicine rather than the illness.
38. See Garrett 1995: 91–94. I would argue in fact that Shenoute's illness discourse reflects a familiarity with both medical knowledge and culturally shared models of suffering.
39. *Canon* 6, XM 190=L.III: 195
40. Crum 1992: 117, nos. 574–75.

4 Shenoute's Place in the History of Monasticism

Stephen Emmel

A LITTLE MORE than 1,500 years ago, inside the massive church whose ruined hulk has come to be known as the White Monastery (Arabic *Dayr al-Abyad*), on an occasion near the middle of the fifth century when the monastery's longtime leader Shenoute was about one hundred years old, and when the White Monastery church was just newly built and being used for worship for the first time, at least by the aged leader himself, Shenoute spoke the following words:[1]

> This great house of such magnitude! And by the providence of God! Not only was it four months that we spent working on it, or all of five, but also with the help of all these things that we gave as wages and expended on it—everything we had! In fact they did not diminish, but rather the Blessed, the Son of the Blessed, God the Almighty, blessed them and added even more to them.

Shenoute thought it miraculous that the monks had been able to afford the expense of building a magnificent new church—and other buildings besides: new monastic dwellings, and also a *niptērion*.[2] Not only were the monks not left materially exhausted by the expense of these major building projects, but according to Shenoute they had been able to be more generous in their service to the poor in that year than ever before.[3] And the

31

miracle of divine providence continued two years later, when an incursion
of barbarians far to the north displaced a large number of people, and some
20,000 souls took refuge in the monastery for a period of three months.
During that time doctors had to treat some of the refugees for wounds,
and nearly one hundred of the refugees died. But about half that number
of women were pregnant when they arrived and gave birth while staying
at the monastery. Some people complained about the accommodations and
the food. But Shenoute was overawed by the fact that the monks were at all
able to accommodate and show hospitality to so many people. He marveled
especially at the seemingly inexhaustible capacity of the monastery's well,
which he described as "little" and said would not have sufficed to provide
water for everyone without God's blessing.[4]

This well has been excavated in recent years, northwest of the church,
and while I cannot say anything about its current capacity to provide water,
I can say that it is a marvelous bit of architecture.[5] We do not know yet
how much of the surviving structure dates from Shenoute's lifetime, but
Peter Grossmann seems to be convinced that at least the basic plan of the
installation might go back to Shenoute himself—whether before or after the
monastery's service as a refugee camp will most likely never be possible to
say. In fact, quite a bit more of the material remains of Shenoute's monastery are visible now as compared with what could be seen just a few decades
ago. For one of the most exciting recent developments in the investigation
of monasticism in the Sohag region in general, and of Shenoute's monastic congregations in particular, is the archaeological excavation that was
begun twenty years ago by the Egyptian Supreme Council of Antiquities
and is now being continued by an international team under the umbrella
of the Consortium for Research and Conservation at the Monasteries of
the Sohag Region, which was formed by Elizabeth S. Bolman and others
in the year 2000.[6] A first season of excavation under the field direction of
Darlene Brooks Hedstrom and Peter Sheehan was undertaken just a few
months before the symposium of which this volume is a record, and further work had already been planned. All of us involved in the consortium
are committed to the steady continuation of this work in accordance with
a plan for scientific investigation and heritage management that respects
the extraordinary value of this region for the history of monasticism and
for Coptic Christian spirituality from late antiquity up to the present day.
Continued cooperation both with the Egyptian antiquities organization and
with the Coptic Church will be essential for the scientific success of our

work, and for appropriate long-term preservation and maintenance of the material remains of seventeen centuries of monasticism in this region in all its spiritual and cultural richness.

Another recent development in the investigation of monasticism in the Sohag region, also specifically to do with Shenoute, is work about which I myself am far more competent to write than I am about archaeology and material culture. I am referring to recent progress in the recovery of the remains of Shenoute's literary legacy, by which I mean progress toward the goal of making it possible for anyone to read as much of Shenoute's writings as we can discover among the Coptic manuscripts that have survived until the present time. Achieving this goal is mainly a matter of editing and translating Shenoute's writings, but also of interpreting them, for Shenoute is not always an author who is easy to understand. (Far from it.) However, editing, translating, and interpreting Shenoute's writings is in fact a much more complex and difficult undertaking than you might think, even if you are aware of the inherent difficulties of working with ancient manuscripts.

For as it happens, Shenoute's writings have survived for us almost solely in manuscripts that were once a substantial part of the library, or libraries, of his own monastery. However, those parchment books in which Shenoute's words had been copied by generations of monastic scribes are now mostly lost. Only parts of about one hundred such 'Shenoute codices' are known to survive. In a few cases, what we have is just a single leaf from one of those books, more often it is something a little more satisfactory, like 10 to 15 percent of the original number of pages. Only twice do we have a Shenoute codex from which more than half the pages survive, and even the better preserved of those two manuscripts is missing 12 percent of its leaves. Furthermore, the surviving fragments—and in the case of the White Monastery library we can speak really only of fragments, even though those fragments exist in large quantities—the many surviving fragments of the once extremely rich and varied White Monastery library are now scattered far and wide, through several dozen museums and libraries: from the Coptic Museum in Old Cairo and the Institut français d'archéologie orientale du Caire to the Bibliothèque nationale de France in Paris, and beyond, in Europe, in North America, and elsewhere. To the extent that progress has been made during the past two centuries in reconstructing Shenoute's corpus of writings from the dismembered and dispersed remains of his monastery's library, it has come through the painstaking piecing together of fragments in and among all these collections of Coptic manuscripts.[7]

The work of reconstruction is not entirely finished, but it is now well advanced, and an international project to edit and translate the surviving corpus of Shenoute's works was organized in 2000.[8] There are many interesting perspectives that Shenoute's large corpus of sermons, tracts, and letters open for us. And despite the many new discoveries that have been made in recent years on the basis of the codicological reconstruction of his corpus, I am confident that much remains still to be discovered. For Shenoute was a truly extraordinary personality, and he left behind an extraordinary literary achievement—extraordinary not just within Coptic literature, where his achievement is completely without parallel, but even within the monastic literature of late antiquity in general, be it Greek, Latin, Syriac, or in whatever other language.

Let me try to highlight just some of the ways in which our knowledge of Shenoute is changing, or has already changed, as a result of fundamental improvement in our access to his literary corpus. It used to be said that the only firm date in Shenoute's biography is the year 431, when he attended the Council of Ephesus with Cyril, patriarch of Alexandria. Firm and precise dates like 431 are still mostly lacking in Shenoute's biography, but in contrast to the situation a century ago, when Johannes Leipoldt wrote the first monograph on Shenoute and could fill only a few pages with a sketch of his biography,[9] today we can begin to imagine using a biographical framework for presenting the totality of Shenoute's activity. At present, when I imagine outlining such a scientific 'Life of Shenoute,' I work with a body of eight provisional main chapters.[10]

The first of these main chapters would be about Shenoute's rise to prominence in his monastery and his selection to become its third leader, or 'Father.'[11] My second chapter would be about Shenoute's style of leadership, particularly as it developed during the first three years of his tenure as the 'Father of These Congregations' in the course of his dealings with the members of the women's monastery to the south.[12] Chapter three, covering the two decades or so around the year 400, would be about Shenoute's anti-pagan activities: his attacks on temples and private shrines, and especially his conflict with the wealthy ex-governor of Thebais (Upper Egypt), Flavius Aelius Gessius.[13] A fourth chapter might be constructed around Cyril of Alexandria's failed effort to make Shenoute into a bishop, Shenoute's subsequent trip with Cyril to the Council of Ephesus in 431, and his efforts on behalf of Alexandrian orthodoxy in Upper Egypt. The next chapter after that would have to treat the years surrounding the construction of the new church, and then the monastery's service as a refugee camp a few years later, events that probably date to the mid- to late-440s.[14]

Somewhere there would have to be a chapter about life in the monastery under Shenoute's leadership, throughout his long tenure as Father.[15] And there would also have to be a chapter about a period of severe illness that Shenoute suffered, so severe that it kept him confined and away from almost all direct human contact for a year or more.[16] A final chapter would try to catch a few glimpses of Shenoute's last years: his reactions to the events that unfolded in Alexandria in the wake of the Council of Chalcedon in 451;[17] his decision to finish out his days on earth in a small abode built for him by his monastic brothers somewhere inside the monastery; and something of his thoughts as he felt the end of his life drawing near.[18]

I have chosen to present this brief overview of Shenoute's biography in the form of a series of imaginary book chapters, in order to be able to under-score a certain point: Quite apart from the inherent interest of Shenoute's life story as such, it is a remarkable thing just that we are in a position to reconstruct his story to the degree that we now can. Even only a decade ago, most people who knew anything about Shenoute still believed that Johannes Leipoldt, writing in 1903, had said more or less the last word about the sparse facts of Shenoute's biography. We now know much more than Leipoldt did.

We owe our newly gained knowledge of Shenoute's life not to the discovery of any entirely new sources, but rather to the continuing care-ful and critical study of sources that have been more or less available for study for several centuries. I mean the manuscripts—or rather, manuscript fragments—of Shenoute's own writings, which have come down to us almost exclusively among the tattered and scattered remains of his own monastery's library. Of course, there is a work of Coptic literature that has become well known, both among scholars and laypeople, as *The Life of Shenoute by Besa*, Shenoute's disciple, and his successor as Father of These Congregations. Because this *Life of Shenoute* was supposedly written by Besa, anyone who reads this work might well expect to learn from it at least the basic facts of Shenoute's biography. But let us look closely at the title of the so-called *Life of Shenoute* in the one Coptic manuscript that has preserved it for us in its entirety, namely the Bohairic text (from Wadi al-Natrun, but now in the Vatican Library), which is what most people mean when they refer to Besa's *Life of Shenoute*.[19] There the title is: "A few of the miracles and marvels which God effected through our holy father the prophet Apa Shenoute, the priest and archimandrite, which the holy Apa Besa, his disciple, witnessed."

Not only does this title make no claim to introduce a narration of Shenoute's biography, but it must be obvious to anyone who reads the work that it also does not in fact narrate his biography. The scholars who gave the title *Life of Shenoute* to this work did so knowing that the designation "Life" in the title of a work like this describes a certain kind, or genre, of ancient literature that in fact cannot necessarily be relied on as a source of historically accurate information. It is also unlikely that Besa was the author of the *Life of Shenoute* as we know it, although it is possible that some of the traditional stories about Shenoute go back to things that Besa said during the years after Shenoute's death, when Besa surely spoke publicly about Shenoute on a regular basis.

However, the *Life of Shenoute* as we know it is a much later work of Coptic literature, belonging to a well-known genre that conforms to certain conventions and serves a particular purpose. The purpose of such a "Life" is to honor, or even to glorify, its subject by every means possible. In the case of a holy man like St. Shenoute, it is especially miracles that he was believed to have worked or to have witnessed that serve to honor and glorify his saintliness, thereby glorifying God and edifying those who read the work or listen to it being read. And so it is no surprise that most of this *Life* is a series of stories narrating miraculous events involving Shenoute, without any attempt even to place the stories in a chronological framework, except that the stories begin with a few miracles from Shenoute's youth, and the work as a whole ends with his death. But between his birth and his death, the exact chronology of events is not important in this *Life*. All that is important is that Shenoute was saintly through and through, as his miraculous *Life* demonstrates in one story after another, page after page.

An important contribution to the study of the so-called *Life of Shenoute by Besa* has been made recently by Nina Lubomierski (2007), and so the only other thing that I want to say about that tradition on this occasion is that I myself remain convinced that the claim that Shenoute lived to be 118 years old[20]—a claim that many people find hard to believe—is at least approximately correct. Here I do not want to go into the complicated details of working out the chronology of Shenoute's biography.[21] However, I do want to emphasize that my conviction about Shenoute's very advanced age at death is based mainly on information that we learn from his own writings, and on one detail in a work by Besa (not in the so-called *Life of*

Shenoute, but in a separately transmitted sermon, which Karl Heinz Kuhn included in his edition of Besa's works under the title "On a Famine").[22] I have spent my own fair share of time trying to analyze the relevant information, and my conclusion remains that Shenoute was born about the year 347 (perhaps on 25 June 347) and died on 1 July 465. This means that in the year 373, when Archbishop Athanasius died, Shenoute was a young man of about twenty-five years.

Scholars have long accepted that Shenoute became the head of his monastery during the few years when Timothy I was patriarch of Alexandria, and I myself think there is good reason to accept Leipoldt's suggestion that it happened around the year 385, just at the time when Timothy died and Theophilus succeeded him.[23] In that case, Shenoute was about thirty-five years old when he became the leading 'Father of These Congregations.' And then he served in that capacity for eighty years.

Something else that scholars have long accepted, up until recently, is that Shenoute directly succeeded Pcol (Coptic *pcōl*), who had founded the monastery in about the middle of the fourth century. I do not know of anything in the *Life of Shenoute*, or in any similar source, that so much as hints at the existence of a second Father who was in charge of the monastery between Pcol and Shenoute. However, Shenoute's own writings—in fact the earliest of all his writings—leave no doubt that he did not become Father of the monastery immediately after Pcol. Rather, another man (whose name we do not know for certain, but there is slight evidence that he might have been called Ebonh, Coptic *ebōnh*)[24] was in charge of the monastery after Pcol died, sometime during the 370s, and then Shenoute succeeded him, thus becoming the monastery's third Father, rather than its second.[25] Furthermore, in these earliest of Shenoute's writings, he tells us quite a lot about a crisis of spiritual leadership that occurred during Ebonh's tenure as Father of the monastery. It was this crisis of leadership that disgraced Ebonh and brought Shenoute to prominence, singling him out as a likely successor to be the monastery's next Father.[26]

Shenoute's earliest writings, which inform us about the events that I have just summarized briefly, are two long open letters to his monastic brothers, written while the crisis was unfolding. Shenoute later regarded these writings as being of such fundamental importance for understanding the ever-present dangers facing the monks, and especially their leaders, as well as for understanding Shenoute's own role as the monks' leading Father, that he made them required reading for every member of the three monastic

congregations under his control, four times each year, as we read here in
Shenoute's own words:

> Let this book . . . remain with the Father . . . of These Congregations at all
> times, so that he might rely on it and not forget or neglect to read its words
> these four times, as is appointed for us. Let the brethren in the village send it
> to him each time they finish reading it, and also let him send it to them each
> time, so that he might understand that it is good to read all its words, not
> omitting any of them. . . . Only these four times each year, even if someone
> hates hearing them, because also he hates his own soul, they will be com-
> pelled to read them all.[27]

The surviving evidence (by which I mean the manuscripts) suggests that
this practice continued for as long as Shenoute's monastery remained a vital
institution, that is, well into the medieval period.[28]

We can say that Shenoute literally 'canonized' his own writings. For
throughout his life he periodically compiled his letters and other communications to the men and women under his guidance, and these compilations
resulted in a set of nine thick books of 'canons.'[29] This is the title that we
find repeated at the end of each of these volumes (to the extent that they
survive; for example, at the end of one manuscript codex *pmehsnau nkanōn*
means "The Second Canon," and a notation immediately following this
title means that the volume contains five works, called *epistolē*, "letters"),
and 'canon' seems also to have been Shenoute's own way of referring to
these volumes, although in exactly what sense, or senses, is a question that
still requires further investigation.[30] The nine volumes of Shenoute's *Canons*
are also now our main source of information about Shenoute's biography.
For it appears that Shenoute organized them chronologically.[31] Certainly,
volumes 1 and 2 contain works from just before and just after he became
Father of These Congregations, while volume 7 contains the works that
have to do with the construction of the new church and the monastery's
service as a refugee camp, and volume 9 reflects the period near the end
of Shenoute's life. Volume 8 contains letters written during the period of
Shenoute's severe illness, and volume 6 might belong to the period just
before that. Throughout all nine volumes, we gain detailed insights into the
organizational structure and everyday life of the monastery.[32]

For various reasons, this biographical interest being not least among
them, it was decided to begin the Shenoute editing project with the nine

volumes of Shenoute's *Canons*. I hope that it will not be too very much longer before the first volume of our edition appears, but it will not be an edition of any of the volumes of the *Canons*. Rather, it will be an edition of a single manuscript in Shenoute's corpus, a parchment codex from the White Monastery library that is known as the 'Florilegium Sinuthianum,' or 'the Shenoute florilegium,' also known as White Monastery Codex XL.[33] The reason for beginning our edition of Shenoute's works with Codex XL is that this unique manuscript contains a series of excerpts from all nine volumes of Shenoute's *Canons*. A 'florilegium' is just such a collection of excerpts, extracted from the works of one or more authors and presented, like a bouquet of flowers, to be enjoyed as an ensemble, a representative sample of the literary garden from which they have been plucked.

The Shenoute florilegium is a beautifully copied manuscript, in my opinion one of the finest examples of the 'Coptic uncial' script that we have. The manuscript is also carefully conceived and laid out, with each excerpt marked out by a heading in red ink, and each 'canonical section'—that is, each group of excerpts coming from a single volume of the *Canons*—marked off by a heading giving the volume number. Interestingly, these rubrics are partly in Greek, even in this manuscript that might have been copied as late as the tenth century, possibly even a few centuries later. For example, by far the most frequent heading that marks the beginning of a new excerpt is the laconic phase *tou autou*, which is Greek for 'by the same (man),' thus indicating that each new excerpt comes from the same author who also wrote the previous excerpts. Presumably, all these statements form a chain that reaches back to the very first page of the book, which unfortunately is missing from among the surviving fragments of this manuscript. But there is no good reason to doubt that on the lost first page of this florilegium there stood the name 'Shenoute,' probably in its Greek form *sinouthios*, which is a form of his name that Shenoute himself seems to have preferred for his literary purposes.

This supposition about the florilegium's missing first page would seem to be confirmed by the heading to the section much later in the book that consists of excerpts from volume 9 of Shenoute's *Canons*. This was the last such heading to be deciphered, because it occurs at the end of a leaf that had been torn in two, with the tear passing down the middle of the heading in the second column.[34] The text says: "Likewise canon 9 of holy Apa Shenoute, prophet and archimandrite. 9."

As it happens, the first surviving page of codex XL is page 41, which—with its tantalizing reference to the letters of St. Antony[35]—comes from the section of the florilegium that concerns volume 3 of Shenoute's *Canons*. Therefore we are missing the entirety of the sections concerning volumes 1 and 2. However, we have the fragmentary remains of a number of copies of both these volumes. Volume 2 consists mostly of a group of letters that Shenoute wrote three years after he became Father of the monastery. From these letters we learn about his difficulties with exercising leadership over the female members of the monastic community.[36] Here is another historical aspect of Shenoute's career about which we learn nothing from the so-called *Life of Shenoute*. From Shenoute's own writings we learn that he was in charge of not just 'a monastery,' but of a group of three monasteries—whence comes Bentley Layton's recent proposal (2002) that we speak of a kind of monastic 'federation' that included both the main monastery, founded by Pcol, and the 'small monastery' founded by Pshoi three kilometers to the northwest of Pcol's foundation (the church of which is now known as the Red Monastery, Arabic *Dayr al-Ahmar*), as well as a monastery for women "in the village to the south," as Shenoute describes it. Shenoute also tells us that Pcol had nothing at all to do with this women's congregation in the village, but that Ebonh had been in the habit of preparing the eucharist for them. Presumably, the village where this women's monastery was located is Atripe (now often called Athribis), and it is tempting to imagine that the women's monastery there was some kind of a private house that had been transformed into a refuge for 'virgins of God,' a kind of urban female asceticism (or monasticism) that we know of in a number of cities elsewhere in Egypt and the Roman Empire.

In his effort to take over from Ebonh the responsibility for the female monks in Atripe, Shenoute at first visited them personally. But his visit resulted only in misunderstanding about his intentions toward the women, and further visits only made the problem worse. And so he abandoned the practice of making personal visits to the women, and for the rest of his life he communicated with them only by means of letters, which he dictated and then sent by the hand of a trusted elder male monk, who also brought back the women's replies or other communications.

Interestingly enough, Shenoute also communicated in this way—by means of letters—with the male members of his monastic federation, that is, the monks in the main monastery (which today we call the White Monastery by generalizing the medieval Arabic name for the church building to refer to the entire surrounding monastic community) and in the smaller men's monastery (which we call the Red Monastery by a similar process of generalization). Why Shenoute did so is hinted at in the *Life of Shenoute*, and it is becoming ever clearer the more deeply we study his own writings: Shenoute himself did not live among his brothers in the monastery, but rather he lived as a hermit somewhere in the surrounding desert. There in some cave or long-since-abandoned tomb (as we may imagine) he had his secretary—his *notarios*—always close by. And probably the trusted monks who carried information back and forth from Shenoute's hermitage to the three federated monasteries came and went more or less daily.

Under normal circumstances, Shenoute and the other hermits living in the desert near the White Monastery federation entered the main monastery only four times each year, at fixed times appointed for a kind of general assembly such as we know of also in the Pachomian monasteries. It was during these periods of assembly that volume 1 of Shenoute's *Canons* was to be read or heard by every member of the three congregations, and it seems likely that these periods of assembly also provided most of the occasions on which Shenoute delivered sermons, whether to the assembled male monks, or to a congregation of people from outside the monastery who came specifically to see and hear him on these special occasions. His sermons were written down by stenographers and then recopied—like his letters—into papyrus codices that were then recopied again and again, in a process that eventually produced the medieval parchment manuscripts from which we can now learn something about Shenoute's life and thought.

In this context, let me return to the *Life of Shenoute* tradition and say something about its claim that Shenoute was only nine years old when he became a monk. I must confess that I am skeptical about this claim. In fact, I am strongly inclined not to believe it, even though I cannot disprove it. Consider this: Shenoute knew Greek, and apparently he knew it pretty well, both to read it and to speak it, as well as to write it. However, if he entered the monastery when he was only nine years old, then where, when, and how did he learn Greek? The question must be posed, for, so far as we can tell, Shenoute's knowledge of Greek was at least partly secular, which is to say that probably he went to school in the big city of Panopolis (Coptic *Šmin*, which is now Akhmim). I think it unlikely that he would have received such an education in the monastery of Pcol.

There is other evidence in Shenoute's writings that he had experienced the world outside the monastery as a young man and not just as a boy, thus making it unlikely that he became a monk at the age of nine. If that were the case, surely his experience of the world effectively ended then and there when he abandoned the *kosmos* in favor of the cell. But I think

it likely that Shenoute was well educated in the normal way of anyone
who was educated in a late antique city like Panopolis, that is, in the
Hellenistic-Greek school system, and so he must have had his education
before he ever became a monk.[37] Furthermore, I suspect that his education and training was significantly better than that of the other monks in
Pcol's monastery, such that soon Shenoute's job there came to be to function as the Father's *notarios*, that is, his secretary. I am beginning to think
that he must have been Ebonh's secretary, and possibly he served in that
capacity already under Pcol. I wish I could prove this hypothesis, because
it helps to explain a number of things about Shenoute's career that are
otherwise very puzzling, such as how he was able to 'publish' his first two
lengthy open letters, at a time when he was—as I used to imagine—just
an 'ordinary' monk.[38]

Another thing that a good education and secretarial training help to explain
in Shenoute is his remarkable literary consciousness, by which I mean his sense
of himself as an author, as he went about producing what was and remained
an extraordinary corpus of Coptic literature, the like of which did not exist
before (except, in some ways, for the Coptic translation of the Bible). To the
extent that Shenoute supervised the compilation not only of his *Canons*, but
also of his sermons and other writings, which we have partly in an organized
set of eight volumes of 'Discourses' (or 'Logoi'), he must have been conscious
of creating a corpus of works that one could set on a bookshelf alongside the
works of great Christian authors from all around the Roman Empire.

Shenoute was undoubtedly a charismatic genius of great personal authority and power. Clearly he had insight into people's hearts and minds, such
that he seemed to his contemporaries to be a prophet. And he was so familiar with the Bible, and so deeply influenced by it (both in Coptic and in
Greek), that he must have felt himself really to be a prophet, a latter-day
Isaiah or Jeremiah, called by God to show His people the narrow path to
salvation. That is why Shenoute not only quoted frequently from the Bible
throughout his letters and sermons, but also sometimes wrote in the same
style as the Bible,[39] as if he was using his own voice to reiterate and rephrase
here and now (in late antique Upper Egypt) the same message that "that
prophetic voice at that time back then" had proclaimed to ancient Israel, in
the time of the Old Testament prophets.

The time is not yet ripe to speak with very much assurance about
Shenoute's thought and teaching, because too much of what he wrote still
remains to be published, translated, and studied. But I do think it is already

safe enough to say what the hard core of his message was, because he repeated it again and again: Repent your sins now, before you die, because there will be no mercy for sinners who die unrepentant! Clearly, Shenoute believed in eternity, and he must have had a very vivid imagination about what eternity means: either eternal bliss, or else eternal misery, the latter especially to be imagined as an amplification of painful things experienced physically in this world here and now. Furthermore, Shenoute was very strict in his view of God's mercy, which he understood to be boundless even for the worst sinner, if he truly repents during this life, but woe upon woe unto all eternity for the unrepentant.[40]

Despite his prominent leadership role—not just within the White Monastery federation, but also in the surrounding districts, where he was famous already during his lifetime as a holy man and champion of the poor, especially against wealthy and oppressive pagan landowners—Shenoute was nevertheless first and foremost a monk, who understood that in the end there was just "one little plot of earth" for which he alone was responsible—by which he meant his own body, with its virtues and its vices, its needs and desires, and its ability to control them or to let them control it.[41]

The monastic life was, in Shenoute's view, no guarantee of success in achieving eternal salvation. Contrary to a view that might have been typical of the early Pachomian monastic communities, and apparently also of Shenoute's predecessor as Father of his monastery, namely that the monasteries were little bits of Paradise on earth, with the monks already like angels sojourning only temporarily among mortals, Shenoute understood that no man or woman alive is completely impervious to the wiles of the devil, and even the most innocent can be misled unwittingly into sin. There is an interesting passage in one of Shenoute's earliest works in which he reports that the Father of the monastery had tried to reassure him that his worries about the existence and spread of sin in the community were unnecessary, because the Father had provided the monastery with a perimeter wall to keep the devil out. To which Shenoute replied: "Did I say that the sins *came in from outside*?"[42]

In Shenoute's view, Satan and his demons and unclean spirits of every sort might be anywhere, constantly at the ready, armed with a wide array of weapons for tempting people to commit evil and to sin.[43] In a sense, however, the devil is an agent of God, Who could destroy him if He wanted to. Human beings have free will, and the role of the devil is to provide people with opportunities to exercise their free will and choose to do good, or at least not to sin. The monastery provides an environment in which certain temptations are limited, in comparison to the frequency of their occurrence in 'the world' outside the monastery, and the strictly regulated life of the monastery makes it relatively easy for a monk to know what he or she is expected to do in order to avoid or resist temptation and sin. Furthermore, the community as such functions as a finely articulated support system in which each individual helps all the other individuals, each and every one, to tend properly his or her own "little plot of earth" in preparation for the judgment of God that will follow upon death.

Like all natural language, scholarly language too has an inherent tendency toward ambiguity, and the title of my presentation at the Sohag monasticism symposium was an example of it. If I take 'the history of monasticism' to refer to 'what really happened' across the years and centuries since the beginning of Christian monasticism, then it seems to me that Shenoute's lifetime marks out a kind of 'golden age' in the evolution of a monastic organization that was basically coenobitic, but incorporated elements of eremitic and semi-eremitic monasticism as well. Shenoute's federation of three physically proximous monasteries was, apparently, 'successful' and widely influential in a variety of ways, both during Shenoute's lifetime and for at least several generations after him. Sadly, our information about the history of Shenoute's monastic federation dwindles to almost nothing under his immediate successors. The papyrus documentary evidence for Shenoute's monastery extends from the sixth century into the eighth, while the surviving dated manuscripts from the White Monastery library belong to the tenth, eleventh, and twelfth centuries. There used to be some inscriptions in the church from as late as the early part of the fourteenth century, after which the monastery seems to have declined and finally fallen to ruin. The influence of St. Shenoute himself, which began already during his lifetime and continues today, is a subject that deserves a study all its own.

However, if on the other hand I take 'the history of monasticism' in my title to refer rather to the scientific discipline that attempts to reconstruct and interpret (what we can know about) whatever it was that really happened, then I must emphasize, first of all, the difficult challenge that we face at present in recovering as much as we can from what survives of Shenoute's writings, and second, the great promise that Shenoute's writings hold for the future. For whatever role Shenoute and his monastic federation played in 'what really happened' in Upper Egypt, the role that his written legacy is beginning to play and, I am sure, will continue to play in the study of Christian monasticism as a whole—not only in Egypt!—is large, and it will grow, precisely because Shenoute's literary legacy is so very rich.

In conclusion, I want to return briefly to the theme with which I began, namely the physical remains of Shenoute's monastery. The ground—the earth—is also a kind of text, written by the activities of human beings and nature. When humans shape the ground to their needs, piling it up into buildings and molding from it the artifacts of daily life, and especially when they turn it not into expressions of the most basic human needs, but into expressions of human spirituality and intellectuality, then they create 'texts' that approach the meaningful heights, or depths, to which language is sometimes capable of giving the most articulate expression. The White Monastery is such a text. The remains of that institution that lie partly now exposed, but mostly still buried by centuries of drifting sand, can speak to us across the centuries going all the way back to the years when Shenoute himself composed his own texts for posterity—including, whether he could imagine it or not, people like us. Just as it is our task—no, rather our duty!—to reconstruct the manuscripts of Shenoute's works so that we may recover as much as possible of his words before any more is lost irretrievably—as so much has already been lost forever—so it is our duty to read the text written in the ground of Shenoute's monastery before it crumbles to dust, irretrievably, forever, as any little plot of earth eventually must. We owe it to Shenoute to do so.

Notes

1. See Emmel 1998: 82–83.
2. Cf. Emmel 1998: 83–84; Grossmann et al. 2004: 372b ("a washing area"), 379b ("a washing place"), fig. A (near the "kitchen area"); Brooks Hedstrom 2005: 9–10 and 19 (= fig. 5).
3. Pleyte and Boeser 1897: 320 col. 2 lines 9–31; Emmel 1998: 83 n. 13.
4. See Emmel 1998, esp. 86–88; on the "amazing little well," see Leipoldt 1906–1913, vol. 3: 70 lines 14–17.
5. So far as I am able to judge; see Grossmann et al. 2004: 379, figs. A and E.
6. Grossmann et al. 2004; Brooks Hedstrom 2005.
7. Emmel 2004b, which includes an extensive bibliography in vol. 2: 951–85.
8. The editorial team comprises at present: Heike Behlmer, Anne Boud'hors, David Brakke, Andrew Crislip, Stephen Emmel (editor-in-chief), Jean-Louis Fort, Bentley Layton, Samuel Moawad, Zlatko Pleše, Tonio Sebastian Richter, Tito Orlandi, Sofia Torallas Tovar, and Frederik Wisse.

9. Leipoldt 1903: 39–47.

10. In addition to the bibliographical references given in the following notes, see also many relevant chapters in the present volume. See now also Emmel 2007: 87–92; Schroeder 2007.

11. Emmel 2004a; Schroeder 2006.

12. Krawiec 1998; Krawiec 2002.

13. Emmel 2002; Emmel (forthcoming).

14. Emmel 1998; Grossmann 2002b; Schroeder 2004.

15. Layton 2002; Layton 2007.

16. Emmel 2004b, vol. 2: 555, 576–79, 593–94.

17. Emmel 2004b, vol. 1: 8 with n. 9; Emmel 2002: 96–98.

18. Emmel 2004b, vol. 2: 556, 570–71, 599.

19. Leipoldt 1906–1913, vol. 1; English translation by Bell 1983.

20. E.g., Bell 1983: 89.

21. Emmel 2002: 95–99.

22. Kuhn 1956, vol. 1: 41, English translation in vol. 2: 40.

23. Emmel 2004b, vol. 1: 7–8.

24. Emmel 2004b, vol. 2: 569.

25. Emmel 2004b, vol. 2: 558–64.

26. Emmel 2004a.

27. Emmel 2004b, vol. 2: 562–63.

28. Emmel 2004b, vol. 1: 13.

29. Emmel 2004b, vol. 1: 111–234.

30. Young 1969.

31. Emmel 2004b, vol. 2: 553–56.

32. Layton 2002; Layton 2007.

33. Emmel 2004b, vol. 1: 111–25.

34. Emmel 2004b, vol. 1: 114 (= pl. 3).

35. Vivian 2005: 82–83.

36. Krawiec 2002; Behlmer 2004.

37. Cf. Timbie 2005: 65–66.

38. Cf. Emmel 2004a: 173.

39. Emmel 2004a: 165–67.

40. Emmel 2006–2007.

41. Chassinat 1911: 99b–100a; French translation by Cherix 1979: 27.

42. Emmel 2004a: 167–69.

43. Brakke 2006: 97–124.

5 Pachomius and the White Monastery

James E. Goehring

IN THE FIRST volume of the *Oxford History of the Christian Church*, entitled *The Church in Ancient Society: From Galilee to Gregory the Great* and published in 2001, Henry Chadwick included the following brief paragraph on Shenoute in his chapter on "Monks: The Ascetic Life."

> In the fifth century the Pachomian monasteries acquired a formidable leader Shenoute; austere and authoritarian, he made discipline tougher (more vehement beatings for lapses) but was admired for generous hospitality and for his onslaughts on pagan temples.[1]

While we historians of Coptic Egypt may give thanks that Shenoute has finally made it into a classic western English language introduction to Christianity, we may also be forgiven for cringing at the historical inaccuracy of enrolling Shenoute himself into the Pachomian federation. And yet there is a way in which history did in fact effect that enrollment, albeit later in date in the community's subsequent articulation of its past. The history of the relationship between Shenoute's White Monastery and the Pachomian federation offers, in fact, a fascinating glimpse into the historical development and creative memory of the Upper Egyptian coenobitic movement. While the evidence is necessarily sparse, enough survives to permit a tentative reconstruction of the various stages involved in the process.

By the middle of the fourth century, when Pcol decided to found his new monastery on the edge of the desert across the Nile from Šmin (Panopolis),[2] the Pachomian Koinonia already administered a cluster of four monasteries in the area on the other side of the Nile. The local bishop of Šmin, an ascetic named Arios, had earlier invited Pachomius to organize a monastery in his city.[3] Its success soon led the federation to expand its operation in the area. Before his death in A.D. 346, the federation added two additional male monasteries, Tse and Tsmine, and a monastery of virgins associated with Tsmine, in the immediate area.[4] The distance of this cluster from the original Pachomian communities centered around Pbow led to an arrangement whereby Petronius, the father of Tsmine, served to oversee the entire cluster.[5] While one need not assume that the Pachomian communities were the only monasteries in the area, it seems probable that their considerable presence made them readily visible and influential in and around the city of Šmin in the middle of the fourth century.

The substantial Pachomian presence in the area leads one to suspect some form of relationship between it and the White Monastery that emerged on the other side of the Nile in the middle of the fourth century. Johannes Leipoldt argued, in fact, that Pcol's success in founding the White Monastery depended on the decline of the Pachomian federation. There is, however, no hard evidence to support this thesis.[6] While it is true that the federation came close to breaking apart upon Pachomius's death, a fact used by Leipoldt in support of his contention, the crisis was averted when Theodore replaced Horsiesius as the federation's general abbot.[7] In order to avoid similar problems in the future, Theodore instituted a new administrative policy, rotating the individual abbots among the various monasteries twice each year.[8] While the silence of the sources allows one to speculate about the fate of the outlying monasteries, it offers no proof that they were either in decline or left the federation. The implementation of the new administrative system suggests rather that they remained within the federation. Additional references indicate, in fact, that the federation continued to grow under Theodore's leadership. Before his death in A.D. 368 he founded two new monasteries, Kaior and Nouoi, further down the Nile beyond Šmin near Hermopolis, and added an additional monastery of virgins at Bechne near the federation's central monastery of Pbow.[9] While problems reemerged when Horsiesius resumed the post of general abbot upon Theodore's death, they did not last long.[10] There is again no indication that any of the federation's monasteries left during Horsiesius's tenure, which lasted at least through A.D. 387. The fact that the federation constructed a major basilica at its central monastery of Pbow in the middle of the fifth century and was involved in the founding of the monastery of Metanoia in the Alexandrian suburb of Canopus argues for its continued strength into the following period.[11]

Given this evidence, there is no reason to assume that the success of the White Monastery near Šmin occurred as a result of the decline of the nearby Pachomian communities.[12] While they certainly declined and disappeared at some point in history, any effort to pinpoint the date rests not on fact but speculation. If one accepts the continuing existence of both communities for some period of time, the more interesting question of their interaction arises. Rather than simply assuming that the White Monastery grew as the nearby Pachomian communities failed, one is compelled to ask about the nature and impact of the relationship between the two. It is to this task that I now turn.

While one will never know why Pcol chose to establish his own community rather than join the Pachomian federation, the significant presence of the federation in the immediate area appears to have influenced his own undertaking. Later sources note that Pcol did not fashion a new way or different rules, but built on the foundation of others, presumably Pachomius and his successors.[13] The so-called *Rule of Pcol*, reconstructed by Leipoldt, supports this claim. Several of its regulations, while formulated differently, address behaviors identical to those found in the *Rule of Pachomius*.[14] Compare, for example, regulations 8 and 9 of the *Rule of Pcol*, as cited by Shenoute, with Praecepta 97 and 96 from the *Rule of Pachomius*.[15]

Rule of Pcol 8
"Cursed is any novice who shaves another novice without being assigned to do so, or who does so out of the sight of others."
Rule of Pachomius, Preacepta 97
"No one shall shave his head without the housemaster, nor shall anyone shave someone else without having been assigned to do so, and nor shall anyone shave someone else while they are both sitting."
Rule of Pcol 9
"Cursed is any novice who removes a thorn from another novice's foot without being assigned to do so, or who does so out of sight of others."
Rule of Pachomius, Preacepta 96
"No one shall remove a thorn from someone else's foot, except the housemaster and his second, or someone who is ordered to do so."

It seems clear from such evidence that Pcol drew from the Pachomian tradition in constructing his own community. One may further assume that his information came from the federation's monasteries in the immediate area. Each new monastery in the Pachomian federation was organized according to the same rule and likely supplied with a copy of it.[16] Whether Pcol learned of the rules through conversations with Pachomian monks or from a copy of the rule acquired for his own community, knowledge of it appears to have influenced the organization and running of his monastery.

The recognition of Pachomius's authority as the founder of the coenobitic life and author of the movement's ancestral rule continued under Shenoute's leadership (385–465).[17] While he guarded the White Monastery's independence, he would on occasion appeal to Pachomius in support of his cause.[18] In his treatise "So Listen," for example, Shenoute harshly condemns an errant monk, suggesting that his activities in the darkness mock the words of "our fathers," which he then narrows down to "Pachomius the Great," citing from his rule "Do not speak with your neighbor in darkness!"[19] By referencing Pachomius and his rule, Shenoute condemns the actions of the errant monk as crimes committed not only against him and his rule, but against the coenobitic institution more generally.

A second reference to Pachomius, although this time not identified as such, occurs in Shenoute's discourse "I Have Heard About Your Wisdom," preached before the governor Flavianus. In this treatise, Shenoute reflects on how a person is to confront the world without becoming an enemy of Christ. At one point, he draws from the *Letters of Pachomius*, declaring: "A good and wise and truly pious father said through his writings in some letters, 'Sing the omega. Do not let the omega sing you'."[20] The passage is a direct quotation from Pachomius's *Letter* 1.[21] While we cannot know for certain why he chose in this instance not to name his source,[22] his use of it again underscores the respect and authority given to Pachomius within the White Monastery.

Additional, more subtle echoes of parallel content and language between Shenoute's writings and the Pachomian dossier further the impression of this connection.[23] One may suspect as well that Shenoute's effort to draw the nearby female community and the Red Monastery into a monastic federation under his centralized control reflects the influence of the Pachomian Koinonia.

Shenoute's successor, Besa (A.D. 465 to after 474), on the other hand, neither quotes from the Pachomian corpus nor refers to the Pachomian federation in his extant letters and sermons.[24] In the later *Life of Shenoute*, however, the Pachomian connection reemerges. It reports that Victor, archimandrite of the Pachomian federation, and Shenoute traveled to the royal city with the Archbishop Cyril of Alexandria to confront the problems raised by Nestorius.[25] The reference probably points to Shenoute's attendance at the Council of Ephesus in 431, and if both his and Victor's participation is historically accurate,[26] it underscores the two coenobitic leaders' recognition within Egypt and establishes a connection between them. If it is not historically accurate, it indicates the later assumption of such contact.

Contact is also assumed for the mid-fifth century in the *Panegyric on Macarius Bishop of Tkôw*, which reports that the Pachomian archimandrite Paphnutius stopped at the White Monastery as he journeyed northward with some brothers to receive a blessing from Shenoute.[27] It is worth noting in this connection that both communities, the White Monastery in Sohag and the Pachomian central monastery of Pbow, constructed great new basilicas with remarkably similar dimensions in the middle of the fifth century.[28] They had become parallel monastic powerhouses in Upper Egypt, and while not precluding some form of competition, the two federations continued to recognize and accept one another, as they always had.

Matters changed dramatically, however, during the reign of the Byzantine Emperor Justinian I (527–565). In the period following the Council of Chalcedon in 451, diversity emerged within the Pachomian federation with respect to the decisions embraced by the council. The differences, however, did not disrupt the federation until the reign of Justinian I, when, according to evidence contained in three fragmentary White Monastery codices, certain pro-Chalcedonian elements within the federation brought accusations against Abraham of Farshut, the archimandrite of the federation's central monastery of Pbow. Based on these charges, Justinian summoned Abraham to Constantinople, where he demanded his allegiance to Chalcedon. When Abraham refused, Justinian stripped him of his position as archimandrite and appointed one of Abraham's pro-Chalcedonian accusers in his stead. Upon his return to Egypt, soldiers accompanied the newly named pro-Chalcedonian archimandrite to Pbow to insure his installation. The sources report that the monks loyal to Abraham, namely, the anti-Chalcedonian element, fled to the desert and other monasteries. As a result, the Pachomian federation, at least as represented by its central monastery of Pbow, became a pro-Chalcedonian organization. Abraham, who managed to return to Egypt with the help of the Empress Theodora, proceeded first to Shenoute's

White Monastery, where he copied the rule and put it in safe storage for later use. He retrieved the copy at a later date when he established his own community near his native Farshut.[29]

The fact that Abraham sought refuge in the White Monastery underscores the close relationship between it and the Pachomian community of Pbow. I have argued elsewhere that the events that befell the Pachomian federation were unique to its own situation. While Justinian I supplied the muscle to effect the enforcement of the Chalcedonian position at Pbow, the impetus for the action came from elements within the Pachomian federation. The emperor's religious policies created an opportunity for the pro-Chalcedonian monks, who used it effectively to gain control of the federation. At the White Monastery, on the other hand, Shenoute's emphasis on the purity of the corporate monastic body and his strict enforcement of the rules insured the community's Coptic orthodoxy. No place existed within the Shenoutean federation where pro-Chalcedonian elements might gain a foothold.[30]

The White Monastery thus offered the exiled anti-Chalcedonian archimandrite welcome and familiar refuge.[31] He used his brief stay there, for example, to make a copy of the rules.[32] While the Synaxarion identifies these as the rules of Shenoute, one wonders whether the identification is anachronistic. It would make more sense for Abraham to make a copy of the Pachomian rule, which, given Shenoute's citation of it in his writings, must have existed in the community's library at that point. In that case, Abraham, shorn of access to his own community, turned to its close Upper Egyptian relative for access to his own Pachomian traditions.

The loss of the Pachomian federation to the pro-Chalcedonian party in the middle of the sixth century removed it as a player in the production of Coptic orthodoxy. The White Monastery, which had existed as one of the two main coenobitic powerhouses in Upper Egypt, became in the process the sole inheritor of the orthodox coenobitic mantle. While insufficient evidence survives to reconstruct the decline of the Pachomian monasteries subsequent to these events, decline they did and ultimately disappeared. One has only to observe the current state of the Pachomian Monastery of Pbow in comparison with that of the White Monastery to recognize this fact.

The transfer of power led as well to a more intimate joining of the early orthodox Pachomian traditions with the continuing orthodox traditions of the White Monastery. As Abraham, when exiled from the newly pro-Chalcedonian and hence heterodox Pachomian federation, had found refuge in Shenoute's White Monastery, so the Coptic orthodox coenobitic tradition found refuge and continuity in the enduring orthodoxy of the White Monastery. The coenobitic family tree shifted to trace its heritage from its early orthodox Pachomian founders to and through Shenoute, who became the tradition's most visible representative in Egypt.

This shift is traceable in the references to Pachomius and Shenoute in the later sources. Prior to the demise of the Pachomian federation, references to Pachomius recognized his authority as the founder of the coenobitic tradition without blurring the distinctive nature of his and Shenoute's federations. Shenoute refers to his coenobitic ancestors as "our fathers," but neither he nor the later *Life of Shenoute* use the phrase to locate the origin of the White Monastery in the Pachomian tradition or to suggest that it has inherited the coenobitic mantle. The usage simply recognizes a more general indebtedness to the earlier Pachomian movement. In the *Life of Shenoute*, for example, the author has Shenoute call out in the midst of a deathbed vision, "My father Apa Pšoi, my father Apa Antony, my father Apa Pachomius, take my hand so that I may rise and worship him whom my soul loves, for behold! He has come with his angels."[33] Note that the use of the term 'father' does not set Pachomius apart. He, like Pšoi and Antony, simply represents the origins of the Egyptian monastic movement, saints who preceded Shenoute to heaven and now return to welcome him into heaven at the moment of his death.

When one turns to the later Panegyrics on Abraham of Farshut, the pattern shifts so as to place Shenoute in the line of early coenobitic leaders. The *First Panegyric on Abraham of Farshut* tells the story of Abraham's vision of his own impending death.

> He looked and saw our holy fathers of the Koinonia, Apa Pachomius and Apa Petronius and Apa Shenoute of the monastery of Atripe. They came to him, and when he saw them, he ran to them (and) greeted them with his face downcast towards the earth. They embraced him, raised him up, (and) greeted him. And they said to him, "Peace to you who has built upon the foundation that we laid."[34]

The author later praises Abraham as "a great one among the saints and an elect and perfect one among the monks, like our ancient fathers and forefathers, that is, Apa Pachomius and Apa Shenoute and Apa Petronius and Apa Horsiesius, the fathers of the world."[35] Shenoute, in these passages, has become one of the founding fathers of the Upper Egyptian coenobitic movement. Gone are the later Pachomian archimandrites, like Apa Victor, who accompanied Shenoute and Cyril to the Council of Ephesus. The coenobitic family tree now moves from Pachomius to Petronius to Theodore to Horsiesius to Shenoute. Shenoute, the archimandrite of the independent White Monastery federation, is here posthumously enrolled in the Pachomian federation.

In similar fashion, Shenoute takes his place alongside Pachomius as the author of the coenobitic rule. In the same *First Panegyric on Abraham of Farshut*, Abraham warns his monks, "And even if the whole world were in prosperity, you would be in need because you abandoned the laws of the Lord that our holy fathers gave us, namely Apa Pachomius and Apa Shenoute."[36] Consider in comparison the passage from Horsiesius's *Fourth Letter.* "Let us remember his [Pachomius's] commandments and laws, which he established for us so that we may observe them in truth. And let us also remember our father Petronius, who passed his short time with us according to the [custom?]. And let us remember our father Theodore."[37] Horsiesius, writing before the events that took place in the reign of Justinian I, thinks historically within the Pachomian tradition. The author of the *First Panegyric on Abraham of Farshut*, on the other hand, writing after those events, thinks more "creatively." He realigns the history of Upper Egyptian coenobitism so that it follows orthodox rather than historical lines of descent. By tracing the coenobitic tradition back through Shenoute to Horsiesius to Theodore to Petronius to Pachomius, the author, whom I take to represent the later tradition, fashions a new line of descent that ignores and therefore bypasses the later heterodoxy of the Pachomian federation.

Let me return in closing to Henry Chadwick's observations that "in the fifth century the Pachomian monasteries acquired a formidable leader Shenoute." The claim, as already noted, is historically inaccurate. While the founders of the White Monastery willingly drew upon the Pachomian example and developed close relationships with the federation, they never became part of it. I would argue, however, that what did not happen historically, happened in the later articulation of history. With the loss of the Pachomian federation to Coptic orthodoxy in the sixth century, Shenoute gained in stature. As the heterodox Pachomian monasteries declined over time and eventually disappeared, Shenoute's position rose within the shared memory of the past. He took his place in a now common coenobitic history that traced its origins back through Shenoute to Pachomius. In this sense then, while Chadwick's assertion is historically inaccurate, it captures the eventual outcome of history. In the aftermath of the events that took place in the reign of Justinian I, the Pachomian tradition, to use Chadwick's words, "acquired a formidable leader, Shenoute."

Notes

1. Chadwick 2001: 402.
2. The precise date of Pcol's founding of his monastery remains unknown. Judging from the date of Shenoute's entry into the monastery circa 356, the founding is usually placed center the middle of the century. Emmel 2004a: 156–57; Layton 2002: 25.
3. Fifth Sahidic *Life of Pachomius* (S5) 54 and the First Greek *Life of Pachomius* (G1) 81; for English translations, see Veilleux 1980–1982, vol. 1: 73–74 and 352–53.
4. For Tse: S5 52 (Veilleux 1980–1982, vol. 1: 72–73) and G1 83 (Veilleux 1980–1982, vol. 1: 354). For Šmin: S5 54 (Veilleux 1980–1982, vol. 1: 73–74) and G1 81 (Veilleux 1980–1982, vol. 1: 352–53). For Tsmine: S5 57 (Veilleux 1980–1982, vol. 1: 77–78) and G1 83 (Veilleux 1980–1982, vol. 1: 354). For the associated monastery of virgins: G1 134 (Veilleux 1980–1982, vol. 1: 393). See also Ladeuze 1898: 174-78; Lefort 1939: 403–404; Goehring 1996: 279 (Goehring 1999a: 101–102).
5. Chitty 1957: 382–85.
6. Leipoldt 1903: 36. His case rests on (1) an assumed loss of power evidenced by the schism that followed Pachomius's death, (2) the fact that this loss of power makes sense of the fact that the later Coptic tradition, while honoring Pachomius, Theodore, and Horsiesius, preserved little more than the names of the subsequent Pachomian abbots, and (3) the fact that the decline of the Pachomian federation explains the rise of the White Monastery. With respect to his second point, it is worth noting that the natural focus of such communities on their founders' stories explains this phenomenon. One could say the same thing with respect to the sources on the White Monastery. In addition, one might point to the Pachomian Archimandrite Victor, who, according to the Coptic Acts of the Council of Ephesus and the *Life of Shenoute*, accompanied Cyril to the Council of Ephesus in 431 C.E. His feast day was later celebrated at the White Monastery (Coquin 1991d: 2308).
7. Sixth Sahidic *Life of Pachomius* (S6) 139–44 (supplemented by the Bohairic *Life of Pachomius* [Bo]); G1 127–131; Veilleux 1980–1982, vol. 1: 195–205, 387–91; Goehring 1986a: 242–44 (Goehring 1999a: 167–70).
8. S6 144; Veilleux 1980–1982, vol. 1: 204–205. This policy is not mentioned in the Greek *Life of Pachomius*.
9. G1 134; see also Bo 202 (= G1 137).
10. Goehring 1999b: 221–40.

11. For the fifth-century basilica, see Coquin 1991b: 1926–1927; Grossmann 1991e: 1927–1929; Goehring 1989: 11–12 (Goehring 1999a: 251–52); Lease 1991. For the monastery of Metanoia, see Gascou 1991: 1608–11. It may be, of course, that not all of the federation's monasteries remained equally strong and/or affiliated with the Koinonia.

12. It should be noted that the existence of a powerful monastery does not necessarily preclude the formation of other independent monasteries in the same area. While various pre-exisiting monasteries did choose to join the Pachomian federation (so Šeneset, Tmoušons, and Tbewe; see Goehring 1992: 245 (Goehring 1999a: 28), others, such as the community near Sne from which Theodore came (Bo 31; G1 33) did not. The later Pachomian monastery of Phnoum at Sne is presented as a new foundation (Bo 58; cf. G1 83) and thus distinct from the independent monastery that Theodore had initially joined. One may point as well to the numerous later monasteries that arose in the vicinity of the White Monastery on the east side of the Nile near Akhmim (Coquin 1991a: 78).

13. Leipoldt 1903: 38 n. 2.

14. Emmel 2004a: 164; Leipoldt (1903: 37–38) indicates that Pcol made the rule somewhat harsher. Emmel notes that Leipoldt's reconstruction of the *Rule of Pcol* has yet to be fully tested against the newly reconstructed *Canons* of Shenoute.

15. Translations from Emmel 2004: 164 *(Rule of Pcol)*; 164–65 n. 39 *(Pachomian Rule)*.

16. Bo 50 (Šeneset); S5 51 (Tmoušons), 52 (Tse); Am 54 (Šmin); Bo 56 (Tbewe), 57 (Tsmine), 58 (Phnoum); cf. G1 54 and 83. The *Life of Pachomius* reports that a copy of the rule was made and deposited in the first associated women's monastery (Bo 27; G1 32). The more distant cluster of four monasteries in the Panololite nome surely had at least one copy of the rule.

17. The dates refer to his period as the third father or leader of the White Monastery. For a thorough discussion of Shenoute's dates, see Emmel 2004: 155–57.

18. I am aware of only two specific references in the surviving corpus of his works.

19. Amélineau 1909: 461; Leipoldt 1903: 99 n. 4. David Brakke alerted me to this passage. The Coptic of the *Pachomian Rule, Praecepta* 94, reads: "No one shall speak to his neighbors in the darkness." While the Coptic differs, the citation of the *Rule* is clear.

20. White Monastery Ms. XH 277.11.35–43; Chassinat 1911: 111; my translation. See Quecke 1968: 155–71.

21. Quecke 1975: 99; cf. Boon 1932: 77. Quecke (1968: 166) identified this passage as the one example in Shenoute's extant writings where he cites Pachomius.

22. Leipoldt (1903: 86 n. 4) suggests that Shenoute may have left Pachomius's name out on the assumption that his non-monastic audience would have been unfamiliar with him.

23. Such echoes are just beginning to be recognized. See Timbie 2005: 70–71.

24. See the indices in Kuhn 1956. It is interesting to note that Besa does quote from the letters of Antony, which one thus assumes were in the monastery's library.

25. *Life of Shenoute* 17–21; English translation in Bell 1983: 47–49. The royal city refers to Constantinople, though one suspects that the passage connects with Shenoute attendance with Cyril at the Council of Ephesis in 431 B.C. (*Life of Shenoute* 128–30).

26. In the Coptic Acts of the Council of Ephesus, Victor's role at the Council of Ephesus is emphasized and Shenoute is not mentioned. See Kraatz 1904: especially 148–71. Janet Timbie brought this reference to my attention. See also Coquin 1991d: 2308.

27. *Panegyric on Macarius* 15.3; Johnson 1980: vol. 415, p. 117 (text) and vol. 416, p. 91 (translation).

28. See above, n. 11; also, Goehring 2006: 3–5.

29. The events are briefly recorded in the Copto-Arabic Synaxarium. See Basset 1916: 682–88; Forget 1906: 411–13 (text); 1921: 401–405 (translation). A brief reference also occurs in the *Panegyric on Apollo*. See Kuhn 1978, vol. 394: 17–18 (text) and vol. 395: 13 (translation). Additional details are preserved in the fragmentary remains of White Monastery Codices GC and GC. The former contains two panegyrics on Abraham of Farshut, and the latter an excerpt on Abraham in a panegyric on Manasseh. See Campagnano 1978: 223–46; 1985b; 1985c. I am currently working on a critical edition of these materials. For a more detailed account, see Goehring 2006: 1–17, and the older dated article, Goehring 1989.

30. Goehring 2006: 17–20.

31. One assumes that some of the others who followed Abraham in leaving Pbow also found refuge at the White Monastery.

32. This information occurs in the Copto-Arabic Synaxarium. Basset 1916: 684–85; Forget 1921: 402.

33. *Life of Shenoute* 185; Bell 1983: 91.

34. White Monastery Codex GC, Coptic page 49A14–B13 (Cairo, IFAO 8r); my translation.

35. White Monastery Codex GC, Coptic page [84]B11–24 (Paris, BN 12913 15v); my translation.

36. White Monastery Codex GC, Coptic page 53A14–B2 (Vienna, BN K9527); my translation. A similar conflation occurs in the *Panegyric on Apollo* (Kuhn 1978, vol. 394: 36.14–22 (text) and vol. 395, 27.25–32 (translation)).

37. Horsiesius, *Ep.* 4 (Veilleux 1980–1982, vol. 1: 163); Veilleux's translation. A similar reference to Pachomius, Petronius, and Theodore occurs in Horsiesius's speech to the brothers after Theodore's death preserved in the Bohairic *Life of Pachomius* 208 (Veilleux 1980–1982, vol. 1: 261–62); Goehring 1999b: 229.

6 The Role of the Female Elder in Shenoute's White Monastery[1]

Rebecca Krawiec

THE WHITE MONASTERY in the fourth and fifth centuries consisted of different communities, or congregations. They were separated physically but united under one set of monastic rules and one main monastic leader, at least during the tenure of its third head, Shenoute. One of these communities was female and was located in a neighboring village; the others were male, and Shenoute began his monastic career living in one of these until a crisis drove him into the desert.[2] Even after taking control of the monastery, Shenoute continued to spend much of his time in the nearby desert, exercising his authority through letters, sermons, and the codification of monastic rules. He also constructed a system of command where various monks, male and female, were entrusted to carry out his orders.

Shenoute had what appears to have been at times a contentious and tense relationship with at least some, if not most, of the women who lived in this monastic system. Although his works survive only in fragments, it has been possible to reconstruct, or re-imagine, these women's monastic experiences and to understand the basis of the disputes that occurred between Shenoute and the women under his care.[3] Despite the recent flurry of scholarly interest in the White Monastery, the role of the female elder is still poorly understood. Three views of the female elder in the White Monastery predominate in scholarship: (1) Susanna Elm presents a thwarted leader who was not given full control over her own community but is instead subordinate both

59

to Shenoute and a male elder who acted as overseer for the female community;[4] (2) Bentley Layton claims she was the equivalent of the male elder, the head of the female congregation second only to Shenoute, just as the male elder in the male congregation was second only to Shenoute;[5] (3) I have argued that she was a figure whose role changed during Shenoute's takeover of the monastery, such that her former independence became subordination, at least during times when she (and other female monks) met with Shenoute, or his agent, the male elder.[6] In order to investigate the tensions among these descriptions, this article examines some of the duties and obligations of the female elder as laid out in the rules that Shenoute both inherited from previous leaders of the monastery and adapts and expanded during his own leadership.[7] Those rules that regulated interaction between the female elder and the male community receive particular attention in order to compare the role of the female elder and the male elder, that is, the man who served as a 'second in command' to Shenoute in the male community of the monastery.[8] I conclude by suggesting that the tensions and contradictions in the female elder's position in the White Monastery's hierarchy illustrate how gender paradoxically contributed to both egalitarianism and inequality in Shenoute's monasticism.[9]

Shenoutean Rule Material

Any analysis of Shenoute's *Canons* requires a clarification of their contents, which include letters,[10] sermons, and rules, of which the last contains various instructions for behavior and the lists of what behavior leads to a person being "cursed." These rules are not limited to any one of the nine *Canons*, but rather are dispersed throughout, mostly in *Canons* 3, 5, 6, and 9, as Stephen Emmel's codicological reconstruction shows. Moreover, as Caroline Schroeder describes, "The rules also contain lengthy narrative descriptions of the ways in which the monks should follow and enforce the rules as well as substantial interpretative, homilectic, and hortatory passages similar in style to Shenoute's letter and sermons."[11] Thus, the rules are not presented in a systematic way to the community but as part of a larger set of complicated literature. Moreover, Shenoute instructs that these *Canons* be read to the monastic community four times a year. Since this instruction follows specific rule material in *Canon* 5 (and since Shenoute uses the word ⲔⲀⲚⲞⲚ, along with ⲈⲚⲦⲞⲖⲎ, "commandment," to refer to the rules themselves), it is unclear whether simply rule material was to be read, or all the literature of the nine *Canons*.[12] This study examines those passages that might most obviously be regarded as rules, passages which are instructions and are meant to set parameters which could then receive further explanation and interpretation in a variety of settings and situations. Information from such rule material, however, cannot be understood independently from the rest of the Canon literature.

The rules do not mention the female elder very often. Her absence is especially notable, given the repeated assertions that the female community was included under the rule. Shenoute constantly reminds his audience that the rules are meant for all monks (see below), thus placing the female monks and community under the authority of the rules, yet he does not mention the female elder as often as the male within the application of the rules. The resulting impression, like reading through the rules themselves, is less of a systematic creation of a hierarchy of authority positions for the monastery and more of a running commentary on those positions as they were evolving. The female elder is presented in three ways in the rule material: (1) rules that establish the male and female elders as parallel authorities for their separate communities; (2) rules that depict the female elder as the authoritative equivalent of the "father of these places," namely, Shenoute; and (3) rules that subordinate the female elder to the male elder. An understanding of the context for these various presentations will explain their inconsistencies. Further, these discrepancies may preserve a record of power negotiations that took place over time between the female community and Shenoute.[13] The rule material therefore is less a synchronic monument of Shenoutean regulation and more a diachronic expression of the changing nature of the authority structures.

The female elder appears in the rule material in much the same way as the female community itself appears: as an addition, or even afterthought, to clarify that how things are done among the men is also how things are to be done among the women. The male and female elders tend to be mentioned in these descriptions when Shenoute needs to set up surveillance (to make sure monks were adhering to the rules) and to allow dispensations. The reciprocity of the rules, alike for men and women, is thus echoed: permission to deviate from the rules comes from the male elder among the men and from the female elder among the women. For example: "Further, the one who will give anything to his companion secretly through fraud among us ourselves or you yourselves, either anything to eat, or clothing, or linen, or a strap, or anything at all secretly, and they did not inform the male elder first among us or they did not inform the female elder first among you, they shall be cursed, because they have transgressed our laws which our fathers have handed down to us."[14] Here Shenoute creates a clear equivalency between the two communities. At times, rules begin as if simply addressing a male community, only to have the female elder and/or female community appear abruptly: "He who will pluck hair which is growing from his armpit or who shaves any place belonging to him in the limbs of his body, unless their head alone, stealthily without the male elder among us [knowing] or without the female elder among you yourselves [knowing] is cursed."[15] Once again, these rules position the male elder and female elder in parallel roles: each is the main, or final, authority for the respective community. Additionally, the absence of a requirement for the male or female elder to consult with Shenoute underscores the control each elder has over his or her immediate community.[16]

The existence of these parallel legislative constructions raises questions about the times that the rule material mentions only the male elder, despite the inclusion of both male and female monks in that very instruction. For example, both male and female monks can make vows to increase their fasting but only the male elder is explicitly authorized to force a monk to eat, despite this vow, if he judges the hardship too great: "And whenever a person among us, or a woman among you, vows not to eat, or not to drink, two days, or three, or four, or more than these, because of God—and others adjure them, misleading them violently to eat, they sin . . . . Whenever the [male] elder sees someone who suffered in asceticism [ⲡⲟⲗⲓⲧⲓⲁ] or rather in another thing because of God, and he compels him to eat, he is responsible for his deeds."[17] What are we to make of the lack of an additional "and so also the female elder" or "and in this way also it is to done among you"? It seems unreasonable, and indeed impractical, to assume the male elder somehow would have this authority in the female community; conversely, it seems reasonable to assume the female elder would do so. Yet the rule is silent on the role of the female elder even though it applies to the female community as a whole.

Moreover, the relationship between Shenoute, the male elder, and the female elder is not set but can be fluid, even within one 'rule.' One example, although dependent on a reconstruction since the text breaks off at a crucial point, shows how the female elder could be simultaneously equivalent and subordinate to the male elder. This passage also questions whether her subordination is due to gender or merely to separation from the 'main' community. Shenoute is discussing the monthly searches of the monks' cells for purloined food; the male elder "will go into all the houses of the community." This formulation could suggest that the women's houses are included as well as the men's. However, Shenoute also orders similar searches "in our other small community which is north of this, so that the father of that place acts also in the same way" along with "the ones who are appointed with him." This "other small community" then has a leader who has the same authority over his community as the male elder has; but he is a "father" and he acts in concert with others. Shenoute continues by instructing that any violations this "father" finds must be reported to the male elder ("he shall inform the male elder about them, and he shall not hide any wicked deed at all"). Finally, Shenoute says, "And the female elder, she shall also act . . . ,"[18] at which point the manuscript breaks off. The parallel construction with the earlier orders to the father of small community, however, suggests that the female elder shall also search the houses in the women's community and that she also reports any transgressions to the male elder. This example illustrates the tension that exists throughout the rule material, in terms of the role and authority of the female elder and of the overall inclusion of women in the monastic rule. On the one hand, the female elder has authority over her community as a separate entity within the monastery since she is in charge of searching it. On the other, all matters are to be vetted through the male elder, who presumably then reports to Shenoute. In addition, the female elder's subordination to the male elder in this case is not due to gender; the other father is just as subordinate. What remains uncertain is the relationship between the male elder and the overall head of the monastery, the "father of the congregations."

Other rules that describe the female elder are less clear on the question of equivalency with the male elder. Instead, they suggest that she is equal in authority to Shenoute. First, on at least one occasion, the wording of a rule equates her with the "father of these places." Both male and female monks were cautioned that they would pay a penalty if they went to work without praying "it not yet having been appointed to them through the father of these places, and without the female elder for her part also who is in the village."[19] Here the final authority for the female community "in the village" is still the female elder, but the comparative authority is not, apparently, the male elder (who is not mentioned) but Shenoute or his successors.

Second, the female elder is at times defined as "the mother" of the female community, a title parallel to the "father of these places."[20] When Shenoute stipulated how those in the female community should communicate with

the men, he designated who should deliver messages: "whenever a need
exists, the female elder herself of the gathering, the mother of the ones in
that place, will go with two other senior women with her."[21] The term,
"mother," however, is itself complicated because soon afterward Shenoute
uses its singular and plural forms in reference to those who should communicate their needs to the male community: "We already have said many
times and we have written it, that the mother or mothers of the ones in the
village will write to us here (about) everything which they need in their
place." Here it appears that Shenoute is referring to the female elder as "the
mother" and then including the mothers, who serve as the head of various houses.[22] Yet the lack of any mention of "elders" (or "senior women")
seems odd. These aberrations thwart any attempts to make a specific reconstruction of the monastery's authority structures. In addition, because the
total number of references to the female elder is relatively few, any variations in Shenoute's references to the woman (or women) in charge are not
easily dismissed. Despite this confusion, these different descriptions do not
alter the main impression created by the material presented thus far: that of a
relatively autonomous female community with an authoritative (and largely
independent) leader.

There is also the question of who appoints the female leaders. Once
again, Shenoute's description of this process uses fluid terminology but con-
veys a clear overall message: God has chosen who should serve as leaders
(presumably including Shenoute).[23] Shenoute writes, "For after the father
of these congregations is his second . . . . Just as God will send this second-
person . . . so also he will send every house-person and their seconds on
behalf of the ones who dwell with them. And just as God will send these
two people and the ones in agreement with them, so also he will send the
mother of the congregation and the one who comes after her, her second,
and all the others who are in agreement with them."[24] That Shenoute uses
"mother of the congregation" indicates a parallel authority system where
each community has a head (father/mother), a second, and their supporters. Since the male community most likely chose Shenoute as its head, one
could expect the female community selected its "mother," although this
process could have changed during the course of Shenoute's leadership.[25]

The rule material thus depicts the female community, and its leadership,
as a separate yet linked community. This dual status, however, also exposes
a tension in the monastic rules: at times, the female elder is her own authority. Yet at other times Shenoute requires the oversight of the male elder,

a decision that subordinates the female elder. The clearest example of this subordination is the requirement that female monks need the permission of the male elder to leave their community: "Nor shall any woman among you escape the gate of the community, or go for any reason, without being ordered by the male elder to go."[26] Besides this rule, most examples of such subordination seem to stem from the letters, which describe actual meetings, more so than from rule material, which remains inconsistent in its depiction of authority positions. For example, the rules for funerals of female monks indicate that the male elder had control over their burial: male monks are sent to the female community to receive the body, singing Psalms chosen by the male elder. No women are allowed to attend the funeral, except for the female elder and "another who is an old woman of many years."[27] Given that monks were most probably buried in the desert, at some distance from the female community in the village, this description is not unexpected. What stands out is less the absence of women, and more Shenoute's careful regulation of the necessary contact between the two communities. Shenoute then segues from funerals to general religious gatherings, saying that "none among us" can skip gatherings for prayer and none can skip "the hour when we lift up the offering . . . unless they are ordered by the male elder among us or the female elder among you." This contrast—between the subordinate female elder of the funeral and the female elder in charge of the gathering in her own community—emphasizes the distinction in place. The male elder leads religious gatherings of both communities, male and female. In those situations when the two communities can remain separate, the female elder has the authority to act independently. Thus, the two communities exist in tension: when separate, they are equal; when together, a male/female hierarchy emerges. Moreover, Shenoute's ideal is for the communities to remain separate since he prefers communication through letters rather than meetings.[28] It is contact between male and female monks that creates anxiety for Shenoute and consequently tension in the rules.

These authority structures are even more complicated by the presence of gatekeepers (literally, 'people appointed to the place of the door') for the female community. The plural in the Coptic is gender neutral and the word ⲢⲰⲘⲈ ('people') is not gender specific. However, Shenoute consistently uses this word ⲢⲰⲘⲈ to refer to monks in the male community as opposed to women in the female (see below). Thus it seems likely that these gatekeepers are men,[29] a supposition that takes on greater weight because of Shenoute's anxiety about contact between the gatekeepers and the female congregation, especially the female leaders who would need to have regular communication with these men. Shenoute writes that these gatekeepers are not allowed "to speak alone with the (woman) at the gate, nor will she herself speak with them, not even regarding the smallest thing, even if she is the daughter of someone from those (men), or his sister or his mother or finally anyone at all either joined to them or not joined to them."[30] One presumes that the woman is not herself a gatekeeper since she is merely at the gatehouse ("in the place of the door") and not "appointed" to it (a gatekeeper). More anxiety appears in another rule, which insists that no material goods should be given to the gatekeepers from the (physically proximate) female community. Rather, these goods are sent from the male gathering, at some distance.[31] These gatekeepers can also not leave the village community, even to visit the sick, unless permission is granted from the male elder.

The presence in the female community of male gatekeepers, themselves part of the male authority system and subordinate to the male elder, supports Elm's contention that the entire female community, although treated as an equal part of the monastery in the rules, was in fact subject to constant male supervision. Yet Layton's contention of equivalency has also been clearly confirmed. It is precisely the fact that the evidence supports two seemingly incongruous portraits that leads me to suggest that the rules preserve a process of power negotiations. For example, the descriptions above suggest various levels of communication between the female and male communities. Shenoute's preferred method allows a woman, who does not a hold a specific title, to come to the gatehouse but not to converse with the men there. If necessary, "whenever the need exists, the female elder herself of the gathering, the mother of the ones in that place, will go with two other great women" to meet with the gatekeepers.[32] Apparently, in these scenarios, only written communication passes from the male gatekeepers to the male community. Finally, however, "whenever the need exists" this same female leadership—the female elder, identified as "mother," and two senior women—can go to the male community, either to deliver the letter themselves or possibly to meet with the male leadership.[33] These complicated descriptions show Shenoute's preference for gender separation, which is made possible by the gatekeepers and which secludes the women, especially the female elder.[34] Such a system, however, cannot have been sufficient, thus forcing Shenoute to allow physical contact between the communities even as he insists that written communication is better.[35]

The Two Communities: Male and Female, Us and You, People and Women

Reading these few passages about the female elder in the context of the overall role of women in the White Monastery suggests that the rule material does not necessarily provide more clarity about the monastic system and its authoritative structures than the letters. Rather, like the letters that accompany them in the *Canons*, they record a tension in the White Monastery in terms of the place and function of the female community. Moreover, the tension appears also in the overall application of the rule material to the women. Elm contends that women lived as part of the monastery from its start and so "Shenoute's rules and '*Canons*' were not originally conceived for a male community only and then simply passed on to a later female addition. They were from the beginning conceived for and addressed to *men and women* alike" (emphasis hers).[36] I would argue that both the position of the female community as part of a larger federation and the authorship and audience of the 'original' rules remains uncertain.[37]

Shenoute uses several phrases to signal an explicit inclusion of women in the monastic rules:[38] (1) "Among us or among you [pl.];" (2) "Among us, either male or female;" (3) "a ⲢⲰⲘⲈ [person/man] among us, or a woman;" (4) "Among you" where "you" is a feminine singular and so refers to the whole federation, including the female community; (5) "Among you [f.s.], either male or female;" (6) "He is cursed, namely a man [not ⲢⲰⲘⲈ], or a woman among you [pl.];" (7) "He is cursed, namely a brother or a sister." Two of these phrases, "either male or female" and "among us and among you" appear frequently in the letters. The first phrase, "either male or female," serves to create an expectation of monasticism that transcends gender, even as it continues to insist on gender identity; while the second phrase, "among us or among you," insists on two communities, an "ours" and a "yours," that are reciprocal but separate.[39] A similar effect is created in the rule material, especially with some of the other five variants. To insist on a rule for all, either male or female, presents a different view of the monastic congregations from a rule for "a man among us, or a woman." In the former case, the rule is presented as egalitarian in its inception; both men and women are submissive to a higher authority (not Shenoute, but rather God, the author of the rules) and this submission marks their monastic identity. In the latter case, women are being asked to adhere to a rule seemingly written for men, which makes the women 'equal' but only as an extension of the male community. As an appendage, the female community accepts not just Shenoute's authority, but an entire system created for a male monastery. In short, they accept a male-dominated surveillance system necessary for Shenoute to exert his control.

This latter view of the female community creates subordination for women even as they are accepted as monks in the federation like the men. As Elm notes: "the mother was forced to subject herself completely to the authority not only of Shenoute but also of another father, again in the name of equality."[40] This point calls into question the term 'equality' when examining the role of gender in Shenoute's monastery. Here modern theoretical investigations about gender equality prove illustrative. These studies have differentiated between a formal sense of equality, "treating likes alike," and a more substantive sense, "addressing disadvantage."[41] Because Shenoute is equal only in the formal sense, he creates inequality. True equality would have to be equal in the substantive sense where the 'disadvantage' is not simply separation from Shenoute (since he also lives apart from the male community) but rather the disadvantage of Shenoute himself not visiting their community and the disadvantage of being a later addition to a monastic system authorized by a distant, and often harsh, male leader. Because of their gender, these women were less and less able to represent themselves to the person in charge of continually shaping and setting their monastic experience; rather, they had to communicate through intermediaries who may or may not have understood or been sympathetic to their arguments. Shenoute's lack of substantive equality in his monastery, even as he strove for reciprocity, helped fuel the tension I have illustrated. He created a system that at times allowed for equality but at other crucial moments revealed the disadvantages the women had as members of the monastic federation.

Notes

1. In addition to the participants of the Sohag Symposium, I would like to thank Caroline T. Schroeder for her comments on the published version of this article.

2. For two accounts of this period of Shenoute's career, see Emmel 2004a and ch. 2 of Schroeder 2002.

3. This is the general subject of Krawiec 2002.

4. Elm 1994: 296–310. Elm uses Johannes Leipoldt's publication of some of the works of Shenoute that includes both rules and fragments of two letters concerning female monks as the basis for her interpretation.

5. Layton 2002: 28–30, esp. Table 1 on 29. For his study, Layton has "read through more or less all the extant remains of the *Canons*" (26).

6. Krawiec 2002: 52–55 and 77–79. For my study, I focused on thirteen letter fragments pertaining to the female community and examined some, but by no means all, of the rule material to set some context for those letters.

7. For previous leaders of the monastery, see Emmel 2004b: 9–10. That the elders, male and female, became crucial to Shenoute's monastic system has been noted by Layton in his suggestion that their role receive further attention (Layton 2002: 51).

8. The Coptic for male and female leadership is ambiguous, although Layton suggests future work must be illuminating: "It will probably be necessary to distinguish two meanings of ΠϨλλO/TϨλλω as follows: (1) 'the male Eldest/female eldest'—the two Elders par excellence (heads of the male and female hierarchies); (2) 'one of the Elders' generically speaking," (Layton 2002: 51 n. 110). Although I understand Layton's use of the superlative 'Eldest' to refer to the head of the group—that s/he is the eldest, not the elder of two—I will continue to use 'elder' in my paper as it remains the usual term in scholarship on monasticism in general, especially throughout the Middle Ages.

9. The tensions, therefore, are not simply in scholarship on the female elder but in the rule material itself. For example, the main passage Layton uses for his description of the monastic hierarchy (see n. 5) does present both elders as in charge of each separate community. Yet, a gender inequality of the sort Elm describes also appears. The particular section (Leipoldt 1906–1913, vol. 3: 156–57) explains the procedures for making reports to Shenoute. Each elder, male and female, creates an account of transgressions ('evil things') based on conversations with heads of houses and senior monks, but the female elder then gives her report to the male elder, who reports everything verbally to Shenoute.

10. The letters recorded in the nine *Canons* include those written to specific individual monks, those written to just the female or male community, and those written to the monastery as a whole. Yet, since Shenoute chose to include these particular letters within this collection, we can infer that whatever the specific original audience, the letter included a more general monastic instruction that Shenoute deemed applicable to all monks, male and female, that was consistent with the rule material with which it was integrated.

11. Schroeder 2002: 88. Also as Layton notes: "In arrangement and style Shenoute's works called *Canons* is not a monastic *regula*," though he also notes Emmel's point that "some materials in *Canons* books 3, 5, and 9 come closest to the literary form of a regula" (Layton 2002: 29 and n. 22).

12. Bentley Layton, in his paper for this symposium ("Ancient Rules of Shenoute's White Monastery Federation"), argued for the existence of two rule books which

would have served as the basis of the rules Shenoute records. Under this theory, these rule books were read to the monks on a regular basis.

13. This argument is not meant to contradict Layton's presentation of the female elder as a static position, since he notes: "For present purposes, I will not take into account the possible evolution of institutional rules and structures over the long span of Shenoute's career" (Layton 2002: 30).

14. Leipoldt, 1906–1913, vol. 4: 122–23. This rule also touches on the issue of Shenoute's codification of rules already in place, and the extent to which he adapts and adds to them. In this case, giving things secretly seems to be the "law" which was handed down from "our fathers." However, that Shenoute also comments on the roles of the male and female elder, as well as how duties were assigned to each, suggests an amalgamation of previous rules and new circumstances: "such that any person, male or female, shall not give anything to his companion through fraud secretly, unless it was appointed to him through the male elder among us or through the female elder who has been set for you among you yourselves."

15. The rule continues, in part, "he who will shave hair in any places belonging to him without the male elder among us or the female elder among you yourselves, they (?) shall be cursed, whether he is a male, whether she is a female. And if the need exists, such that they shave sick parts (of the body), they shall inform the male elder first among us or they shall inform the female elder among you yourselves" (Leipoldt 1906–1913, vol. 4: 171).

16. Since Shenoute lived outside the monastery, the male community needed a person to provide daily oversight as much as the separate female community did.

17. Leipoldt 1906–1913, vol. 4: 59–60.

18. Ibid.: 58.

19. Ibid.: 106. A parallel for this passage appears in Young 1993: 48–59.

20. Though Layton also points to Shenoute's use of the phrase "congregational parents among us whether male or female" (Layton 2002: 29, Table 1, n.s 2 and 3).

21. Here Shenoute uses the phrase, "Senior Women," with ⲚⲞϬ ⲚϬ2ⲓⲘⲈ, which Layton argues is the term for female elder monks and which functions as the equivalent for "the elders" (Ⲛ2ⲀⲖⲞ), implied male. Young translates the Coptic phrase as "older women" but he also translates ⲐⲖⲖⲰ as "mother superior" (Young 1993: 56).

22. These heads of monastic houses are also at times called ⲈⲓⲞⲦⲈ, a gender neutral 'parents.' See Layton 2002: 29.

23. This view is in keeping with Shenoute's overall understanding of his leadership, as I argue (Krawiec 2002: 51–72), and with the general presentation of God as the author of the rules for the monastery, as Schroeder argues (Schroeder 2002: 103–107).

24. Leipoldt 1906–1913, vol. 4: 44.

25. On the process of Shenoute's having become head of the monastery after his complaints about the previous leader, see Schroeder 2002: 76–85 where she lays out the "political" implications of his rhetoric. For appointments of female leaders, compare the problem in *Abraham, Our Father* from *Canon* 3, where a female monk seems to have been reluctant to receive an increase in her rank (Krawiec 2002: 38–40).

26. Leipoldt 1906–1913, vol. 4: 61.

27. Ibid.: 61–62.

28. "For the letter is for us and for you yourselves the firmness and the greater benefit of our gathering" (Ibid: 108). See Young 1993: 56: "Corresponding (by letters) is indeed the assured enhancement of our assembling."

29. As Layton argues (2002: 34–35).

30. "At any time within these congregations, whenever the necessity arises, such that the people who have been appointed to the place of the door of the congregation which is in the village must speak with the ones in that place, or such that the ones in that place themselves say a word to us or a message" (Leipoldt 1906–1913, vol. 4: 107).

31. Ibid.: 106.

32. Ibid.: 107.

33. See n. 21 above.

34. Indeed, the passage in question ends with the specific admonition that the gatekeeper system allows the female elder and senior women to "remain there with their companions together" (Leipoldt 1906–1913, vol. 4: 107).

35. See note 28 above.

36. Elm 1994: 300.

37. I here follow Schroeder's arguments about the authorship and origins of the rule material (see Schroeder 2002: 100–103).

38. In some cases, rules do not mention women at all. Further exploration is necessary to determine whether their absence means the rule does not apply to them or whether their inclusion is implied.

39. Krawiec 2002: 95–100, esp. 99.

40. Elm 1994: 308–309.

41. Kapur 1999: 144.

7 The Ancient Rules of Shenoute's Monastic Federation

Bentley Layton

WORK IS NOW well under way to produce a critical edition of Shenoute's vast work entitled *Canons*. My own editorial task is volumes 4 and 5 of the *Canons*. Now, this title—*Canons*—is a bit odd. In Christian usage of the Greek language, 'canons'—*kanones*—meant 'rules' or 'laws,' and so it is no surprise to find that volumes 4 and 5 do contain a large number of monastic rules.[1] However, as you read these volumes, and indeed all nine volumes of the *Canons*, two very peculiar problems immediately catch the eye.

First, for the most part, these nine books do not consist of monastic rules or laws. Instead, they consist mainly of monastic diatribe, filled with reproach and warning, directed to fellow monks and nuns. Why, then, were these diatribes entitled *Canons*?

Second, interspersed throughout the *Canons* we *do* find a certain number of monastic rules floating here and there. However, Shenoute usually quotes these rules without making any obvious connection to the theme or argument of the work in which they occur. What is the function of the rules that occur haphazardly in the midst of diatribe? Why are they there, and not collected together in one book? How do they belong to the text? Or, to put the question more broadly, what is the *Canons*, why does it exist, who gave it this name, what was its intended function, and in what environment was it used? So far, we have no answer to these questions, and I am not going to answer them all in this paper.

In order to edit and translate Volumes 4 and 5 as accurately as possible, I decided to collect and study all the rules and policy statements that occur in *all* books of Shenoute's *Canons*. My corpus now amounts to more than five hundred rules, that is, short passages that seem to be, or to cite, or to reflect, a monastic rule. Since many, many parts of the *Canons* have not survived down to the twenty-first century, the original, complete text of the *Canons* must have contained even many more rules than I have collected—let us imagine, a thousand or more. The quantity of the surviving rules is nothing short of sensational.

Now, the genre of Christian monastic rule had already been invented by Pachomius two generations before Shenoute. However, only one hundred or so Pachomian rules now survive, and mostly in a Latin version, whereas, in the Shenoute corpus, we have over five hundred items, a really extensive set of commands and policies in the original Coptic. This enables us to understand the administration of an early coenobitic monastic federation, both in detail and in its overall structure. As readers may know, much of my recent research has been devoted to analyzing the structure of Shenoute's monastic world on the basis of these rules.[2]

Let us return to the rules. What is the source of authority for these rules? Who was their reputed author? In seeking to answer these questions, it is very important to remember that Shenoute was not the founder of the White Monastery federation: this was apparently Apa Pcol. As Professor Emmel has demonstrated,[3] Shenoute was the third leader of the federation, the successor of a certain Apa Ebonh. Thus: Pcol, Ebonh, Shenoute. During Shenoute's leadership as third abbot of the federation, the time of experimentation and surprise had passed. Patterns of daily life had become well established, taken for granted, and typified.[4]

Now, in quoting monastic rules, Shenoute speaks of "us," thus including himself, as having inherited the rules from predecessors. He refers to the "canons" or "traditions" or "commands" or "commandments" or "laws" that a group called "our fathers" either "established" or "laid down" or "wrote" or "commanded to us" or "that we have," or something similar.[5] It is clear that Shenoute is not the author of the five hundred or so monastic rules in my corpus—at least, certainly not all of them.

Furthermore, Shenoute's federation possessed and used distinct books of ancient rules, which Shenoute mentions in several places. These books do not survive. But we know how they were used. In fact, many of the rules quoted by Shenoute probably came from these books. According to statements made by Shenoute, these ancient books were used in several different institutional contexts by the leaders of the federation.[6] In order to describe the uses of these lost rule books, I must first describe the organizational structure of the White Monastery federation.[7]

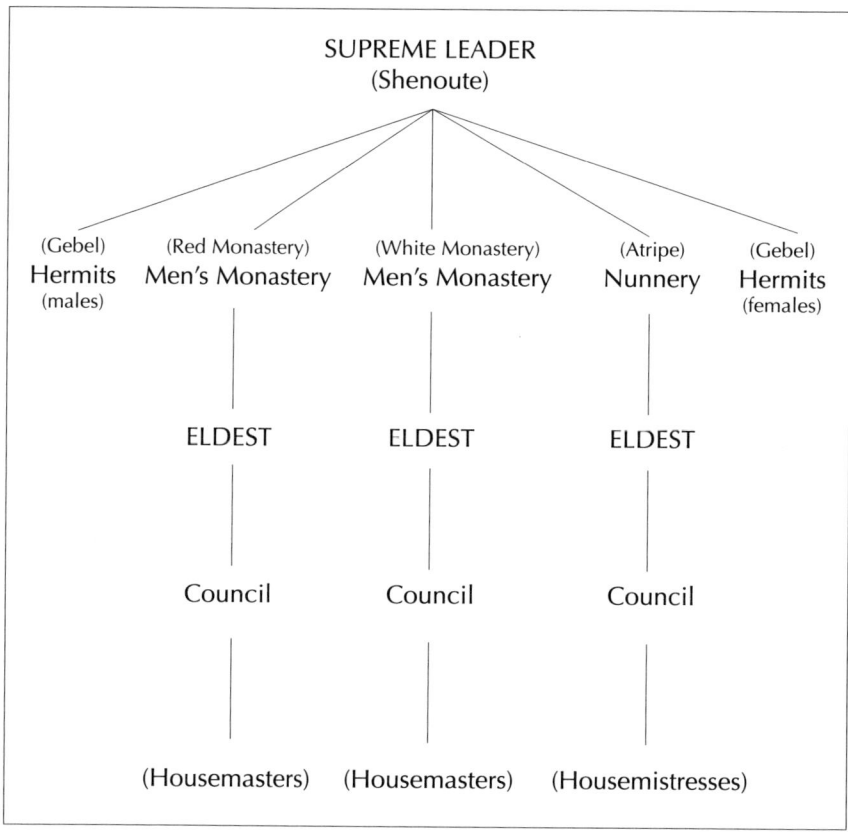

Fig. 7.1. The Organizational Structure of the Federation.

As Fig. 7.1 indicates, Shenoute's monastic federation consisted of three congregations, comprising two monasteries for men (located at the White Monastery and the Red Monastery); a nunnery for women, located in the village of Triphiou (probably the archaeological site of Atripe); as well as a cluster of male and female hermits living along the base of the Gebel or valley wall. A supreme leader (Shenoute, for example) headed the federation as a whole. Under him, each of the three congregations was headed by an officer called the Eldest; and each congregation had its council of elders who served as advisors. The monastic population of each congregation was enclosed by a wall and was divided into units called houses. Each house was headed by a housemaster or housemistress.

The daily schedule[8] of the monks or nuns consisted of six events, which were obligatory for all healthy monks or nuns. As Fig. 7.2 indicates, just before dawn a great assembly was held in each of the three individual congregations for prayer, instruction, and communal handiwork. At 6 a.m., a smaller meeting for prayer and handiwork was held in each of the houses of each congregation; and the same repeated at (probably) 9 a.m. At 12 noon there was a communal meal in each individual congregation. At 3 p.m. was another meeting in each of the houses for prayer and handiwork, and in the evening, another great assembly for each entire congregation.

---

1. Just before dawn, a great assembly, that is, a collective meeting for prayer and handiwork in each entire congregation (in the church building?)
2. 1st hour (6 a.m.), prayer and handiwork in the houses
3. [. . .] hour (9 a.m.?), prayer and handiwork in the houses
4. 6th hour (12 noon), the daily meal
5. 9th hour (3 p.m), prayer and handiwork in the houses
6. Evening, a great assembly

Fig. 7.2. The Daily Schedule of Monastic Life.

Twice a week, we are told, on Wednesdays and Fridays, one of the smaller meetings included a catechesis—an instruction. And three times a week, on Wednesdays, Fridays, and Saturday nights, one of the great assemblies also included an instruction.[9]

I will now return to the ancient rule books that Shenoute mentions. How were these books used in the federation?

The answer to this question comes from Shenoute's own statements,[10] which tell us the following. At the most intimate organizational level, passages from these rule books were sometimes read aloud or interpreted in catecheses or instructions that were given twice a week in each house by the housemaster or mistress. This would have taken place at a smaller meeting held, at either 6 a.m., 9 a.m., or 3 p.m., in each House. Here, personal spiritual intimacy was the tone. The housemaster or mistress was the most significant spiritual advisor to the individual monk and nun, and indeed, these officers were also called "Congregational Parents."[11] These officers monitored the spiritual state of each monk and nun, and their twice-a-week catecheses were an occasion for learning, participation, group response, and bonding—moments of great emotional significance. Here the rules were translated into patterns of daily life at the most personal level, under something like parental guidance.

Second, higher leaders also occasionally used or interpreted the ancient rule books to instruct a large audience. Such plenary instructions were given in one of the great assemblies consisting of all the monks or nuns in a given congregation.

Third, the rule books were required to be publicly read out in their entirety during each of the four weeks of annual plenary meeting,[12] in which all the members of a given congregation were told to scrutinize their words and deeds in the light of the written rules. Possibly these weeks were the first week of Lent, Easter week, and two other weeks of the year.

Fourth, and finally, when any newcomer came to the gate of the monastery and announced his desire to become a monk,[13] he was first scrutinized by the gatekeeper and then examined by the supreme leader (Shenoute, in this case). Finally, he was led into the church, and before the altar he had to swear a solemn oath that he would agree to the way that the monks live and comply with any and all rules on pain of expulsion. This was a vague and insubstantial promise to keep all existing rules, even though he did not know what they were. For, there would have been far too many rules to learn at once—a thousand or more, probably—and anyway, most of them would make absolutely no sense without a prior knowledge of the terminology, roles, and organization of the monastery, which the newcomer had not yet internalized. Yet, in making his monastic vow, he learned that formal rules existed and that they would somehow be used in the future. Here we see the use of rule books as an idea or mental icon without yet, as it were, opening their covers.

In summary, there were at least four ways that rule books were used in the White Monastery federation. First, in some of the small-scale instructional meetings in the individual houses. Second, in some of the large-scale great assembly meetings of the individual congregations. Third, to be ritually read aloud in their entirety before each individual congregation, during each of the four weeks of annual scrutiny. And fourth, as an object of unknowing obedience, to which reference was made whenever a new monk or nun took their oath of submission.

There is no indication that low-level, ordinary monks ever possessed, borrowed, or even touched a rule book, and it is most unlikely that they would have done so. Such books were instructional, disciplinary, and ritual tools, meant to be used, interpreted, or altered by authorized leaders of the federation. They were material for the use of teachers and supervisors.

So, what did these rule books look like? Exactly what did they contain? Unfortunately, I cannot find any way to reconstruct their exact contents. Nor do I know how they were arranged. However, it is possible to make a few observations based on the forms of the surviving rules that are quoted by Shenoute in the *Canons*.

I have studied the formal style of the White Monastery rules collected in my database[14] and discovered that about 40 percent—nearly half—have the same form as the Coptic rules of Pachomius, as published by Lefort. These rules are practical and casuistic. They are both affirmative and negative. Affirmatives usually express the main command by Coptic *efna-* (sometimes *efe-*), and negatives by *nnef-*. Casuistic conditions are expressed by formal conditional sentences *(if . . . then . . .)* or by adverbial elements such as *at any given time, anyone in this congregation, anyone in this congregation whether male or female, except with permission of such-and-such an officer, except in case of emergency or of sickness,* etc.—in other words, practical administrative rules geared to daily application. In my current research on the White Monastery rules, I am in the process of comparing these rules with the somewhat earlier rules of Pachomius. Shenoute, of course, knew about Pachomius, who had died[15] one year before Shenoute was born.

Shenoute mentions Pachomius by name in the *Canons* and knows about the story that Pachomius received his rules from an angel.[16] Occasionally Shenoute speaks of his own monastic federation as a *"Koinonia"*[17]—favorite jargon of the Pachomian monks. And the two surviving Coptic manuscript fragments of Pachomius's rules, which were copied in the early Middle Ages, once belonged to the White Monastery library, according to Orlandi.[18] So the Pachomian connections are unmistakably there. Yet, Shenoute does not claim the authority of Pachomius when citing any of the White Monastery rules. For example, once he quotes what we can recognize as an actual rule of Pachomius (*Praecepta* 95, about the distance that two monks must leave between themselves when they walk or sit).[19] But he attributes this rule only vaguely to "those who have said." It appears that Pachomius was not considered to be the patron of the Pachomian type of rules that were used in Shenoute's federation, however much they may owe historically to Pachomius.

A second important formal group of ancient rules—accounting for about 15 percent of the surviving rules—are curses.[20] Half of these begin with the phrase "Cursed be anyone who (does so-and-so)" *(fshouort nci- . . .).* Another third have the curse at the end: "Anyone who (does so-and-so) shall be under a curse" *(. . . efešōpe efshouort).* This form is unique in early monastic rules. It has a biblical basis in Deuteronomy 17.

It is extremely interesting that in three of the manuscripts of Shenoute's *Canons,* curse rules are accompanied by numbers written in the margin.[21] Only a few numbered curses have survived. They include curses numbered 5–11, 56–60, 116–119, 128–139, 192–195, and 204. Though only a few have survived, we can see from the numbering that originally there were more than two hundred of them. This suggests (although it does not prove) that Shenoute had access to an ancient rule book in the form of numbered curse rules.

There is more that can be said about the structure and origins of the ancient rule books used in Shenoute's monastic federation. For the moment, however, I would like to conclude by referring to the problem with which this paper began: namely, the question of the literary context—Shenoute's work entitled *Canons*—in which these rules are quoted. Earlier in this chapter I cited Shenoute's own statement about various institutional settings in which the ancient rules were used.[22] One of these was the large assembly of all monks or nuns, held twice a day in each of the three congregations of the federation. Three times a week (Wednesday, Friday, Saturday night) one of these great assemblies included a catechesis or instruction given by a senior leader of the congregation.[23] Here, the rule tells us, excerpts from the rules might optionally be read out by the instructor, as the instructor exhorted the assembled persons to scrutinize their words and their deeds in the light of the ancient rules. Might it be that Shenoute's *Canons* gives us some examples of the kind of urgent rhetoric that was delivered in the great assembly meetings, before an entire congregation, where instructors occasionally made use of the ancient rule books, just as Shenoute does in his *Canons*? If so, this would provide a partial answer to the question I raised at the beginning of this chapter—namely, what are Shenoute's *Canons*?

Notes

1. By my count of surviving leaves, *Canon* 1 contains 27 rules; vol. 2 contains 3 rules; vol. 3 contains 97 rules; vol. 4 contains 46 rules; vol. 5 contains 120 rules; vol. 6 contains 36 rules; vol. 7 contains no rules; vol. 8 contains 6 rules; vol. 9 contains 207 rules.

2. Layton 2002; Layton 2006; Layton 2007; Layton (forthcoming). A few passages of the present paper reproduce the wording of one or another of these essays.

3. Emmel 2004b: 9–10.

4. Layton 2007: 45–46.

5. Layton (forthcoming).

6. Shenoute writes (or perhaps quotes), "If they happen to read them (the rule books) in the Houses, nothing stands in the way. And also if they happen to read from them, whenever they want to, on days when all are gathered in the assembly, scrutinizing their words and their deeds according to our rules (canons), nothing stands in the way. However—on these four yearly occasions (the four annual weeks of scrutiny, cf. note 12) they shall all be read without fail, even if there is someone who hates to hear them because he hates his very soul": *Canon* 1, YW210, based on text as collated by Stephen Emmel; an imperfect transcription of the same text is given by Munier 1916: 117.

7. For further details, consult Layton 2002: *passim*, and Layton 2007: 53–54.

8. Layton 2007: 51–53 ("The Hierarchy of Time").

9. "Just as the housemasters give catechesis each fast day, also the heads of these abodes shall give catechesis in the assembly three times per week: the two fasts and the eve of Sunday" (*Canon* 9).

10. Shenoute, quoted above in note 6; Layton 2007: 65–69.

11. Layton 2002: 29, table 1.

12. "Four weeks per year . . . everyone who dwells in the desert in our territory shall assemble with the monks or nuns and come together" (*Canon* 3); "We scrutinize our words and deeds during the four weeks when we assemble" (*Canon* 9).

13. Layton 2007: 58–64.

14. In Layton (forthcoming): *passim*.

15. 9 May 346.

16. *Canon* 4, BZ10=Leipoldt 1908: 120.

17. *Canon* 1, YW78=Paris, *BN copte 1302* f.78 verso; vol. 3, YA313=Leipoldt 1913: 122; vol. 9, FM96=Leipoldt 1913: 89 and BV283=Leipoldt 1913: 172.

18. Orlandi 2004: "Pacomio." (Consulted on 29.12.2004.) The manuscript sigla are MONB.BC and MONB.BF.

19. *Canon* 9, DF145–46 = Leipoldt 1913: 95, speaking of "those [that is, Pachomius] who have said, You shall leave a cubit between yourselves and them."

20. Studied in Layton (forthcoming).
21. Codexes GI, YA, and YD. For the marginalia of GI, cf. Emmel 2004: 162; for
    YA, Emmel 2004b: 147–48; and for YD (fragment 2 verso), Cairo, Institut français
    d'archéologie orientale du Caire, ms. inv. 2349A (Emmel *per litt.* 26.08.2004; not
    mentioned in Emmel 2004b).
22. Text in note 6, above.
23. See note 9, above.

8 The Fate of the White Monastery Library

Catherine Louis

THE LIBRARY OF the White Monastery, founded during the fourth century by Apa Pegol, an uncle of Shenoute, went through an outstanding period in the centuries that followed its creation. During the fourteenth century, however, the Arab occupation and the Mamluk attacks sounded the death knell for this bastion of Christian culture in Egypt. The manuscripts it contained were stored, under circumstances that still remain obscure, in hidden rooms from which they were only rescued after several centuries.

In 1778 Cardinal Borgia purchased, without knowing their exact origin, a portion of more than 2,300 pages and fragments, today preserved in the libraries of Naples and Rome. For about fifty years a number of libraries of the world were able to purchase important collections of manuscripts without being able to determine their origin. This source seemed to have dried up until Gaston Maspero, in 1882, purchased from a dealer of Cairo, probably Marius Tano, some very beautiful pages that he bought for the Institut français d'archéologie orientale du Caire (IFAO). Tano informed him that these pages "had been found in the Deir Amba-Chenoudah by a monk"[1] who had sold them to him. However, among these pages were some whose writing was clearly evocative of those bought in the past by Cardinal Borgia. As a result, the origin of all these manuscripts acquired earlier was established.

Up to now we know very little about Maspero's purchase of the Coptic manuscripts from the White Monastery. However, while preparing the catalogue of Coptic manuscripts kept in the IFAO, my interest in the history of this deposit led me to consult the letters received by Gaston Maspero, currently preserved in the Institut de France in Paris.[2] Now, these letters throw quite a new light on the circumstances that surrounded the discovery of these manuscripts by Maspero, and in particular their acquisition by the Bibliothèque nationale de France (BN). I am going to try therefore to summarize this history as it is described in this correspondence.[3] However, before starting this narration, I would like to add that a third hidden room was discovered, in 1906, at the time of the works of restoration undertaken in the monastery. This room contained the last pages that the monastery revealed.[4]

In 1882, Maspero learned of the existence of a hidden room concealed somewhere inside the White Monastery that contained a large number of pages of Coptic manuscripts. Having arrived there, he made acquaintance with a French expatriate in Egypt named Auguste Frènay, director of the French mill at Akhmim.[5] Conscious of the importance of his discovery, Maspero arranged, with the help of Frènay, whom he made his correspondent and his spokesman with the monks, for the entirety to be bought by the BN. As this discovery was still little known, the price of the pages was very low. It was therefore important that it remain thus, so that Maspero could buy them all for an affordable price. This necessitated total secrecy concerning this fabulous find of several thousands of pages in order to avoid the antiquities dealers driving up prices through arguing about their purchase. Frènay then started negotiations with the superior of the White Monastery, but the latter hesitated and only accepted the sale center the end of 1884.

At this time Eugène Grébaut had just been named as director of the IFAO. A letter that he sent to Maspero on 14 December 1884 states:

"I have the intention to send M. Amélineau and Virey to join you in Thebes to attend your excavations . . . . M. Amélineau informed me of a project of which he will already have spoken you and that you would approve, he has told me. What should one think about this purchase of Coptic papyri? Perhaps our budget would be sufficient; but should we risk the deal? I lack information."[6]

Thanks to this letter, we learn, on the one hand, that the secret Maspero wanted to keep had been discovered, since Amélineau had been informed and had spoken of it to Eugène Grébaut. One can suppose that the informant could be Xavier Charmes, who was then Minister of Public Instruction in France, and also the protector and the friend of Amélineau, but there is no proof at the present time that this information came from him. However, we know from a letter sent on 17 December 1884 by Grébaut to Maspero that Xavier Charmes had promised Amélineau he would finance a part of his purchase.[7] On the other hand, Grébaut seems to have only very little information about this discovery: he still ignores the fact that the manuscripts are essentially composed of fragments of parchment and are not papyri. What seems strange in this letter is the fact that Amélineau asserts that he has already raised the question of the White Monastery manuscripts with Maspero. However, this affirmation seems very doubtful. Indeed, Grébaut, having no answer from Maspero on 10 January 1885, wrote to Maspero that he had just allowed Amélineau to make these purchases, and that he was financially sustained by Xavier Charmes. A few days later, Grébaut wrote again to Maspero to inform him that he had news from Amélineau:

> A letter from M. Amélineau warns me that he has finished his research and that he is going to depart to Luxor (where he was supposed to join Maspero). He will give you the details. His success would be satisfactory: the manuscripts will be in Cairo towards the beginning of February. Aly Bahgat[8] will bring them to me, according to the instructions of M. Charmes . . . . M. Amélineau wanted to bring you his loot to Luxor, but I received from the ministry . . . special instructions that compelled me to ensure that the manuscripts were brought immediately to the Mission in Cairo.[9]

Thus Amélineau went to the White Monastery where he would have made the acquisition of Coptic manuscripts. Immediately after this he had to join Maspero in Luxor, and then things began to get complicated because it seems that Maspero took a long time before writing to Grébaut what he thought about this expedition. But here is the letter that Grébaut wrote to Maspero on 2nd March, 1885:

> Dear M. Maspero,
> From the moment I received your last letter but one—the one that concerned Amélineau—I was intending to write you. Your letter stoppped me, and made me so puzzled that I wanted, before answering you and writing to Amélineau, to collect if it was possible, some information. I don't want to cause the Mission any trouble!
> Aly Bahgat questioned by me time and again said nothing to me: either he knows nothing or he doesn't want to say anything.

Artin Pasha,[10] seen four times in fifteen days, either at home, or at the mission, did not show me anything. Nevertheless we talked about Amélineau and Aly Bahgat. He had asked the latter for a report. Aly Bahgat showed me a project written for him by Amélineau. Amélineau committed the very serious mistake of taking Artin for a very simple child. The report was puerile, but I could not see anything compromising there. However, with prudence—you had so scared me—I cut and abridged without mercy. . . . To redo.

Aly Bahgat re-did his work in Arabic; he read me a translation of it. I found his report interesting, but not compromising. *Amélineau is not named there*. Aly Bahgat, the hero of the journey, counts the monks, their mills, their maronites; he copied in Arabic Joanne's guide that he had borrowed from me! *Of Coptic manuscripts, no mention*. Artin was delighted, he wants the report to be read in the Institut . . . .

As for the object of the Amélineau mission, I swear to you that I believed you to be better informed about it than me. . . . On my arrival, I understood that he was about, in advance of you, to execute a project that you had not only approved, but conceived yourself. I wrote of it to you only as a matter of form. . . . Amélineau assured me that all was agreed with you, that you had sent him to me to settle this matter immediately once and for all; that I could speak in your name to Artin Pasha. I wrote to M. Charmes to commend Amélineau to him . . . . M. Charmes invited me by telegram to 'advance' 4,000 fr. to Amélineau. . . . Amélineau had asked for a minister's commission . . .

The result is sparse enough so far. Amélineau did not give me any report.

The entire information he wrote to me is that I would receive from Aly Bahgat a case of manuscripts (I had asked him, in accordance with the instructions of M. Charmes, to send it as soon as possible to Cairo). Amélineau added that his mission was not finished, that he would go again to a convent where several important manuscripts were being copied for him. Aly Bahgat confirmed this good news to me. . . .

The manuscripts contained in the famous case are of little importance. Most of them are copies, more or less complete, more or less damaged, of the remnants from a Coptic Mass book. In them I can see prayers, epistles, and gospels for all the feasts of the year. Half of these texts are in Arabic.

The result is up to this point sparse. . . .

However I am inviting Amélineau, by a letter that will leave at the same time as this one: 1 to keep silent, 2 to behave with the utmost prudence. I will let him believe—which is not exact, but you made me understand the necessity to make him very prudent—that the patriarch has some fears. Let Amélineau finish his mission as well as he can, but without creating trouble for us.[11]

Here is how I believe one should interpret this letter: Amélineau, having learned that a very important collection of Coptic manuscripts were kept inside the walls of the White Monastery, applies to Xavier Charmes to obtain funds from the French Government, of which he receives 4,000 francs; he then asks Grébaut for other funds, of which he receives 2,000 more francs, while affirming to him that Maspero himself has put him in charge of going to buy the set of the White Monastery manuscripts for him. Then, Grébaut writes to Maspero to inform him of it and to tell him that Amélineau, once his purchases are done, will join him directly at Luxor. Maspero, from then on aware of the situation, does not immediately answer Grébaut about Amélineau; probably he is expecting Amélineau to join him in Luxor in order to explain himself directly to him. The letter from Grébaut I have just quoted shows that, in fact, Maspero did not know anything of the projects of Amélineau before he had been warned by Grébaut, since theoretically Maspero had charged Frènay, not Amélineau, to negotiate the purchases. The great sum of money (6,000 francs) that Amélineau had obtained was supposed to be used to buy the entire contents of the cell, that is to say perhaps about four or five thousand leaves and fragments. However, the manuscripts brought back by Amélineau were very few and of very little value; they are kept today in the Bibliothèque nationale de France (BN) under the numbers 112 to 128.[12] These are liturgical manuscripts written on paper in Bohairic and Arabic, the oldest of them dating to the fifteenth century—that is to say that they were far from being worth the sum that Amélineau spent to acquire them. His insistence on obtaining the manuscripts from the White Monastery and the fact that he was willing to pay a great deal for manuscripts that, all things considered, were of little value, had the effect of inflating the prices. Maspero, who hoped to acquire the whole collection for a moderate sum, had to give up this project; and, as was foreseeable, when the matter became known antiquities dealers and collectors hurried in large number to buy, almost leaf by leaf, the contents of the room. As we know, this resulted in the scattering of its contents among several libraries in the world.

Maspero and Frènay therefore had to find more substantial financing, but the prices had become so elevated that it was henceforth impossible to hope to acquire the entirety of the collection for the BN. In the month of December 1885, Xavier Charmes finally officially granted 5,000 francs to Maspero[13] so that he could finance a significant purchase. Frènay had already been able to acquire some pages on several occasions, which he often had to pay for himself, while waiting for financing by the French Government. But he was thus able to acquire, between March 1885 and January 1886 and through five successive purchases, a batch consisting of about 1,700 pages and fragments that were deposited in the BN on 19 March 1886.

However, the antiquities dealers, who did not stop searching for manuscripts, made the prices rise again as a letter sent in January 1886 by Frènay to Maspero shows us.[14] Also, institutions such as the British Museum had sent their own purchasers there, and Frènay had to let go more and more manuscripts.[15] In spite of everything, Frènay succeeded in acquiring about 1,500 pages for Maspero and sent them to him in June 1886, whereas the latter, having given up his work at the Museum of Boulaq, had gone back to France. However, the case, which had stayed somewhere in the museum for two months, arrived at the BN only on 17 February 1887, that is to say eight months later. Moreover, while opening it, Maspero noted with alarm that of the 1,500 pages he expected there remained only 828. What had happened to the other half? He asked Frenay for an explanation, who answered him in these words:

> I'm terribly annoyed because of the problems that this unhappy consignment of fragments has caused you and I regret not having sent them through the Consulate. Someone has certainly, during the two months that they remained in Boulaq, checked them, browsed through them, and, during this period, Arabs, who knew their value, could have diverted part of them . . . . All I can say is that I wrote your letter only after having filled the case, that is to say that my account was correct . . . .[16]

During the same period, Amélineau had acquired funds from Émile Guimet in order to buy new Coptic manuscripts; he found some that came from the White Monastery at Tano, and this collection was then offered by Guimet to the BN, where it arrived on 20 May 1887.[17]

As for Maspero's purchases, after the misadventures undergone by the second collection that he had obtained it seems that the French Government grew reticent, and it became difficult for Maspero to obtain the necessary funds. This is how a fragment of St. John's Gospel that Frènay offered to

Maspero was finally boughtby Golenischev toward the beginning of the year 1889.[18] Maspero succeeded, however, in obtaining, not without difficulty, a last collection of about one hundred pages and a box of fragments, that arrived at the Bibliothèque nationale de France on 14 October 1887.

This succession of purchases, therefore, with its attendant difficulties, ends on a somewhat depressing note. In spite of it, about 3,500 sheets and fragments of parchment were able to join the Coptic fund of the BN between March 1886 and October 1887, making this library "the most important in the world from this point of view."[19]

Notes

1. Maspero 1907: 322–23. For a summary of what we know so far about the discovery of these manuscripts, see Louis 2005: 7–12.
2. Later abreviated IdF.
3. More detailed versions of this research can be found in Louis 2005: 7–39, and Louis 2007.
4. According to Maspero 1907: 323: "J'ajouterai qu'en 1906, des réparations ayant été faites au Deir par les soins de l'administration des Wakfs, une chambre de débarras nouvelle fut exploitée par les ouvriers, et qu'il en sortit, outre des cuivres superbes, une masse considérable de manuscrits. Le service des Antiquités saisit quelques centaines de feuillets qu'il remit au patriarcat copte jacobite du Caire, puis, quand la surveillance archéologique des travaux lui fut retirée, des livres entiers et des centaines de fragments parurent sur le marché . . . ."
5. Here is how Maspero describes this cell and the circumstances of its discovery: "C'est en 1882 qu'ayant vu entre les mains d'un marchand du Caire de très beaux fragments de manuscrits coptes, je les fis acheter par l'Institut français; je m'inquiétai en même temps d'en rechercher la provenance, et il ne me fut pas difficile d'apprendre qu'ils avaient été trouvés au Deir Amba-Chenoudah par un moine qui les avait vendus à mon marchand. Je tâchai donc de nouer des relations directes avec le couvent, et grâce à l'obligeance de M. Frénay, directeur du moulin français d'Akhmîm, je sus bientôt qu'on avait découvert dans une partie des bâtiments à laquelle on accède par un couloir caché, une chambre pleine de vieux livres. Comme les musulmans, les coptes répugnent à penser qu'un papier sur lequel le nom de Dieu est écrit peut être foulé aux pieds ou souillé d'une manière abominable: ils enferment ceux de leurs livres qui deviennent hors d'usage dans des chambres secrètes où ils les oublient. Le dépôt que M. Frénay me signalait devait donc contenir les débris de la bibliothèque du Monastère, et comme les manuscrits des collections du XVIIIe siècle, notamment

ceux de la collection Borgia, avaient été acquis au Deir par les Franciscains de la mission d'Akhmîm, je pensai que nous avions grand chance de trouver là des portions
manquantes de ces manuscrits. Une première tentative pour se les procurer que fit
l'Institut français, échoua par la faute de celui qui fut chargé de l'opération, et nous
n'aurions rien eu si M. Frénay n'était de nouveau venu à notre secours. Il acheta au
moins, pour une somme minime, une caisse qui contenait les plus beaux spécimens
de la cachette, des volumes presque entiers, ou des feuillets chargés de miniatures,
comme ceux qui furent arrachés à un exemplaire illustré des Épîtres de S. Jean; puis,
à différentes reprises, il réussit à obtenir des lots moins importants. Cependant, le
bruit s'en étant répandu, les marchands et les voyageurs se mirent en campagne, et le
premier résultat de leur intervention fut de relever les prix: les feuillets, qui valaient
d'abord cinquante centimes ou un franc montèrent rapidement à deux francs, puis
à cinq, puis à vingt. La prompte action de M. Xavier Charmes et la libéralité de
M. Léopold Delisle me permirent d'assurer à la Bibliothèque la moitié au moins de
ce trésor: le reste s'est dispersé dans les différentes bibliothèques de l'Europe . . . "
(Maspero 1907: 322–23).

6. IdF, ms. 4020, fol. 540.

7. See IdF, ms. 4020, fol. 544–45.

8. Archeologue.

9. IdF, ms. 4020, fol. 548.

10. An Egyptian statesman who contributed to the organization of the journey.

11. IdF, ms. 4020, fol. 549–50.

12. According to a note actually preserved in the Archives Nationales in Paris, under the
    ref. F/17/2931.

13. According to a letter written by Charmes to Maspero: IdF, ms. 4010, fol. 470–71.

14. IdF, ms. 4018, fol. 481–82.

15. IdF, ms. 4018, fol. 483–84.

16. IdF, ms. 4018, fol. 501–502.

17. See Amélineau 1907–14, vol. 2.

18. This fragment has been published by Elanskaya 1994, nr. 15: 451–454 and
    pl. CLXXV–CLXXVI.

19. Quotation from Maspero. Cf. David 2003: 237.

9 The Coptic Life of Shenoute

Nina Lubomierski

THE COPTIC LIFE *of Shenoute* is best known in its Bohairic version. In Bohairic, a virtually complete version of the *Vita Sinuthii*, that is the *Life of Shenoute*, has come down to us. It gives an account of Shenoute's life from his birth to his death and is attributed to Shenoute's successor, Besa. The Bohairic manuscript, which stems from the Monastery of St. Macarius, is now conserved in the Biblioteca Apostolica Vaticana and was published by Amélineau in 1888 with a French translation and again eight years later by Leipoldt in his well-known edition.[1]

The *Vita Sinuthii* has also come down to us in the Coptic Sahidic dialect. In Sahidic only twenty-six leaves of the *Vita Sinuthii* from the library of Shenoute's monastery have survived. They are conserved in the Bibliothèque nationale in Paris, the Biblioteca Nazionale in Naples, the Coptic Museum in Cairo, the British Library in London, and the Papyrus Collection of the Österreichische Nationalbibliothek in Vienna. Only two of these leaves, the single one from Vienna and one fragment from Naples, are unpublished, the rest of the fragments were published by Amélineau, Crum, and Munier.[2] Unfortunately Amélineau's edition, which consists of twenty fragments from Paris, Naples, and Cairo, is not reliable.

The codicological relationship between the fragments of the *Vita Sinuthii* from Shenoute's monastery have been systematically investigated for the first time with the result that—apart from two leaves—the fragments can be related to four different codices.[3] The main bulk of fragments, thirteen leaves altogether, belong to Codex MONB.FR, which was reconstructed by Orlandi as part of his work on the *Corpus dei Manoscritti Copti Letterari* (CMCL). Emmel put together three leaves to form Codex MONB.WX, which is parallel to codex FR. Codex MONB.WU, consisting of two leaves, and Codex MONB.WV, consisting of six leaves, were established during the course of my work.

Furthermore, two Sahidic fragments of the *Vita Sinuthii* of unknown origin have come down to us. One of them, a single parchment bifolio in the Department of Egyptian Antiquities of the British Museum, was published by Shore.[4] The other one, consisting of six leaves from a paper manuscript, is kept in the Biblioteca Apostolica Vaticana and has not yet been published. These leaves are in poor condition as they had once been folded and used to increase the strength of a book cover. They once belonged to the private collection of Raphael Tuki and were incorporated into the Borgian Collection of the Biblioteca Vaticana as late as 1913 by Henry Hyvernat.[5]

The discovery of eight unpublished leaves, the fact that most of the editions of the published fragments can only be called preliminary, and the results of the codicological reconstructions underline the necessity of a new edition of all the Sahidic fragments of the *Vita Sinuthii*.

The *Vita Sinuthii* has also been translated into Arabic, Syriac, and Ethiopic. In Arabic and Ethiopic, complete manuscripts of the *Vita Sinuthii* survive. Amélineau published an Arabic version, using four different manuscripts for his edition.[6] Again Amélineau's work cannot be relied upon, and already Leipoldt has called for a new edition.[7] This call is supported by the fact that two unpublished Arabic versions of the *Vita Sinuthii* can be found in the British Library alone.[8] The Arabic version is more than twice as long as the Bohairic version. Its length results—generally speaking—from additional episodes and from material added to episodes that are also reported in at least one of the other versions. In 1982 Colin published a critical edition of an Ethiopic version, based on three witnesses, with a French translation.[9] With regard to its length the Ethiopic version takes an intermediate position between the shorter Bohairc and the longer Arabic version. In Syriac, two versions of the *Vita Sinuthii* have been published, one of them only in very fragmentary condition.[10] The other one has survived in a complete manuscript and is now conserved in the Bibliothèque nationale in Paris. It is far shorter and simpler than the other versions. In contrast to this short Syriac version, I will refer to the Bohairic, Arabic, and Ethiopic versions collectively as 'long versions.'

After the different versions of the *Vita Sinuthii* had been published, the main question was which version represented the presumable Sahidic original. Nearly all scholars agree that the presumable original was written in Sahidic.[11] Amélineau, Ladeuze, Leipoldt, and others noticed that the Sahidic fragments also represented different recensions and they were even sure that some of them did not derive from Besa.[12] According to Leipoldt, the Sahidic fragments had lost their "*pristina puritas*," their earlier purity.[13] But which version has preserved it?

As the Ethiopic version had not been published at that time and since the knowledge about the Syriac fragments was limited, the main question was whether the original text was preserved in the Arabic or the Bohairic version. Amélineau voted for the longer Arabic version, calling the Bohairic version an "*abrége*,"[14] that is an abridgement, of the original version. According to Amélineau the translator of that version was interested only in the edifying and miraculous parts of the *Vita* and omitted all the historical information in the Sahidic original. Furthermore, the translator left out or changed the connecting phrases between different episodes of the *Vita* so substantially that some parts of the text remain more or less incomprehensible. In addition to that, the title of the Bohairic version states that the text gives an account only of a few of Shenoute's miracles. Amélineau interpreted that as a signal of a translator who did not want to report *all* the miracles, but only a few of them.

But Amélineau's point of view did not convince any of his fellow scholars. Ladeuze, Nau, and Leipoldt held that the Bohairic version is closer to the presumable Sahidic original than the Arabic version.[15] Their objections against Amélineau's line of argumentation are as follows: Besa himself states in his introduction to the Bohairic *Vita* that he is able to talk about only a small selection of Shenoute's miracles. Besides, those parts in the Arabic *Vita* that are better understandable than their Bohairic parallels probably underwent later revisions. Moreover, the Arabic version reports many more miraculous deeds of Shenoute, and it even exaggerates miraculous talents as compared with the Bohairic version. This also seems to be the work of a later editor. Furthermore, Ladeuze pointed out that those episodes that are reported only in the Arabic version were most probably added in the course of the revisions of the text.[16]

A comparison of the Bohairic and the Arabic versions shows that both Amélineau and his opponents are right in some respects. The Arabic version gives more detailed information about life in Shenoute's monastery, as

Amélineau suggested. For example, only the Arabic version states how many men and women belonged to the White Monastery.[17] On the other hand the Arabic version relates more miraculous deeds than the Bohairic version, as Leipoldt stated. But this is mostly due to the fact that the Arabic version is more than twice as long as the Bohairic version. However, the Arabic version shows a special affinity for angels. In this respect the supernatural element is indeed exaggerated in the Arabic version or neutralized in the Bohairic version. With regard to the depiction of Shenoute's asceticism, of his work as the leader of the White Monastery, and of his commitment to the poor there are hardly any differences between the two versions. Again the Arabic version merely gives *more* examples than the Bohairic.

In two respects, however, the Arabic and the Bohairic versions differ considerably from one another. In the Arabic text Shenoute is shown to be very self-assured and combative with regard to the Church, that is, the local clergy and the patriarchs in Alexandria. In the Bohairic (and the Ethiopic version) the conflict between Shenoute and the Church is levelled out. In addition to that, Shenoute's fight against pagans, but especially against the heretic Nestorius, is depicted much more aggressively in the Arabic version.

Therefore one can say that the Arabic version seems to be much more rooted in Shenoute's monastery. It draws a more detailed picture of Shenoute and his monastery, whereas the Bohairic (and the Ethiopic) version gives a more generalized account of Shenoute's life and work. The Arabic version seems to address people who are closely linked with Shenoute and his monastery, whereas the Bohairic version appeals also to a wider public. Regarding the contents, it is much more plausible that the Bohairic version is a shortened and generalized form of the presumable original, as Amélineau had suggested.

Does the Arabic version therefore represent Besa's original text? Before this question can be answered let us have a closer look at the Sahidic fragments. As already mentioned, it has been observed that the Sahidic fragments also represented different recensions of the *Vita*. An analysis of the newly established codices led to the same results. Some of them are very close to either the Arabic or the Bohairic version, and will not be referred to individually in the following remarks. In contrast to that, the parallel Codices FR and WX show a high degree of independence from the other versions. For example, they differ from the long versions with regard to the manner in which the individual episodes are introduced. Most of the episodes narrated in FR and WX have long introductory sentences in which a speaker frequently addresses his listeners directly, for example like this: "But lest we protract this speech, I am going to tell of a miraculous deed that [Shenoute] himself wrote down in his holy sermons."[18] It is obvious that FR and WX are composed as speeches. In contrast to that, only the prooimia of the long versions make it clear that they are introductions to speeches. The episodes in the main body of the long versions, namely, the Bohairic, Arabic, and Ethiopic versions, usually start with a formula equivalent to "once upon a time"[19] without any reference to a narrator or an audience.

It is one even more striking feature of FR and WX that they do not seem to have been written by Besa. Besa is not mentioned in any pericope of FR and WX, not even in the account of Shenoute's death where he plays an important role in the long versions. Furthermore, the narrator of FR and WX never states that he saw any of Shenoute's wonderful deeds with his own eyes, but he constantly names witnesses, sometimes very vaguely with formulas such as, "it has been said that,"[20] sometimes more precisely, for example: "and our monastic fathers, who lived at the time of our father Apa Shenoute, have [also] said that,"[21] or "those who have met him in his body have testified to us that."[22] The last two phrases propose that the author of FR and WX was neither an eyewitness to the miracles performed by Shenoute nor one of his contemporaries. Therefore the author of FR and WX was by no means Shenoute's disciple and successor, Besa. Amélineau, Ladeuze, and Leipoldt had already noticed this peculiarity and excluded some of the Sahidic fragments, which are now designated to Codex FR, from the *Vita Sinuthii.*

In contrast, the long versions are attributed to Besa in their titles and—in correspondence with that—'Besa' emphasizes in their introductions that he saw the miracles of Shenoute with his own eyes, or that at least he heard about them from Shenoute himself. Furthermore, the impression that Besa was the author of the long versions is reinforced by the fact that he is mentioned in many of their episodes. Besa appears as the first-person narrator of these episodes, introducing himself either as "I, Besa," or just "I" without the name. However, the number of times Besa appears in the long versions varies considerably from version to version. In the Bohairic and Ethiopic versions, he is mentioned in 15 percent of the episodes, whereas he is mentioned in 25 percent of the episodes of the Arabic version. This difference is explained by the fact that—on the one hand—Besa plays a role in episodes that are narrated only in the Arabic version. On the other hand, in some episodes Besa is mentioned only in the Arabic version despite the fact that the same episode also occurs in the Bohairic and Ethiopic versions. Furthermore, it is remarkable that the figure of Besa shows hardly any original features, except for a few episodes which were probably all taken from a single source, namely the panegyric on Macarius of Tkôw.

We may therefore conclude that neither the speeches in the Sahidic codices FR and WX nor the long versions of the *Vita Sinuthii* were originally composed by Besa. This is in accordance with Volkmar Keil who already in 1978 expressed his doubts about the traditional opinion that saw Besa as the author of the *Vita Sinuthii*.[23]

The genesis of the *Vita Sinuthii* may have taken place in the following way: In correspondence with the Coptic tradition, speeches of praise were given in honor of Shenoute every year on the day of his commemoration in his monastery. At least some of these speeches were preserved and copied, but also revised in the monastery library. For the scribes not merely copied the texts but also reworked them, as Tito Orlandi has pointed out, thus "creating new texts from pieces of existing ones."[24] With regard to the speeches in commemoration of Shenoute, the scribes seem to have extended the part concerning the life and miraculous deeds of Shenoute by inserting episodes known, for example, from oral tradition or from Shenoute's own writings. During the course of these revisions, those parts of the texts that showed the features of a speech, such as the rhetorical introductions to individual episodes, mostly vanished.

The revisions of the texts probably served a special purpose, which was described by Karl Heinz Kuhn with regard to a commemorative encomion on John the Baptist. Kuhn asked: "Is it not possible that books of homilies were compiled for certain occasions, in this case for the commemoration day of John the Baptist? Any preacher, or any copying scribe, would be at liberty to select from the material assembled there, and thus to produce a refashioned sermon suitable in length and character for his particular public."[25] This model could explain the contents of codex FR, which contains either two speeches of praise or one speech plus an appendix. At some stage there seemed to have been a desire to collect everything known about Shenoute in one work. This compilation probably was the size of the Arabic version. Parts of it have come down to us in three Sahidic fragments.[26] It is the expression of a self-confident monasticism in Shenoute's monastery. Furthermore, an introduction was added to this long compilation, which attributed it to Besa, presumably because he was felt to give final authority to the contents. Because of the elaborate style, the prooimium seems to have been inserted by a scribe who was highly educated and who knew the rules of ancient rhetoric. At what time all this happened is difficult to say because of the fragmentary state of the Sahidic texts and the poor editorial state of the Arabic version. However, if we presume that the long compilation had the full extent of the Arabic version published by Amélineau, its genesis must be dated to the end of the seventh century, because it referred to the Arab invasion and the following fighting.[27] This long compilation was already shortened in Shenoute's monastery, as can be seen from the fragmentary codex WU. As the work spread across the walls of Shenoute's monastery it was generalized in such a way that people who did not belong to the White Monastery could also identify themselves with the story narrated. The Bohairic and the Ethiopic version are examples of such abridged versions.

To sum up, the so-called *Vita Sinuthii* should not be regarded as a biography of Shenoute originating from a single Urtext written by Besa. Rather, the texts known to us mark different stages in the text's development, from speeches of praise, delivered on the day of commemoration of Shenoute, to collections of episodes from Shenoute's life, many of which are surely the product of someone's pious imagination. It was only at some later stage of this process that the texts were attributed to Besa in order to give the work complete authority.

Notes

1. Amélineau 1888–95: 1–99; Leipoldt 1906–1913, vol. 1: 7–76. Fragments of the Bohairic Version were published by Evelyn-White 1973: 163.
2. Amélineau 1888–95: 237–47, 633–49; Crum 1905: 164–65; Munier 1916: 63–65, pl. XIII.
3. The Sahidic Codices from Shenoute's monastery are designated according to the system that has been established by the CMCL. The prefix MONB standing for *Monasterio Bianco* is omitted in this study once the codices have been introduced.
4. Shore 1979: 134–39, pls. XXIV–XXV.
5. Hyvernat 1896: 549. The fragment has been assigned the call number Borg. Copt. 134 ff. 2–7.
6. Amélineau 1888–95: 289–480.
7. Leipoldt 1964: 53; cf. Crum 1904: 130 n. 3.
8. Cureton and Rieu 1846–1871: 670; Rieu 1894: 26–28.

9. Colin 1982.
10. Guidi 1889 (only in fragmentary form); Nau 1899–1900.
11. Except for Nau 1899–1900: 361–63.
12. Amélineau 1888–95: LIX; Ladeuze 1898: 124; Leipoldt 1903: 13f.
13. Leipoldt 1906–1913, vol. 1: 2.
14. Amélineau 1888–95: VII.
15. Leipoldt 1898: 12; Ladeuze 1898: 125–27; Nau 1899–1900: 360.
16. Ladeuze 1898: 136.
17. Amélineau 1888–95: 331.
18. Amélineau 1888–95: 237, 12–238,1.
19. E.g. the formula "ⲁⲩϣⲱⲡⲓ *[ⲇⲉ] [ⲟⲛ]* ⲛⲟⲩⲉϩⲟⲟⲩ " can be found in the beginning of the paragraphs (Leipoldt 1906–1913, vol. 1) §§ 14; 22; 25; 36; 42; 68; 70; 73; 74; 91; 93; 94; 115; 119; 125; 138 and 151.
20. FR 45 i.28 (Amélineau 1888–95: 642, 9) and FR 58 i.6 (Amélineau, *Monuments*, 240, 3): ⲁⲩϫⲟⲟⲥ ⲇⲉ ⲟⲛ. WX frg. 2r ii.26f : ⲡⲉϫⲁⲩ. (Amélineau 1888–95: 244, 8).
21. FR 47 ii.19–27.
22. FR 59 ii.23–27.
23. Keil 1978: 40–41. Cf. Emmel 2004b: 92 note 149.
24. Orlandi 2002: 220.
25. Kuhn 1966: (textus), XVIII.
26. Kodex WV, GB-BL Or. 3581B f. 72 and VA-V Borg. Copt. 134 ff. 2–7.
27. Cf. Amélineau 1888–95: LVIII; Leipoldt 1898: 14.

10 Shenoute as reflected in the *Vita* and the *Difnar*

Nashaat Mekhaiel

EVERYONE WHO IS familiar with Coptic history and culture a little will have various associations with the name Shenoute. It is not surprising that this multilayered fourth-century personality (A.D. 348–466) has stayed alive through literary means, not only by his own writings, but also in works that want to remind of him. Two of them are to be compared here in their statements about Shenoute, which are the *Difnar* and Shenoute's *Vita*,[1] which had originally been composed in Sahidic by Shenoute's successor, Besa. This chapter will discuss the conceptions and expectations that are found in a text like the *Difnar*, pursue its literary tradition, and also portray a possible source of the *Difnar*.

This investigation is divided into three sections. After a short introduction to the *Difnar* the passages in the text are discussed, which are reproduced in the *Vita* and in the *Difnar* literally or almost literally. Doing so, certain epithets have to be taken into consideration which are attributed to Shenoute. Subsequently, epithets and passages are compared which, although not literally identical, are of equal content, but which are still comprehensible on their own in the *Difnar*. Finally, allusions in the *Difnar* that presuppose knowledge of the *Vita* are referred to.

The *Difnar* is an important component of the liturgical literature in the Coptic Church.[2] For example, it contains hymns that refer predominantly to the lives of important and holy personalities of the Coptic

Church, and furthermore memorial texts dealing with angels, apostles, prophets, synods, and parish fairs as well as special celebrations like the birth of Christ. The special importance of the *Difnar* is stressed by Bishop Matthäus in his preface to the 1985 edition of the *Difnar*,[3] where he referred to its meaning as *"Teil der täglichen Psalmodie"* and its *"Benutzung zur Verehrung und zum Lob der Märtyrer und Heiligen."*[4] The encomiums of the *Difnar*, read out in the entire Coptic Church over centuries, contributed essentially to its survival. For a long time the authorship of the *Difnar* was attributed to the patriarch Gabriel ibn Turik (1131–1145), who played an important role using the Arabic language in the liturgy of the Coptic Church.[5] Due to many corresponding passages in the *Difnar* and the *Synaxarion* it can be concluded that the *Difnar* is based to a certain extent on the *Synaxarion*.[6]

Gawdat Gabra assumes that the *Difnar* was originally not written in one piece, but that its composition developed over several centuries.[7] This development continued at the latest until the fourteenth century when the *Difnar* was eventually at the disposal of many copyists. The oldest remaining edition of the *Difnar* originates from the Antonius Monastery. It was copied from an unknown source in the year A.M. 1101 (A.D. 1385).

The *Difnar*, a two-piece hymn sung to the melody of "Adam and Batos," is dedicated to Shenoute on his memorial day, 7 Abib.[8] Since the *Difnar* represents a compilation from different sources, one may not expect the hymn to have an all-too-harmonic structure. Although there are corresponding parts, which can usually be recognized as a unity from the beginning of the sentences, one is regularly confronted with repetitions, a sudden change in the artistic means as well as direct juxtapositions of contrasting elements. To sum up, the text has not been processed and smoothed to the point that its seams can no longer be recognized.

1) The most evident argument for taking the Shenoute-*Vita* as a source for the author or reviser of the Shenoute hymn in the *Difnar* are their identical passages. Such parts exist indeed, although they are very rare in relation to the overall dimensions of the text. The question of their importance must be clarified later. Four passages in the text are relevant in this context:

a) Shenoute is appointed archimandrite by divine providence:

Vita: ⲀⲞⲨⲤⲘⲎ ⲰⲰⲠⲒ ⲰⲀⲢⲰⲞⲨ ⲈⲂⲞⲖ ⲂⲈⲚⲦⲪⲈ ⲈⲤⲬⲰ ⲘⲘⲞⲤ ⲬⲈⲀⲨ ⲐⲀⲰⲰⲈⲚⲞⲨϯ ⲚⲀⲢⲬⲎⲘⲀⲚⲀⲢⲒⲦⲎⲤ ⲈⲠⲒ ⲔⲞⲤⲘⲞⲤ ⲦⲎⲢϥ ⲘⲪⲞⲞⲨ (§ 9).

Difnar: ⲱ ⲪⲎ ⲈⲦⲀϥⲤⲰⲦⲈⲘ ⲚϯⲤⲘⲎ ⲈⲐⲞⲨⲀⲂ ⲬⲈⲀⲨⲐⲰⲰ ⲚⲰⲈⲚⲞⲨϯ ⲚⲀⲢⲬⲎ ⲘⲀⲚⲦⲢⲒⲦⲎⲤ (27r, 5–8).

The call of the voice from the sky sounds at first like a literal quotation from the *Vita*. The preceding context, however, is arranged in a different way in the *Difnar* from Shenoute's view and also the relation to the entire world is missing, which lends the sentence in the *Vita* a more profound meaning. It was probably intended that this call of God was not changed and falsified thereby. It is conceivable that it was also passed on separately.

b) When Shenoute is dying he calls upon other monk fathers:

Vita: ΠΕΧΑϤ ΟΝ ΧΕΠΑΙⲰΤ ΑΠΑ ΠϢΟΙ ΠΑΙⲰΤ ΑΠΑ ΑΝΤⲰΝΙΟⲤ ΠΑΙⲰΤ ΑΠΑ ΠΑϨⲰΜ ΑΜΟΝΙ ΝΤΑΧΙΧ ΝΤΑΤⲰΝΤ ⲈΘΡΙΟⲨⲰϢΤ ΜϤΗ ΕΤΑΤΑѰⲨΧΗ ΜΕΝΡΙΤϤ (§ 185).

Difnar: ΠΕΧΑⲔ ΧΕΑΒΒΑ ΠϢΟΙ ΠΑΙⲰΤ ΑΒΒΑ ΑΝΤⲰΝΙ ΝΕΜΑΒΒΑ ΠΑϨⲰΜ ⲀΜΟΝΙ ⲚΤΑⲚΧΙΧ 2ΙΝΑⲚΤΑΟⲨⲰϢΤ ⲘΠΑⲤ̅Ⲥ̅ ΙⲎ̅Ⲥ̅ ϤΗ ⲈΤΑΤΑѰⲨΧΗ ΜΕΝΡΙΤϤ ⲈΜΑϢⲰ (28v, 8–15).

Again, Shenoute's call corresponds to the first part word for word. The final clause could have been formulated independently; this sentence contains a quotation, the meaning of which the author/reviser wanted to preserve. And again, this utterance could have been passed on alone, without encouraging the endeavor to search for a source such as the *Vita*.

c) The end of Shenoute's life is described in the following words:

Vita: ΤΟΤΕ ΑϤϯ ΜΠΕϤΠⲚ̅Ⲁ̅ ⲈΝΕΝΧΙΧ Μϥϯ ΜΠΙ Ⲉ2ΟΟⲨ ΕΤΕΜΜΑⲨ ΝⲤΟⲨⲌ ΝΕΠΗϤ (§ 186).

Difnar: ⲈΤΑⲔϯ ⲘΠΙ ΠⲚ̅Ⲁ̅ ⲈΝΕΝΧΙΧ ⲘΠⲞ̅Ⲥ̅ (28v, 16–17).

Here we find a coherent connection of words, though it would thus be unwise to draw hasty conclusions. While the *Vita* focuses on as exact a dating as possible, the *Difnar* cares only for the fact that Shenoute hands himself over to the Lord.

d) Furthermore, similarities are found with the names and epithets of Shenoute. The *Difnar* indicates that we have here in part an older source.

Vita: ⲤΜΟⲨ ⲈΡΟΝ ΠΕΝΙⲰΤ ⲈΘΟⲨΑΒ ΗΛΙΑⲤ ΝΒΕΡΙ (§ 19).

Difnar: ϤΗ ⲈΤΑⲨϯΡΕΝϤ ΧΕⲎ̅ΛΙΑⲤ ⲘΒΕΡΙ (28r, 3–4).

Might the author/reviser refer to the *Vita* here? That is conceivable but not sufficiently proven. The only thing certain is that, at the time the *Vita* assumed the form it is known in today, Shenoute was commonly known by the name "the new Elias."

None of the remaining passages in the text justify the label '(almost) literal correspondence.'

2) The circumstance of Shenoute's being seen in vicinity to the prophets both in the *Difnar* and in the *Vita*—although not in literal correspondence—

may have contributed to the conception of "the new Elias." This shows in such epithets as we see here.

In the *Vita* Shenoute is labelled "prophetic father" several times,[9] which is supported by various episodes in which Shenoute proves his foretelling skills. Shenoute stands in general contact with the prophets,[10] but also certain figures of the Old Testament are mentioned.[11] The author of the hymn in the *Difnar* describes Shenoute as "great prophet" or even as "venerable prophet," and Christ himself is the one to put the prophet's garment on him.[12]

In the eyes of the author Shenoute is "a second Moses."[13] Both prophets, Moses and Shenoute, share the fact that they gave laws to the faithful. For, in the *Difnar* we find exactly this connection: Shenoute is assumed as the one called "prophet and chosen legislator."[14] In this formulation we can find another reference to the fact that this designation was familiar to the author/reviser of the *Difnar*.

At an early point in the hymn it is pointed out to whom the laws are addressed: ΠΙ ΡΕϤϹΕΜΝΕΝΟΜΟϹ ⲚⲚΙ ΜΟΝⲀΧΟϹ ΝΕΜΝΙ ΚΟϹΜΙ ΚΟΝ (28r, 7–9). In the *Vita* we find familiar conceptions: Here, it is Besa and his brothers who list in detail why Shenoute is deservedly designated "legislator."[15] Already at this point we can sum up as an intermediate result what has to be elaborated in detail later: the *Difnar* alludes, gives keywords; the *Vita* provides the background, describes closely, works out details.

Shenoute, however, is not only distinguished by his proximity to the prophets, but also to the angels and saints. Again, the *Vita* and the *Difnar* agree on this point.[16]

Vita: 2ⲀΝϹΟΠ ΕΡΕΝΙ ⲀⲄⲄΕⲖΟϹ ΟΥΟΝ2 ΕΡΟϤ (§ 121); ΠϹΟΝ ΝΝΗ ΕΘΟΥⲀⲂ ΤΗΡΟΥ (§ 188).

Difnar: ⲠΙ ⲰϕΗΡ Ⲛ<Ⲛ>ⲀⲄⲄΕⲖΟϹ (26r, 15); ΠΙ ⲰϕΗΡ ⲚΤΕΝΗ ΕΘΟΥⲀⲂ (27v, 13).

The strongest connection to the divine, however, that differentiates Shenoute from the mortal world, is established by his intense relation to Christ. The *Vita* describes this in lively colors, and several times allows him to have a dialogue with Christ in the form of visions.[17] Thus a further parallel between *Vita* and *Difnar* is found. Shenoute is appointed bearer of secret knowledge, through which he stands separate against the common believers.

Vita: ΕϤΧⲰ ΕΡΟΙ Ν2ⲀΝΜΥϹΤΗΡΙΟΝ (§ 25).

ΠΙ ϹⲰΤΗΡ ⲀΕ ⲀϤⲀΜΟΝΙ ΝΤΧΙ Χ ΜΠⲀΙ ⲰΤ ⲀΠⲀ ⲰΕΝΟΥ† ⲀϤΜΟⲰΙ ΝΕΜⲀϤ ⲰⲀ†ΡΙ

ΕΤ2Ι ΠⲰⲀϤΕ ΕΥϹⲀΧΙ ΝΕΜΝΟΥΕΡΗΟΥ ⳉΕΝ2ⲀΝΝΙ Ⲱ† ΜΜΥϹΤΗΡΙΟΝ (§ 160).

Difnar. ⲱ ⲫⲏ ⲉ̅ⲧ ⲁⲡ̅ⲭ̅ⲥ̅ ⲁ ⳸ⲥ ⲁ ⲭ ⲓ ⲛ ⲉ ⲙ ⲁ ⳸ ⲟⲩⲟ ⲍ ⲁ ⳸ ⲉ ⲱ ⲡ ⲡ ⲛ ⲁ ⳸ ⲛ̅ ⲍ ⲁ ⲛ ⲙ ⲩ ⲥ ⲧ ⲏ ⲣ ⲓ ⲟⲛ (27r, 13–16).

Likewise, Shenoute stands in a special relation to the Father as "Beloved One of God" and "Chosen One by God," as testified in the *Vita* and the *Difnar* in the same way.[18] Blessed by God with special grace and gifts, Shenoute's influence is not limited to his monastic environment but covers the whole world.

This is merely alluded to in the *Difnar* by use of the phrase "he whose words have spread over the face of the whole earth;"[19] in the *Vita*, however, this is broadly represented in many individual occurrences. As a counselor for prominent personalities such as office-holders and travelers Shenoute was well respected, his fame reaching even the ears of the emperor.[20] In particular, the relationship and mutual contacts with Emperor Theodosius are the subject of several chapters (§§ 53–67). A similar case is represented in the *Difnar* where Shenoute is characterized as "he who went to the synod with our father Cyril and blamed Nestorius."[21] The *Vita* provides three chapters concerning the scene, describing the meeting between Cyril, Shenoute, and Nestorius, followed by Shenoute's appointment as archimandrite (§§ 128–30). However, it is sufficient for the author of the hymn to simply remind the reader of the event. In contrast to the *Vita*, the *Difnar* is neither capable of nor willing to give any details. It is therefore limited to praising Shenoute in general phrases.[22] This may have conjured up the appropriate images and sayings to the believers, to whom Shenoute was familiar from the liturgy as well as from literary and iconic tradition. A further example may clarify this. In the *Difnar* it is stated that Shenoute "strengthened the kings through the comforting spirit" and that the kings "brought gifts and sacrifices to his holy monastery in honor and glory,"[23] without, however, any names or details being given. Thus, we might have here an allusion to the three holy kings who bring gifts to the newborn Jesus to praise him. On the other hand, one might as well take it, against the background of the *Vita*, as a description of the friendly relationship between Shenoute and Theodosius,[24] which was characterized by mutual respect and appreciation. The author of the hymn accepted this ambiguity, which he took to be deliberately open—for his goal was the glorification of the holy one, not the entertainment of the listeners. We thus also have to take into consideration the differing purposes of the texts that are discussed here.

3) In a certain passage, however, the *Difnar* takes up the opposite approach. Here the author narrows the view to one detail and, by mentioning this small

detail, directly preassumes a familiarity with the stories around Shenoute. The *Difnar* says: "O he who has been lifted upon a cloud until it brought him to the monastery." And a little later: "He who has crossed the depth of the sea without a ship."[25] Here it has to be known that, in the *Difnar*, the cloud is used several times by Shenoute as a means of traveling where urgent haste is due or secrecy required.[26] For example, this is the help granted by God when Shenoute is denied passage by ship (§ 18). This detail, the flying cloud, thus represents Shenoute's abilities, which distinguish him from other humans. It is an expression of his holiness and his special relationship to God.

Finally, with all the things in common, one aspect has to be pointed out that does not play an unimportant role in the *Vita*, but that is completely omitted in the *Difnar*. This is Shenoute's part in violent actions against paganism. Might this not have fitted in with the conception of Shenoute as the *Difnar* portrays him? There Shenoute is characterized as an idol to the believers. He has led a perfect life through his purity, his patience, and love of mankind,[27] which could also lead the way to eternal life for the believers. Hereupon their hopes and expectations are based.[28] For the *Vita* no contradiction results. Here individual narrations are additively assembled, telling, each on its own, of the miracles of the hero and where it is not forgotten to weave in his appraisal. The hymn in the *Difnar* lacks, as mentioned, a constant organizational principle as well as a leading idea. However, the text is much shorter and accordingly denser and must therefore portray Shenoute's holiness and virtues in the invocations in a much more pointed style to elicit imitation.

As demonstrated, there are numerous parallels between the *Vita* and the hymn in the *Difnar*. It can be reasonably assumed that the *Vita* was familiar to the author of the hymn in the *Difnar*. It is more difficult, however, to try to prove a direct use of the original source. The similarities remain 'mosaic pieces,' which assemble to provide a many-faceted image of Shenoute. In the hymn this picture is merely sketched out in dots, whereas it is fully painted in all its details in the *Vita*.

Notes

1. The text quoted here follows the reprint edition of Leipoldt 1906–1913 [1951].
2. Cf. Malak 1964: 19f; Burmester 1967: 108; Quecke 1970:1.88.132.
3. Matthäus 1985.
4. Cf. Gabra 1996: 42.

5. Cf. Graf 1944–1953b: 327; Graf 1944–1953a: 512; Moftah 1991: 1728. This is, however, a controversial source, especially rejected by Walter E. Crum: Crum 1909: 213.

6. Cf. for example, Gabra 1993: 63ff.; Gabra 1989: 15; cf. also Cramer 1981: 207; Ishaq 1991: 901; Aziz 1991: 2173f. Especially Crum and O'Leary consider the *Synaxarion* to be the main source for the *Difnar*, however, they do not consider other sources impossible. Crum 1909: 211–13. See also the preface in O'Leary 1926–1930.

7. Cf. Gabra 1998: 64.

8. The quotation follows the above mentioned Antonius manuscript from the fourteenth century (A.D. 1385) the text of which will soon be made available to the scientific community in my dissertation. The hymn can be found there at fol. 26r, 12–31r, 5.

9. E.g. in §15: ΠΑΙ ⲰⲦ ⲆⲈ ⲚⲀⲒ ⲔⲈⲞⲤ ⲞⲨⲞ2 ⲘⲠⲢⲞⲪⲎⲦⲎⲤ ⲀⲠⲀ ⲰⲈⲚⲞⲨ† (similar to §§ 25, 53, 76, 92 and 20, where his deeds are compared to those of the prophets and apostles: ⲪⲎ ⲈⲦⲈⲚⲈⲯ2ⲂⲎⲞⲨⲒ ⲰⲞⲠ ⲃⲈⲚⲞⲨⲈⲢⲰⳘⲰⳘ ⲘⲪⲢⲎ† ⲚⲚⲒⲠⲢⲞⲪⲎⲦⲎⲤ).

10. As in §121 within an enumeration of Shenoute's "dialogue partners": 2ⲀⲚⲤⲞⲠ ⲞⲚ ⲚⲀⲯⲤⲀⳘⲒ ⲚⲈⲘⲚⲒⲠⲢⲞⲪⲎⲦⲎⲤ. See similar parts at §124.

11. An example is the Prophet Jeremias (ⲈⲢⲈⲠⲈⲚⲒ ⲰⲦ ⲘⲠⲢⲞⲪⲎⲦⲎⲤ ⲀⲠⲀ ⲰⲈⲚⲞⲨ† ⲘⲞⳘⲒ ⲚⲈⲘⲠⲒⲚⲒ ⲰⳘ† ⲘⲠⲢⲞⲪⲎⲦⲎⲤ ⲒⲈⲢⲈⲘⲒ ⲀⲤ, § 94) or Ezechiel (ⲚⲀⲯⲘⲞⳘⲒ ⲆⲈ ⲞⲚ ⲚⲞⲨⲤⲞⲠ ⲚⲈⲘⲠⲒⲠⲢⲞⲪⲎⲦⲎⲤ Ⲓ ⲈⳘⲈⲔ ⲒⲎ ⲚⲬⲈⲠⲈⲚⲒ ⲰⲦ ⲈⲐⲞⲨⲀⲂ, § 95).

12. ⲠⲒ ⲚⲒ Ⲱ† ⲘⲠⲢⲞⲪⲎⲦⲎⲤ (27v, 11); ⲚⲦⲈⲚⲈⲢⲰⳘⲀⲒ ···ⲈⲠⲒ ⲠⲢⲞⲪⲎⲦⲎⲤ ⲈⲦⲦⲀⲒⲎⲞⲨⲦ (29v, 11–12); ⲱ ⲪⲎ ⲈⲦⲀⲠⲬⲤ̅ ⲘⲞⲢⲯ ⲘⲠⲒ ⲤⲬⲎⲘⲀ ⲈⲐⲞⲨⲀⲂ ⲚⲦⲈⲠⲒ ⲠⲢⲞⲪⲎⲦⲎⲤ ⲠⲒⲚⲒ Ⲱ† ⲚⲀⲒ ⲀⲤ (27r, 9–12).

13. ⲠⲒ ⲘⲀ2Ⲃ̅ ⲘⲘⲰⳘⲤⲎⲤ (27v, 15).

14. ⲀⲨⲘⲞⲨ† ⲈⲢⲞⲯ ⲬⲈⲠⲒ ⲠⲢⲞⲪⲎⲦⲎⲤ ⲞⲨⲞ2 ⲠⲒ ⲚⲞⲘⲞⲐⲈⲦⲎⲤ ⲈⲦⲤⲰⲦⲠ (30r, 3–4).

15. ⲀⲯⲤⲈⲘⲚ Ⲛ2ⲀⲚⲔⲀⲚⲰⲚ ⲚⲚⲒⲘⲞⲨⲚⲀⲬⲞⲤ (§ 11); ⲀⲔⲘⲞ2 ⲘⲠⲒ ⲔⲞⲤⲘⲞⲤ ⲦⲎⲢⲯ ⲃⲈⲚⲚⲈⲔⲔⲀⲚⲰⲚ ⲈⲐⲞⲨⲀⲂ ⲚⲈⲘⲚⲈⲔⲤⲀⳘⲒ ⲚⲤⲞⲪⲒ Ⲁ ⲚⲎ ⲈⲦⲀⲯ† ⲈⲢⲬⲀⲢⲒⲌⲈⲤⲐⲈ ⲘⲘⲰⲞⲨ ⲚⲀⲔ ⲀⲚⲈⲔⲖⲞⲄⲞⲤ ⲚⲈⲘⲚⲈⲔⲚⲞⲘⲞⲤ ⲚⲈⲘⲚⲈⲔⲞⲨⲀ2ⲤⲀ2ⲚⲒ ⲚⲈⲘⲚⲈⲔⲈⲚⲦⲞⲖⲎ ⲚⲀⲠⲞⲤⲦⲞⲖⲒ ⲔⲞⲚ ⲘⲞ2 ⲘⲠⲒ ⲔⲞⲤ̅ ⲘⲞⲤ ⲦⲎⲢⲯ (§ 179).

16. The relationship to the apostles, in the *Vita* for example, to Paul (§§138–39), is not discussed in the *Difnar*. In the *Vita* Shenoute is considered an apostle himself (§172).

17. To provide just a few examples, § 72, § 121 and §154f. are mentioned here.

18. "Beloved One by God" in the *Vita*: ⲪⲘⲈⲚⲢⲒ Ⲧ ⲘⲪ† (§ 120, uttered by the martyrs), in the *Difnar*: ⲠⲒ ⲘⲈⲚⲢⲒ Ⲧ ⲚⲦⲈⲪ† (27v, 12); "Chosen One by God" in the *Difnar*: ⲠⲒ ⲤⲰⲦⲠ ⲚⲦⲈⲪ† (26r, 14).

19. ⲪⲎ ⲈⲦⲀⲚⲈⲯⲤⲀⳘⲒ ⲰⲈ ⲚⲰⲞⲨ 2Ⲓ ⲬⲈⲚⲠ2Ⲟ ⲘⲠⲔⲀ2Ⲓ ⲦⲎⲢⲯ (30r, 1–2). See also at the above mentioned quotation of the appointment as archimandrite.

20. 2ⲀⲚⲚⲒ Ⲱ† ⲘⲘⲎⲒⲚⲒ ⲚⲈⲘ2ⲀⲚⲰⳘⲪⲎⲢ Ⲓ ⲈⲨⲞⳘ...ⲈⲦⲀⲨⲘⲞⳘⲒ ⲈⲂⲞⲖ ⲰⲀⲦⲞⲨⲘⲀ2Π2Ⲟ ⲘⲠⲔⲀ2Ⲓ ⲦⲎⲢⲯ 2ⲰⲤⲀⲈ ⲚⲦⲈⲠⲈⲯⲤⲰⳘ Ⲧ ⲪⲞ2 ⲰⲀⲚⲒ ⲞⲨⲢⲰⲞⲨ ⲚⲈⲨⲤⲈⲂⲎⲤ ⲞⲨⲞ2 ⲚⲤⲈⲬⲞⲤ ⲚⲰⲞⲨ (§ 53).

21. This refers to the Council of Ephesus in A.D. 431

22. Here it must be considered that the hymn in the *Difnar* prefers biblical formulations and phrases. Such a language that is strongly tainted in the style of the Old Testament will inevitably make use of statements that are kept in a general tone, which renders them universally applicable.

23. ⲫⲎ ⲈⲦⲀⲚⲒ ⲞⲨⲢⲰⲞⲨⲒ ⲚⲒ ⲚⲀϤ ⲚⲀⲚⲀⲰⲢⲞⲚ ⲚⲈⲘⲀⲚⲰⲞⲨⲰⲞⲨⲰ Ⲓ ⲈⲠⲈϤⲘⲞⲚⲀⲤⲦⲎⲢ Ⲓ ⲞⲚ ⲈⲐⲞⲨⲀⲂ ϧⲈⲚⲞⲨⲰⲞⲨ ⲚⲈⲘⲞⲨⲦⲀ Ⲓ Ⲟ̇ (30r, 9–12).

24. Cf. *Vita* for example, § 60f.

25. ⲱ̇ ⲫⲎ ⲈⲦⲀⲨⲦⲀⲖⲞϤ Ⲉ̇2ⲢⲎⲒ ⲈⲦ6ⲎⲠⲒ ⲰⲀⲦⲈⲤⲈⲚϤ Ⲉ̇2ⲢⲎⲒ Ⲉ̇ⲠⲒ ⲘⲞⲚⲀⲤⲦⲎⲢ Ⲓ ⲞⲚ (27v, 2-5); ⲫⲎ Ⲉ̇ⲦⲀϤⲬⲒⲚⲒ ⲞⲢ ⲘⲠⲒⲠⲈⲖⲀⲄⲞⲤ ⲚⲦⲈⲫⲒⲞⲘ ⲬⲰⲢⲒⲤ ⲬⲞⲒ (28r, 11–13).

26. Cf. for example, §§ 18f., 58 and 63.

27. Purity: 26r, 16; 26v, 7–10; patience: 26v, 16; love for mankind: 26v, 17.

28. The hymn ends with this hope: ⲀⲔⲤⲰⲬⲠ ⲚⲀⲚ ⲘⲠⲈⲔⲂ Ⲓ ⲞⲤ ⲚⲈⲘⲚⲈⲔⲤⲀⲬⲒ ⲚⲢⲈϤ† ⲘⲠⲰⲚ2 ⲚⲎ ⲈⲐⲘⲞⲰ Ⲓ ⲚϧⲢⲎⲒ ⲚϧⲎⲦⲞⲨ ⲫ†ⲚⲀⲰⲰⲠⲒ ⲚⲈⲘⲰⲞⲨ ⲚⲒ ⲀⲄⲄⲈⲖⲞⲤ ⲚⲀⲀ̇ⲢⲈ2 Ⲉ̇ⲢⲰⲞⲨ ⲰⲀⲦⲞⲨⲈⲢⲠⲈⲘⲠⲰⲀ ⲘⲠⲒ ⲰⲚ2 ⲚⲈⲚⲈ2 (30v, 12–31r, 4). ⲂⲒⲞⲤ probably refers to the virtuous way of living rather than the literary work and is then a synonym to ⲠⲞⲖ Ⲓ ⲦⲈⲒ Ⲗ· ⲤⲀⲬⲒ alludes to his sermons and letters.

11 The Relationship of St. Shenoute of Atripe with His Contemporary Patriarchs of Alexandria

Samuel Moawad

WHEN WE SPEAK about the relationship of St. Shenoute with the Alexandrian patriarchs, we speak indeed about a traditional relationship between Coptic monasticism and the official church of Egypt. The basis of this relationship was already established at the dawn of Coptic monasticism by the patriarch Athanasius (328–373), who recognized the important role that the monks could play on behalf of the Church. To understand the relationship between Shenoute and his patriarchs or between the monastic organization and the official church in the time of Shenoute, it is necessary to present briefly the main features of this relationship as it developed from the time when the monastic system first appeared up until the time of Shenoute.

The Church and Monasticism
Although monasticism came into existence independently of the official church, we cannot consider it as an opposition movement against the church, as some scholars have seen it.[1] In contrast to this opinion, we can consider the *Vita Antonii* of Athanasius as recognition by the church of the 'legality' of the monastic movement. When Athanasius chose his bishops from among the monks, he did not try to weaken monasticism and put it under his authority. He trusted the monks and could not ignore their popularity among the simple people. His letter to the monk Dracontius, who refused to carry out his duties as a bishop, shows no opposition, but only that Athanasius saw

monasticism from a different perspective than that from which the monks saw it.[2] It was Athanasius who gave monasticism a new perspective: that it is more than hunger and thirst, as many monks had thought.[3]

Athanasius cultivated good contacts with the different monastic systems and regions. He welcomed Antonius in Alexandria,[4] visited the Pachomian monks[5] and received them in Alexandria,[6] and was the adviser of some virgins.[7]

Most of the monks were not theologians and did not try to be. They could not and did not try to access the theological sources, for the majority of them could not understand the Greek language. They found it enough to follow the opinions of their patriarchs and to read their works, especially the festal letters.[8] One should not be surprised to find agreements between the monks' fathers and the patriarchs, especially with regard to church dogma and heretical opinions. A comparison between the nineteenth chapter of the *Vita Antonii* and the fortieth festal letter of Athanasius concerning the martyr cult, or between Shenoute's work *And It Happened One Day* and a letter of Cyril, confirms the influence of the patriarchs' thought on the monks.[9]

The pontificate of Patriarch Theophilus (385–412) was a turning point in the relationship between the church and the monastic organization. The festal letter of Theophilus from the year 399 rejected and condemned those monks who believed in the anthropomorphology of God.[10] The monks of Scetis crowded around the house of the patriarch and asked him to condemn Origen, who rejected the literal interpretation of the Scriptures and the anthropomorphology of God. At the same time Theophilus quarrelled with the Tall Brothers, who admired Origen. To take revenge on the Tall Brothers, and at the same time to satisfy the monks of Scetis, the patriarch pursued and drove away all the followers of Origen and burned their cells and books.[11]

For the first time in the history of monasticism, the monks believed in and struggled for a dogma that the Church had condemned, and the patriarch meddled in monastic affairs to achieve personal aims. Through this situation, both the patriarchs and the monks realized the kind of role the monks could play in the politics of the church and also in the theological struggles in which the church was engaged.

Shenoute and Athanasius
When we investigate the relationship between Shenoute and his contemporary patriarchs, we do not find any change in the nature of this relationship.

It remained as it had been in the past. Shenoute (347–465) was contemporary with seven patriarchs, from Athanasius to Timothy Aelurus, and as a head of his monastery (ca. 385–465) he was in contact with the last four.[12] Some of his correspondence with these patriarchs has been preserved and offers us some good material for investigating this relationship.[13] Although this began with the career of Shenoute as abbot of the White Monastery, it was in its beginning a common and normal relationship between an abbot and his patriarch. Shenoute had no personal contact with Athanasius, but it is clear from his writings that he was reading not only this patriarch's festal letters, which existed in Coptic, but also his other Greek writings, especially his four books against the Arians, and attacked, like Athanasius, the Arians, the Meletians, and the apocryphal books.[14] The sources of Shenoute's teachings were the same as Athanasius's, namely the Holy Bible and the fathers of the church. Therefore, his rejection of the apocryphal books is to be expected, based on the thirty-ninth festal letter of Athanasius. He quoted Athanasius explicitly in his writings, such as in *I Am Amazed* and *Acephalous Work A 17*.[15]

The divinity of Jesus, the Son of God, was also the main theme in the writings of Shenoute against the Arians, as it is also in the writings of Athanasius, even if Shenoute began to inveigh against other heresies as well. He connected all the heresies with the divinity of Jesus. In his work *I Am Amazed*, he attacked one of the apocryphal books just because it had the title "The gospel of Jesus, the Son of God, and the begotten of the angels."[16] Also in his work *And It Happened One Day*, which was addressed against the teaching of Nestorius instead of speaking about the nature of Christ, he spoke only about the eternity of the Son.[17]

Compare the following excerpts from Shenoute's *I Am Amazed* with various works of Athanasius:

Shenoute of Atripe	Athanasius of Alexandria
As the great wise man Apa Atha-nasius, the archbishop, revealed the evil of those who say these impieties and their other wicked words, which are these: The Father has not always been a Father, and the Son has not always existed, but rather the Son of God too came into existence from what was not, and like everything that was created he too is a creature and a creation; and there was a time, when the Word of God did not exist; and before he was begotten he did not exist; and also that he is not by nature the Son of God; and also that he is one of those begotten and created; and that he is a creature and a thing made and a thing; and that God was existing alone and no one was being with him. And when he wanted to make us, then he created this one and called him logos and Son; and like everything that did not exist before and (then) existed by the will of God, he also did not exist before, but he existed by the will of God; and that he also existed by a grace. (Shenoute, *I Am Amazed* §§ 325–28, ed. Orlandi 1985: 24, 26.)	And the mockeries which he [Arius] utters in it [Thalia], repulsive and most irreligious, are such as these:—"God was not always a Father"; but "once God was alone, and not yet a Father, but afterward He became a Father." "The Son was not always"; for, whereas all things were made out of nothing, and all existing creatures and works were made, so the Word of God Himself was 'made out of nothing,' and 'once He was not,' and 'He was not before His origination,' but He as others 'had an origin of creation.' 'For God,' he says, 'was alone, and the Word as yet was not, nor the Wisdom. Then, wish-ing to form us, thereupon He made a certain one, and named Him Word and Wisdom and Son, that He might form us by means of Him.'. . . and that the Son again, as partaking of it, is named Word and Son according to grace. Athanasius, *Contra Arianos* 1.2:5 (Schaff and Wace 1994, II, vol. 4: 308–309.)
	Arius and those with him thought and professed thus: 'God made the Son out of nothing, and called Him His Son'; 'The Word of God is one of the crea-tures'; and 'Once He was not'; and 'He is alterable; capable, when it is His Will, of altering.' Athanasius, *De Synodis* 15 (Schaff and Wace 1994, II, vol. 4: 457.)

	Because they have perfected themselves in a lying and contemptible science; and as to the ignorant and simple, they have led them astray by evil thoughts concerning the right faith established in all truth and upright in the presence of God. Athanasius, *ep. fest.* 39,1 (Schaff and Wace 1994, II, vol. 4: 551.)
The Scriptures of the living water are enough that the thirsty people drink. (Shenoute, *I Am Amazed* § 0426, ed. Orlandi 1985: 46.)	These are fountains of salvation, that they who thirst may be satisfied with the living words they contain. Athanasius, *ep. fest.* 39,6, trans. (Schaff and Wace 1994, II, vol. 4: 552.)

Although he was influenced by Athanasius, who read Origen and praised him,[18] Shenoute rejected all Origen's writings, as we see in *I Am Amazed* and *And It Happened One Day.*[19] He also had a different point of view from Athanasius about the martyr cult. While Athanasius was very strongly opposed to this,[20] Shenoute allowed it with certain conditions, such as that one must behave at a martyr's shrine as if one is in a church, with respect and worship.[21]

Now, how can we interpret these disagreements between the abbot and his patriarch, whom Shenoute honored and admired? Here we have to note that the thought of Shenoute was always in agreement with the *current* thought of the church and not absolutely with the thought of the church in general. In the fifth century the Alexandrian Church under Patriarch Theophilus rejected Origen, all his teachings, and the teachings of his disciples, much like a holy war against so-called 'Origenism.'[22] This fact explains why Shenoute fought against Origenism only in those sermons delivered after the episcopate of Theophilus,[23] and why he quoted Theophilus at such length in his work *I Am Amazed.*[24] We can also say the same about the attitude of Shenoute center the martyr cult. It was Cyril who was the first patriarch to allow the erection of martyr chapels to supersede the Egyptian pilgrimage.[25]

Shenoute and Theophilus

Concerning theology, Theophilus did not offer any significant writings. We cannot consider his fighting against the Origenists as a theological matter, because he himself had no problem with Origen's writings until 399. He even wanted to ordain Evagrius Ponticus, the most popular Origenist in the fourth century, as a bishop.[26] However, Theophilus was the one who stimulated the struggle between Christians and pagans by destroying the Serapeum in Alexandria in 392.[27] The situation became dangerous at the time of Cyril, when the Christians in Alexandria murdered Hypatia, a famous pagan philosopher.[28] That act was considered by Shenoute and his fellow monks in Upper Egypt as permission to do the same in their regions. These Christians relied also on the edicts of Emperor Theodosius I from 391 and 392, which outlawed paganism and gave the Christian officials many privileges in comparison with the non-Christians.[29] Another edict, from 399, allowed the destruction of pagan temples.[30]

This fight against paganism was more violent in Upper Egypt than in Lower Egypt, and especially so in the region of Akhmim. The *Vita* and the writings of Shenoute testify to his struggle against paganism.[31] Shenoute was not satisfied with destroying the temples just in his immediate neighborhood, but he also helped others to do it elsewhere.[32] He did not tolerate paganism, either in public, or in secret. This attitude motivated him to search the house of his enemy Gesius twice, with and without his permission, to ascertain whether he possessed idols or not.[33] Like other Christians, Shenoute also justified his violence against non-Christians on the basis of the edicts of the emperors.[34] It was not by accident that Shenoute began his own struggle against paganism after that struggle had already begun in Alexandria, with the blessing of his patriarchs and above all the Patriarch Theophilus.

Shenoute and Cyril

With the pontificate of Cyril (412–444) the relationship between the church and the monastic organization developed another feature. It became more close and personal. The wish of Cyril to crown Shenoute as a bishop[35] (which is something that Athanasius did not try with Antonius) and his rather private invitation to the abbot to attend the Council of Ephesus in 431,[36] reveal a new dimension in this relationship and in the relationship between the Church and the monastic organization in general.

Although the monks were not theologians, and the Church did not want them to become such, they played a role that the Church intended for them, namely to support their patriarchs. In his letter to the monks of Egypt, Cyril advised them not to be involved in theological matters: "It would be better for you to pay no attention at all to such inquiries and not at all to dig up difficult questions . . . . For the finer distinctions of speculations transcend the comprehension of the less instructed. However, you have not remained completely ignorant of such discussions. . . . I thought it necessary to say some few words to you concerning these matters. I do not do this that you may have a greater battle of words; rather, I intend that you may escape the danger of going astray."[37]

The narrative in the Bohairic *Life of Shenoute*[38] about how he struck Nestorius, and how Cyril rewarded him and appointed him as an archimandrite, is untrustworthy,[39] but nevertheless shows how the relationship between the church and the monks had come to appear. Cyril could not ignore the monastic organization that possessed hundreds of monasteries and thousands of monks, and he could not ignore the most famous abbot in Egypt. His invitation to attend this council was the beginning of the participation of monasticism in shaping the politics of the church, and later when the majority of Alexandrian patriarchs and bishops were chosen from among the monks, the monastic organization effectively became the leadership of the church and could finally incorporate the Church into its own organization, thus making the Coptic Church into a monastic church.[40] As we have seen in his relationship with Athanasius, Shenoute's fight against heresies was influenced by his patriarchs. Their writings were considered by him as laws in and of themselves.[41] He rejected the apocryphal books because Athanasius had rejected them,[42] he rejected the teachings of Origen because Theophilus had rejected them, and he allowed the martyr cult because Cyril allowed it. His struggle against Nestorius was also influenced by the writings of Cyril. Shenoute understood Nestorius's heresy as Cyril had understood and interpreted it.[43] That is confirmed by the fact that not all the quotes of Nestorius in the writings of Shenoute are to be found in the writings of Nestorius himself.[44] In his defense of Nestorius, Shenoute depended on the writings of Cyril. In his *And It Happened One Day*, he wrote: "But Nestorius who was given the title 'bishop'. . . said: "She gave birth to a human Christ who was like Moses, David, and others."[45] We find similar words in a letter of Cyril to Nestorius: "If you believe that he was a prophet like Moses, then neither Moses nor any of the prophets was able to bear the sins of the world."[46]

In his sermons *And It Happened One Day* and *I Am Amazed*, Shenoute spoke about the Eucharist and how the bread and the wine are transformed into the body and the blood of Christ, seeing a certain relationship between the divinity of Christ and the transformation of the bread and the wine in the Eucharist. It is difficult to understand this relationship until one reads the third letter of Cyril to Nestorius (ep. 17,12), in which he says:

> Proclaiming the death according to the flesh of the only begotten Son of God, that is, of Jesus Christ, and confessing his resurrection from the dead and his ascension into heaven, we celebrate the unbloody sacrifice in the churches, and we thus approach the spiritual blessings and are made holy, becoming partakers of the holy flesh and of the precious blood of Christ, the Saviour of us all. And we do this, not as men receiving common flesh, far from it, nor truly the flesh of a man sanctified and conjoined to the Word according to a unity of dignity, or as one having had a divine indwelling, but as the truly life-giving and very own flesh of the Word himself.

Here Cyril can explain that if Christ is not the eternal Son of God, the Eucharist loses its mysterious efficacy. We do not find such an explanation in Shenoute's writings, and that is one of the great differences between a theologian like Cyril and a monk like Shenoute.

In his letters, Cyril used the example of the union between the body and the soul to explain the union between the two natures of Christ.[47] Shenoute used the same example regarding the two natures: "The Godhead did not leave the humanity when He was on the cross. When someone is murdered, does one say that a body was murdered? Is it not said that we murdered the whole man, although the soul does not die, but only the body? It is also the same with the Lord. He died in his humanity, but in his soul he did not die."[48]

In his letter to the monks of Egypt we can observe how Cyril used a style of language that the monks could understand, and it is very similar to the language of Shenoute when he puts rhetorical questions or imagines, as in a diatribe, that his opponents ask him questions, and so on.[49] And because he knew the value that Athanasius had for the monks, Cyril mentioned him twice in his letter to them, and he quoted from his work *Contra Arianos*.[50]

Shenoute of Atripe	Cyril of Alexandria
Why did all our holy fathers, especially our father Apa Athanasius, the archbishop, the man of the true knowledge, not accept them [the apocryphal books], but rejected them strongly? (Shenoute, *I Am Amazed* § 0308, ed. Orlandi 1985: 22.) Who are those who destroy the snares of those people and uproot them? They are the teachers of the Scripture from the prophets, the apostles, and the orthodox fathers in every time. (Shenoute, *I Am Amazed* § 0323, ed. Orlandi 1985: 24.) There is no deed or word that man can hear, or understand, or give fruits within, that the prophets or apostles or faithful fathers and true teachers of the church did not reveal fully. (Shenoute, *I Am Amazed* § 0360, ed. Orlandi 1985: 32.)	If we abide by the teachings of the holy Fathers and are earnest in considering them of great value, and test ourselves, "whether we are in the faith" according to the Scripture, it will truly come about that we most fitly will mold our thoughts to their upright and blameless judgments. (Cyril, *ep.* 4,2, trans. McEnerney 1987: 39.)
He [Nestorius] did not persuade these, saying of Christ: "He is a man in whom God dwells and after he was born from Mary the *logos* went into him." (Shenoute, *I Am Amazed* § 0464, ed. Orlandi 1985: 50.)	For an ordinary man was not born of the Holy Virgin and then the Word descended into him. (Cyril, ep. 4,4, trans. McEnerney 1987: 40.)

Shenoute of Atripe	Cyril of Alexandria
Then the one whom the Virgin has born is a god. Therefore it is necessary to confess that Mary is the bearer of God, as our fathers said. (Shenoute, *I Am Amazed* §§ 0482, ed. Orlandi 1985: 54.)	Nor do we say that they are conjoined to one another by dignity and authority… Neither do we say that the Word of God dwelled, as in an ordinary man, in the one born of the Holy Virgin, in order that Christ might not be thought to be a man bearing God. (Cyril, ep. 17,9, trans. McEnerney 1987: 83.)
	We shall find that the holy Fathers have thought in this way. In this way, they have not hesitated to call the Holy Virgin the Mother of God. (Cyril, *ep.* 4,7, trans. McEnerney 1987: 41.)

Shenoute and Dioscorus

It seems that the attempts of the church to prevent the writings of Origen from being read were unsuccessful. Up to the pontificate of Dioscorus, the writings and the opinions of Origen were disseminated not only among the laymen or the monks of Nitria, but also in the monasteries of Upper Egypt. A monk called Helias was condemned and dismissed by Dioscorus because he was an Origenist. To ensure that these measures would be carried out, Dioscorus sent a letter to Shenoute to announce his decisions to the clerics and laymen and to drive away this monk from all monasteries and churches.[51] Dioscorus, who invited Shenoute with Macarius of Tkôw to attend the Council of Chalcedon,[52] trusted no one but Shenoute to execute his orders and to announce them even to the bishops of these regions.

Notes

1. Heussi 1936: 184; Brakke 1998: 83. Against this, cf. Ranke-Heinemann 1964: 104; Heussi 1936: 182.
2. Athanasius, *ep. Drac.* (Schaff 1994: II,4: 557–60).
3. *The History of the Patriarchs* (ed. Seybold 1912: 57).

4. Athanasius, *Vita Antonii* 70 (Schaff 1994: II,4).

5. *Vita Pachomii Prima* (Veilleux 1980–1982, vol. 1: §§ 30, 143–44); *Vita Pachomii Bohairic* (Veilleux 1980–1982, vol. 1: §§ 28, 200–201); *Vita Pachomi Arabic* (Amélineau 1889: 384–85, 693–96); Ammon, *Ep. Thphl.* § 34 (Goehring 1986).

6. *Vita Pachomii Prima* (Veilleux 1980–1982, vol. 1: §§ 113, 120); *Vita Pachomii Bohairic* (Veilleux 1980–1982, vol. 1: §§ 96, 134); *Vita Pachomii Arabic* (Amélineau 1889: 642–43, 659).

7. See note 3.

8. *Apophthegmata Patrum*, Sisoes 25 (Miller 1998); *Vita Pachomii Prima* (Veilleux 1980–1982, vol. 1: § 94b); *Vita Pachomii Bohairic* (Veilleux 1980–1982, vol. 1: § 189); Shenoute, *I Am Amazed* §§ 0308, 0319, 0329–0330 (Orlandi 1985); Barnard 1997: 7, 9.

9. See notes 45 and 46 below.

10. This letter is lost, but Gennadius mentioned it. Cf. Gennadius, *Vir. ill.* ch. 34 (Schaff 1994: II,3).

11. Socrates, *h. e.* 6,7 ; Sozomenus., *h. e.* 8,11–12 (Schaff 1994: II,2); Palladius, *v. Chrys.* chs. 6–8 (Schläpfer 1966); *Vita Aphu* §§ 5–11 (Bumazhnov 2006); Evelyn-White 1973, vol. 2: 125–44; Clark 1992: 105–21; Dechow 1988: 402–14. Until the end of the fourth century, there was no antiorigenist movement in Egypt. The works of Origen were read by many people and even by the Alexandrian patriarchs and church fathers like Athanasius (Ath., *ep. Serap.* IV. 9–10; Ath., *decr.* 27; Soc., *h. e.* 6,13) and Didymus the Blind (Soc., *h. e.* 4,25). The writings and the opinions of Origen were spread among the monks of Nitria by some foreigners like Evagrius Ponticus, Palladius, and John Cassian, who all visited and settled in Wadi al-Natrun. The struggle concerning Origenism began outside of Egypt between Epiphanius, Bishop of Salamis, and John of Palestine.

12. Emmel 2004b, vol. 1: 8; Emmel 2005: 8318b; Behlmer 1996: LV–LX.

13. A letter to Timothy [I?] (Zoega, 1810: 428; Leipoldt 1906–1913, vol. 3: 13–14, no. 2); to Theophilus (?) (Leipoldt 1906–1913, vol. 3: 14–15, no. 4); from Cyril (Leipoldt 1906–1913, vol. 3: 225–26, Add. I.A,B,C); to Cyril (?) (ed. Young 1993: 175); from Dioscorus (Thompson 1922: 367–76); to Dioscorus (Leipoldt 1906–1913, vol. 3: 13, no. 1); to Timothy [II?] (Leipoldt 1906–1913, vol. 3: 14, no. 3). See Emmel 2004b, vol. 1: 8 n. 9, 273, 280.

14. Moussa 1998–1999: 20–25.

15. Shenoute, *I Am Amazed* §§ 308, 319, 325, 330, and 815 (Orlandi 1985); Shenoute, *Acephalous Work A17* (Lefort 1935: 56–58). Cf. Brakke 1998: 289 n. 3.

16. Shenoute, *I Am Amazed* § 0309 (Orlandi 1985).

17. Shenoute, *And It Happened One Day* 87v–82r = MONB.AV 228–229 (Lefort, ed., 1955: 41–42).

18. Athanasius, *ep. Serap.* IV. 9–10; Athanasius, *decr.* 27 (Schaff, trans., 1994: II,4); Socrates, *h. e.* 6,13 (Schaff, trans., 1994: II,2).

19. Shenoute, *I Am Amazed* § 0359 (Orlandi 1985), MONB.DQ 113–114 (Wessely 1909–1917, vol. 1: 131–32), MONB.DS 190–92 (unpublished), MONB.DQ 123 (Wessely 1909–1917, vol. 1: 133), MONB.DS 197:i.26–199:ii.1 (unpublished), MONB.DS 221 (Emmel 1995: 95); Shenoute, *And It Happened One Day* 84r = MONB.AV 233 (Lefort 1955: 43).

20. Athanasius, *ep. fest.* 41 (Schaff 1994: II,4).

21. Shenoute, *Those Who Work Evil* (Amélineau 1907–1914, vol. 1: 211–20); Horn 1986: 5; Baumeister 1972: 69–70.

22. Jerome, *ep.* 92, 96 (Schaff 1994: II,6).

23. It is clear that *And It Happened One Day* was written after 450, because Shenoute mentioned the death of Nestorius, and *I Am Amazed* ca. 445. See Emmel 2004b, vol. 2: 648, 665–66.

24. Emmel 1995: 95–96.

25. Montserrat 1998: 261–263; Baumeister 1972: 69–70.

26. Socrates, *h. e.* 4,23 (Schaff 1994: II,2).

27. *Theodoret, h. e.* 5,22 (Schaff 1994: II,3); Bauer and Strzygowski 1905: 152, plate 6 verso; Hahn 2004: 78–94.

28. Socrates, *h. e.* 7,15 (Schaff 1994: II,2); John of Nikiu, *The Chronicle* 84, 87–103 (Charles 1981).

29. Pharr 1952: 16.10.1,2,4–7,10–14; Hussey 1966: 42–44; Martin 2001: 110.

30. Pharr 1952: 16.10.16.

31. *Vita Sinuthii Bohairic* §§ 83–84, 125–27 (Leipoldt 1906–1913, vol. 1; Bell 1983); *Vita Sinuthii Arabic* (Amélineau 1888–1895: 385–86, 425–26, 439–46); *Panegyric on Macarius* §§ VIII–IX (Johnson 1980); Shenoute, *Let Our Eyes* (unpublished, see Emmel 2004b, vol. 2: 680, 865); Emmel (forthcoming); Shenoute, *Not because a Fox Barks* (Chassinat 1911: 38–50, 211; Leipoldt 1908: 77–84; Barns, trans., 1964); Emmel 2002: 102–13; Leipoldt 1903: 175–82; Hahn 2004: 254–60.

32. *Panegyric on Macarius* §§ VIII–IX (Johnson 1980); *Vita Sinuthii Arabic* (Amélineau 1888–1895: 429).

33. Shenoute, *Not because a Fox Barks* (MONB.XH 209:ii.2–210:i.8, Chassinat 1911: 43–44; MONB.DU 172, Leipoldt, 1906–1913, vol. 3: 81–82; Barns, trans., 1964: 157); Shenoute, *Let Our Eyes* (unpublished; see note 31 above); *Vita Sinuthii Arabic* (Amélineau 1888–1895: 425–26).

34. Shenoute, *Let Our Eyes* (*WW* 27:ii.3–25, unpublished; see note 31 above).

35. Leipoldt 1906–1913, vol. 3: 34–35; Emmel 2004b: 8; Grillmeier 1979–2002: 213.

36. Zoega 1810: 28–29; Leipoldt 1906–1913, vol. 3: 35, 219; 225 B; *Vita Sinuthii*

Bohairic § 17 (Leipoldt 1906–1913, vol. 1; Bell 1983); *Vita Sinuthii Arabic* (Amélineau 1888–1895: 426); *Panegyric on Macarius* § IV,1 (Johnson 1980); Emmel 2004b: 8 nn. 9 and 10; Weiss 1969–1970: 183 n. 2; Grillmeier 1979–2002, vol. 2, part 4: 213.

37. Cyril, ep. 1,4 (McEnerney 1987).

38. *Vita Sinuthii Bohairic* §§ 128–130 (Leipoldt 1906–1913, vol. 1; Bell 1983); *Vita Sinuthii Arabic* (Amélineau 1888–1895: 427–28).

39. Leipoldt 1903: 1 n. 2, 41; Bell 1983: 108 n. 85; *The History of the Patriarchs* (Seybold 1912: 73); Grillmeier 1979–2002, vol. 2, part 4: 218–19; Hahn 2004: 223.

40. Brakke 1998: 99; Krause 1981: 58.

41. Shenoute, *I Am Amazed* §§ 0323, 0360, 0482 (Orlandi 1985).

42. Shenoute, *I Am Amazed* § 0308 (Orlandi 1985).

43. Weiss 1969–1970: 186–92; Grillmeier 1979–2002, vol. 2, part 4: 214–17.

44. Grillmeier 1979–200, vol. 2, part 4: 215.

45. Shenoute, *And It Happened One Day* 84r = MONB.AV 233 (Lefort 1955: 43).

46. *The History of the Patriarchs* (Seybold 1912: 71).

47. Cyril, *ep.* 1,36, 50,6 (McEnerney 1987).

48. Shenoute, *I Am Amazed* §§ 0473–0474 (Orlandi 1985).

49. Cyril, *ep.* 1, 19, 24, 26, 32 (McEnerney 1987).

50. Cyril, *ep.* 1, 6–9 (McEnerney 1987).

51. Dioscor. Al., *Ep. ad Sinuth.* (Thompson 1922); Dechow 1988: 237–40.

52. *Panegyric on Macarius* § X II,7 (Johnson 1980); *Vita Sinuthii Arabic* (Amélineau 1888–1895: 429–31, 467–68).

12 Manichaeism and Gnosticism in the Panopolitan Region between Lykopolis and Nag Hammadi

Siegfried G. Richter

To DEAL WITH the religious movements of Manichaeism and Gnosticism in the area of Sohag presents a good many problems and raises several questions that will perhaps never be answered. This fact depends on our lack of evidence concerning these two strong 'enemies' of the Christian 'orthodox' faith, a faith that was defended by officials of the Church and of Monasticism like Shenoute, the famous abbot of Sohag. I am not able to enlarge our knowledge of this topic, but I try in this article to mention several aspects and to restrict the field of information.

In scholarly literature the city of Panopolis "has often been taken as a test case for the religious situation in Egypt in Late Antiquity."[1] This depends on the fact that a lot of sources tell of several philosophical and religious activities and also of conflicts, especially in this area. In general one could say that in the early fourth century, paganism was still strong. Approximately at the same time a kind of competition between Gnostic groups, the Manichaean religion, several Christian tendencies, and a developing institutional Christian Church, formed by men like Bishop Athanasius of Alexandria, reached a culmination point.[2] At the very end of this century pagan religions lost their dominance. Nevertheless a well-educated pagan elite was still active and famous in the fifth century, demonstrated also by their activities in the area of Panopolis. Famous, for example, was Horapollon, who wrote the well-known interpretation of more than one hundred hieroglyphic signs.[3] Stories like the struggle between Shenoute and Gessios led to the conclusion that Panopolis was a kind of castle (or *qasr*) against Christian influence.[4] However, the view of the past as a kind of permanent struggle between paganism and Christianity does not reflect reality at all. In general, the conversion of a society to another religion, as living together in daily life between different religious groups, is marked by a diversity of factors. In the case of Panopolis the information we have should not lead to the conclusion "of a fierce battle between opposing forces or a religious war."[5]

Beside 'the pagans,' Gnosticism and Manichaeism also played an important role as counterparts of institutional Christianity. However, in the case of the region of Panopolis it is difficult to find strong historical facts for these two groups. One has to keep in mind that the borderline between several religious beliefs is often flittering and porous and depends on ancient and modern definitions, which are changeable.[6]

An early witness may be the alchemist Zosimus, who was suspected to be involved in Gnostic circles. He must have been active in about 300 and in several ancient sources is connected to the city of Panopolis. Michèle Mertens listed a considerable quantity of relations to Gnostic texts, but concluded: "However, the question of how Zosimus came into contact with hermetism and gnosticism remains open," and two lines later: "It is very likely, but in the texts that have come down to us from Zosimus, there is not a scrap of evidence allowing us to claim that he frequented this kind of circles."[7]

From Lykopolis to Nag Hammadi

In some ways it is remarkable that one of the most important abbots of Egyptian monasticism, a man who has been described as a kind of pragmatic warrior for the orthodox faith, is to be centered in the middle of two places that for historians are famous for their non-Christian and heretical activities.

About 110 kilometers to the north lies the city of Lykopolis, often mentioned as the center of Manichaean activities. The Coptic Manichaean library of Madinat Madi in Fayoum and the texts of Kellis, found in the house of a Manichaean community, were written in the Lykopolitan dialect. This dialect also plays an important role in the most famous find of Coptic manuscripts, the find of Nag Hammadi, which marks the counterpole in the south. For this reason the dialect and the city of Lykopolis were often connected with the Manichaeans or other 'heretics.'

About eightly kilometers away from Sohag in the area of Nag Hammadi thirteen papyrus-codices were found in December 1945. This so-called 'Gnostic Library' includes several non-Gnostic texts, for instance Christian philosophical writings or hermetic tractates. From this point of view, the different religious texts could be read by various readers of different religious faiths, involved in different official or non-official groups. So the readership has to be imagined as a very complex one. It was not possible to clarify the archaeological context of the finding of the library. For this reason, the context of the texts could only be reconstructed by the contents of the codices, observations in the order of the scriptures, mysterious colophons, and certain facts such as several versions of the same texts, duplicates, and some documents used for the book-binding. The thesis of a relationship to the nearby Pachomian monasteries was discussed in several works but could not be proved.[8]

The Lack of Basic Historical Information

We do not know all of the texts created in the 'Age of Spirituality,' as so often called and we are not able to estimate the original number of copies that exist. In fact, however, we know some. In contrast to this we have a much poorer knowledge about archaeological remains or names of normal people who belonged to Gnostic or Manichaean groups. We do not possess information on their number and their spread in villages and towns.

Moreover, even the biographical data of some famous persons are poor. In Manichaean studies the name of Lykopolis is associated with the neo-Platonist Alexander of Lykopolis. His antimanichaean tractate was written about 300 and was transmitted through the centuries because of its importance in the debates with the sect of the Paulicans in the ninth century. Photius (c. Manich. 1,11) tells of him that he converted to Christianity and became bishop of Lykopolis (as predecessor of Meletius)—a piece of information that is unreliable. We do not know anything more about Alexander, and to my knowledge it is not absolutely sure where he was in touch with the Manichaeans: whether in Lykopolis or in Alexandria.[9] His statements about Manichaean missionary work concern the whole of Egypt.

For several reasons the theory was developed that the Cologne Mani Codex, the smallest codex preserved from antiquity, was translated from an East Aramaic dialect to Greek in this area.[10] The thesis of such a translation is based on certain particularities in Greek. The localization of such a scribal activity to this area is possible, but since the codex was bought in the antiquity trade, there exists no certain evidence for its origin. In spite of the sources we have, the gaps in our view of 'heretic' history are frustrating and no one can say how far from historical reality it might be.

What about Shenoute and the Manichaeans?

But what about the area of Sohag? Do we have any evidence that Shenoute himself was in touch with Manichaeans? D.W. Johnson collected the available data of "Coptic Reactions to Gnosticism and Manichaeism," including some reflections on the Manichaean religion in the *Corpus Sinuthianum*.[11] Besides a so-called gray area, where he listed some polemics against Gnostics and Manichaeans, he listed—if I count right—six passages that argue directly against Mani or the Manichaeans. In fact it is not an argumentation but a blaming of forbidden thoughts from a Christian point of view: the rejection of the Old Testament and the prophets, and the Manichaean belief that Jesus was not born of a woman. It is no surprise that these two points especially are mentioned in the works of Shenoute. From the very beginning of conflict in the Church, or between different theologians, schools and so on, the neglect of the Old Testament was not tolerated. Different opinions concerning questions of Christology were the main reason for struggle and schisms in the Church itself and in the fight against Gnostics or Manichaeans.

It is proved that Shenoute was a well-known person in his area, and that many non-Christians visited him and debated with him.[12] As far as I know, however, it is not recorded whether he personally met any believers of the Manichaean faith.

That there existed Manichaeans in Middle and Upper Egypt even a long time after Shenoute is verified by a certain other Shenoute, who functioned as dux in the seventh century. It is told that he burnt two Manichaean priests in the year 643.[13]

Back to our Shenoute: two sources have a little more quality in their argument against Manichaeans.

References to the Acta Archelai

The fragment BN Copte 130³ fol. 39f., assigned to volume 8 of the Discourses of Shenoute (codex GP), bears a small Antimanichaicon.[14] However, although the *Acta Archelai*, which were composed some years after 325 and contain a fictitious debate between a certain Bishop Archelaios and Mani, are mentioned, almost nothing can be found about Manichaeism itself. The text shows that Shenoute—possibly because of this region—was estimated to know something about Manichaeans and that he dealt with this subject. Shenoute stated that a presbyter of Side, a city in Asia Minor, wanted to know something about the Manichaeans. We do not know any other facts about this presbyter and his relationship to the famous abbot. However, it is possible that they met personally during Shenoute's journey through Asia Minor on his way to the Council of Ephesus or on other occasions.

Already at the beginning Shenoute refers to the *Acta Archelai*: "Archelaios, the bishop of Carchar in Mesopotamia, also made a few remarks while opposing Mani, the root of Manichaeism."[15] Although the acts contain various statements on the history of the Manichaeans and details of their theological system, the homily of Shenoute offers no further information. After the short introduction, he cited the gospels and inveighed against the Pharisees. In fact there are no further relations to the *Acta Archelai* or excerpts in this text.

We can only conclude that the use of the term 'Manichaean' for Shenoute and for the audience was common.

Further references to the *Acta Archelai* shows BN Copte 131⁴ fol. 158 recto col. B, which belongs to codex ZM of the White Monastery and contains varia.[16] In the fragment some pagan opinions about the fate of the soul after death are mentioned. This is a kind of brief list without profound information, but written in a neutral way. Such lists in the form "some say . . . others say" are also known in Manichaean literature. The unpublished *Kephalaia* of Dublin contain a chapter about different Christological thoughts written in the same form.[17]

In the section on Manichaean thought, which follows the foregoing pagan part, the author cites sentences from the *Acta Archelai*.[18] It is told that a soul that murders will be transferred into the body of a leper. The next statement that the air is the soul of animals, men and so on could be a misunderstanding or false interpretation of some Manichaean doctrines. Normally the air is only one of the five elements. Further on, our author is right to point out that in the Manichaen view the body does not belong to God but to dark matter and that the prophets are neglected.

Although the statements show a certain knowledge of the Manichean doctrine, they are very general. On the one hand it depends on the focus of the text, namely to register imaginings of the afterlife of the soul. On the other hand, it is normal in a certain sense that polemics against the Manichaeans describe the myth with so many details. In the texts of Sohag we have not so far found such descriptions. There is a large difference between the poor information about the Manichaean doctrine we find in these texts and the theological discourses of Augustine for example, who himself had been a Manichean for several years. It seems that Shenoute had no interest in such details. Augustine tried to prove it wrong; Shenoute already knew that it was wrong.

Worshiping the Sun and Magical Texts

In the works of Shenoute one can find several statements against the worship of stars or of the sun and the moon, in other words polemics against astrological ideas. In the famous struggle with Gessios he wrote: "Could I have hidden the sun in the sky and the moon and the stars, which you worship? Or could I there, where the sun sets, build walls to hinder your praying to the West?"[19] In another place we read: "Woe to him who puts his hand on the mouth, gives them kisses and says: 'Hail, sun,' or, 'Be strong, moon,' thanking the creatures and worshiping them more than the creator himself."[20]

First of all, this is a tirade against pagan traditions. Jaques van der Vliet remarked that this precise formula could be in common use in the environment of the White Monastery.[21] It is possible that Shenoute also observed this custom among Manichaeans, who were known even in Rome as busy admirers of the sun. Even in the fifth century the popes of Rome lamented the Manichaean custom of praying to the sun before entering a church. The same words Shenoute used can be proved in the Coptic Manichaean Psalm Book of Madinat Madi. In a group of sun hymns—testimonies in several languages are preserved from the East, or Middle Asia, to the West—one psalm starts with the words: "Hail, sun," the same wording mentioned by Shenoute. Since this salutation was iterated after each strophe of the Coptic psalm, one could say that it was a well-known expression.[22]

Traces of Gnosticism

Among the descriptions by Shenoute of the objects in a pagan sanctuary some "books full of all manner of magic" are mentioned. It is possible that scriptures like the Books of Jeu, which are counted as Gnostic but have a lot of connections to magical works, were characterized in this way.[23] In these two books the way of the soul through the spheres of heaven is described. Beneath a dialogue between Jesus and the apostles, magical spells, diagrams and descriptions of the localities should enable the soul to pass through.

D.W. Johnson in his article mentioned above, and D.W. Young in a contribution about the background to the Nag Hammadi codices, collected several possible relations of Coptic literature to Gnostic works.[24] Among these sources an allusion to Eve and Cain in the *Life of Pachomius* could be the "most unambiguous reference to a Gnostic doctrine."[25] Some allusions to the Gospel of Philip and the Gospel of Thomas are in discussion. H. Behlmer showed that some terms in the scriptures of Shenoute such as "kingless," a term found in Sethian texts, or "the illuminator" are not necessarily linked to Gnostic texts as previously thought.[26] In his sermon "De iudicio," Shenoute argues against a group of heretics who could be influenced by Gnostic thoughts.[27] These heretics, so Shenoute said, dismissed material property and wealth. Furthermore—that is the important point—material wealth would belong to the devil or to the sphere of the devil, a formulation near to the Gnostic thought that all matter is evil.

In this brief overview there is no opportunity to mention all details, but it is obvious that the traits of Manichaeism and Gnosticism in this area depend only on textual references, often with a limited historical value.

This lack of sources has several causes. Here I want to deal with one of them and raise the simple question: How visible or invisible was a believer of Gnostic thought or a member of the Manichaean religion? It is very likely that in the course of the fourth and fifth centuries non-Christians and non-orthodox Christian believers went further and further underground.[28] For pagan religions the official temple cult, and also several kinds of sanctuaries and idols—paintings and sculptures—were characteristic and visible. This type of religious practice was castigated not only in Christian but also in Manichaean literature. Instead of worshiping idols the 'heretics' (all non-institutional Christians, Gnostic groups and the Manichaean communities) read the Gospels, the epistles of Paul and what are called today the apocryphal texts. It is true that they read with their own eyes and established their own interpretations.

In other words, several Gnostic groups, Manichaeans, and orthodox Christians would meet in the same bookshop. We can assume that the appearance of a member of a Gnostic or Manichaean community did not differ much from other Christian believers. This is despite some reports in anti-heretical Christian texts that Manichaeans were pale in complexion because of fasting too much. Fasting (and giving alms) was also a Christian practice, and the tendency to exaggerate the practice was a known problem.

Comparing the evidence of various sacraments we find similar obser-vances, for example, in the Gospel of Philip and in Christian orthodox ritual.[29] Most differences can be found on the level of interpretation or in details of practice. To speak about Gnostic cultic behavior in general raises several difficulties because of the ambiguous source material. By contrast, the rituals of the Manichaeans are much better documented. Most rituals could be celebrated in normal houses: Worshipers sang psalms and listened to hom-ilies or readings of their holy books. Even special assemblies such as vigils or gatherings of the Electi did not require a special building. An essential cus-tom like the *Seelenmesse*, celebrated for the soul to find its way through the stars, was noted only for praying, singing psalms and giving alms[30] and could be carried out in a familiar environment. As far as we know the so-called Manichaean monasteries were located in ordinary houses.

There was only one exception: the feast of the Bema, which ran over two days. A raised chair was built and it was celebrated in the open air.[31]

Except for some Church Fathers who speak about this feast in general, there are no local reports—for example, in the scriptures of Shenoute—about such a representative feast, which was celebrated, as we assume, by everyone in the wider neighborhood. Perhaps it is only an accident of transmission ('Zufall der Überlieferung'), but perhaps the Manichaean com-munities were so small in number in Panopolis that the individuals had to travel to other villages or towns to celebrate their main feast days.

These few remarks may show the difference between the struggles of Shenoute against pagans on the one hand and Gnostic or Manichaean groups on the other. In spite of the historically transmitted sources, the evidence for these two religious phenomena is noted for its gaps in our knowledge.

Notes

1. Van Minnen 2002: 180 with references.
2. Drawing a distinction between the mentioned religious directions has been the focus of scholarly studies up to today. See the outline of the state of research by Logan (2006) and Marjanen (2005) and the newest attempts for definitions of Gnosticism by King (2003) and Layton (1995).
3. Thissen 2001: esp. XII–XIII.
4. Van der Vliet 1993; cf. to the conflict between Shenoute and Gessios Thissen 1993; see the new interpretation of Gessios as a kind of *crypto-pagan* by Emmel 2002: 108–109.

5. Van Minnen 2002: 181.

6. This phenomenon is described well by Khosroyev (1995).

7. Mertens 2002: 175.

8. See Logan 2006: 15–17 and the detailed discussion in Khosroyev 1995: 77–103; see also Rousseau 2007.

9. Cf. Khosroyev 1995: 105 f. n. 303; to the work of Alexander see Van der Horst and Mansfeld 1974; Villey 1985.

10. Koenen 1973 and Koenen 1983: 95 with references (cf. Khosroyev 1995: 106 n. 305).

11. Johnson 1987.

12. Behlmer 1998.

13. Klein 1992: 373.

14. Klein 1992; Emmel 2004b, vol. 1: 281; 2004b, vol. 2: 660.

15. Translation by Johnson 1987: 207.

16. Lefort 1929; Van der Vliet 1993: 124; Emmel 2004b, vol. 1: 353.

17. Funk 1990: 528.

18. Polotsky 1932.

19. Leipoldt 1906–1913, vol. 3: 81–82.

20. Zoega 1810: 456 f.

21. Van der Vliet 1993: 118.

22. Richter 2000 esp. 484 f.

23. Johnson 1983: 202.

24. Ibid.; Young 1970.

25. Johnson 1983: 201.

26. Behlmer 1996: XC f.; concerning "kingless" see Painchaud and Janz 1997, who raised the question of a link on p. 460.

27. Behlmer 1996: LXXXVIII f., 267 n. 593.

28. Vinzent 1998: 46 f.

29. See Schenke 2001 with bibliography. In general see Logan 2006: 76–82.

30. Richter 1997.

31. See the study of the feast of the Bema by Wurst 1995.

13 Monks and Scholars in the Panopolite Nome
The Epigraphic Evidence

Sofia Schaten and Jacques van der Vliet

DURING THE CONFERENCE "Perspectives on Panopolis," which took place in Leyden in 1998, Lucia Criscuolo discussed the evidence of the Greek inscriptions, including Christian ones, from the Panopolite nome, the present-day Sohag–Akhmim area. Already in the beginning of her paper, she observed that it would be "impossible to sketch a coherent picture of Panopolis on the basis of its Greek inscriptions."[1] Regrettably, the same judgment applies to the exclusively Christian sources from late antique and medieval times that are the subject of the present contribution. It is not that Christian inscriptions from the region are scarce, rather to the contrary, but the record is discontinuous and often lacks the context that might give it historical significance. Further problems, as we will see, concern the heuristics and the accessibility of parts of the material.

In the following pages, some problems and challenges of the epigraphic evidence for the Christian history of the region will be briefly discussed. Our discussion will be guided by the geographical distribution of the texts. In fact, most of the inscriptions from Christian Panopolis can be traced to one of four main provenances. First, on the east bank, the necropoleis in the vicinity of the town, and, secondly, stretching into the eastern desert, Wadi Bir al-'Ayin; then, on the opposite bank of the Nile, the White Monastery and its surroundings; and, finally, the more modest site of the Red Monastery. Wadi Bir al-'Ayin and its inscriptions have received considerable attention in Klaus Kuhlmann's book on the archaeology of the Akhmim area,[2] whereas the inscriptions in the church of the Red Monastery will be published in a volume that is due to appear under the editorship of Karel C. Innemée in the series "La peinture murale chez les coptes" (Institut français d'archéologie orientale, Cairo). As the reader can easily be referred to the publications mentioned, only two out of the four geographical clusters of epigraphic material will be dealt with below. First, the numerous group of tombstones from late antique Panopolis, intriguing on account of their idiosyncrasy, will be discussed by Sofia Schaten. Then, Jacques van der Vliet will review the rich and varied record from perhaps the most impressive Christian site of Egypt, the White Monastery.

"Rive droite": The Town

From the point of view of epigraphy, the town of Panopolis, modern Akhmim—a town that was a well-known production center of linen fabrics, and had a flourishing Greek-style urban life and a rich monastic hinter-land—appears to be a desert region. All the epigraphic witnesses of urban life, such as inscriptions commemorating the foundation or restoration of churches and other public buildings, seem to have disappeared. The only epigraphic material that we do have originates from funerary contexts.[3] The area around Akhmim had extensive cemeteries and, from the early second half of the nineteenth century, the discovery of tombs, mummies, and fine mummy clothes made the town famous for its splendid textiles.[4] Cäcilia Fluck's contribution to the present volume discusses these textile finds in detail and gives extensive information about the various areas and cemeteries from where these may have come (Chapter 21). The publications about the textile finds that followed the earliest so-called excavations (for which see C. Fluck's contribution) contain information about several necropoleis but, to the best of my knowledge, do not mention Christian stelae. The bulk of the funerary inscriptions said to be from Akhmim (some 115 stelae in Lefebvre 1907 alone) were found in the second half of the nineteenth and the begin-ning of the twentieth century, and made their way into various museums.[5] None of these stelae, however, were found during regular excavations, and no doubt some of them have been given an Akhmim provenance in order to make them more interesting for the antiquities market.[6]

In spite of the relatively large numbers that have survived, many Christian stelae from the Akhmim region, as from the rest of Egypt, must have been lost. Thus, the lack of decorated stelae in various styles is conspicuous, even though there are a few stelae with an *anch*-shaped cross depicted in the center of the stone.[7] Their assignment to Akhmim is often uncertain, however.[8] Like other regions and cities that were centers of Greek culture with inhabitants of both ethnic backgrounds (Greek and Egyptian), workshops in Panopolis must have produced elaborate decorated stelae with Hellenistic and, later on, Byzantine characteristics. Variations in usage can be observed even within the same sites. In all probability, the decorated stelae from the Panopolite region were destroyed owing to natural circumstances or reused in constructions outside the cemeteries.

Stelae with inscriptions only were sometimes set in a niche in the wall of a tomb. Since very few Coptic cemeteries have been found intact, it is difficult to determine whether stelae like those from Akhmim were placed in a niche or erected on top of a grave. The type that is commonly called typical for Akhmim is a roughly triangular stela with an inscription, a model that seems restricted to this particular region. All stelae in this class are from limestone, mostly roughly cut; their sizes may vary, but only a few measure more than 30 x 60 cm. Their shape suggests that they were erected on top of a tomb, as their relative great thickness gives them considerable stability. A second group in the more common rectangular shape but with a typical inscription possibly shares the same local background. Both groups show an individuality in the textual formulae that deserves further discussion.

Inscribed funerary monuments from medieval Christian Egypt followed the tradition of calling upon the visitor to commemorate the deceased, and recitation was thought to create a relationship between the deceased and the living person. The typical stelae from Akhmim bear a Greek inscription that consists of the introductory formula "stela of the deceased N.N.," followed by the verb "he (or she) lived" and the age of the deceased. Although variations are possible, the date of death is usually given in the form: month name, day of the month (in numbers) and number of the indiction-year, a way of dating that does not allow the assignment of absolute dates.[9] In a few cases short prayers or acclamations follow, such as "do not be sorrowful, no one is immortal." The use of the word "to die" is avoided here as in other areas of Egypt, where it may be replaced with expressions like "to lay down the body" or "to go to rest." In Panopolis, the word "stela" takes the place of these phrases, which is unique for Egypt. A lot of these stelae are damaged, but the formulaic pattern of the inscriptions allows suggestions for the restoration of the missing parts. Within this stereotypical group, some variation can nevertheless be observed. Thus, a few inscriptions start with formulae like "God is one, who helps" or "Oh God, have mercy on the soul" that are also known from stelae in the Hermonthis area.[10] Small crosses or an alpha and omega are the only decorative elements that are sometimes added to the text.

The second, much smaller group of stelae, has the more common rectangular shape and also bears a different text (in Greek or in Coptic). Like many inscriptions from Hermonthis, they state that the deceased "ended his life" or "went to his/her rest."[11]

The only provenance given for all these stelae is Akhmim. No more precise indications are ever given. It would be interesting to investigate whether all these pieces may have come from one place or from different cemeteries, and whether they have been picked up in small compounds, belonging to one or more communities of either laymen or clergy. For questions of prosopography, demography, and causes of death, an extensive research into the Akhmim stelae, covering names and occupations,[12] as well as age, gender, and the month of death, would undoubtedly yield more and more precise results.[13] Also, dating the stelae from Akhmim (like similar stelae from other regions in Egypt) remains a problem, not only on account of the absence of absolute data but also owing to the lack of information about find circumstances. On various grounds, they may be dated to the sixth or early seventh century, however.[14]

"Rive gauche": The White Monastery
Shenoute and His Patrons

Very few inscriptions in the White Monastery can be linked to its most famous abbot and the builder of its monumental basilica, St. Shenoute. The commemorative text inscribed on the inner face of the granite lintel above the main southern entrance to the church is a major exception.[15] Its six lines of Greek are dedicated to "the eternal memory" of "the founder" of the building, a high-ranking official, the Count (*komes*) Caesarius (Kaisarios), the son of Candidianus (Kandidianos). The inscription is an invaluable document for several reasons. It is, first of all, an independent, non-literary witness to the importance of Shenoute's social network, confirming that he counted his patrons among the political and economic elite of his time. The text formally identifies one of these patrons, the Count Caesarius, who is known also from the writings of Shenoute, as the principal sponsor of the church. Furthermore, the language of the text, Greek, underlines the sociolinguistically significant observation that Coptic came only to be used for public inscriptions well over a century after the death of Shenoute.[16] Finally, although the inscription is not dated, the activity of Caesarius in this part of Egypt can with a high degree of probability be situated in the very middle of the fifth century.[17] This, in turn, yields a reliable date for the building of the monastery's great church.

Further inscriptions that might shed light on the chronology of Shenoute date from a far later period. They belong to a considerable group of Coptic dipinti in and around the northern conch of the church sanctuary, which have now for the greater part disappeared.[18] Two of these (Crum A.1 and A.2) contain a concise *curriculum vitae* of Shenoute himself, which provides precise, though not necessarily accurate dates for his life and times. They may date from as late as the late thirteenth or early fourteenth century.[19] Modern scholars tend to be wary of using this information, and they are obviously right, also because of the uncertainties and the lacunae in the published texts. Nevertheless, it may be observed that, while being all but contemporary, they are at least based on intentional computing, whereas contemporary sources rather tend to produce accidental information. Nor can it be excluded that the medieval chronologist had information at his disposal that is not available to the modern biographer. Thus, according to Crum's dipinto A.2, Shenoute was born in A.D. 348 or 349,[20] while, according to A.1, the great church of the monastery was consecrated in the 106th year of his life.[21] Combining these data yields the year 454 or 455 for the latter event, which is certainly not far off the mark. This calculation could be based upon a now lost hagiographic or epigraphic source, perhaps even a foundation inscription that, unlike the lintel of Count Caesarius, did not survive to the present.

Also near the sanctuary of the church another late antique dedicatory inscription is found, one much less known than the Caesarius lintel.[22] Regrettably, its relationship with the construction works undertaken by Shenoute remains doubtful. This brief text, again in Greek, is situated several meters above the floor, on the shaft of the northernmost of two marble columns that originally marked the entrance to the triconch of the sanctuary, but are now partly walled in. Although noticed as early as the late seventeenth century, the inscription has never been properly published and the few authors that mentioned it failed to interpret it correctly.[23] It consists of three lines of beautifully engraved majuscules surmounted by a large Latin cross, also carefully executed in raised relief.[24] The text reads (in translation):

"In fulfillment of a vow by Heliodoros and Kallirhoe and their children." The inscription, therefore, commemorates a Christian family who erected this column with its sculptured cross as an ex-voto.

At first sight, it might seem indisputable that Heliodoros too, like Caesarius, numbered among the wealthy patrons who had assisted Shenoute in financing and erecting the great monastery church. Some objections can be raised, however. First, according to Peter Grossmann, the present columns at the entrance to the sanctuary were erected there in a relatively late stage, in replacement of earlier, larger columns.[25] Then, palaeographically, the text is rather different from the Caesarius lintel, which is certainly contemporary with Shenoute. Finally, and most compellingly, in February 1909 a similar marble column with an exactly identical inscription and decoration was discovered, not in the White Monastery, but built into a house to the southeast of the town of Akhmim.[26] If both columns once belonged to one and the same building, as seems plausible, the find of the second column is not in favor of identifying this building with the White Monastery church. Although various scenarios can be envisaged, it seems more likely that the columns were originally part of another Christian or christianized building, perhaps situated in or near the town of Panopolis, which was demolished or destroyed at an unknown date and plundered for various other building or restoration works. Thus Heliodoros and his family may have contributed only indirectly and unwittingly to the construction of Shenoute's church.

Medieval Patrons, Artists, and Scholars

Before the early-twentieth-century restoration that stripped the walls of the church almost entirely of their plaster coating, these must have been covered with numerous inscriptions, both painted and engraved.[27] The very few that survive or have been recorded in the past tell not only about leaders and patrons of the monastery in medieval times, long after Shenoute's death, but also about the use and development of the monastery church as sacred space. Obviously, several of these inscriptions belong to the class of dedicatory inscriptions, connected with building, restoration, or decoration works. The most sensational among them are undoubtedly the bilingual, Armenian and Coptic, set of texts that accompany the monumental painting of Christ enthroned, still visible in the central apse of the church. They comprise both legends and prayers for the artist, the Armenian painter Theodore, and the various Armenian and Coptic sponsors of the project that was apparently completed in A.D. 1123–24.[28] The whole setup is reminiscent of similar "multicultural" decoration projects in Dayr al-Surian, in Wadi al-Natrun. Even if the White Monastery has never really become a "Monastery of the Armenians," the scale and the central position of the apse painting clearly indicate the importance of Armenian patronage in the early twelfth century.

Another set of inscriptions in the northeast area of the church concerns reconstruction and decoration works that took place about a century later. Two of these texts mention a major rebuilding that was completed in the year 1259 under the Archimandrite Ioannes.[29] The former is a long dipinto that can still be seen today on the front of the brick pier to the north of the central apse; the latter, much briefer, was situated between two niches in the northern conch. They record the erection of "four columns" in order to reconstruct the roofing of two "tabernacles" and their adjacencies, which had become "uncovered" as the result of an earthquake. In view of the position of one of the texts (A.6) and the use of a Coptic term for "canopy" in both, it may be supposed that they commemorate the reshaping of the original, late-antique triconch into its present form, with a central dome carried by four brick piers.[30]

Other texts in the same general area commemorate the donation and execution of a decoration program in this part of the church, but the nature of the works is not always entirely clear. Only in one case, a priest and monk, Phibamon, who is also styled a scribe and architect, is clearly credited for sponsoring the painting of an archangel, probably St. Michael, still vaguely visible above the door to the northern pastophorion.[31] In addition to their obvious interest for the architectural history of the church, these dedicatory inscriptions provide lots of accidental information. Thus Crum's text A.6 gives in passing a brief biography of the Archimandrite Ioannes (l. 17–23) as well as a hint of the (very negative) popular opinion about the rule of "the Turks," the first Mamluks (l. 16–17).

A final group of dipinti from the same northeast part of the church, the famous library inscriptions, must date from the same general period as the ones quoted above (twelfth–fourteenth century).[32] They have recently been discussed and partly republished by Tito Orlandi,[33] and need only be mentioned briefly here. Written on the walls of the north pastophorion,[34] they list titles of books with their quantities, and in addition contain a number of apotropaic charms written in Arabic in Coptic characters as well as prayers for the scholarly priest who wrote the inscriptions, a certain Klaute (Claudius). It would seem that they combine a shelving system with an inventory of the library that was kept in the room.

In spite of their obvious interest, some cautionary remarks about the documentary value of these inscriptions are due here, some of which have been made already by earlier authors. First, we have very little idea of the disposition of the texts on the walls, which hampers any reconstruction of the library—if that it was—as a physical and functional unit. Secondly, whereas the room in question may have stored a library, as is not unusual for a sacristy,[35] it cannot automatically be equated with *the* library of the monastery. The place where the inscriptions were situated, the north pastophorion, would suggest that the books stored there were primarily those used for liturgical reading. However, even if this room really did contain a more comprehensive library, the inscriptions can only give an indication of what it may have looked like at an unknown, but certainly quite late stage. A library, even a monastic library, is not a static unity, but subject to constant renewal. This is all the more so when it passes through periods of language shift, as occurred in the White Monastery, which saw two major language shifts in the course of its history: first from Greek to Coptic, and then from Coptic to Arabic. The library inscriptions reflect the final stages of the last of these shifts. Even if they cannot, therefore, provide a reliable guide to *the* White Monastery library, they do remain an important witness to medieval Coptic literary culture, and as such they deserve further study.

Outside of the sanctuary area, medieval painted inscriptions can be found even today at various places where the original plaster still holds—thus, in particular, on the medieval masonry piers, erected within the so-called 'southern narthex,' which was perhaps originally a chapter-house.[36] As far as they can be deciphered, they seem to be mostly commemorative in character, combining names and brief prayers. Some are published, like the Coptic prayers for workmen copied in the early years of the twentieth century,[37] others appear to have been never recorded. On the south wall of the same room, a more remarkable text, the Great Doxology in Greek, survived against all odds.[38] In some way, this long and formal liturgical text, enclosed in a *tabula ansata*, must have been connected with the function that this part of the "southern narthex" had in medieval times.

Adding Pieces to a Puzzle

The walls of the basilica are not the only source for the epigraphy of the White Monastery. The extensive ruins that surround it also yielded many inscriptions, which often still await publication. Some of these afford vivid glimpses of past monastic life. Perhaps the most stunning of them is a unique stone lintel that was found in the 1990s by an Egyptian mission, and is as yet unpublished.[39] It gives a graphical representation of what the White Monastery 'federation' must have looked like hierarchically a few centuries after Shenoute's death. In polychrome relief, it depicts eight standing monastic dignitaries, represented *en face*, four to the left and four to the right of a central motif, presumably a cross, now missing. The Coptic inscription that frames the relief panels mentions their names and titles, starting from the left with "the great archimandrite," perhaps called Apa Paniskos. As the fourth in the series, a woman appears, undoubtedly the head of the nunnery. The last person portrayed is an architect and deacon, Apa Stephanos. According to the inscription, he was the founder of the monastic building for which the lintel was intended. The monument's lower architrave bears a prayer for the sculptor.

The top of the hierarchy of the White Monastery is again immortalized on a far later and very different monument. The largest of the impressive ceremonial keys from Sohag that are now in the Coptic Museum in Cairo is inscribed in copper and silver inlay.[40] The inscriptions commemorate the monastic dignitaries who ordered it, among whom was an Archimandrite Iohannes. It has recently been suggested that he might be the same person as the like-named archimandrite who directed the rebuilding of the church sanctuary in the middle of the thirteenth century, according to the mural inscriptions quoted above.[41] The fabrication of such a monumental key would indeed well fit the wave of architectural renewal attested by these inscriptions.

In addition to other textual remains, the Egyptian mission mentioned earlier also appears to have discovered funerary inscriptions, otherwise hardly known for the White Monastery.[42] This would open an as yet unexplored field of research. Until now, the funerary epigraphy from the White Monastery area seemed to be virtually limited to a single Coptic stela, now apparently lost, which belonged to a monk, Pamin, and was published more than a century ago by W. de Bock.[43] The publication of the recent finds could pave the way for a study of local funerary habits and formulae as is possible for other centers in Upper Egypt.

This brief review may give an indication of the interest and broad variety of the epigraphic material from the White Monastery. It also shows how much work remains to be done. Even within the relatively well-explored area of the great church, many inscriptions wait to be published or even identified. Others are available only in old or substandard publications. Already quite a lot have vanished completely or are doomed to vanish soon.

About recent finds made in the vicinity, almost all information is lacking. It must therefore be urgently recommended that, whatever conservation or research projects are considered for the White Monastery or the surrounding area, they should on principle include a systematic and comprehensive survey of the epigraphic material, either lost or surviving. In reconstructing the long but poorly known history of this important center of learning and piety, the evidence of the inscriptions cannot be dispensed with.

Notes

1. Criscuolo 2002: 56.
2. Kuhlmann 1983: 6–9, with pl. 5–15; two previously unknown texts discovered by Kuhlmann were published by Guy Wagner (1982; cf. Łajtar 1993).
3. For further information about funerary stelae, Greek and Coptic, from Christian Egypt and their classification, see Crum 1902 (catalogue of Christian stelae in Greek and Coptic in the Egyptian Museum; most of these are in the Coptic Museum today), Lefebvre 1907 (catalogue of Christian inscriptions in Greek from collections in Egypt and abroad), Zuntz 1932 (an attempt to locate stelae in different areas and places), Krause 1991a (general introduction to Christian epigraphy in Egypt), Wietheger 1992 (analysis of the inscriptions from the Monastery of St. Jeremiah at Saqqara), *SB Kopt* I–III (Coptic "Sammelbuch" including many funerary inscriptions), Thomas 2000 (about decorated stelae). Stelae from Akhmim were first collected in Lefebvre 1907 and 1911; for recent reviews of this material, see Timm 1984–1992, vol. 1: 90, n. 44–46, and Criscuolo 2002, to which may be added: Łajtar and Twardecki 2003: nos. 94–95 (Adam Łajtar), and Gascou 2004.
4. For the archaeological remains in the area, see Kuhlmann 1983, McNally and Dvoržak Schrunk 1993.
5. Most of them are now in the Greco-Roman Museum in Alexandria, a few others in the Coptic Museum, Cairo, and in various collections in Europe and the United States. As yet no special publication has been devoted to them; most of the stelae in Alexandria are known only from Lefebvre 1907, where no pictures are given.
6. Thus, in Lefebvre 1907 and 1911, over fifty pieces are labeled "Akhmim?."
7. Cramer 1955: 20–26, fig. 19–21; Cramer 1957: no. 22.
8. E.g., in the case of the stelae Crum 1902: nos. 8575 (= Coptic Museum inv. no. 8656) and 8603.
9. For the indiction, a fifteen-year cycle introduced for fiscal purposes in the early fourth century, see now Bagnall and Worp 2004.
10. E.g., Lefebvre 1907: nos. 263, 294, 345.

11. Lefebvre 1907: no. 673, cf. Pellegrini 1907: no. 3; Lefebvre 1911: 238–45.

12. Cf. Timm 1984–1992, vol. 1: 90, n. 46.

13. Thus, Scheidel 2001 records seasonal mortality in Egypt from ancient to modern times; his "Appendix one" lists months of death after epitaphs from ancient and medieval Egypt and Nubia, including stelae from Akhmim quoted after Lefebvre 1907.

14. See Krause 1991a: 1293–94.

15. *SB* III, no. 6311; *ed. princeps* with facsimile: Lefebvre 1920a: 470–75; see also Lefebvre 1920b; Monneret de Villard 1923; Monneret de Villard 1925–26, vol. 1: 18–22; Emmel 1998: 94. The information in Timm 1984–1992, vol. 2: 608, n. 44–45, is misleading: the lintel is no tombstone and the text is entirely unambiguous.

16. Cf. Bingen 1999: 613–14.

17. As can be inferred from works by Shenoute that mention him; see Emmel 1998: 94, taking up earlier discussions by Monneret de Villard (1923; 1925–1926, vol. 1: 18–22). A Coptic fragment edited by Johnson (1976: 10, 1 *verso*, col. a, l. 29) associates Caesarius with the death of Nestorius, which would date his activity again around 445–55, but the text smells of hagiographical embroidery. No other independent sources for Caesarius appear to exist (cf. Martindale 1980: 249–50). Lefebvre (1920a: 475) dates the inscription palaeographically to the first half of the fifth century.

18. Published by W.E. Crum (1904c) after copies by the English clergyman W.J. (not W.T.) Oldfield (1857–1934; *Who Was Who 1929–1940*: 1021).

19. If the commemoration of the artist Merkouri in A.1, l. 23–25 (cf. Crum 1904c, vol. 1: 555; Monneret de Villard 1925–1926, vol. 1: 28; Coquin 1975: 277–78) indeed belongs to the same text.

20. Crum 1904c: 555–56.

21. Crum 1904c: 554, l. 13–16.

22. Van der Vliet, forthcoming, offers a fuller discussion of this inscription than is possible here.

23. Vansleb (J.M. Wansleben; 1677: 374) erroneously describes it as an epitaph. Coquin and Martin (1991: 765) think it belonged to a pagan temple, which may be correct for the column, but not for the inscription. They are followed by Criscuolo 2002: 60–61, who tentatively links it to a far older and entirely unrelated monument of a Triphis priest (*SEG* 43, no. 1124). According to Monneret de Villard (1925–1926, vol. 1: 25, n. 6) it had disappeared; other descriptions of the church do not appear to mention it.

24. It is technically impossible that the cross is a Christian addition, post-dating the inscription. The two belong together, as in the column's exact counterpart quoted below.

25. Grossmann 2002b: 127; cf. 2002a: 533–34 (where he dates the capitals on top of the present columns to the sixth century).

26. Lefebvre 1910: 62–63, no. 815 (*SB* I, no. 1597). This column was transported to Cairo in 1909, but I have been unable to trace it.

27. Cf. Crum 1904c: 552.

28. See Kapoïan-Kouymjian 1988: 16–17 (includes photos and extensive bibliography); also Crum 1904a: 556–57.

29. Crum 1904c: A.6 and A.7.

30. Cf. C.R. Peers *apud* Crum 1904c: 569; Monneret de Villard 1925–1926, vol. 1: 28–31; Grossmann 2002a: 535–36.

31. Crum 1904c: A.10; Monneret de Villard 1925–1926, vol. 1: 30, tends to make this Phibamon the architect responsible for the restoration works described by the other inscriptions, but this is far from certain.

32. The texts are now completely lost; the copies by W.J. Oldfield as published by Crum 1904a: 564–69, nos. B.12–31, are our only source.

33. Orlandi 2002: 213–15; cf. Khosroyev 2003; Takla 2005.

34. See Crum 1904c: 552–53; *pace* Orlandi 2002: 211–12.

35. Cf. Crum 1904c: 553, n. 4.

36. See Grossmann 2000a: 531–32.

37. Lefebvre 1920a: 485–86, 488, fig. 3660.

38. Lefebvre 1907: no. 237; 1920a: 485, fig. 3658; cf. Leclercq 1921: 2511–12; 1925: 2891–93; Quecke 1970: 276; Van Haelst 1976: no. 773; Tidda 2001: 118–19.

39. I owe my knowledge of this piece to a set of photographs made by the excavators. It presently consists of two blocks of about 36 x 46 cm. each; it can be dated to about the seventh–ninth century with the greatest caution only.

40. Inv. no. 5915; see Bénazeth and Boud'hors 2003 (*editio princeps* of the texts and extensive discussion).

41. Bénazeth and Boud'hors 2003: 31 and 36.

42. Known to me only in inexpert transcriptions.

43. De Bock 1901: 69, no. 81 ("une stèle calcaire trouvée près des ruines de la ville d'Athribis").

14 Searching for Shenoute
A Copto-Arabic Homilary in Paris, BN arabe 4796

Mark N. Swanson

Introduction and Review

Will students of the Arabic literature of the Copts be able to contribute
to the current intensive study of the literary corpus of St. Shenoute the
Archimandrite? The idea that they might is by no means farfetched. After
all, Arabic recensions of Coptic texts have frequently proved invaluable to
Coptologists, sometimes providing a template for the identification and
reconstruction of fragmentary Coptic originals.[1] Might not Arabic texts
provide the same service for works of Shenoute?

Unfortunately, the results up to now are, in Stephen Emmel's word,
"disappointing."[2] We do, of course, possess the Arabic translation of the *Life*
of Shenoute attributed to his disciple Besa,[3] as well as that of *Good is the Time
for Launching a Boat to Sail*.[4] An edition of the Arabic version of the pseudo-
Shenoutian *Sermon on Christian Behavior* has been announced,[5] and there are
at least three Arabic apocalyptic texts (fictitiously) attributed to the saint.[6]

There was not much more than that to report when, in January 2004,
Mr. Hany Takla invited me to give some attention to two collections
of homilies found in manuscripts of the Bibliothèque nationale (BN) in
Paris.[7] The first of these collections is a seventeenth-century manuscript
of seventy-one folios catalogued as BN ar. 4761.[8] Since I have reported
on this collection elsewhere,[9] I will limit myself to a very brief description here. The manuscript consists in a set of nine homilies attributed to

St. Shenoute, for the seven Sundays of Lent. Significantly, a statement of
waqf on its final folio shows that it was once a part of the White Monastery
library. The homilies are consistent in theme: they commend the disci-
plines of fasting, prayer and almsgiving, as well as the good works of love,
forgiveness, and long-suffering. With great urgency they stress the necessity of attending to one's eternal salvation through repentance now in this
life, before death makes repentance impossible; of prayer for forgiveness;
and of the good works that alone will avail a person before God on the
Day of Judgment.

While these ideas are not necessarily foreign to St. Shenoute, it quickly
becomes apparent that the collection of BN ar. 4761 is *not* a translation from
Coptic, but rather an Arabic composition that reflects an Islamic environment and that fits in well with other late medieval Copto-Arabic literature.
The preacher uses Qur'anic terminology freely, and indulges in several
bursts of *saj'* or rhymed Arabic prose. Soteriological passages reflect ideas
common in Copto-Arabic catechetical texts of the eleventh and twelfth
centuries. Illustrative material comes from a variety of traditions, many of
them shared by medieval Christians and Muslims: stories of Alexander the
Great;[10] the sayings of Luqman the Wise;[11] and the story of Barlaam and
Yuwasaf (known in the West as Iosaphat).

This collection is interesting in itself, providing a fine display of late-
medieval Copto-Arabic resources for preaching. More than that, it provides
tantalizing clues as to how St. Shenoute was remembered and portrayed in
his own monastery, where the manuscript was once housed and read. The
Shenoute of BN ar. 4761, like the original, preaches the necessity of repentance in this life, before it is too late. What is intriguing (and perhaps a little
ironic) is the way that the Shenoute of BN ar. 4761 becomes a profoundly
enculturated preacher, ready to commend to his congregation the figures of
Alexander (the Macedonian pagan conqueror!), Yuwasaf (who began his literary career as the Buddha!), or Luqman (the sage of Qur'anic renown!).[12]

Paris, BN ar. 4796: Homilies for Sundays at the Evening Raising of Incense

Let us move on to the other collection, a set of twenty-six homilies for the
evening raising of incense for Sundays in the first half of the church year,
preserved as the first work in the manuscript Paris, BN ar. 4796. (A brief
table of contents, with the Gospel passages on which each homily is based,
is given in the Appendix.) The manuscript is a copy that Amélineau had

made of a manuscript that contained a statement of *waqf* to the benefit of the Monastery of St. Antony in Luxor. The manuscript's first few leaves are missing, but Troupeau attributed the collection to St. Shenoute on the basis of the colophon at fol. 82r: "the *maymar* of the great saint, Anba Shinudah the Archimandrite, is complete."[13]

The homilies are quite brief, and space allows that I give here a translation of one of them, appointed for the eve of the third Sunday in Hatur.

A Sample Homily (English Translation)
Paris, BN ar. 4796, fols. 30v–32r

The eleventh homily, appointed for His saying, "Come, you who are weary, and I will give you rest. Take my yoke upon you and learn from me, for I am gentle, humble and calm of heart." [Matthew 11:28–29] It includes a well-grounded argument that the yoke of our Lord is lighter than concern for worldly things. It is read on the night of the third Sunday of the month of Hatur.

It is necessary for us that we hasten to put down the weight of our concern for worldly matters, and that we are always found gentle, humble and glad, bearing the yoke of our Lord, so that he might give us the bliss of the Kingdom.

Now if someone says: "You there, how is it that his yoke is light, since he stipulates for his followers that they deny themselves, renounce their passions, abandon their fathers, mothers, children, brothers and sisters, and [all] worldly pleasures—since otherwise they are not worthy of being his followers?"—Then I say:

We must understand that whether the load carried by human souls is light or heavy depends solely on the reward that is their end. For example, let us suppose that two men, laborers in the employ of a certain king, worked exceedingly hard for one day. When they had completed their work, the king commanded that one of the men be granted a rest for one day, to be spent in happiness and [delight[14]], after which he would return to that work. As for the other [laborer], he too was granted a rest—but permanently, forever! Would not his labor be called exceedingly 'light,' by comparison with the duration of his rest? He could well say: "I labored for one day, and I have received eternal happiness!" As for the first man, he could well call his labor 'heavy,' by virtue of his speedy return to burdensome toil.

Thus it is necessary for us to understand that bearing the yoke of our Lord, while it entails toil for a time, will gain everlasting life; and the hope of that life will by no means be 'heavy' but rather 'light' in the view of those who have knowledge.[15]

And I say: Why do we not compare bearing the yoke of our Lord with the burdens of the world and the distress that they cause us? Which is lighter to bear?

Let us imagine two men: one an ascetic monk, and the other a rich man in [what we call] easy circumstances. Is it not true that the monk has only to be concerned with a single soul in matters of food, drink, clothing, shelter and so on—and that all of these requirements are very light and easily available, however they are obtained? As for the rich man in 'easy' circumstances, in his quest for pleasures he requires aides, retinue, maidservants, slaves, various people carrying out tasks, and so on: some preparing food, and others drink; some cleaning his houses, others making the beds, and others specialized in bodily pleasures. His costs and expenditures increase. He resorts to stratagems to gather up from every direction enough [money to finance his household]. Then perhaps he is plunged into [bad] times when making money is impossible. His costs double. He is pelted with the arrows of illness, symptoms of disease, the loss of beloved things, the increased difficulty of the demands on him . . . and he will see that his condition is the harshest of all conditions and the most exceedingly difficult for the soul. He will reckon it the 'heaviest' of all burdens. So! Has it not now become clear that it is the condition of the first man [that is, the monk] which is 'light' and 'easy'?

That condition is the one to which our Lord has called us (to him be glory!), saying: "Come to me, you who are weary, and I will give you rest, you who bear heavy burdens." His meaning in saying this is that you are only laboring like this in order to obtain rest for your souls. This present world of yours is not the world of [true] pleasures and rest; indeed, you seek [true pleasures and rest] from a thing [that is, this world] that does not possess them—and you end up losing *both*. But if you bear with difficulties for a little while, in obedience to your Lord, and labor for a short time, then you shall obtain all the pleasures prepared for you, divested of any kind of toil or any sort of defect.

Our path, then, is to put down from our necks the weight of care about transitory matters, and to hasten to bear the yoke of our Lord with joy and happiness, so that we might obtain the life prepared for us in the Kingdom of Heaven.

And to our Lord be glory forever, Amen.

Characteristics of the Homilies

The foregoing homily is, in a number of ways, typical of the entire collection. Each homily has an introduction (printed in italics in the example above) that announces the appointed Gospel passage and a particular topic that the homily will address. The question and answer form—"If someone says . . . ," "Then I respond . . . "—is common throughout the collection. Simple images from life—in the example above, the king and the laborers, or the monk and the rich man—are likewise common. Nearly all the homilies end with a summary sentence introduced by *fa-sabiluna*: "Our path, then, is . . ." (as follows). And the message of the above homily, that one must put worldly things aside and turn to the things that lead to the bliss of the kingdom, is the constant theme of the entire collection.

The homilies frequently begin with *rebuke*. The preacher regularly compares his hearers with characters in the Gospel texts appointed for the evening, for example: the disciples, who by faith performed miracles;[16] the women who followed and served Jesus;[17] the sick who went to extraordinary lengths to seek out healing;[18] or even the demons who acknowledged and obeyed Christ.[19] The preacher's constant question is: If *they* did these things, what about *you*?

The preacher can also turn to situations in human life as grounds for his rebukes. People are on their very best behavior when in the court of an earthly king; so *what about you*, who talk business in church?[20] People make haste to seek out a physician when ill in body, and carefully follow his instructions, no matter how unpleasant; so *what about you*, who are in dire need of physicians of souls?[21]

The preacher can be quite specific and colorful as he rebukes his hearers' attachment to worldly things. To the women (in Homily 13) he says: "What benefit is it to you that you wear sumptuous robes, hang precious jewels around your neck, and put bracelets on your hands and earrings in your ears?"[22] He comments that taking pleasure in such worldly things is like a prisoner taking pleasure in his prison![23] In another homily (Homily 17), the preacher addresses the men:

> I see you, you there, going out from us and frequenting the beauty shops: you go and sit there, take a mirror in your hand, and look—sometimes at your face, and sometimes at the hair of your beard, and sometimes at the hair of your head. And then [the barbers] trim and adorn; they describe the current fashions and ask those who are seated around you to tell you how fine

their handiwork is. Perhaps you are an old man—but you are not ashamed to
be ornamented like a youth!

> How strange it is that you expend such concern on the well-being of
> your transitory body, and neglect the matter of your eternal soul![24]

The preacher is especially harsh in his condemnation of drunkenness,
which causes people "to fall from the rank of human beings so that they
resemble irrational animals."[25]

> If you say, "How does a human being who speaks of good things resemble an
> irrational animal?" —I respond:
>
> Even if they differ in appearance, they resemble them in their actions.
> This is because drunkenness and gluttony make people [wallow] in the
> unclean things of the earth like swine; others dig up corpses like dogs; others
> growl in rage like lions; others neigh after women and boys like horses; oth-
> ers snatch at things like wolves; others are deceptive like foxes; others engage
> in horseplay, strip themselves and tear their clothes, bash in their heads, and
> throw themselves into wells and other dangerous places like madmen. Truly
> I am ashamed to mention one by one all of the kinds of depravity that issue
> from drunkenness![26]

Whatever the specific rebuke, the preacher soon turns to exhortation:
Turn away from passing, worldly concerns! Awake from your slumber! And
turn to prayer and good works, to almsgiving and deeds of mercy, to the
study of Scripture and other spiritual books—that is, the things that lead to
the bliss of the Kingdom of the Lord, God and savior Jesus Christ.

Is There a Connection to St. Shenoute?

Does this collection of homilies have anything to do with St. Shenoute?

As one reads the last of the homilies (Homily 26), one encounters a sudden break between fol. 78 and fol. 79: one passes in mid-sentence from an
analogy involving sailors using all their expertise at sea to the words, "O
friend of God, behold, the gates are opened so that you may enter!" In
fact, the collection of homilies breaks off at this point. The next four folios
turn out to be the end of an entirely different text—in fact, the very end
of the Arabic *Life* of Shenoute. *That* is the "*maymar* of the great saint Anba
Shinudah the Archimandrite" mentioned in the colophon on fol. 82.[27] The
collection of homilies, in its present state, lacking both beginning and end,

is simply *anonymous*. It contains no attribution to St. Shenoute; nor is there any reason for us to propose this attribution.

This is undoubtedly another disappointing result for those who are looking for material of direct relevance to the study of the Shenoutian corpus. Even the four-folio fragment of the Arabic *Life* of Shenoute is less than exciting; it offers a text very close to the fragment published by Galtier over a century ago,[28] and thus offers very limited help to a future editor of the Arabic *Life*.

Still, the collection of homilies is itself not without interest. Since each homily is based—rather loosely!—on a particular text from the Gospels, the collection provides a witness to the lectionary used by the community. A preliminary summary of results may be seen in the Appendix. We note that the lectionary assumed by the homilary of Paris, BN ar. 4796 appears to be very close to the *katameros* of Lower Egypt used in the Coptic Orthodox Church today and over the past several centuries,[29] although there are a few deviations that may be of interest to liturgical scholars. Quite apart from any technical liturgical information that may be squeezed out of the collection, these homilies give us a window into the life and piety of the Coptic Orthodox community, where preachers used texts from the Gospels and a variety of examples taken from everyday life in order to cajole and scold members of their flock who, like most of us, enjoyed the distractions of this passing world.

Appendix

Paris, BN ar. 4796, fos. 1–78

Homilies for Sundays at the evening raising of incense

Homily	Sunday	Folios in PA 4796	Gospel quotations or allusions in the titles and incipits★	Gospel readings according to the present katameros★★	Comments (x marks a match)
1	Tut 1	(missing)	(missing)	Matthew 11:11–19	
2	Tut 2	1r–3r	(beginning missing)	Luke 4:38–41	
3	Tut 3	3r–7r	Mark 1:32–34 or parallels	Mark 1:29–34	x
4	Tut 4	7r–11r	Matthew 9:23–26 or parallels	Matthew 9:18–26	x
5	Babah 1	11v–16r	John 6:26	Matthew 14:15–21	feeding of the 5,000
6	Babah 2	16r–18v	Matthew 17:24–27	Matthew 17:24–27	x
7	Babah 3	18v–21r	Mark 5:1–20 or parallels	Mark 4:35–41	adjacent passages
8	Babah 4	21r–23v	Matthew 14:23 or parallels	Matthew 14:22–36	x
9	Hatur 1	24r–27v	Mark 4:12 or parallels	Mark 4:10–20	x
10	Hatur 2	27v–30v	Matthew 6:28	Matthew 6:28b–33	x

11	Hatur 3	30v–32v	Matthew 11:28–29	Matthew 11:25–30	x
12	Hatur 4	32v–37v	Matthew 17:17 or parallels	Matthew 17:14–21	x
13	Kihak 1	37v–42r	Matthew 28:9? or Luke 7:38 / John 12:3?	Mark 14:3–9	parallel passages
14	Kihak 2	42v–46v	Luke 7:36–50	Luke 7:36–50	x
15	Kihak 3	46v	= Babah 3 (Mark 5:1–20 or parallels)	Mark 1:23–31	different exorcism
16	Kihak 4	46v–49r	Luke 8:1–3	Luke 8:1–3	x
17	Tubah 1	49r–51r	Luke 4:38–39 or parallels	Luke 4:40–44	adjacent passages
18	Tubah 2	51v–54v	Matthew 14:28–29	Matthew 14:22–36	x
19	Tubah 3	54v–58v	John 5:2–9	John 5:1–18	x
20	Tubah 4	58v–62v	John 5:31, 39, 46	John 5:31–46	x
20a	Amshir 1	63r	(not given)	John 6:15–21	
21	Amshir 2	63r–64v	John 4:46–53	John 4:46b–53	x
22	Lent 1	64v–67v	Matthew 6:34	Matthew 6:34, 7:1–12	x

23	Lent 2	68r–70v	Mark 1:12–13, Matt. 4:1–11 or Luke 4:1–13	Mark 1:12–15	Paris ms. fits Mt./Lk. best
24	Lent 3	71r–73r	Matthew 15:2	Matthew 15:1–20	x
25	Lent 4	73r–75r	Matthew 6:25–34	Luke 12:22–31	parallel passages
26	Lent 5	75v–78v	Luke 18:1–8 (end missing)	Luke 18:1–8	x

★   Sometimes the homilies do not permit a choice between parallel passages in the synoptic Gospels (Matthew, Mark, and Luke). Then the text listed is the one that provides the best comparison with the next column, followed by the words "or parallels."

★★ According to Anonymous 1983.

Notes

1. Good recent examples of this include van Esbroeck 1998 and Boud'hors and Boutros 2001.
2. Emmel 2004b, vol. 1: 67.
3. Amélineau 1888–1895, fasc. 1: xlviii–xciii and 289-478; Galtier 1905.
4. Leipoldt 1906–1913, vol. 4: 173–97.
5. Lucchesi 2000: 422.
6. Amélineau, 1888–1895, fasc. 1: lii–lviii and 338–46; Grohmann 1914; van Lent 1999.
7. I am grateful to Mr. Hany Takla both for his invitation to undertake this investigation and for providing me with copies of the manuscripts in question.
8. Some attention had already been given to this collection. See the provisional English translations of some of the homilies in Hanna and Takla 1994–1997, and an edition and French translation of one of the homilies in Ghica 2001.
9. See Swanson 2005, with details supporting the paragraphs that follow.
10. See Ghica 2001 for the homily centered on a story about Alexander.
11. On the use of Luqman in these homilies, see Swanson 2006.
12. Swanson 2005: 37–42.
13. Troupeau 1972–1974, vol. 2: 47.

14. Reading *ibtihaj* for *niyah*.

15. The function of the four words that follow in the manuscript is not very clear to me ("Then–they gave—returning—to you"), and they have been omitted from the translation.

16. Paris, BN ar. 4796, fol. 51v (Homily 18).

17. Paris, BN ar. 4796, fols. 46v–47r (Homily 16).

18. Paris, BN ar. 4796, fols. 54v–55r (Homily 3).

19. Paris, BN ar. 4796, fol. 3rv (Homily 13).

20. Paris, BN ar. 4796, fols. 21v–22r (Homily 8).

21. Paris, BN ar. 4796, fol. 63rv (Homily 21), fols. 76v–78v (Homily 26).

22. Paris, BN ar. 4796, fol. 38rv (Homily 13).

23. Paris, BN ar. 4796, fol. 38v.

24. Paris, BN ar. 4796, fol. 49v (Homily 17).

25. Paris, BN ar. 4796, fol. 16v (Homily 6).

26. Paris, BN ar. 4796, fol. 16v–17r.

27. Indeed, had the colophon referred to the homilies one would have expected the plural, *mayamir*, rather than the singular, *maymar*.

28. Galtier 1905. Compare the fragment preserved in Paris, BN ar. 4796, fols. 79–82 with Galtier 1905: 110, line 5–112, line 8.

29. I used a recent edition of the *katameros* with commentary: Anonymous 1983. On the characteristics of the Coptic Orthodox lectionary of Lower Egypt, see Zanetti 1984 and Zanetti 1985.

15 Biblical Manuscripts of the Monastery of St. Shenoute the Archimandrite

Hany N. Takla

THIS CHAPTER WILL deal primarily with the survey of the published biblical manuscripts that came from the library of the Monastery of St. Shenoute. In addition to the history and the state of research on the subject, I will include brief comments on the extent and the character of this part of the collection. Based on manuscript evidence identified so far, it will also address the role that the Fayoum area may have played in shaping the contents of the library.

For more than two centuries scores of scholars have contributed to identifying and publishing the remains of the biblical codices of this once great library. However, without the recent labors and publications of P. Nagel,[1] Franz J. Schmitz,[2] Karlheinz Schüssler,[3] and Tito Orlandi,[4] the study presented here would have been nearly impossible to prepare in the short period of time it took.

History of the Library[5]

The library of a monastery is an indicator of the vision of its abbots and the literary usage of its monks. Its contents reveal the history of that usage. Its current fate, however, is a measure of its decline. In that respect we had the greatest Coptic library in Upper Egypt in the fifth century and I dare to say the greatest Coptic library ever assembled in all of Egypt to date. During the ninth to twelfth centuries the library of the monastery was estimated by Orlandi to contain at least 1,000 codices of varying sizes that may have

reached 500 pages each.[6] His average of 200 pages per codex would yield at
least 200,000 pages, of which he estimates that we know of about 10 percent. A library with such a long history would probably have gone through
the typical three major stages that Coptic manuscripts have undergone: the
papyrus stage from the fourth to the eighth and ninth centuries, the parchment stage from the ninth to the thirteenth centuries, and the paper stage
from the thirteenth to fourteenth centuries and later. According to Walter
E. Crum, St. Shenoute in his writings mentioned the existence of what is
commonly understood to be papyrus codices,[7] although among the surviving fragments of the library they are virtually absent. The evidence of the
parchment stage of the library[8] provides us with the typical codex material
found there according to Orlandi.[9] The paper stage is not voluminous but is
understandingly less dismembered, and would be primarily for liturgical purposes. In summary, we can imagine a library in the fifth and sixth centuries
with thousands of small or medium papyrus volumes, especially of biblical
codices, to serve the thousands of monks and nuns that were there. When
parchment replaced papyrus, there was more emphasis on larger, lectern-
sized, mainly biblical and literary volumes arranged for liturgical functions.
Both the Fayoum scriptoria and the monastery scriptorium were involved
in this massive conversion process. The paper stage in the thirteenth and
fourteenth centuries came at the time when the monastery and its Sahidic
dialect was on the decline, so lectionaries became more abundant, Arabic
translation of the bare essential liturgical texts were made, and numerous
biblical and literary works were lost in their entirety. However, there is
nothing to explain the loss of virtually the entire papyrus collection or the
totally missing biblical and literary works that would not be expected to be
lost at that stage. Either a catastrophic event befell them or they were buried
in a location at this monastic site that has not yet been discovered. Although
I fear the former, I am hopeful of the latter.

History of Research on Biblical Manuscripts of the Monastery

The location of the library of the monastery, being conjectured as the mysterious parallel narthex of the church,[10] was moved at a later date to the
upper back room north of the Sanctuary area, a room, based on the published accounts of Crum[11] and later Orlandi,[12] that must have served as the
staging area for the new parchment volumes being produced. I am basing
this on the Coptic inscription in the north wall of the chamber room that

Orlandi republished, which can be loosely translated as "small and larger unbound Four Gospels."[13] This is an indication of storage of an unfinished product that was manufactured in the monastery scriptorium. It is interesting to note that only the mention of the Gospels, Catholic Epistles, and Acts on the north wall and psalms on the west wall were visible. Could it be that the rest were copied elsewhere, or is this all that Canon W.T. Oldfield[14] could have read at the time of his visit?

In any case, the library continued to exist in what was probably considered a sacred room, which apparently was later, in the late eighteenth century, regarded as a treasure room. In about 1778 the librarian of the Vatican Library, J. Assemani (?), may have obtained the Borgia folios.[15] His success may have alerted Professor Charles G. Woide of Oxford and Admiral Jacobo Nani of Venice, who were able to obtain a significant number of folios from this collection by 1784. Before 1808 France was a recipient of some of these treasured folios.[16] In the nineteenth century, French collectors[17] and others, especially English travelers, secured more of that collection for the libraries of their countries or for their own research.[18] It seems that most of the transactions were kept confidential or were conducted through agents of the monastery. Acquisitions by the Institut français d'archéologie orientale du Caire (IFAO)[19] in Cairo in the last quarter of the nineteenth century may have alerted French scholars in Egypt that there was a treasure well of these manuscripts that had not yet run dry. So through the efforts of Gaston Maspero,[20] Émile C. Amélineau, and others in the mid 1880s, France acquired everything that was left in that small chamber, including the small scraps of parchment.[21] About four thousand folios and fragments in all made their way to the Bibliothèque nationale (BN) in Paris.[22] However not everything that belonged to the library was there at the time, because there were still hundreds of folios that were later acquired by a host of institutions in Europe, Egypt, and the United States. Biblical manuscripts were well represented in most of these acquisitions. As a result, many orphan folios and fragments of the same biblical codices resided in multiple collections in many countries. Some are currently scattered over as many as ten different collections.[23]

The first copies of the biblical codices appeared in Giovanni L. Mingarelli's edition of the Nani folios,[24] followed by Friedrich C. Münter's publication of the Daniel fragments a year later,[25] and Agostino Giorgi's publication of fragments of the Gospel of John from the Borgia collection later in that decade.[26] Then, a decade later, Woide used the Oxford folios

in the appendix to his edition of the Greek New Testament.[27] The catalog
edition of the Borgia Coptic collection by Georg Zoega in 1810[28] prompted
more publications of biblical parts of this collection such as that of W.F.
Engelbreth[29] who republished the Fayoumic fragments from that collection.
Later in the century C. Cuegney published some of the biblical fragments
that were in Paris at the time.[30]

However, thanks to Amélineau's cataloguing[31] of the massive French acquisitions that began in 1890[32] and his publications of fragments from the BN
and other collections,[33] publication of these texts came into vogue. In the late
nineteenth and early twentieth centuries, Agostino Ciasca[34] and P.J. Balestri[35]
published the Borgia biblical collection and even integrated the folios that
Mingarelli and others had published earlier. In 1892, Maspero published the
Old Testament folios of the BN,[36] catalogued earlier by Amélineau. This was
followed by the publications of Marius Chaine[37] and Louis J. Delaporte[38] of
some of the New Testament fragments of that collection in the early twentieth
century. Within the next few decades after 1883 Oscar von Lemm published
many of the biblical fragments of St. Petersburg, Moscow, and Berlin.[39] Carl
Wessely published the Vienna fragments[40] and J. Schleifer published the British
library fragments.[41] Also, Pierre Lacau,[42] E. Chassinat,[43] and Henri Munier[44]
published much of the IFAO and the Egyptian Museum fragments in Egypt.
These publications started to take shape in a diplomatic edition rather than
the continuous text format of Amélineau, Ciasca, and Maspero. In England
G. Horner was compiling an edition of all the fragments of the Sahidic New
Testament.[45] He used most of the fragments that were known in his time,
including the hundred of fragments he acquired for the British Museum in
1875. This publication is still referenced whenever Sahidic New Testament
texts are published in lists or texts.

In 1912–1913, Adolphe Hebbelynck published two articles,[46] listing
all the manuscripts in the Borgia Collection of this library from the Old
Testament and the Gospels with the known related fragments from other
collections. He relied on the earlier works of Crum,[47] Wessely,[48] and others
in compiling the list. Later A. Vaschalde published a series of articles[49] listing
all the published fragments of the Coptic Bible. This ushered in a new era
of publications that included works by Hebbelynck,[50] Walter C. Till,[51] and
others, which published some of the fragments from the above collections
that escaped the first round of publishing.

In the 1980s, Franz J. Schmitz and Gerd Mink began to expand the
scope of Hebbelynck's work by publishing lists of all the known fragments

of the Sahidic New Testament, whether they belonged to this library or
to others. This yielded three volumes on the Gospels[52] and one on the
Catholic Epistles.[53] Nagel, then in East Germany, was working on a similar project for the Old Testament. This yielded two articles that primarily
used Hebbelynck's edition in being limited to Borgia's first 32 codices.[54]
However, he put more emphasis on the codicology of these codices and
identified more fragments. In the 1990s, Schüssler began to compile his
own listing of the codices of both Old and New Testaments.[55] His work has
yielded seven volumes so far, with data on 180 codices. However, this created three different reference numbers to the biblical codices of the library
over and above Orlandi's overall scheme of identifying the library's codices
as a whole. Also, more fragments from the library were published during
the same period by Nagel,[56] Schüssler,[57] and Anne Boud'hors.[58] The latter published material from among the smaller fragments that Amélineau
placed together in BN Copte 132 and 133 as well as the material from De
Ricci's collection that were catalogued under BN Copte 161. She also published fragments from the library that are now in the Louvre Museum[59] and
Strasbourg University.[60] Further, whole book publications from other locations either included a collation against or selections from codices belonging
to this library such as those of James Drescher[61] and Frank Feder.[62]

The Current Extent of the Biblical Collection

In Orlandi's published article about the monastic library, he mentions
ninety-four Biblical codices out of about 325 identified codices or about 29
percent.[63] In his recently published Internet site[64] the number has grown to
about 100. These are arranged as follows:

A. Old Testament: 36
   1. Pentateuch[65]   10
   2. Historical[66]   6
   3. Poetic[67]   12 (10 are Psalm codices)
   4. Major Prophets[68]   6
   5. Minor Prophets[69]   2
B. New Testament: 64
   1. Gospels[70]   52
   2. Pauline[71]   4
   3. Catholic Epistles[72]   2
   4. Acts[73]   5
   5. Apocalypse[74]   1

The surviving manuscripts of the Old and New Testament books preserve
the text in a mostly fragmentary way with portions of the same verse even
being preserved in different collections. They are spread among twenty-
seven collections in twelve different countries over three continents. The
Paris, Vatican, and Vienna collections, in that order, hold the largest number of known biblical fragments. The least fragmentary and most complete
is Job, and to a lesser extent Ecclesiastes. The least preserved are the Minor
Prophets with only fragments from four of the twelve books identified so
far. Several of the Old Testament historical books did not survive in the
library on the basis of what has been identified so far. The New Testament
books, though fragmentary, preserve the majority of the text.

The Fayoum Connection

Arnold Van Lantschoot in his study of Coptic colophons[75] showed that
Fayoum was the producing center for some of the codices found in the
library. This concept was expanded decades later in Nanka S.H. Jansma's
work on the illuminations of the library manuscripts,[76] which showed that
the more elaborately illuminated manuscripts were productions of Fayoum
scriptoria. Lantschoot's publications of these colophons showed that there
were manuscripts produced in Fayoum for use in Fayoumic religious institutions, which were later rededicated to this monastery. All this indicates that
by the tenth century, the authorities of St. Shenoute's Monastery turned to
the Fayoum scriptoria to help in the massive conversion of the library from
the ancient papyrus codices to parchment. This, however, did not last, as
these scriptoria were made extinct during the time of Caliph al-Hakim in
the early years of the eleventh century.[77]

In 1808 Étienne Quatrèmere, in his study of Egypt and the available Coptic
manuscripts in European collections in his time, published Fayoumic texts
from BN Copte 78.[78] He referred to them with the designation Bashmuric.
Zoega[79] later published his famous catalog of Coptic manuscripts in the Borgia
collection, of which all the non-Bohairic fragments were acquired from the
monastery circa 1778. In that catalog, Zoega published twelve folios from
three manuscripts of what he also referred to as Bashmuric texts.[80] These folios
were immediately republished by his fellow Dane Engelbreth and were com-
mented on by Jean F. Champollion in a later work.[81]

Later in the century von Lemm published five folios from the Golenshiev
collection in St. Petersburg[82] belonging to the Gospels manuscript of the
Borgia collection. This was later republished by Alla Elanskaya in 1969 in

her catalog of the Coptic collection of the State Public library of Leningrad.[83] In 1887, Jakob Krall[84] published one folio from among the 1,000 folios from the monastery that the Austrian National Library in Vienna had obtained. Two years later Maspero[85] published one of the folios in this dialect that he found in the BN collection. Also in the same year Urbain Bouriant published several of the fragments obtained by IFAO in Cairo from the monastery collection.[86] They were later republished in a better edition by Émile Chassinat in 1902. This publication ushered in the designation used in reference to these codices until today, that is, Manuscripts A, B, and C. In 1909 Wessely[87] republished the lone folio from Manuscript C, the Pauline Epistles, found in Vienna along with the folios from the same manuscript in Cairo that Bouriant and Chassinat had published earlier. In 1910 J. David[88] published the Paris BN fragments of the Gospel of St. Matthew from Codex B, the Gospels. Then Hebbelynck[89] published one of the folios of fragments from Corinthians I found in the same collection from Manuscript C. Lastly, in 1987 Boud'hors[90] published some of the smaller fragments from manuscripts A and C that she identified. She also included a brief summary of where the manuscripts are and who published what. There is no doubt that a publication of all that remained of these manuscripts is sorely needed.

Now we ask the question, what are these manuscripts doing hundreds of kilometers away from where one would expect to find them? There are fragments from other Fayoumic manuscripts that were identified among those attributed to the library, but only the three manuscripts discussed above will be addressed. The identified complete folios or fragments of these three manuscripts can be summarized as follows:

- Ms. A. Isaiah and Jeremiah: fifteen folios (Borgia, BN, IFAO)
- Ms. B. The four Gospels (only fragments from Matthew, Mark, and John): fifteen folios (Borgia, St. Petersburg, BN)
- Ms. C. Pauline Epistles (fragments from 10 of the fourteen epistles): eighteen folios (Borgia, St. Petersburg, BN)

These manuscripts are typical of those that would be read by monks. The order of the biblical books included in manuscripts B and C is typical of other manuscripts found in the monastery and in the Hamuli collection.[91] The size of manuscripts A and C is typical of a church reading book. One possible conclusion that can be drawn from such observation is that these manuscripts were once the property of a monastery (or a church) in the Fayoum area that was ruined some time in the tenth to twelfth centuries. They were probably carried to the Monastery of St. Shenoute along with other manuscripts by monks from Fayoum who joined the monastery. They may have been put to use for a while by such monks, but this would be very difficult to conclude from the available evidence.

The Character of the Collection

Because of the seemingly mixed origin of the present parchment collection, it can be assumed that there are at least two different types of biblical texts. The ones that were produced in the monastery would probably tend to exhibit a more standard Sahidic reading, which would be native to the monastery. The ones that were copied in Fayoum, and more probably those that were rededicated from that district, would exhibit a higher degree of vowel usage, which is typically found in Fayoumic.[92] This would serve as a good criterion for classifying and perhaps dating the manuscripts of the monastery, assuming that further study of the text can substantiate such a distinction.

The order of the Coptic Bible found in the monastery is very difficult to determine because we never had the entire text of either the New or the Old Testament included in a single manuscript, but the following observations can be made:

- The Pentateuch was arranged in the regular order found in the Septuagint with Genesis, Exodus, Leviticus, Numbers, and Deuteronomy in that order.
- The historical books are more difficult to place in order. From the catalogued material it seems as if Tobit followed Joshua in Codex MONB.IL and may have followed Judith, although none of that book survived in that codex. Judges was followed by Ruth and/or either by Kings (I and II Samuel and/or I and II Kings). There are no surviving fragments catalogued so far from Chronicles, Ezra, Nehemiah, Esther, or Judith.
- The Major Prophets would have Isaiah and Jeremiah in that order or in separate manuscripts. Ezekiel seems to have been written in a separate manuscript. Daniel seems to have followed Judges in one codex (MONB.IN) and followed Genesis in Codex MONB.IA. In any case it was treated more as part of the Historical Books than either the Major Prophets or even the Minor Prophets as it usually occurs in the Bohairic.[93]
- The Minor Prophets is not well preserved in either of the two manuscripts catalogued so far. The only notable order is Amos being followed by Micah in Codex MONB.JG.

- The Gospels followed the traditional order of Mathew, Mark, Luke, and John whenever they all were grouped in the same manuscript
- The Pauline Epistles followed the typical Coptic order of I and II Corinthians followed by Hebrews. This occurred in both the Sahidic and Fayoumic manuscripts in the monastery.
- The Catholic Epistles always began with I and II Peter, followed by the three John epistles, James, and concluding with Jude.
- The Acts of the Apostles is usually found in separate manuscripts. Only in the Sahidic-Greek codex MONB.LU does one find it inserted between the Pauline Epistles and the Catholic Epistles. This was probably a more ancient text than the other ones found of that book.
- Apocalypse may have followed the Catholic and Pauline Epistles, revealing an earlier version of a manuscript of selected books of the Bible.[94]

Conclusion

In conclusion, there is much work to be done on this subject. This can be summarized as follows:

1. The acceleration of publishing the lists of grouped fragments under a codex as well as properly identifying their provenance.
2. The inclusion of enough codicological data as well as sample photographs. This is being done by Schüssler, but it is insufficiently done in the Schmitz publications.
3. Classifications of manuscripts according to origin, whether they were produced in the monastery, produced in Fayoum on commission from the monastery, or rededicated from another place to the monastery. This can be done by first establishing the character of each of these origins, using colophons; illuminations based on Jansma's study, and other codicological features.
4. The preliminary publishing of the grouped fragments by codex in a diplomatic edition. Electronic media is the most appropriate method at this stage.
5. The compilation of a concordance of biblical quotations from St. Shenoute's writings and other abbots from the monastery to support the classification process mentioned above.
6. The making available of preliminary data of all of the above to researchers and students in a similar fashion to Orlandi's Internet site.

7. The character of the bilingual, Greek–Sahidic texts need to be studied further, especially to determine the relationship between the Greek and the Sahidic texts. Is the Sahidic a translation from the included Greek text? Or were they placed together from two different sources, such as was observed in Bohairic–Arabic texts of the fourteenth century and later?[95]

To accomplish the above tasks, the academic community needs to draft an army of scholars, who can work at Amélineau's energetic pace with the traditional precision of German scholarship. For such an army, all of us live in hopeful anticipation.

Notes

1. Nagel 1983–1984.
2. Schmitz and Mink 1986–1991, Schmitz 2003.
3. Schüssler 1995–2004.
4. Orlandi 2003.
5. Cf Takla 2005.
6. Orlandi 2002: 225–26.
7. Crum 1905: xi–xii.
8. According to C. Kotsifou there was documentary evidence of the monastery purchasing parchment for use in manuscripts prior to the classical date of the eighth–ninth centuries that Takla 2005 has assigned as the beginning of that period. This can be reconciled by the fact that such earlier volumes may have been smaller in size than the ones belonging to that parchment age of the library. Cf. Takla 2006: 24–25 and C. Kotsifou article in this volume.
9. Orlandi 2002: 220.
10. Grossmann 2002a: 141 n. 132.
11. Crum 1904a.
12. Orlandi 2002.
13. Orlandi 2002: 213.
14. Crum 1904a.
15. Orlandi tentatively credits Assemani with the acquisition of the White Monastery fragments, now in the Vatican Borgia Collection, cf. Orlandi 2002: 228. Prof. S.L. Emmel relayed to me that Giorgi, in his publication of some of these fragments, has identified that a different person brought these fragments to the collection (Giorgi 1789). However, it was J. Assemani who did the initial cataloguing of the material.

16. Bibliothèque nationale de Paris (BN). *BN Copte 78.*

17. *BN 102,* Orlandi 2002: 227.

18. Rev. G. Horner has obtained a few hundreds of these folios in 1875, Orlandi 2002: 228.

19. Institut français d'archéologie orientale.

20. Maspero 1892: 1 indicates that his discovery of the room was in 1883.

21. Jansma 1973: 9 indicates that these manuscripts came to the library in four lots between March 1886 and October 1887. For more details on this purchase, consult Catherine Louis's article on the subject in this volume.

22. Orlandi 2002: 228.

23. Codex MONB.LB [Gospels], and Codex MONB.LU [Pauline Epistles]. The designation used here is based on the reference system used in Orlandi 2003.

24. Mingarelli 1785: vi–lxxviii.

25. Münter 1786.

26. Giorgi 1789.

27. Woide 1799.

28. Zoega 1810. In this publication he listed the contents of the biblical codices with no text except for Fayoumic fragments discussed below.

29. Engelbreth 1811.

30. Cuegney 1880.

31. Amélineau's *Catalog* is unpublished but its manuscript is available at the BN.

32. Jansma 1873: 12.

33. Amélineau 1884, Amélineau 1886-1888a, Amélineau 1886–1888b.

34. Ciasca 1885–1889.

35. Balestri 1904.

36. Maspero 1892.

37. Chaine 1905.

38. Delaporte 1905, Delaporte 1906, Delaporte 1908.

39. Lemm 1885a; Lemm 1885b; Lemm 1890–1892; Lemm 1890–1906; Lemm 1912.

40. Wessely 1908; Wessely 1909–1917; Wessely 1913; Wessely 1914.

41. Schleifer 1909–1914; Schleifer 1912.

42. Lacau 1901.

43. Chassinat 1902.

44. Munier 1914; Munier 1916; Munier 1919–1923.

45. Horner 1911–1924.

46. Hebbelynck 1911–1912.

47. Crum 1905; Crum 1909.

48. See note 40.

49. Vaschalde 1919–1933.

50. Hebbelynck 1913; Hebbelynck 1922a; Hebbelynck 1922b.

51. Till 1933; Till 1934; Till 1937; Till 1939.

52. Schmitz and Mink 1986–1991.

53. Schmitz 2003.

54. Nagel 1983–1984.

55. Schüssler 1995–2004.

56. Nagel 1987; Nagel 1989a; Nagel 1989b.

57. Schüssler 1974–1975.

58. Boud'hors1987.

59. Boud'hors*et al.* 1996.

60. Boud'hors 1998.

61. Drescher 1970.

62. Feder 2002.

63. Orlandi 2002: 225.

64. Orlandi 2003.

65. Refers to books of Genesis, Exodus, Leviticus, Numbers, and Deuteronomy.

66. Refers to books of Joshua, Judges, Ruth, I & II Samuel, I & II Kings, I & II Chronicles, Judith, Tobit, Esther, Ezra, Nehemiah, and I & II Maccabees.

67. Refers to books of Job, Psalms, Proverbs, Ecclesiastes, Song of Songs, Wisdom of Solomon, and Wisdom of Ibn Sirach.

68. Refers to the books of the four Major Prophets and their associated books: Isaiah, Jeremiah, Lamentations, Baruch, Epistle of Jeremiah, Ezekiel, and Daniel.

69. Refers to the twelve Minor Prophets Books: Hosea, Joel, Amos, Jonah, Obadiah, Nahum, Micah, Habakkuk, Zephaniah, Haggai, Zachariah, and Malachi.

70. Refers to the Four Gospels: Matthew, Mark, Luke, and John.

71. Refers to the fourteen epistles of St. Paul: Romans, I & II Corinthians, Ephesians, Galatians, Colossians, Philippians, I & II Thessalonians, Hebrews, I & II Timothy, Titus, and Philemon.

72. Refers to Epistles of James, I & II Peter, I & II & III John, and Jude.

73. Or the Acts of the Apostles.

74. Or the Book of Revelation.

75. Van Lantschoot 1929.

76. Jansma 1973.

77. Depuydt 1993: cxv.

78. Quatrèmere 1808: 228–53.

79. See note 29.

80. Zoega 1810: 139–168.

81. Champollion 1818.

82. Von Lemm 1885a.

83. Elanskaya 1969: 96–120.

84. Krall 1887, vol. 1: 67–69; 2–3, 69–71.

85. Maspero 1889.

86. Bouriant 1889.

87. Wessely 1908: 6–12.

88. David 1910.

89. Hebbelynck 1922b.

90. Boud'hors 1987: 87–98.

91. Cf. Depuydt 1993.

92. In compiling the text of Tobit from two different manuscripts, the manuscript used to fill the gap in the middle chapters was similar to the Sahidic Old Testament manuscripts of the Hamouli collection. Cf. Takla 1996–1997.

93. E.g., BN Copte 96.

94. E.g., British library *Or. 7594*, Papyrus codex.

95. E.g., Vatican Copte 1, a tenth-century parchment codex of the Pentateuch with a fourteenth-century parallel Arabic column translation.

16 Once More into the Desert of Apa Shenoute

Further Thoughts on BN 68

Janet Timbie

THE MANUSCRIPT KNOWN as BN Copte 68, a trilingual (Coptic-Greek-Arabic) paper codex written in the fifteenth to sixteenth centuries and containing instructions for worshipers and liturgical readings, was the object of brief notices and descriptions in the nineteenth century.[1] Hans Quecke, in 1970, was the first to offer an extended discussion and suggest solutions to some of the text's puzzles.[2] Yet it is surprising to see how often he states that a term in the text is "puzzling" or "incomprehensible."[3] In every case of initial puzzlement, Quecke goes on to offer possible solutions after weighing the evidence. Stefan Timm does the same in the 1985 section of the multi-volume work, *Das christlich-koptische Ägypten in arabischer Zeit*, since the rite described in BN 68 seemed to contain information about the complex of buildings that made up the monastery of Apa Shenoute.[4]

My intention was to build on the foundations laid by Quecke and Timm when I analyzed BN 68 and its rite in two publications that appeared in 1995 and 1998.[5] The longer publication appeared in *Pilgrimage and Holy Space in Late Antique Egypt*, edited by David Frankfurter, and offered a provisional explanation of the text as a series of instructions to worshipers who came to participate in a stational liturgy for the "feast of the desert of Apa Shenoute."[6] The sequence of places visited and actions undertaken in the rite—as I understood them at the time of that essay—will be summarized before re-visiting some of the problems. The pilgrims/worshipers

169

go up to the mountain (ⲧⲟⲟⲨ), which refers to the entire domain of
Shenoute.[7] They assemble at the corner of the choir-leader (ⲧⲕⲉⲗⲭⲉ
ⲙⲡⲥⲁ2)[8] and later turn north to the ⲉⲧⲣⲓⲅⲁⲙⲟⲨ (Copticized Greek, for
apeirogamos, 'without experience of marriage') church, a shrine dedicated
to the Virgin Mary and founded by Shenoute, Pgol, and Pshoi.[9] After
arriving at the church, the people chant while walking to the ⲑⲁⲗⲗⲥⲥⲁ
of Apa Shenoute, which I then argued was a receptacle for his remains.[10]
A sermon by Shenoute, *Good is the Time for Launching a Boat to Sail*, is
read, and then Mass is celebrated (following a five-page gap in the text).[11]
The worshipers then "go down" to the monastery of Apa Shenoute and
enter the church of the Virgin Mary and St. George.[12] The monastery
indicated at this point is the central, main monastery of the domain of Apa
Shenoute. Within its walls the large church contained sanctuaries dedicated to the Virgin Mary, St. George, and Shenoute.[13] Instructions for
prayers and singing follow, and then the manuscript breaks off.[14] In general,
according to my earlier reconstruction, the program was "assemble, process to a church containing the relics of Shenoute, celebrate mass, process
to his main monastery, . . . and (probably) return from the mountain."[15]
Some of these statements were working hypotheses offered as explanations of difficult language in an unusual text. I hoped that other scholars
would read, evaluate, and correct my interpretations, as I attempted to do
with the earlier work of Quecke and Timm.

In 2004, Peter Grossmann published an essay in which he disagreed with
many points in my reading of BN 68.[16] His point of departure is not simply
this manuscript, but various historical traditions about the burial of Shenoute
and how they relate to the terrain around the White Monastery and to the
archaeological remains of the monastery. All this is examined in an effort to
locate the burial place or places of Shenoute.[17] After summarizing the data,
Grossmann concluded that Shenoute was first buried by the community and
then secretly re-buried by Besa and a few other monks. Later, the remains
were removed to the main church and finally hidden there in 1167, under
the apse.[18] The remains were lost at some point after that.

BN 68, in Grossmann's interpretation, describes a rite that stays very
close to the main monastery and church. ⲉⲧⲣⲓⲅⲁⲙⲟⲨ is another name for
the large, central church.[19] He argues that there is no walk to the site of
Shenoute's cell and an associated church, since it would be too difficult.[20]
The ⲧⲟⲡⲟⲥ mentioned in BN 68 could be his residence in old age, which
was in main monastery.[21] And given the burial sequence for Shenoute's

body, the ΘΑΛΑCCΑ is not a container for remains, but the great spring of the main monastery that miraculously provided water for thousands of refugees in Shenoute's lifetime.[22]

It seems that my 1998 essay and the 2004 study by Grossmann interpret BN 68 in ways that disagree both on specific points and on the overall interpretation of the rite. Does the rite direct the worshipers around the entire domain of Apa Shenoute or does it confine them to the small area around the main monastery? What is the ΘΑΛΑCCΑ of Apa Shenoute? New evidence has come to light that may assist in answering these questions. It will briefly be reviewed before I turn to the sermon of Shenoute, *Good is the Time for Launching a Boat to Sail*, which was read during the rite. Does the sermon help us understand the rite?

If the sequence of burial, secret re-burial, and removal to a chamber in the church for the body of Shenoute is correct, then ΘΑΛΑCCΑ cannot be a container near the altar for the physical remains of Shenoute. Grossmann argued that it referred to the spring of the monastery; Quecke also examined "watery" explanations without reaching a conclusion.[23] Yet no Coptic or Greek texts that I have located use ΘΑΛΑCCΑ in that way. In the *Life of Shenoute*, the miraculous spring is ϨΟΝΒΕ.[24] Burmester, citing A. J. Butler, described an altar cavity called a *thalassa* that was used for the relics of saints or martyrs.[25] Perhaps the *thalassa* did not contain the physical remains of Shenoute, but valuable relics associated with him. Andrea Jördens has published a sixth-century papyrus in which the head of a women's monastery states that she is sending a fragment of the "sticharion of abbas Sinouthios" to bring about healing of a demon-possessed nun.[26] This special item of clothing, perhaps the one that is the focus of so much discussion in Shenoute's letters to the women's monastery,[27] could qualify as a relic since it had been in contact with his body during his lifetime.[28] The ΘΑΛΑCCΑ would still be a container of some sort for non-bodily relics, which would solve the vocabulary problem (that is, non-occurrence of ΘΑΛΑCCΑ as spring or well).

However, this would not address the question of where this ΘΑΛΑCCΑ was located: in the main church of the White Monastery or in another church or chapel within the domain. Does BN 68 describe a rite enacted at widely separated locations in the domain of the White Monastery or one tightly focused on the main monastery and church? The directions in the manuscript—go up to the mountain (BN 68.4r), turn north to the ΕΤΡΙΓΑΜΟΥ church (BN 68.32r), go down to the monastery of Shenoute (BN 68.100r, 137r)—could apply in either case.[29] This is a fifteenth- to sixteenth-century manuscript that collects a variety of biblical, liturgical, and homiletic materials (in Sahidic, Bohairic, Greek, and Arabic) and, at best, records the directions for a rite as it was performed at some time prior to the writing of BN 68. It is possible to imagine a progression whereby the original 'rite for the feast of the desert' covered widely separated sites in the domain, but by a later date (that is, one closer to the date of BN 68) the rite was confined to the main monastery. BN 68 would then preserve the directions of the earlier stage, which were "symbolically" re-enacted by later worshipers. The stations of the cross, as a rite of prayer, offer an analogy: early Christian pilgrimage to the Holy Land led to later depictions of the stations in monasteries, chapels, and churches, and finally to a series of fourteen crosses in the nave of the church representing the stations.[30]

More archaeological investigation of the White Monastery site may help us understand that what was done at the time BN 68 was written and what might have been done at earlier time. Work by Bentley Layton on the *Canons of Shenoute*—the writings directed to a monastic audience that reveal the day-to-day operation of the community—has sketched in the outlines of the domain: the large monastery including the main church, a village with the women's monastery, a "little" monastery, cells for hermits (and Shenoute) at the valley wall, the house of Apa Pshoi, and the "church of our father."[31] These sites were well known to the community in the lifetime of Shenoute (385–465?) and probably for some time after. Further study of both the literary and archaeological evidence may show whether these sites were visited in a rite that eventually became the rite recorded in BN 68.

There is evidence that some kind of rite of the 'desert' was practiced long before BN 68 was written. The sermon by Shenoute that is preserved in this manuscript, *Good is the Time for Launching a Boat to Sail*, also survives in two fragmentary codices from the White Monastery.[32] In Codex YP 1: i.1–2 (a tenth–eleventh century manuscript), a liturgical heading appears before the sermon and indicates the day on which it should be read: "the Monday they go to the desert."[33] This heading in Codex YP suggests that there was a ritual procession that used this sermon several centuries prior to writing of BN 68. The reference to "Monday" is not inconsistent with the direction in BN 68, "the Monday of the second week in the holy forty days."[34] Does the content of the sermon, "Good is the Time for Launching a Boat to Sail," shed any light on the origins or character of an earlier ritual procession or help us understand the directions given in the rite described in BN 68?

Shenoute begins the sermon (in my somewhat colloquial translation of the Coptic NAÑOYⲠNAY): "It is a good time to launch a boat to sail. It is also a good time to moor in the harbor. But it is sinking that is bad."[35] The sermon, and the rite of BN 68, is intended for a mixed audience of laity, clergy, and monks. And let us recall that the first stage of the BN 68 procession for those coming from Panopolis would be to 'launch' a boat and then 'moor' on the west bank of the Nile. Shenoute continues: "This is what I am saying: it is a good time to go to the church of God."[36] There are two points in which the rite of BN 68 directs the worshipers to a church: the ⲈTⲢⲒⲄAMOY church at fol. 32 and the church of the Virgin Mary and St. George at fol. 139. These directions bracket the reading of the sermon, which occurs on fols. 54–64.[37] Shenoute then says: "It is good to go up (BⲰK Ⲉ2PⲁⲒ) on a high mountain (TOOY) at any time or any day for the benefit in good things. Coming down (ⲈⲒ Ⲉ2PⲁⲒ) from it is good also, by means of the turns in the path, for what we need below it. But it is bad to fall off (the mountain) so that you utterly perish!"[38] Here, too, the sermon is echoed in the instructions in the rite of BN 68. On the first page of the manuscript (fol. 4r), "all the people go up (BⲰK Ⲉ2PⲁⲒ) to the mountain (TOOY) to gather at the corner (KⲈⲀXⲈ) of the teacher (Cⲁ2)."[39] After the worshipers take part in several actions of the rite, including a mass and the reading of the sermon, they recite while "coming down" (NHY ⲈⲠⲈCHT, fol. 100r) before entering "the door of the monastery of our holy father, Apa Shenoute" (ⲠPO MⲠMONⲀCTHPⲒON MⲠⲈNⲈⲒⲰT ⲈTOYⲀⲀB ⲀⲠⲀ ⲰⲈNOYTⲈ, fol. 137r). There are verbal parallels between sermon and rite in the use of BⲰK Ⲉ2PⲁⲒ for 'go up' and ⲈⲒ/NHY for 'come down.'

Shenoute returns to the theme of falling off the path at little later in the sermon, this time with a clear moral interpretation: "It is falling off the path and perishing in sin that is bad."[40] This is one of many points at which he exhorts his listeners, both lay and monastic, to make special efforts at spiritual practice for a time and to make a serious effort to "stay on the path" at all times. All this is appropriate for a Lenten sermon read on "the Monday of the second week of the holy forty days," as stated at the beginning of BN 68.[41] What are some of the practices that Shenoute recommends? First of all, "fasting is good" at one time, "eating is good" at another.[42] "Those who serve their belly are rejected, just as the apostle (Paul) scorned them in the conclusion of the first letter."[43] This refers to Paul in Romans 16:18: "such people do not serve our Lord Christ but their own appetites." Later in the sermon, Shenoute notes that "the apostle said, 'For the kingdom of God is not eating and drinking,'(Romans 14:17) though it is God who created eating and drinking, but not being insatiable."[44]

Different types of sexual continence are recommended. "(A) period of abstinence from your wife is good" and "marriage is also good." Of course, Shenoute says, "I am speaking to lay people who are in proper marriage, not to monks who have taken up their cross (and) followed the savior."[45] For "there is no single skill or single work . . . there are many. . . . Some (are) virgins, others keep their beds pure."[46] He exhorts the audience to keep both thoughts and bodies pure: "If it is with difficulty that Jesus dwells in the man who tries to purify his heart daily of thoughts that are defiled . . . then how will He remain at all in . . . one who sleeps with animals . . . and even in male and female fornicators?"[47] The sermon calls the audience to avoid impure actions, then to purification of thoughts.

Shenoute also recommends acts of charity: care for strangers and being "merciful" if his listeners simply "have the necessities of life without riches."[48] The important thing is to maintain a record of "good works." One "who has many good works for a season, now not only becomes weak in good works, but even commits . . . worthless acts" and will suffer the same fate as Jerusalem: "I will give Jerusalem to removal and as a dwelling place of snakes" (Jeremiah 9:11).[49] The former favor of Jerusalem—and of the one who used to do good—will not save it (or him) if behavior changes. And prayer is important: "It is good to run to God every day and every hour and every moment. We call on Him so that He guards us from evil here and makes us worthy of a place of rest in the place to which we go."[50]

There are calls to repentance scattered throughout the sermon. Repentance is compared to waking from sleep. "Christ came to the world. We sin and we did not repent. Indeed, 'it is the time and the hour of rising from sleep' (Romans 13:11)."[51] Those in the audience may sin without being aware of it, so they need to make a broad commitment to repentance. "Repent, O man who thinks God forgave you, though He did not forgive. . . . According to the prophet, 'Gray hairs grew on us but we did not know (it)' (Hosea 7:9); that is to say, we did great evil, while being forgetful, (acting) as though they were not sins. . . ."[52] All efforts to repent for past sins and change behavior will be rewarded. "If you are amazed at everything you see on earth, then how much will you be amazed at what you see in heaven! . . . When you see the heavenly Jerusalem, how much will you be amazed!"[53]

Shenoute calls his audience to special efforts in fasting (from food and sex), prayer, and acts of charity *for a period of time*. That is the sense of "fasting is good" and "eating is also good."[54] This call is combined with a broad warning about the need to repent for past sins, making the sermon a perfect choice for a Lenten rite. The opening of BN 68 specifies "the Monday of the second week of the holy forty days," meaning during Lent, but the heading of this sermon in codex YP, "the Monday when they go to the desert," could point to the same time in the liturgical year.[55]

There is one more theme in the sermon that is consistent with the penitential quality of a rite of the desert. Shenoute talks about sunrise and the need to get up and get moving: "The night is good . . . but the day is preferable since with the sun's rising all the beasts of the field . . . sleep in their dens and 'man goes out to his work and to his task until the hour of evening' (Psalm 103:22–23)."[56] And "if disgrace comes to those who sleep and get drunk in the evening, then how great is the . . . disgrace of those who sleep during the day!"[57] Shenoute also offers spiritual interpretations of sunrise (Jesus as sun of righteousness, citing Malachi 4:2 and John 11:27), but this does not necessarily dilute the message of his quote from Romans: "It is the time and the hour of rising from sleep" (Romans 13:11).[58] The reading of his sermon reminded the listeners to get up and get moving, either on "the Monday when they go to the desert" or in the rite recorded in BN 68.

In conclusion, I ask the following questions. When did the 'rite of the desert of Apa Shenoute' begin? When did Christians from Panopolis begin to "go to the desert" for a stational liturgy? Was there a Lenten rite for laity and monks even during the lifetime of Shenoute (d. 464/5)?[59] I cannot conclusively answer these questions at this time, or solve all the puzzles of BN 68. However, careful reading of *Good is the Time for Launching a Boat to Sail* reinforces the penitential nature of the rite that BN 68 places in Lent. At its core, therefore, the rite is not about Shenoute (whose feast day is 1 July), but about the effort made by the worshipers as they walk from place to place—praying, singing, and participating in the mass. In its early stages of development, perhaps even during Shenoute's lifetime, the rite might have required a strenuous hike around the domain of the White Monastery.[60] As the legend of Shenoute grew in the centuries after his death and was preserved in versions of the *Life of Shenoute*, the rite might have acquired a Shenoutean focus to supplement the basic penitential character of the earlier practice. "When they go to the desert", in Codex YP, becomes "the feast of the desert of Apa Shenoute" in BN 68. It is also possible that the strenuous procession around the domain evolved into a limited circuit of the main church and monastery. In the same way, the stations of the cross evolved from devotions at Jerusalem sites to artistic tableaux set up in Europe to fourteen crosses (with or without artistic representations) in the nave of a church.[61]

Relying on his unequaled knowledge of Christian architecture in Egypt, Peter Grossmann has reconstructed the sequence of burials and resting places for the physical remains of Shenoute.[62] However, until some textual support is found for the Greek loanword 'ΘΑΛΑССΑ' being used in Coptic to mean well or spring, I prefer to explain it as an 'altar cavity' that was one stop on the path of the rite described in BN 68. Perhaps it held special items that belonged to Apa Shenoute, such as the sticharion.[63] Scientific excavation around the White Monastery and the publication of improved texts and translations of the works of Shenoute (especially the *Canons*) may eventually give clear evidence of the location of destinations in the 'rite of the desert,' both at the time of the composition of the text preserved in BN 68 and at an earlier, formative period.

Notes

1. Hyvernat 1896: 549; Quatremère 1808: 299–300.
2. Quecke 1970: 488–99.
3. Ibid.: 490, ΤΚΕΛΧΕ ΜΠCΑ2, is "unverständlich;" on 493 it is "rätselhaften." Other terms that Quecke struggles with are ΕΤΡΙΓΑΜΟΥ (490), ΠΕ2ΟΟΥ ΜΠΕCΝΑΥ (489), and ΘΑΛΑССΑ (490 n. 15).
4. Timm 1984–1992, vol. 2: 601–33, section on "ad-Der al-Abyad."
5. Timbie 1998: 415–41; Timbie 1995: 89–93.
6. Ibid.: 415–41.
7. Ibid.: 424–27.
8. Ibid.: 428–29.
9. Ibid.: 430–34.
10. Ibid.: 432–36.
11. Ibid.: 432–34. On this sermon, see Emmel 2004b: 675.
12. Ibid.: 434.
13. Meinardus 1965: 292, and for the most complete description of the church, Grossmann 2002a: 528–36.
14. Timbie 1998: 440.
15. Ibid.: 440.
16. Grossmann 2004: 85–105.

17. Ibid.: 85.

18. Ibid.: 102.

19. Ibid.: 92, arguing that it is unlikely that two churches would be dedicated to the Virgin Mary.

20. Ibid.: 102.

21. Ibid.: 99–100, discussing the text cited by Crum in which Shenoute orders the monks to destroy his cell.

22. Ibid.: 86.

23. Ibid.: 86; Quecke 1970: 490 n. 15.

24. See Crum 1939: 691a for ϨⲞⲚⲂⲈ. Förster 2002: 326 lists occurrences of ⲐⲀⲖⲀⲤⲤⲀ in Coptic documentary texts.

25. See Timbie 1998: 432–35 for bibliography.

26. Kohlbacher 1999, vol. 2: 144–54 and Jördens 2004: 142–56.

27. Krawiec 2002: 150–54.

28. See the definitions and historical review in Chiovard 2003: 50–56.

29. Timbie 1998: 418 for a review of these directions.

30. Brown 2003: 499–501.

31. Emmel 2004b: 553–605 discusses the contents of the *Canons*; Layton 2003 deals with the territory of the WM federation.

32. Emmel 2004b: 675, 862. In addition to BN 68, the sermon survives in part in YP and XD.

33. YP 1=FR-BN 130.5 f. 78r. ⲠⲈⲤⲚⲀⲨ ⲈϢⲀⲨⲂⲰⲔ ⲈⲠⲬⲀⲒ̈Ⲉ.

34. BN 68 f. 4r.

35. Leipoldt 1906–1913, vol. 4: 174: ⲚⲀⲚⲞⲨⲠⲚⲀⲨ ⲚⲔⲀⲠⲬⲞⲒ ⲈⲂⲞⲖ ⲈⲢϨⲎⲦ. ⲚⲀⲚⲞⲨⲠⲚⲀⲨ ⲞⲚ ⲘⲘⲞⲞⲚⲈ ⲈⲦⲈⲘⲠⲰ. ⲰⲘⲤ ⲆⲈ ⲠⲈⲦϨⲞⲞⲨ.

36. Ibid.: 174.

37. See Timbie 1998: 418.

38. Leipoldt 1906–1913, vol. 4: 175.

39. Timbie 1998: 426–28 discusses the interpretation of the terms mountain, corner, and teacher. All present problems.

40. Leipoldt 1906–1913, vol. 4: 176.

41. BN 68 f. 4r; see Quecke 1970: 489 n. 10 for discussion of the dating problem.

42. Leipoldt 1906–1913, vol. 4: 174.

43. Ibid.: 193.

44. Ibid.: 195.

45. Ibid.: 174–75.

46. Ibid.: 177–78.

47. Ibid.: 192–93.

48. Ibid.: 176, 178.
49. Ibid.: 186.
50. Ibid.: 175–76.
51. Ibid.: 178.
52. Ibid.: 182.
53. Ibid.: 189.
54. Ibid.: 174.
55. BN 68 f. 4r and YP 1=FR-BN 130.5 f. 78r.
56. Leipoldt 1906–1913, vol. 4: 176.
57. Ibid.: 179.
58. Ibid.: 177–78.
59. Emmel 2004b: 6–12 on the chronology of Shenoute.
60. See Grossmann 2004: 102; what is too strenuous for one era may not be so for another.
61. Brown 2003: 500.
62. Grossman 2004: 102.
63. See Jördens 2004: 142–56 for sticharion reference.

17 Bohairic Liturgical Texts Related to St. Shenoute[1]

Youhanna Nessim Youssef

IN LIGHT OF the fact that many scholars chose as the focus of their papers on the White Monastery the life and works of Shenoute in the early centuries, I decided to provide an overview on the Bohairic liturgical texts related to St. Shenoute.

The Psalis of St. Shenoute

The bibliography of St. Shenoute by P.A. Frandsen and Richter-Aeroe[2] does not include any psali dedicated to this saint. There are two authors who wrote psalis for St. Shenoute; the first being Nicodemus, whose works were published for the first time in 1906[3] with an Arabic translation in 1913, and republished in 1993 by Bishop Matteaus (abbott of the Syrian Monastery in Wadi al-Natrun).[4] The second author is Gabriel, whose psali was published by Leipoldt.[5]

ГЄ ГАР ПІΝІϢϯ СЄΝΟΥΘΙΟС ΠΙΟΥΗΒ ΠΙ ΑΡΧΗΜΑΝΑΡΙΤΗС ΑϤСΑΧΙ ΝЄΜ ΠΟΥΡΟ ΠΧ͞С ΜϕΡΗϯ ΜΜϢΥСΗС ΠΙΝΟΜΟ-ΘΙΤΗС	*For* the great **Senuthius, the priest** *the archimandrite*, spoke with *Christ* **the King** like Moses the *Lawgiver.*
ΔΑΥΙΔ ΠΟΥΡΟ ΠΙΘΜΗΙ ΑϤСΑΧΙ ΧЄ ΠΙΘΜΗΙ ЄϤЄϕΡΙ ϧЄΝ ΠΗΙ ΜΠΟ͞С ΜϕΡΗϯ ΜΠΙϢЄΝСΗϤΙ ЄΤЄ ϕΑΙ ΠЄ СЄΝΟΥΘ͞ΙΟС	David the righteous king said: "the righteous shall flourish like a cedar in the house of the Lord"[6] who is Senuthius.
ЄϤЄϢϢΠΙ ΝΧЄ ΠΙΘΜΗΙ ΔЄ ΟΝ ЄΥΜЄΥΙ ЄΝЄϨ ΑΛΗΘϢС ΝΘΟΚ Ϣ ΔΙΚЄΟΝ ΑΚϬΙ ΜΠΙϢΝϧ ΝЄΝЄϨ	"The righteous will be ever mindful"[7] *Truly* you O *righteous one* deserved[8] eternal life.
ΙΗ͞С ΠΧ͞С ΠΙ ΔΗΜΙΟΥΡΓΟС ΑϤΤΑΜΟΚ ЄΠΙΜΥСΤΗΡΙΟΝ ϧЄΝ ΝΙ ϧΑЄ ΝΝΙ ΧΡΟΝΟС Ϣ ΠΙΝΙϢϯ ϧЄΝ ΠЄϤΑΓϢΝ	**Jesus** *Christ, the Creator,* **informed you** about the *mysteries* **of the end of** (all) *ages;* O **great in his struggles.**
ΚΥΡΙΟС ΑϤСϢΤΠ ΜΠΙ ΑΓΙΟС ΙСΧЄΝ ΤЄϤΜЄΤΚΟΥΧΙ ΚΑΛϢС ΠΙΟΥΗΒ ΜΜΗΙ СЄΝΟΥΘΙΟС ΠΙϢϕΗΡ ΝΝΙ ΑΓΓЄΛΟС	*The Lord* had *well* chosen the *holy* **one,** since his childhood; O **true priest Senuthius, the friend of the angels.**
ΡΑϢΙ ΘЄΛΗΛ Ϣ ΝΙΜΟΝΑΧΟС ЄΤϧЄΝ ΠΙ ΜΟΝΑСΤΗΡΙΟΝ ΝΤЄ ΠЄΝΙϢΤ СЄΝΟΥΘΙΟС ΠΙ ΔΙΚЄΟС ΠΙ ΤЄΛΙΟΝ	**Rejoice and be happy, O** *monks,* **of the** *monastery* **of our father Senuthius, the** *perfect righteous one.*
ϕΝΗΒ ϕϯ ΠЄΝΒΟΗΘΟС ϬΙСΙ ΜΠΤΑΠ ΝΝΙ ΧΡΙСΤΙΑΝΟС ϨΙΤЄΝ ΝΙ ϯϨΟ ΝϯΘЄΟΤΟΚΟС ΝЄΜ ΠΙ ΘΜΗΙ ΠΙΝΙϢϯ СЄΝΟΥΘΙΟС	Lord God, our *Helper,* exalt the horn of the *Christians*[9] through the demands of the *Theotokos* and the righteous one the great Senuthius.
ΧЄΡЄ ΝЄ Ϣ ϯΠΑΡΘЄΝΟС ΜΑΡΙΑ ΘΜΑΥ ΜΠΙ ΔЄСΠΟΤΗС ΧЄΡЄ ΠΙΝΙϢϯ ΝΘЄΟϕΟΡΟС ΑΒΒΑ ϢЄΝΟΥϯ ΠΙ ΑΡΧΗΜΑΝΑΡΙΤΗС	Hail to the *Virgin,* Mary the mother of the *Lord,* Hail to the great *theophore* Abba Shenoute the *archimandrite.*
ϯΨΥΧΗ ΝΙ ΒЄΝ ΜΟΙ ΝϢΟΥ ΝΟΥΧΒΟΒ ϨЄΝ ϕΜΑΝϢϢΠΙ ΝΝΙ ΠΑΡΘЄΝΟС ΝЄΜ ΑΒΡΑΑΜ ΙСΑΑΚ ΝЄΜ ΠΙΘΜΗΙ ΠΙΝΙϢϯ СЄΝΟΥΘΙΟС	All the *souls* give them coolness in the dwelling of the *Virgins,*[10] Abraham, Isaac and Jacob, the righteous one the great Senuthius.

ⲱ ⲡⲉⲛⲟ̄ⲥ ⲓ̄ⲏ̄ⲥ ⲡⲭ̄ⲥ̄ ⲉⲑⲃⲉ ⲧⲉⲕⲙⲁⲩ ⲙⲡⲁⲣⲑⲉⲛⲟⲥ ⲁⲣⲉϥⲙⲉⲩⲓ ⲙⲡⲓⲉⲗⲁⲭⲓⲥ-ⲧⲟⲥ ⲱⲡⲧⲉⲛ ⲋⲱⲛ ⲛⲉⲙ ⲛⲉⲕⲡⲓⲥⲧⲟⲥ	Our Lord Jesus *Christ*, for your Mother the *Virgin*, remember the *humble* and count us also among Your *faithful*.

Psali of Adam for St. Shenoute to be recited on the first day of Kiahk, for the commemoration of the great saint St. Shenute the archimandrite.

ⲓ̄ⲏ̄ⲥ ⲡⲓⲙⲁⲓⲣⲱⲙⲓ ⲁϥⲥⲱⲧⲡ ⲙⲡⲓⲁⲓⲕⲉⲟⲥ ⲓⲥⲭⲉⲛ ⲧⲉϥⲙⲉⲧⲕⲟⲩⲭⲓ ⲡⲓⲉⲑⲟⲩⲁⲃ ⲥⲉⲛⲟⲩⲑⲓⲟⲥ	**Jesus the lover of mankind had chosen the *righteous one* since his childhood, the holy Senuthius.**
ⲛⲉⲛⲓⲟϯ ⲙⲙⲟⲛⲁⲭⲟⲥ ⲉⲩⲉⲣϣⲁⲓ ⲛⲁⲕ ⲕⲁⲗⲱⲥ ⲱ ⲡ̄ⲛ̄ⲁ̄ⲧⲟⲫⲟⲣⲟⲥ ⲡⲓⲉⲑⲟⲩⲁⲃ ⲥⲉⲛⲟⲩⲑⲓⲟⲥ	**Our fathers the *monks* will make well your feast, O *Pneumatophore*, the holy Senuthius.**
ⲱ ⲡⲉⲛⲛⲏⲃ ⲁⲣⲓ ⲫⲙⲉⲩⲓ ⲙⲡⲉⲕⲃⲱⲕ ⲛⲓⲕⲟⲩⲁⲓⲙⲟⲥ ⲟⲩⲟⲋ ⲭⲱ ⲛⲁϥ ⲛⲛⲉϥⲛⲟⲃⲓ ⲉⲑⲃⲉ ⲡⲓⲉⲑⲟⲩⲁⲃ ⲥⲉⲛⲟⲩⲑⲓⲟⲥ	O our Lord, remember your servant **Nicodemus**, and forgive him his sins for the (sake of the) holy Senuthius.

Commentary

The author of these psalis had no knowledge of the life of Shenoute, but he mentioned a few events concerning St. Shenoute that have been highlighted above in bold type.

1- In the first stanza, the author referred to what is known as the visions of Shenoute,[11] or the apocalypse of Shenoute.[12]
2- He highlighted that God had chosen St. Shenoute since his childhood.
3- He mentioned that St. Shenoute was a priest, and this aspect has been mentioned in the Arabic life, but without any details.[13]
4- The author of the psalis showed clearly that in his time the monastery of St. Shenoute was inhabited by monks.
5- Except for these aspects, the author knew nothing about the works and the deeds of St. Shenoute.
6- Nicodemus,[14] the author of the psalis, was from Upper Egypt, but spent most of his life in Cairo where he wrote the psalis. He attended

the feast of St. Shenoute (in the seventeenth /eighteenth centuries and so he applied the same psalm [Psalm 92[91] 10–11], which is recited during the liturgy.[15]

He adapted the response of the Gospel as a stanza in his psali.[16]

ΠΙ ΔΓΙΟϹ ϹΕΝΟΥΘΙΟϹ ΠΙ ΟΥΗΒ ΝΤΕ ⲫϯ ΕΤϬΟϹΙ ΕΤϨΕΝ ΠΕϤΑΡΙΜΟϹ ΝΑϹΤΙΟϹ ΕϤΜΕϨ ΝΟΥϨΗΤ ΝΑΤϬΟϹΙ	ΠΙ ΔΓΙΟϹ ϹΕΝΟΥΘΙΟϹ ΠΙ ΟΥΗΒ ΕΤϬΟϹΙ ΕΤϨΕΝ ΠΕϤΑΡΗΜΟϹ ΝΑϹΤΑΤΟϹ ΕϤΜΕϨ ΝΟΥΧΑΙ ΕΤϬΟϹΙ
The holy Senuthius, the priest the High God who is in his *beautiful wilderness* with a tireless burning heart.	*The holy* Senuthius, the high priest who is in his *beautiful wilderness* full of sublime salvation.

From what we can gather, one may assume that the author of the psalis applied their knowledge of the liturgical texts recited during the feast of St. Shenoute, to the life of the saint. In fact, these sentences taken from liturgical texts may be applied to any saint.

Historical data is very insufficient. These two psalis of fifty-six stanzas cannot be compared with the Doxology of St. Shenoute, which is nine stanzas.

Before concluding this section, one must ask an important question: why were the psalis only written in the seventeenth to eighteenth centuries?

In addition to laymen playing an active role during this period,[17] the seventeenth and eighteenth centuries saw a renaissance in the Coptic Orthodox Church, evident in the various building activities that took place during this time:

1- Many churches were built with a distinctive architectural style consisting of a square building containing up to twelve copulas[18] and three sanctuaries. Examples can be seen in churches such as the church of Amir Tadros in Old Cairo,[19] the church of Manyal Shihah,[20] the church of Tammouh,[21] the church of the Virgin Mary in Abu Far,[22] the church of the Virgin Mary in Oskor,[23] the church of the Apostles in Atfih,[24] the church of Mari Girgis in Ishnin al-Nasara,[25] the church of Dair al-Sanquriyah,[26] the church of St. Castor Bardanuha,[27] the church of St. Athanasius in Kufur al-Suliah (Matai),[28] the church of St. Pigol in Tallah,[29] the church of St. Kir and St. John in Manhari,[30] the church of Theodore in Abu Qurqas,[31] the church of the Angel in Hur,[32] the church of the Angel in Rayramun,[33] in addition to the church buildings in the Red Sea monasteries of St. Antony[34] and St. Paul.[35]

2- Refurbishment of ancient churches with wood art. We can mention as examples the outstanding wooden pulpit that can be seen in the church of Abu Sayfayn in Harit Zuwayla,[36] as well as the screens of the church of Abu Sayfayn in Old Cairo.[37]

3- These centuries also saw the emergence of a new school in Coptic icon writing. Amongst the leading iconographers were Ibrahim al-Nasikh[38] and Yuhanna al-Armani,[39] as well as Matari.[40]

4- The reappearance of wall-painting art after many centuries of disuse, such as those painted in the monastery of St. Paul near the Red Sea.[41]

5- The copying of manuscripts such as those from 'Dayr al-Adawiyyah.'[42]

6- The translation of several works from different languages, among them the works of Bar Hebraeus.[43]

7- The composition of theological books; such as those of Yusab, the Bishop of Girga.[44]

8- The composition of new liturgical texts in both the Coptic and Arabic languages; the authors are Nicodemus and Patriarch Mark VIII.[45]

9- The concoction of the Myron in A.D. 1703[46] by the patriarch John XVI after an interruption of 242 years.

10- The ceasing of persecutions.

11- Relations with Ethiopia—the patriarchs sent several letters containing sermons and doctrines.[47]

12- Relations with other denominations, including the Roman Catholic Church.

During the eighteenth century, the Roman Catholic Church tried to win over the Coptic Orthodox patriarch Pope John XVII (1726–1745) and his successor Mark (1745–1769) to the cause of the union. They were unsuccessful because joining the union meant becoming a 'Frank' (that is, an alien with French culture).[48]

There are two other psalis[49] written by the deacon Gabriel, as his name appears in the last stanza of the psali Batos.

ⲱ ⲡⲉⲛⲥⲱⲣ̅ ⲛⲁⲅⲁⲑⲟⲥ ⲉⲑⲃⲉ ⲧⲉⲕⲙⲁⲩ ⲥⲉⲛⲟⲩⲑⲓⲟⲥ ⲁⲣⲓ ⲫⲙⲉⲩⲓ ⲡ̅ⲥ̅ ⲙⲡⲉⲕⲃⲱⲕ ⲅⲁⲃⲣⲓⲏⲗ ⲡⲓⲇⲓⲁⲕⲱⲛ ϧⲉⲛ ⲧⲉⲕⲙⲉⲧⲟⲩⲣⲟ ⲛⲉⲙ ⲛⲓⲡⲓⲥⲧⲟⲥ	O our *Savior*, for the sake of Your mother and Senuthius remember O Lord your servant **Gabriel the *deacon*** in Your Kingdom, with the *faithful ones*.

And in the last stanza in the psali Adam:

ⲱ ⲡⲉⲛⲛⲏⲃ ⲁⲣⲓ ⲫⲙⲉⲩⲓ ⲙⲡⲉⲕⲃⲱⲕ ⲅⲁⲃⲣⲓⲏⲗ ⲛⲉⲙ ⲡⲥⲉⲡⲓ ⲛⲛⲓⲡⲓⲥⲧⲟⲥ ⲉⲑⲃⲉ ⲫⲏⲉⲑ̅ⲩ̅ ⲥⲉⲛⲟⲩⲑⲓⲟⲥ	O our Lord remember Your servant **Gabriel** and the rest of the *faithful* ones for (the sake of) the holy Senuthius.

Gabriel the deacon is also the author of a psali that concludes the *Theotokia* of Sunday during the month of Kihak. This psali is composed according to the reverse order of the Coptic alphabet as it ends with six stanzas; the initial letters of which spell the name of the author.[50] Gabriel had a sincere devotion to St. Shenoute, evident in the stanzas of the psali of Kihak.

ϩⲱⲃⲥ ⲉϫⲱⲓ ⲡⲁⲛⲟⲩϯ ϧⲉⲛ ⲧϧⲏⲓⲃⲓ ⲛⲧⲉⲕⲙⲉⲑⲛⲟⲩϯ ⲙ̀ⲫⲣⲏϯ ⲛⲁⲃⲃⲁ ϣⲉⲛⲟⲩϯ ⲛⲉⲙ ⲁⲃⲃⲁ ⲡⲁⲫⲛⲟⲩϯ	Cover me my God with the shadow of Your Divinity like Abba Shenoute and Abba Paphnoute.

The knowledge of Gabriel concerning the life of Shenoute is more than that of Nicodemus, as evident in the following:

ϫⲁⲡⲱϣⲓ ϧⲉⲛ ⲑⲙⲏϯ ⲛⲧⲥⲓⲛⲟⲇⲟⲥ ⲛⲧⲉ ⲛⲉⲛⲓⲟϯ ⲛⲟⲣⲑⲟⲇⲟϧⲟⲥ ⲱ ⲡⲉⲛⲓⲱⲧ ⲉⲑ̅ⲩ̅ ⲥⲉⲛⲟⲩⲑⲓⲟⲥ ⲕⲁⲧⲁ ⲡⲥⲁϫⲓ ⲙⲡⲉⲛⲓⲱⲧ ⲕⲩⲣⲓⲗⲗⲟⲥ	You are elevated in the midst of the *council* of our *Orthodox* fathers, our holy father Senuthius *according* to the word of our father Cyril.

However, this knowledge is not based on written texts but on oral tradition, which accounts for the confusion between Constantine and Theodosius, who was a contemporary of Shenoute:

| KOCTANTINOC ΠΙΜΑΙ ΠΧC ΑϥΝΑΥ ΕΠϢΟΥ ΝΝΙΜΟΝΑΧΟC ΜΑΛΙCΤΑ Ν2ΟΥΟ ΜΠΙΑΙΚΕΟC CΕΝΟΥΘΙΟC ΠΙΠΡΕCΒΥΤΕΡΟC | Constantine the God–loving one saw the glory of the monks, and *moreover* the *righteous* Senuthius *the priest.* |

Like Nicodemus, Gabriel used the previous liturgical works to compose his *psali,* and hence one finds that part of a stanza of the Adam *psali* is taken from the Doxology of St. Antony:

BⲰΛ ΕΒΟΛ ϪΕΝ ΝΕΤΕΝ2ΗΤ ΝΝΙΜΟΚΜΕΚ ΝΤΕ †ΚΑΚΙΑ	BⲰΛ ΕΒΟΛ ϪΕΝ ΝΕΤΕΝ2ΗΤ ΝΝΙΧΡΟϥ ΝΕΜ ΝΙ ΦΘΟΥΝΟC
Take out from your hearts the thoughts of evil.	Take out of your hearts guile and *jealousy.*

There are similarities in the works of Gabriel and Nicodemus, such as the prayer for those who have reposed in the second last stanza. While there are only three known psalis of Gabriel, it seems he may have been a contemporary of Nicodemus.

The Doxologies of St. Shenoute[51]

The author of the Coptic Doxology of St. Shenoute had access to a different version of the Coptic *Life of Shenoute.* We will show here some comparisons:

A- The Doxology Batos

The author of the *Doxology Batos* focuses on several events in the life of Shenoute. The first stanza is taken from the Bohairic **Life of Shenoute**:

Doxology[52]	Vita
ΝΘΟΚ ΟΥΜΑΚΑΡΙΟC ΠΕΝΙⲰΤ EΘY ΑΒΒΑ ϢΕΝΟΥ† ΧΕ ΑΚϢⲰΠΙ ΝΟΥΑΠΟCΤΟΛΟC ΟΥΟ2 ΜΠΡΟΦΗΤΗC ΕΥCΟΠ	ΝΕϥ2ΒΗΟΥΙ ΕΤΑΥϢⲰΠΙ ΕΒΟΛ2ΙΤΟΤϥ ΕΥΟΝΙ ΝΝΑ ΝΙΠΡΟΦΗΤΗC ΕΘΟΥΑΒ ΝΕΜ ΝΙΑΠΟCΤΟΛΟC ΝΤΕ ΠCC
You are *blessed,* O our holy father St. Shenoute, for you became an **apostle and also a prophet.**	The deeds ... which he did, resemble those of the **prophets and the apostles** of the Lord.[53]

ⲔⲈ ⲄⲀⲢ ⲀⲔⲤⲈⲘⲚⲒ ⲚⲞⲘⲞⲤ ⲚⲀⲚ ⲈⲚⲒ ⲀⲢⲈⲦⲎ ⲈⲦⲬⲎⲔ ⲈⲂⲞⲖ ⲀⲔⲀⲢⲈⳉ ⲈⲚⲒ ⲈⲚⲦⲞⲖⲎ ⲈⲦⲤⳋⲎⲞⲨⲦ ⳋⲈⲚ ⲠⲈⲨⲀⲄⲄⲈⲖⲒⲞⲚ	ⲞⲨⲞⳉ ⲀϤⲤⲈⲘⲚⲒ ⲚⳉⲀⲚⲔⲀⲚⲰⲚ ⲚⲚⲒⲘⲞⲚⲀⲬⲞⲤ ⲚⲀϤⲬⲰ ⲠⲈ ⲚⳉⲀⲚⲘⲎϢ ⲚⲈⳉⲎⲄⲒⲤⲒⲤ ⲈⲨⲘⲈⳉ ⲚⲈⲚⲦⲞⲖⲎ
You have set for us a *law* **of** perfect *virtues*, and kept the **commandments** written in the *Gospels*.	**You have set for us** *laws* **for** the *monks* and said many *exegesis* full of **commandments**.[54]

It seems that the following stanza refers to the story mentioned only in the Arabic version of the *Life*:

Doxology	Vita[55]
Ⲁ ⲠⲤⲐⲞⲒⲚⲞⲨϤⲒ ⲚⲦⲈ ⲚⲈϤⲀⲢⲈⲦⲎ ⳁⲘⲠⲞⲨⲚⲞϤ ⲚⲚⲈⲚⲮⲨⲬⲎ ⲘⲪⲢⲎⳁ ⲘⲠⲒ ⲀⲢⲰⲘⲀⲦⲀ ⲈⲦⲢⲎⲦ ⳋⲈⲚ ⲠⲒⲠⲀⲢⲀⲆⲒⲤⲞⲤ	
The incense of his *virtues* delighted our *souls*, like the blossomed *aroma*, the *paradise*	One day a monk gave to Shenoute an apple, the fruit of paradise, which he received from heaven. Shenoute planted the seeds which bore fruit.

The following stanzas of the *Doxology* refer to another tradition not reported in the Coptic *Vita*, however, the beginning and the end are similar:

Doxology	Vita[56]
ⲀⲖⲎⲐⲰⲤ ⲀⲔϬⲒⲤⲒ ⲈⲘⲀϢⲰ ⳋⲈⲚ ⲐⲘⲎⳁ ⲚⳁⲤⲨⲚⲞⲆⲞⲤ ⲚⲦⲈ ⲚⲈⲚⲒⲞⳁ ⲚⲞⲢⲐⲞⲆⲞⳅⲞⲤ ⳋⲈⲚ ⳁⲠⲞⲖⲒⲤ ⲈⲪⲈⲤⲞⲤ	ⲀⲤϢⲰⲠⲒ ⲆⲈ ⲞⲚ ⲚⲞⲨⲤⲎⲞⲨ ⲈⲐⲢⲞⲨⲐⲰⲞⲨⳁ ⲈⳁⲤⲨⲚⲞⲆⲞⲤ ⲚⳉⲈ ⲚⲈⲚⲒⲞⳁ ⲈⲐⲞⲨⲀⲂ ⲈⲨⲢⲞⲨⲈⲢⲔⲀⲐⲈⲢⲒⲚ
ⲀⲔⳁϢⲒⲠⲒ ⲚⲚⲈⲤⲦⲞⲢⲒⲞⲤ ⲠⲒⲠⲀⲦⲢⲒⲀⲢⲬⲎⲤ ⲚⲀⲤⲈⲂⲎⲤ ⲞⲨⲞⳉ ⲀⲔⲈⲢⲞⲘⲞⲖⲞⲄⲒⲚ Ⲛ ⳁⲞⲘⲞⲖⲞⲄⲒⲀ ⲈⲐⲚⲀⲚⲈϤ	ⲘⲠⲒ ⲀⲤⲈⲂⲎⲤ ⲚⲈⲤⲦⲞⲢⲒⲞⲤ

ϢEN OYMETOYAI NϯTPIAC NPEϤTANϢO NOYMOOCIOC ϢIⲰT NEM ΠϢHPI NEM ΠIⲠⲚⲀ ⲈⲐⲨ Ⲅ NPAN OYNOYϯ NOYⲰT	
OYOϨ AKCⲰTEM ETCMH ECⲰϢ EBOⲖϢEN TϢE EϤXⲰ MMOC XE AYEPAΓIAZIN MMOϤ CENOYΘIOC NAPXHMANAPITHC	OYOϨ NAYⲰϢ EBOⲖ THPOY NXE NAϮCYNOⲆOC XE AϮIOC AϮIOC AϮIOC APXHMANTPITHC
Truly you were greatly exalted in the midst of the *council* of our *orthodox* fathers, in the *city* of Ephesus.	I happened at the time when our holy fathers assembled at the *Synod* in order to condemn the impious Nestorius.
You put to shame Nestorius, the *impious patriarch*, and you have *confessed* the good *confession*: "One in [essence] is the *Trinity*, *consubstantial* and life-giving, the Father, the Son and the Holy *Spirit*, three names—one God.	
And you heard the voice from heaven, proclaiming and saying: "You are *sanctified* O Shenoute the *archimandrite*."	And those of the *synod* sung: "*Worthy, worthy, worthy O archimandrite*."

The resemblance to Moses is mentioned in Shenoute's *Vita* as well as his conversations with Christ:

Doxology	**Vita**[57]
ⲰOYNIATK Ⲱ ΠIⲆIKEOC ABBA ϢENOYϯ ΠI APXHMANAPITHC XE NΘOK AKCAXI NEM ΠⲬⲤ MϢPHϯ MMⲰYCHC ΠINOMOCITHC	XE A ΠⲞⲤ EPXAPIZECΘE NHI MΠA2I MMⲰYCHC ΠAPXHΠPOϢHTHC ACϢⲰΠI ⲆE ON NOYE2OOY EϤ2EMCI NXE ΠENIⲰT AΠA ϢENOYϯ ϢATEN ΠI ⲖAK2 MΠETPA NΘOϤ NEM ΠENⲞⲤ ⲦHC ΠⲬⲤ EYCAXI NEM NOYEPHOY

| Blessed are you O *righteous* Abba Shenoute the *archimandrite*, for you spoke with *Christ* like Moses the *Law-giver*. | For the Lord has *granted* to me (Shenoute) the age of Moses the *great prophet*.
It happened one day that our father was sitting next to the corner of the rock speaking together with our Lord Jesus Christ.[58]
It happened one day that our father was sitting next to our Lord Jesus Christ speaking together.[59] |

B- The Doxology Adam

There are two hymns included in the book of glorifications.[60]

ΜΠΕ ΠΑΙⲰΤ ϢΕΝΟΥϯ ⲤⲰⲂⲒ ΕΝΕ2 ΝΑΥ ΕΡΟΚ ⲬⲤⲰⲂⲒ ΜⲪΟΟΥ ϯΠΑΡΑΚΑⲖΙΝ ΜΜΟΚ ΜΑΤΑΜΟΙ ΕΠΙΜΥⲤΤΥΡΙΟΝ	My father Shenoute, I never saw you laughing. You are laughing today, I *beg* you my father inform me of this *secret*.
ΠΑΡΑⲖΕⲜ 2ΗΠΠΕ ΑϥΟΥⲰϢ ⲚϪΕ ΚⲰⲤΤΑΝΤΙΝΟⲤ ΠΟⲖΙⲤ ΕΙΡΙ ΝΟΥ2ΑΠ ΝΑΙΚΕΟⲤ Ⲁ Ⲫϯ ΝΤΕ ΤⲪΕ ΡΑϢΙ ΕⲬⲰϥ	*Paralexis* Behold, Constantine (the *city*) wished to judge with *justice* and God of Heaven rejoiced.
Ⲁ Π ΟΥΡΟ ΚⲰⲤΤΑΝΤΙΝΟⲤ ΠΟⲖΙⲤ ΙΡΙ ΝΟΥΕ2ΟΟΥ ΜΜΙⲤΙ ΚΑΤΑ ΤⲤΥΝΙΘΙΑ ΝΝΙΟΥΡⲰΟΥ	King Constantine (the *city*) wished to celebrate the birthday *according to* the *custom* of the kings.
ΑϥΟΥⲰΡΠ ΑϥΘⲰΟΥϯ ΝΝΕϥⲆΥΝΑΤΟⲤ ΝΙ ⲬⲰΡΙ ΝΤΕ ΤΕϥΜΕΤΟΥΡΟ ΑϥⲤΟΒϯ ΝⲰΟΥ ΝΤΕϥⲤΙ ⲰΟΥΝΙ ΝΤΟΥⲬⲰΚΕΜ ΜΠΑΤΟΥ2ΕΜⲤΙ	He sent to assemble the *mighty* strong (men) of his kingdom, he prepared for them his bath in order that they wash before sitting.
ΕΤΑΥϢΕΝⲰΟΥ ϢΑϯⲤΙ ⲰΟΥΝΙ ΑΠΟΥΡΟ ΤⲰΝϥ ΑϥϢΕ ΝΕΜⲰΟΥ ⲬΕ ΜΗΠⲰⲤ ΝⲤΕΜΕΥΙ ΕΡΟϥ ⲬΕ ΟΥΟΝ ΟΥΠ- ⲚⲀ̅ ΜΜΕΤ6ΑⲤ2ΗΤ ΝΕΜΑϥ	When they went to the bath the king arose with them *lest* they think that he is possessed with the *spirit* of arrogance.

ЄΤΑ ΠΟΥΡΟ ϢЄ ϢΑ †СΙ ϢΟΥΝΙ ΑϥΧΟΥϢΤ ΑϥΝΑΥ ЄΠΙΠΑΡΑΧΙΤΗС ЄΡЄ ΟΥϢϢΝΙ СΑϨΟΥΝ ΜΜΟϥ Α ΠЄϥΗΤ ΜΚΑϨ ЄϨΡΗΙ ЄΧϢϥ	When the king arrived to the bath he looked and saw the *bath attendant* had a burn, and his heart was sad.
ΜΠΙΝΑΥ ЄΡΟΚ ЄΚСϢΒΙ ЄΝЄϨ ΠϢС ΑΚСϢΒΙ ϨЄΝ ΠΑΙ ЄϨΟΟΥ ΠЄΧЄ ΒΙСΑ ΠΙΜΑΘΗΤΗС ЄϥСΧΙ ΝЄΜ ΑΒΒΑ ϢЄΝΟΥ†	I never saw you laughing, *how* is it that you are laughing today, said Besa the *disciple* while talking with Abba Shenoute.
СϢΤЄΜ ΠΑϢΗΡΙ ΟΥϨϢΒ ΝϢϕΗΡΙ ΟΥϨΑΠ ΜΜΗΙ ЄΤΑ ΠΟΥΡΟ ΑΙϥ ΧЄ Αϥ† ΜΠΙΠΑΡΑΧΙΤΗС Є†ΜЄΤΝΙϢ† ΝСΤΡΑΤΙΑΑΤΗС	Listen my son to an amazing thing, a right judgement which the King did, for he gave the *bath attendant* the greatness of a *general*.
†ΒΙΡ ΝЄΜ †С2ΙΜΙ ΜΠΙΠΑΡΑΧΙΤΗС ΑϥΤΗΙ ΤΟΥ ΜΠΙСΤΡΑΤΙΑΑΤΗС Α ϕ† ΝΜ ΝΙ ΑΓΓЄΛΟС ΡΑϢΙ ΑΝΟΚ ϨϢ† ΝΤΑΡΑϢΙ	The [basket] with the woman of the *bath attendant*, he gave them to the *general* God with the *angels* are happy so I should be happy.
ΤϢΒϨ ΠΑϬ͞С ΝΙ ϢΤ ΝΑСΚΥΤΗС ΑΒΒΑ ϢЄΝΟΥ† ΠΙ ΑΡΧΗΜΑΝΑΡΙΤΗС ΝΤЄϥΧΑ	Pray our lord father the ascetic man Abba Shenoute the *archimandrite*, so that . . . .

Commentary

1- This story did not survive in the Bohairic or the Ethiopian *Vita*.[61] The Arabic *Life of Shenoute* and the Sahidic version are fragmentary.

2- The birthday of the kings always relates to the wicked kings such as Pharaoh (Genesis 40:20) and Herod (Matthew 14:6). It appears occasionally in the Coptic martyrdom such as that of Epima, where we find that the boat of the saints arrived on the birthday of the kings.[62] It is amazing to have this theme for a pious king (Constantine/Theodosius).

3- The theme of the bath is frequent in Coptic martyrdoms, so that, "The governor went to the bath," as in the story of Panesnew,[63] Epima,[64] Shenoufe,[65] Macarius of Antioch,[66] and Claudius of Antioch.[67]

Going to the bath is considered as an act against asceticism. Constantine of Asyut, while praising St. Athanasius, mentioned among virtuous deeds: "fasting . . . and not taking a bath."[68] In the *Life of John of Lycopolis* it mentions how sedition started in the bath during the reign of Theodosius.[69] The *Life of Severus of Antioch* mentions that from the time he became a monk he never entered the bathhouse until his last days.[70] It is therefore unique to find this Doxology intertwining the two themes (the birthday of the king and the bath) in such a positive way.

The Second Doxology Adam

ⲑⲱⲟⲩϯ ⲧⲏⲣⲟⲩ ⲙⲫⲟⲟⲩ ⲱ ⲛⲓ ⲭⲣⲓⲥⲧⲓⲁⲛⲟⲥ ϩⲓⲛⲁ ⲛⲧⲉⲛϯⲱⲟⲩ ⲙⲡⲉⲛⲟ̅ⲥ̅ ⲓ̅ⲏ̅ⲥ̅ ⲡ̅ⲭ̅ⲥ̅	Assemble O all *Christians* today in order to glorify our Lord Jesus Christ.
ⲟⲩⲟϩ ⲛⲧⲉⲛⲧⲁⲓⲟ ⲙⲡⲉⲛⲓ ⲱⲧ ⲛⲇⲓ ⲕⲉⲟⲥ ⲁⲃⲃⲁ ϣⲉⲛⲟⲩϯ ⲡⲓ ϣⲫⲏⲣ ⲛⲛⲓ ⲁⲅⲅⲉⲗⲟⲥ	And to honor our father the *righteous* Abba Shenoute the friend of the *angels*.
ⲟⲩⲟϩ ⲛⲧⲉⲛⲱϣ ⲉⲃⲟⲗϧⲉⲛ ϩⲁⲛⲥⲙⲏ ⲛⲑⲉⲗⲏⲗ ϫⲉ ⲭⲉⲣⲉ ⲁⲃⲃⲁ ϣⲉⲛⲟⲩϯ ⲡⲓ ⲁⲣⲭⲓ ⲙⲁⲛⲇⲣⲓ ⲧⲏⲥ	And to sing with a joyful voice: *Hail Abba Shenoute the archimandrite!*
ϯ ϩⲓ ⲣⲏⲛⲏ ⲛⲁⲕ ⲙⲫⲟⲟⲩ ⲡⲉⲛⲓⲱⲧ ⲁⲃⲃⲁ ϣⲉⲛⲟⲩϯ ⲡⲓ ⲁⲣⲭⲓ ⲙⲁⲛⲇⲣⲓ ⲧⲏⲥ ⲫⲁ ⲡⲓ ⲧⲱⲟⲩ ⲛⲁⲑⲣⲓ ⲡⲓ	*Peace* be with you today O our father Abba Shenoute the *archimandrite*, who has the desert of Atripe.
ϯ ϩⲓ ⲣⲏⲛⲏ ⲛⲁⲕ ⲙⲫⲟⲟⲩ ⲡⲓⲛⲓ ⲱϯ ⲙⲡⲣⲟⲫⲏⲧⲏⲥ ⲡⲓ ⲙⲉⲛⲣⲓ ⲧ ⲛⲧⲉ ⲛⲏⲉⲑ̅ⲩ̅	*Peace* is with you today O great *prophet* the beloved of the saints!
ϯ ϩⲓ ⲣⲏⲛⲏ ⲛⲁⲕ ⲙⲫⲟⲟⲩ ⲡⲓ ⲙⲁϩ ⲃ̅ ⲙⲙⲱⲩⲥⲏⲥ ⲫⲏⲉⲧⲁⲩϯⲣⲉⲛϥ ϫⲉ ⲏⲗⲓⲁⲥ ⲙⲃⲉⲣⲓ ϫⲉ ⲁⲕⲧⲉⲛⲑⲱⲛⲕ ⲉⲣⲟϥ	*Peace* be with you today the second Moses, who was called the new Elijah for you resembled him.
ϯ ϩⲓ ⲣⲏⲛⲏ ⲛⲁⲕ ⲙⲫⲟⲟⲩ ⲡⲓ ⲣⲉϥⲥⲉⲙⲛⲉ ⲛⲟⲙⲟⲥ ⲛⲛⲓ ⲙⲟⲛⲁⲭⲟⲥ ⲛⲉⲙ ⲛⲓ ⲕⲟⲥⲙⲓ ⲕⲟⲛ	*Peace* is with you today, who provides a *law* for the *monk*, and for the *worldly* (men).
ϯ ϩⲓ ⲣⲏⲛⲏ ⲛⲁⲕ ⲙⲫⲟⲟⲩ ⲫⲏⲉⲧⲁϥⲉⲣⲭⲓⲛⲓⲟⲣ ⲙⲡⲓ ⲗⲁⲅⲟⲥ ⲛⲧⲉ ⲫⲓⲟⲙ ⲭⲱⲣⲓⲥ ϫⲟⲓ	*Peace* is with you today, who crossed the *deep* sea *without* a ship.
ϯ ϩⲓ ⲣⲏⲛⲏ ⲛⲁⲕ ⲙⲫⲟⲟⲩ ⲡⲉⲛⲓⲱⲧ ⲁⲃⲃⲁ ϣⲉⲛⲟⲩϯ ⲛⲉⲙ ⲡⲉⲕϫⲓⲛⲉⲣⲁⲡⲁⲧⲁⲛ ⲙⲡⲉⲕⲟ̅ⲥ̅ ⲛⲕⲁⲗⲱⲥ	*Peace* is with you today our father Abba Shenoute and your *good meeting* with your Lord.

ⲱ ⲫⲎⲈⲦⲀ ⲠⲬⲤ ⲈⲢⲬⲀⲒⲢⲈⲤⲐⲈ ⲚⲀϤ ⲘⲘⲀ2Ⲓ ⲘⲘⲰⲨⲤⲎⲤ ⲠⲒⲚⲒⲰϯ ⲘⲠⲢⲞⲫⲎⲦⲎⲤ	O that one whom *Christ granted* to him the power of Moses the great *prophet*!
ⲱ ⲫⲎⲈⲦⲀϤⲈⲚⲔⲞⲦ ⳍⲈⲚ ⲠϢⲰⲚⲒ ⲘⲠⲈϤⲘⲞⲨ ⲈⲢⲈ ⲚⲎⲈⲐⲞⲨⲀⲂ ⲐⲎⲢⲞⲨ ⲞⲒ ⲚⲬⲀⲞⲘ ⲈⲢⲞϤ	O who rested in the sickness of his death while all the saints were crowning him!
ⲠⲈⲬⲎⲒ ⲬⲈ ⲀⲂⲂⲀ ⲠⲒϢⲰⲒ ⲠⲀⲒⲰⲦ ⲀⲚⲦⲰⲚⲒ ⲚⲈⲘ ⲀⲂⲂⲀ ⲠⲀⳍⲰⲘ ⲀⲘⲞⲚⲒ ⲚⲦⲀⲬⲒⲬ 2ⲒⲚⲀ ⲚⲦⲀⲞⲨⲰϢⲦ ⲘⲠⲀ6Ⲥ ⲒⲎⲤ ⲫⲎⲈⲦⲀ ⲦⲀⲯⲨⲬⲎ ⲘⲈⲚⲢⲒ ⲦϤ ⲈⲘⲀϢⲰ	I said: O Abba Pishoi, my father Antony and Abba Pachom stretch out my hand *in order that* I may prostrate before my Lord Jesus, whom my *soul* extremely loves.
ⲈⲦⲀⲔϯ ⲘⲠⲒ ⲠⲚⲀ ⲈⲚⲈⲚⲬⲒⲬ ⲘⲠ6Ⲥ ⲀϤⲞⲖϤ ⲈⲠϢⲰⲒ ⲚⲈⲘⲀϤ ⲈⲚⲈϤⲘⲀⲚⲈⲘⲦⲞⲚ	When you gave *up your* spirit in the hand of the Lord, He took you with Him in His resting places.
2Ⲓ ⲦⲈⲚ ⲚⲒ ⲈⲨⲬⲎ ⲚⲦⲈ ⲠⲈⲚⲒⲰⲦ ⲚⲀⲤⲔⲨⲦⲎⲤ ⲀⲂⲂⲀ ϢⲈⲚⲞⲨϯ ⲠⲒ ⲀⲢⲬⲎⲘⲀⲚⲀⲢⲒ ⲦⲎⲤ Ⲡ6Ⲥ ⲀⲢⲒ 2ⲘⲞⲦ	Through the *prayers* of our father *the ascetic* Abba Shenoute the *archimandrite*, *may the* Lord grant . . . .

Commentary

This doxology stresses several points such as the comparison between Shenoute on the one hand and Moses and Elijah on the other, which also occurs in the Sahidic *Alphabeticon* (Acrostic hymn).

The stanza concerning the repose: "I said: O St. Pishoi, my father Antony and St. Pachom . . . " is taken directly from the Bohairic *Life of Shenoute*.

Conclusion

The comparison between the psalis and the doxologies shows that the doxologies are an important source on the *Life of Shenoute*.

The psalis are of late dates. They are attributed to Nicodemus of the seventeenth to eighteenth centuries and Gabriel who was also a contemporary of Nicodemus. The authors of the psalis did not have firsthand knowledge of the life of Shenoute.

This paper demonstrates once more the importance of the book of Glorifications as a source and witness of Coptic literary texts.

Appendix

Psali Batos

ⲀⲢⲈⲌ ⲈⲢⲞⲚ Ⲱ ⲠⲬⲤ ⲠⲈⲚⲞⲨϮ ⲌⲒ ⲦⲈⲚ ⲚⲒⲠⲢⲈⳡⲂⲨⲀ ⲚϮⲠⲢⲞⳤⲦⲀⲦⲎⳤ ⲘⲀⲢⲒⲀ ⲐⲘⲀⲨ ⲘⲠⲬⲤ ⲠⲈⲚⲚⲞⲨϮ ⲚⲈⲘ ⲀⲂⲂⲀ ⳈⲈⲚⲞⲨϮ ⲠⲀⲢⲬⲒⲘⲀⲚⲀⲢⲒⲦⲎⳤ	Preserve us, *O Christ* our God, by the *intercessions* of the *protectress* Mary the mother of *Christ* our God and St. Shenoute the *archimandrite*.
ⲂⲞⲚ ⲞⲨⲦⲀⲒⲞ ⲈⲢⲠⲢⲈⲠⲒ ⲚⲀϤ ⲠⲒ ⳡⲪⲎⲢ ⲚⲚⲒⲀⲠⲞⳤⲦⲞⲖⲞⳤ ⲞⲨⲞⲌ ⲞⲚ ⳤⲈⲈⲢⳡⲀⲒ ⲚⲀϤ ⲈⲦⲈ ⲪⲀⲒ ⲠⲈ ⳤⲈⲚⲞⲨⲐⲒⲞⳤ	The honor *is worthy* to him, the friend of the *Apostles* and also he is commemorated, that is, Senuthius.
ⲄⲈ ⲄⲀⲢ ⲠⲒⲚⲒⳡⲦ ⳤⲈⲚⲞⲨⲐⲒⲞⳤ ⲠⲒ ⲞⲨⲎⲂ ⲠⲒ ⲀⲢⲬⲎⲘⲀⲚⲀⲢⲒⲦⲎⳤ ⲀϤⳤⲀⳒⲒ ⲚⲈⲘ ⲠⲞⲨⲢⲞ ⲠⲬⳤ ⲘⲪⲢⲎϮ ⲘⲘⳠⲤⲎⳤ ⲠⲒ ⲚⲞⲘⲞⲐⲈⲒⲦⲎⳤ	*For the great Senuthius, the priest the archimandrite, spoke with Christ the king like Moses the Lawgiver.*
ⲀⲀⲨⲒⲀ ⲠⲞⲨⲢⲞ ⲠⲒ ⲐⲘⲎⲒ ⲀϤⳤⲀⳒⲒ ⲬⲈ ⲠⲒ ⲐⲘⲎⲒ ⲈϤⲈⲪⲒⲢⲒ ⳘⲈⲚ ⲠⲎⲒ ⲘⲠ⳪ ⲘⲪⲢⲎϮ ⲘⲠⲒ ⳡⲈⲚⳠϤⲒ ⲈⲦⲈ ⲪⲀⲒ ⲠⲈ ⳤⲈⲚⲞⲨⲐⲒⲞⳤ	David the righteous king said: "The righteous shall flourish like a cedar in the house of the Lord[71]" who is Senuthius.
ⲈϤⲈⳡⲰⲠⲒ ⲚⲬⲈ ⲠⲒ ⲐⲘⲎⲒ ⲀⲈ ⲞⲚ ⲈⲨⲘⲈⲨⲒ ⲈⲚⲈⲌ ⲀⲖⲎⲐⲰⳤ ⲚⲐⲞⲔ Ⲱ ⲀⲒⲔⲈⲞⲚ ⲀⲔ⳪Ⲓ ⲘⲠⲒ ⲰⲚⳠ ⲚⲈⲚⲈⲌ	"The righteous will be ever mindful.[72]" *Truly* you O *righteous* deserved[73] eternal life.
ⲌⲈⲞⳡ ⲚⲈ ⲚⲈⲔⲠⲞⲖⲎⲦⲒⲀ Ⲱ ⲠⲒ ⲚⲒⳡⲦ ⳤⲈⲚⲞⲨⲐⲒⲞⳤ ⲚⲈⲘ ⲦⲈⲔⲬⲞⲌ ⲚⳤⲀ ⲦⲈⲔⲀⲄⲚⲒⲀ Ⲱ ⲠⲒ ⳡⲪⲎⲢ ⲚⲦⲈ ⲪϮ ⲠⲒ ⲖⲞⲄⲞⳤ	Numerous are your *virtues* O great Senuthius, and your zeal for *chastity* O friend of God the *Word*.
ⲎⲠⲠⲈ ⲀⲚⲞⲚ ⲦⲈⲚⲈⲢⳡⲀⲒ ⲚⲀⲔ ⳘⲈⲚ ⲌⲀⲚϮⲀⲀⲘⲞⳤ ⲚⲈⲘ ⲌⲀⲚⲌⲰⳤ ⲈⲚⲰⳡ ⲈⲂⲞⲖ ⲬⲈ ⲬⲈⲢⲈ ⲚⲀⲔ Ⲱ ⲠⲒ ⲚⲒⳡⲦ ⳤⲈⲚⲞⲨⲐⲒⲞⳤ	Lo, we commemorate you with psalms and odes, saying: "*Hail* to you O great Senuthius."
ⲐⲈⲖⲎⲖ ⲘⲪⲞⲞⲨ Ⲱ ⲦⲬⲰⲢⲀ ⲚⲬⲎⲘⲒ ⲚⲈⲘ ⲠⲒ ⲖⲀⲞⳤ ⲚⲦⲈ ⲚⲒⲠⲒ ⳤⲦⲞⳤ ⳠⲈⲚ Ⲡ ⳡⲀⲒ ⲘⲠⲒ ⲢⲈϤⲈⲢ ⲌⲈⲘⲒ ⲠⲒ ⲀⲄⲒⲞⳤ ⳤⲈⲚⲞⲨⲐⲒⲞⳤ	Rejoice today, O *country* of Egypt with the *faithful people*, in the feast of the guide the holy Senuthius.

Ī̄H̄C̄ ΠX̄C̄ ΠΙ ΔΗΜΙΟΥΡΓΟС ΑϤΤΑΜΟΚ ΕΠΙΜΥCTHΡΙΟΝ ϧΕΝ ΝΙ ϧΛΕ ΝΝΙΧΡΟΝΟС Ꞷ ΠΙ ΝΙϢϮ ϧΕΝ ΠΕϤΑΓꞶΝ	**Jesus** *Christ the Creator,* informed **you** about the *mysteries* of the end *of* (all) *ages;* ***O Great in his struggles.***
ΚΥΡΙΟС ΑϤСꞶΤΠ ΜΠΙ ΑΓΙΟС ΙСΧΕΝ ΤΕϤΜΕΤΚΟΥΧΙ ΚΑΛꞶС ΠΙ ΟΥΗΒ ΜΜΗΙ СΕΝΟΥΘΙΟС ΠΙ Ϣ϶ΗΡ ΝΝΙ ΑΓΓΕΛΟС	*The Lord* had *well* chosen the *holy* one since his childhood; ***O true priest Senuthius, the friend of the angels.***
ΛΑΟС ΝΙΒΕΝ ΝΟΡΘΟΔΟ϶ΟС ΕΥΕΡΧꞶΡΕΥΙΝ ΜΠΕΝΙꞶΤ ΠΙΝΙϢϮ ΠΙ СꞶΤΠ ΠΙ ΠΝΕΥΜΑΤΟϤΟΡΟС ΠΙ ΑСΚΗΤΗС ΑΒΒΑ ϢΕΝΟΥϮ	All the *orthodox people will commemorate* our father, the great chosen *spirit-bearer,* the *hermit* Abba Shenoute.
ΜΑΡΕΝΘꞶΟΥϮ Ꞷ ΝΑΜΕΝΡΑϮ ΝΤΕΝΤΑΙΟ ΜΠΙ ΑСΚΗΤΗС ΠΙ ΟΥΗΒ ΝΤΕ ϤϮ ϢΕΝΟΥϮ ΠΙ СꞶΤΠ ΠΙ ΑΡΧΗΜΑΝΔΡΙΤΗС	Let us assemble, O beloved, in order to honor the *hermit,* God's priest, Shenoute, the chosen *archimandrite.*
ΝΑΙ ΝΑΝ ΟΥΟ2 СꞶΤΕΜ ΕΡΟΝ ΝΑ2ΜΕΝ ΕΒΟΛ϶ΕΝ ΝΙ ΔΙꞶΓΜΟС ꞶΛΙ ΜΠΕΚΧꞶΝΤ ΕΒΟΛ2ΑΡΟΝ ΕΘΒΕ ΠΙ ΕΘΟΥΑΒ СΕΝΟΥΘΙΟС	Have compassion upon us and listen to us, save us from *persecutions,* take away Your anger from us, for (the sake of) the holy Senuthius.
϶СΜΑΡꞶΟΥΤ Ꞷ ΠΕΝΝΗΒ ΠX̄C̄ ΝΕΜ ΠΕΚΙꞶΤ ΝΑΓΑΘΟС ΝΕΜ ΠΕΚ⎯Π⎯Ν⎯Α⎯ ΜΠΑΡΑΚΛΗΤΟС ΝΑΙ ΝΑΝ ΕΘΒΕ СΕΝΟΥΘΙΟС	You are blessed, O our Lord *Christ,* and Your Good Father, and Your *Spirit the comforter,* have mercy upon us for (the sake of) Senuthius.
ΟΥΝΙϢϮ ΠΕ ΠΤΑΙΟ ΝΝΙ ΑΓΙΟС ΜΑΛΙСΤΑ ΠΙ СꞶΤΠ ΝΑСΚΥΤΗС ϤΗΕΤ2ΕΜСΙ ΝΕΜ ΠΟΥΡΟ ΠX̄C̄ ΑΒΒΑ ϢΕΝΟΥϮ ΠΙ ΑΡΧΗΜΑΝΔΡΙΤΗС	Great is the honor of the *saints, moreover* the chosen *hermit,* who sat with *Christ* the king, Abba Shenoute the *archimandrite.*
ΠΙ ΑΓΙΟС СΕΝΟΥΘΙΟС ΠΙ ΟΥΗΒ ΝΤΕ ϤϮ ΕΤСΟСΙ ΕΤ϶ΕΝ ΠΕϤΑΡΙΜΟС ΝΑСΤΙΟС ΕϤΜΕ2 ΝΟΥ2ΗΤ ΝΑΤϬΟСΙ	*The holy* Senuthius, the priest of the High God who is in his *beautiful wilderness*[74] with a tireless burning heart.[75]
ΡΑϢΙ ΘΕΛΗΛ Ꞷ ΝΙ ΜΟΝΑΧΟС ΕΤ϶ΕΝ ΠΙ ΜΟΝΑСΤΗΡΙΟΝ ΝΤΕ ΠΕΝΙꞶΤ СΕΝΟΥΘΙΟС ΠΙ ΔΙ ΚΕΟС ΠΙ ΤΕΛΙΟΝ	**Rejoice and be happy, O** *monks* **of the** *monastery* **of our father Senuthius, the** *perfect righteous one.*

COMC OYO2 CWTEM ЄPON W ПENCWTHP NAΓΛΘOC WΛI MПEKXWNT ЄBOΛ2ΑPON ЄΘBЄ ПINIWϯ CЄNOYΘIOC	Look and listen to us, O our *good Saviour*, take away from us Your anger for the (sake of the) great Senuthius.
TЄNTWB2 MMOK ЄΘBЄ NIMWOY NЄM NICIϯ NЄM NIKΑPПOC NЄM NIMOYN2WOY CMOY ЄPWOY ЄΘBЄ ПIЄΘOYΑB CЄNOYΘIOC	We beseech you, concerning the waters, the plants, the fruits and the rain, bless them, for the (sake of the) holy Senuthius.
ȲC ΘC ΑPЄ2 ЄNЄNIOϯ NЄM NЄNCNHOY NIΔIΑKONOC NΑ2MOY ПЄNNHB ЄBOΛ2Α 2Oϯ NЄM NI2OX2ЄX NTЄ ПΑIKOCMOC	Guard, *O Son of God*, our fathers and our brethren the *deacons*, save them our Lord from fear and distress in this *world*.
ФNHB ϕϯ ПЄNBOHΘOC ϬICI MПTΑП NNIXPICTIΑNOC 2ITЄN NIϯ2O NTΘЄOTOKOC NЄM ПIΘMHI ПINIWϯ CЄNOYΘIOC	Lord God our *Helper*, exalt the horn of the *Christians*[76] through the demands of the *Theotokos* and the righteous one the great Senuthius.
XЄPЄ NЄ W ϯПΑPΘЄNOC MΑPIΑ ΘMΑY MПIΔЄCПOTHC XЄPЄ ПINIWϯ NΘЄOФOPOC ΑBBΑ WЄNOYϯ ПIΑPXHMΑNΑPITHC	Hail to the *Virgin* Mary the mother of the *Lord*, Hail to the great *theophore* Abba Shenoute the *archimandrite*.
ϮYXH NIBЄN MOI NWOY NOYXBOB ϬЄN ФMΑNWWПI NNIПΑPΘЄNOC NЄM ΑBPΑΑM ICΑΑK NЄM ПIΘMHI ПINIWϯ CЄNOYΘIOC	All the *souls* give them coolness in the dwelling of the *Virgins*,[77] Abraham, Isaac and Jacob, and the righteous one the great Senuthius.
W ПЄNŌC IHC ПX̄C ЄΘBЄ TЄKMΑY MПΑPΘЄNOC ΑPЄФMЄYI MПIЄΛΑXICTOC WПTЄN 2WN NЄM NЄKПICTOC	Our Lord Jesus *Christ*, for (the sake of) your Mother the *Virgin*, remember the *humble* and count us also among your *faithful*.

Psali of Adam

ⲀⲒⲦⲰⲂⲎ ⲘⲘⲞⲔ ⲠⲀϬⲤ ⲬⲰ ⲚⲎⲒ ⲈⲂⲞⲖ Ⲱ ⲠⲒⲀⲄⲀⲐⲞⲤ ⲈⲐⲂⲈ ϮⲐⲈⲞⲦⲞⲔⲞⲤ ⲚⲈⲘ ⲠⲒ ⲈⲐⲞⲨⲀⲂ ⲤⲈⲚⲞⲨⲐⲒⲞⲤ	I pray to you O Lord to forgive me O *Good One*, for the (sake of the) *Theotokos* and the holy Senuthius.
ⲂⲞⲎⲐⲒⲚ ⲈⲢⲞⲒ ⲠⲞⲤ Ⲱ ⲠⲬⲤ ⲠⲈⲚⲚⲞⲨϮ ⲈⲐⲂⲈ ⲦⲈⲔⲘⲀⲨ ⲦⲀϬⲤ ⲚⲈⲘ ⲠⲒ ⲐⲘⲎⲒ ϢⲈⲚⲞⲨϮ	*Help* me Lord O *Christ* our God, for (the sake of) Your mother my Lady, and the righteous Shenoute.
ⲄⲈ ⲄⲀⲢ ⲚⲐⲞϥ ⲀϤϬⲒⲤⲒ ϦⲈⲚ ⲚⲒⲀⲄⲒⲞⲤ ϤⲀ ⲠⲒⲤⲰⲒⲦ ⲈⲦϬⲞⲤⲒ ⲠⲒ ⲈⲐⲞⲨⲀⲂ ⲤⲈⲚⲞⲨⲐⲒⲞⲤ	*For* you became higher than the *saints*, O you who have the high reputation, the holy Senuthius.
ⲆⲀⲨⲒⲆ ϦⲈⲚ ⲦⲈⲚⲘⲎϮ ⲚⲈⲘ ⲚⲒⲆⲒⲔⲈⲞⲤ ⲈⲐⲂⲈ ⲠⲦⲀⲒⲞ ⲘⲠⲒⲚⲒϢϮ ϤⲎⲈⲐⲞⲨⲀⲂ ⲤⲈⲚⲞⲨⲐⲒⲞⲤ	David and the *righteous ones* [come] into our midst, to honor the holy Senuthius.
ⲈⲖⲈⲎⲤⲞⲚ ⲎⲘⲀⲤ Ⲱ ⲠⲈⲚⲚⲎⲂ ⲈⲐⲂⲈ ⲦⲈⲔⲘⲀⲨ ⲘⲀⲢⲒⲀⲤ ⲚⲈⲘ ⲠⲒ ⲈⲐⲞⲨⲀⲂ ⲤⲈⲚⲞⲨⲐⲒⲞⲤ	O our Lord *have mercy upon us*, for (the sake of) Your mother Mary and the holy Senuthius.
ⲌⲈⲞϢ ⲄⲀⲢ ⲚⲈ ⲚⲈⲔⲚⲒϢϮ ⲘⲠⲞⲖⲎⲦⲒⲀ Ⲱ ⲠⲈⲚⲒϢⲦ ϢⲈⲚⲞⲨϮ ⲠⲀⲖⲒⲚ ⲚⲈⲘ ⲦⲈⲔⲤⲞϤⲒⲀ	*For* numerous are your great *virtues* O our father Shenoute, *and also* your *wisdom*.
ⲎⲆⲈⲞⲤ ⲀϤϬⲒⲤⲒ ⲈⲌⲞⲦⲈ ⲚⲒⲘⲞⲚⲀⲬⲞⲤ ⲬⲈ ⲚⲐⲞϤ ⲀϤϨⲈⲘⲤⲒ ⲞⲨⲞϨ ⲀϤⲤⲀⲬⲒ ⲚⲈⲘ ⲠⲞⲤ	He became *pleasantly* higher than the *monks*, and he sat and spoke with the Lord.
ⲐⲰⲞⲨϮ Ⲱ ⲚⲒⲖⲀⲞⲤ ⲘⲘⲀⲒⲚⲞⲨϮ ⲒⲎⲤ ⲠⲬⲤ ⲚⲦⲈⲚⲦⲀⲒⲞ ⲔⲀⲖⲰⲤ ⲘⲠⲒ ⲈⲐⲞⲨⲀⲂ ⲤⲈⲚⲞⲨⲐⲒⲞⲤ	Gather, O *people* who love the God Jesus *Christ*, in order to *well* honor the holy Senuthius.
ⲒⲎⲤ ⲠⲒⲘⲀⲒⲢⲰⲘⲒ ⲀϤⲤⲰⲦⲠ ⲘⲠⲒⲆⲒⲔⲈⲞⲤ ⲒⲤⲬⲈⲚ ⲦⲈϤⲘⲈⲦⲔⲞⲨⲬⲒ ⲠⲒ ⲈⲐⲞⲨⲀⲂ ⲤⲈⲚⲞⲨⲐⲒⲞⲤ	**Jesus the Lover of mankind, had chosen the *righteous one since his childhood, the* holy Senuthius.**
ⲔⲀⲖⲰⲤ ⲀⲔⲒ ϢⲀⲢⲞⲚ ⲘϤⲞⲞⲨ Ⲱ ⲠⲒⲆⲒⲔⲈⲞⲤ ⲠⲒⲚⲒϢϮ ϦⲈⲚ ⲠⲈϤⲀⲄⲰⲚ ⲠⲒ ⲈⲐⲞⲨⲀⲂ ⲤⲈⲚⲞⲨⲐⲒⲞⲤ	You are welcome today, O *righteous* one and great in his *struggle*, the holy Senuthius.

ΛΑΟC ΝΝΙΠΙCΤΟC ΕΥΕΡΧΩΡΕΥΙΝ ΚΑΛΩC ΜΠΙΡΩΜΙ ΝΤΕΛΙΟC ΠΙ ΕΘΟΥΑΒ CΕΝΟΥΘΙΟC	The *faithful people will decently celebrate,* (in honor of) the perfect man the holy Senuthius.
ΜΑΡΕΝΘΩΟΥ† ΤΗΡΕΝ Ω ΝΙΧΡΙCΤΙΑΝΟC ΝΤΕΝΕΡΩΑΙ ϨΕΝ ΦΡΑΝ ΜΠΙ ΕΘΟΥΑΒ CΕΝΟΥΘΙΟC	Let us all gather O *Christians,* in order to commemorate the name of the holy Senuthius!
ΝΕΝΙΟΤ ΜΜΟΝΑΧΟC ΕΥΕΡΩΑΙ ΝΑΚ ΚΑΛΩC Ω ΠΝΑΤΟΦΟΡΟC ΠΙ ΕΘΟΥΑΒ CΕΝΟΥΘΙΟC	**Our father the *monks* will make well your feast, O *Pneumatophore,* the holy Senuthius.**
ϪΑΠϢΩΙ ΕΜΑϢΩ ϨΕΝ ΘΜΗΤ ΝΟΥΡΑΝΟC ΕϨΟΤΕ ΝΗΕΘΟΥΑΒ ΤΗΡΟΥ ΠΙ ΕΘΟΥΑΒ CΕΝΟΥΘΙΟC	You are extremely higher in the *heavens,* more than all the saints, the holy Senuthius.
ΟΥΝΙϢΤ ΠΕ ΠΕΚΤΑΙΟ Ω ΠΙ ΑCΚΥΤΗC ΠΙ ΕΘΟΥΑΒ CΕΝΟΥΘΙΟC ΠΙ ΑΡΧΗΜΑΝΑΡΙΤΗC	Great is your honor, O *hermit,* the holy Senuthius the *archmandrite.*
ΠΕΚΡΑΝ ΜΕϨ ΝCΟΦΙΑ Ω ΠΙΔΙΚΕΟC ϨΕΝ ΤΕϤΟΙΚΟΝΟΜΙΑ ΠΙ ΕΘΟΥΑΒ CΕΝΟΥΘΙΟC	Your name is full of *wisdom,* O *righteous* one in his *economy.*
ΡΑϢΙ Ω ΝΙΠΙCΤΟC ϨΕΝ ΦΡΑΝ ΝΙΗC ΠΧC ΝΕΜ ΠΙ ΔΙΚΕΟC ΠΙ ΕΘΟΥΑΒ CΕΝΟΥΘΙΟC	Rejoice, O *faithful ones* in the name of Jesus *Christ* and the righteous holy Senuthius.
CΟΜC CΩΤΕΜ ΕΡΟΝ ΕΘΒΕ ΝΙΜΩΟΥ ΝΕΜ ΝΙΚΑΡΠΟC ΝΕΜ ΝΙCΙ† ΔΕΟΝ ΜΑΡΟΥΑΙΑΙ ΚΑΛΩC	Look and listen to us (as we ask) for the water, the *fruits, and also* the plants, let them multiply *well.*
ΤΕΝΤΩΒϨ ΜΜΟΚ ΝΑΙ ΝΑΝ ΠΙ ΑΓΑΘΟC ΕΘΒΕ ΤΕΚΜΑΥ ΝΕΜ ΦΡΑΝ ΜΠΙ ΕΘΟΥΑΒ CΕΝΟΥΘΙΟC	We beeseech You, have mercy upon us O *Good One,* for (the sake of) Your mother and the name of the holy Senuthius.
ΥC ΘC ΠΕΝΝΟΥ† ΝΟϨΕΜ ΜΠΕΚΛΑΟC ΕΒΟΛϨΑ ΝΙϨΟΤ ΝΕΜ ΠCΟϬΝΙ ΝΙ ΕΘΝΙΚΟC	O *Son of God,* save Your *people* from fear and the counsel of the *gentiles.*
ΦΤ ΠΙΜΑΙΡΩΜΙ ΟΥΟϨ ΝΑΓΑΘΟC ΧΩ ΝΑΝ ΕΒΟΛ ΝΝΕΝΝΟΒΙ ΕΘΒΕ CΕΝΟΥΘΙΟC	Good God, the Lover of mankind, forgive us our sins for (the sake of) Senuthius.

ⲬⲈⲢⲈ ϮⲠⲀⲢⲐⲈⲚⲞⲤ ⲐⲘⲀⲨ ⲚⲒⲎⲤ̄ ⲠⲬⲤ̄ ⲬⲈⲢⲈ ⲠⲒⲆⲒⲔⲈⲞⲤ ⲠⲒ ⲈⲐⲞⲨⲀⲂ ⲤⲈⲚⲞⲐⲨⲒⲞⲤ	*Hail* to the *Virgin*, the mother of Jesus *Christ, Hail* to the *righteous* one the holy Senuthius!
ⲮⲨⲬⲎ ⲚⲦⲈ ⲚⲈⲚⲒⲞϮ ⲘⲀⲈⲘⲦⲞⲚ ⲚⲰⲞⲨ Ⲱ ⲠⲬⲤ̄ ⲈⲐⲂⲈ ϮⲘⲀⲤⲚⲞⲨϮ ⲚⲈⲘ ⲠⲒ ⲈⲐⲞⲨⲀⲂ ⲤⲈⲚⲞⲨⲐⲒⲞⲤ	Our fathers' *souls* give them rest O *Christ,* for the (sake of the) mother of God and the holy Senuthius.
Ⲱ ⲠⲈⲚⲚⲎⲂ ⲀⲢⲒ ⲪⲘⲈⲨⲒ ⲘⲠⲈⲔⲂⲰⲔ ⲚⲒ ⲔⲞⲨⲆⲒⲘⲞⲤ ⲞⲨⲞⲆ ⲬⲰ ⲚⲀϤ ⲚⲚⲈϤⲚⲞⲂⲒ ⲈⲐⲂⲈ ⲠⲒ ⲈⲐⲞⲨⲀⲂ ⲤⲈⲚⲞⲨⲐⲒⲞⲤ	O our Lord, remember Your servant Nicodemus, and forgive him his sins for (the sake of) the holy Senuthius.

Notes

1. For the lack of space the Sahidic texts are not included in this paper cf. Kuhn and Tait 1996: 136–45; Junker 1977: 214–19.

2. Frandsen and Richter-Aeroe, 1981: 147–76.

3. Leipoldt 1906–1913, vol. 4: 226–33. (Repr. 1960.)

4. Al-Maqari and Girgis, 1913: 253–64.

5. Leipoldt 1906–1913, vol. 4: 234–42. (Repr. 1960.)

6. Ps. 92 [91] 10–11.

7. Ps. 112[111]: 5.

8. Lit. "took."

9. Ps. 89 [88]:17?

10. Matt. 25:1–13.

11. Leipoldt 1906–1913, vol. 3: 198–204 (1955 repr.). Translated into Latin by Weismann 1952.

12. Amélineau 1888 : 340–46. Cf. Martinez 1990: 247–59; Grohmann 1913: 187–267; 1914: 1–14.

13. Amélineau 1888: 370.

14. For this author cf. Youssef 1994: 625–33; 1998: 383–402.

15. Al-Suriani 1986, vol. 2: 255; 1986, vol. 3: 185.

16. Al-Suriani 1986, vol. 2: 255.

17. Girgis 2000: 23–44.

18. Grossmann 1991a: 552a–555a.

19. Grossmann 1991b: vol. 2, 660b–661b.

20. Al-Suriani and Habib 1990: 160.

21. Ibid.:159. Meinardus 1977: 347–48.

22. Ibid.:157.

23. Ibid.: 152–53.

24. Ibid.: 151–52.

25. Ibid.: 136–37.

26. Ibid.: 135–36; Meinardus 1977: 361–62.

27. Ibid.: 134.

28. Ibid.: 133.

29. Ibid.: 126.

30. Ibid.: 124–25.

31. Ibid.: 123–24.

32. Ibid.: 121–22; Meinardus 1977: 361–62.

33. Ibid.: 121.

34. Meinardus 1991, vol. 3: 719b–729a.

35. Van Moorsel 2002: 14–15.

36. Archbishop Basilios 1991: 111a–112a.

37. Coquin 1991b: 549–52.

38. Guirguis 2004: 939–52.

39. Skálová and Gabra 2003: 137–41; Youssef 2003: 443–48.

40. Skálová and Gabra 2003: 132–36. Van Moorsel, Immerzeel, and Langen 1994: 47.

41. Van Moorsel 2002: 47–120.

42. Coquin and Martin 1991: 712b–713a.

43. Khalil 1991a: 345–46.

44. Graf 1951: 138–42; Khalil 1991b: 2360a–2362a.

45. Shoucri 1991.

46. Muyser 1944: 116–76, esp. p. 168.

47. Kamil 1942: 89–143, and esp. 97.

48. Bilaniuk, 1991.

49. Leipoldt 1906–1913, vol. 1: 82; Leipoldt 1906–1913, vol. 4: 234–42.

50. 'Abd al-Masih 1958: 86–87.

51. For the doxologies cf. 'Abd al-Masih 1938: 97–113; 1942: 31–61; 1946–1947: 95–158; esp. *BSAC* 8: 51–52.

52. Nahdat 'l-Kanais 1949: 422–24.

53. Leipoldt 1906–1913, vol. 1: ch. 2.

54. Leipoldt 1906–1913, vol. 1: ch. 11.

55. Amélineau 1888 : 415–20.

56. Leipoldt 1906–1913, vol. 1: 57–59; ch. 128–131. There is also an episode about Nestorius and Shenoute in the Arabic life cf. Amélineau 1888: 426–28.

57. Leipoldt 1906–1913, vol. 1: 73, ch. 174.

58. Ibid., 19, ch. 25.

59. Ibid., 35, ch. 70.

60. This Doxology was partly published by Leipoldt (1906–1913, vol. 1: 82) and a German translation in Cramer 1969: 54–55.

61. This Bohairic life is an abridged version; some fragments published by Leipold show clearly that there are many episodes not included in the actual life cf. Leipoldt 1906–1913, vol. 1.

62. Mina 1934 : 13; Balestri and Hyvernat 1907: 133.

63. Till 1935: 96.

64. Mina 1937: 24; Balestri and Hyvernat 1907: 144.

65. Reymond and Barns 1973: fol. 121R I 16, p.105.

66. Hyvernat 1886: 50.

67. Godron 1970: [28].

68. Orlandi 1974: 32.

69. Till 1935: 147.

70. Kugener 1904: 259–60; McVey 1993, lines 845–860

71. Psalm 92[91] 10V11

72. Psalm 112[111]: 5

73. Lit. "took."

74. For this word, cf. Lefort 1935: 411–15.

75. Grammatically wrong, the translation is based on the Arabic.

76. Psalm 89 [88]:17.

77. Matthew 25:1–13

18 Liturgy in the White Monastery

Fr. Ugo Zanetti

LITURGY IS AN essential part of the life of a monastery, and we can hardly feel an interest for the White Monastery without being interested in its liturgical life as well.[1] Unfortunately we still know little about this subject, as recently stated by Heinzgerd Brakmann, a most distinguished scholar in the field of Coptic liturgy: " . . . even the simplest questions concerning [the White Monastery's] liturgy and that of Southern Egypt do not meet a satisfactory answer. At present, scholarly literature has very little, if anything, to offer on how services were conducted in the course of time: daily Hours, Commemorations and Feasts, and the structure of sacramental and other services."[2]

The reason is well known: the liturgical manuscripts, as well as all other manuscripts of this library, have been dismembered,[3] and a liturgical document is interesting only if complete since the structure of the service concerns us more than its contents, which are usually known from elsewhere. This holds true even more here, since we have no liturgical commentaries dating from the first millennium to help us to understand how services worked.

Available Material

Here are the sources from which we can collect information:
- fragments from the White Monastery manuscripts, when we are able to locate them and to reconstruct the original manuscript, as well as

correctly to understand their contents not forgetting that, there as elsewhere, services changed over time;

- comparison material from the Pierpont Morgan manuscripts, which belonged to the monastery of St. Michael in Hamuli in Fayoum;
- mentions of the Upper Egypt liturgy found in the *Lamp of the Sanctuary (Missbah al-zulma fi idah al-khidma)* of Abu-l-Barakat Ibn Kabar (d. 1324).[4]
- additional material for comparison: a detailed description of the consecration of the *Myron* (Holy Chrism) in the year 1374, written in about 1377 by Bishop Athanasius of Qus,[5] some prayers and hymns preserved in present Coptic services,[6] and possibly some remnants in the liturgy of Ethiopia.[7]

Preliminary Remarks

Liturgical books were usually divided: the priest's book comprised the *anaphorae* and the blessings, that of the deacon, the parts which were proper to him (*diakonika*), and possibly also the responses made by the people; there were several books for the use of the cantors.

The *typika* (also called *directory* or *index*)—liturgical books built as an *ordo* and summarizing in a few lines the directions for a whole service—are of special interest for us. Indeed, each fragment, even in isolation, allows us to reconstruct several contiguous services; if we are able to gather some contiguous sheets of a *typikon* we can reconstruct a coherent portion of the liturgical year.

Coptic liturgy has always been bilingual: still today, the deacons' biddings, and some chants, can be taken in Greek. Greek was widely used in the White Monastery; Arabic is sometimes found, at least in rubrics.

A. The Priests' and Deacons' Books

1. The Missal

Among all liturgical books of the White Monastery, only the *Missal* (*Euchologion*) —that is, the book containing everything that the celebrating priest has to say at mass and other sacraments and services—has been published in a scholarly way.[8] This edition has been out of print for some time, and the author is preparing a new and revised one. Since we have 29 sheets out of the at least 120 found in the original manuscript, we can evaluate how great the loss is; however, fragments from other missals from the White Monastery might compensate for that loss, at least in part.

2. The Deacons' Books

To explain how important the deacon's book is for the liturgical historian, Brakmann found a nice comparison: the priest's and the deacon's books are "like the two sides of a zip fastener," which are of no use separately. The missals have very few rubrics, but the deacon's books allow one to understand how the service proceeded; since the *diakonika* underwent very little change, they give us a sure reference mark. Brakmann is cataloguing them at present, after having offered a list of fragments in his detailed review of Henner's thesis.[9]

Next to the deacon's biddings, one should mention the *Diptyka*: during the *anaphora*, the deacon commemorates "our fathers in the faith," the saints, the deceased patriarchs and the acting hierarchs. A paper on this subject is currently being prepared.[10]

3. The Lectionaries

The situation has undergone little change since my rapid survey written twenty years ago,[11] and the specific research about the Catholic Epistles.[12] Lists of readings have been published: the analysis of the full lectionary M 573,[13] and the contents of the lectionary M 615 (gospels only).[14] A number of other fragments are known: some of them were listed long ago,[15] others have lately been pointed out.[16] However, these witnesses only rarely agree with each other. To understand how the readings worked in the White Monastery, we cannot avoid making use of the *typika*; I shall return to this topic in a specific paper.

Despite the differences between Upper and Lower Egypt, Burmester was long ago able to publish a 'middle' edition of the Holy Week Lectionary; much research has still to be done, but we can at least have an idea of how the Holy Week services were conducted in the White Monastery.[17]

4. Typika

As said above, the *typika* were used by all the participants, the priests, the deacons, and the cantors, since they described how services were to be performed and specified the variable parts, including the readings. Some of them contain only information for mass, while other ones describe the vigils and other services, and some seem to be all-inclusive. Few papers have been published about them, one giving two pages taken from two different *hermeniai typika*,[18] and one reconstructing a part of a *typikon* for Mass.[19] Fortunately, we can also refer to the precious transcripts given in some manuscript catalogues.[20] I shall detail this point elsewhere.

B. The Liturgical Day in the White Monastery, and the Contents of the Divine Service

Gathering all the information available in the liturgical documents (but not in the literary texts: this should be done by some other scholar), as well as in literature,[21] we can obtain an idea of how daily services were conducted in the White Monastery. However, we should never forget that, because of the scarcity of resources, we are in danger of taking as universal certain details which were valid only locally and for a limited time.[22]

1. The Liturgical Day in the Pachomian Monasteries

Before talking about the White Monastery, let us recall how literary texts describe the office in the Pachomian monasteries: there were two daily services, one at dawn and another in the evening; the morning service was held in church, while the evening one was said together by the monks of each 'house' before retiring.[23] Their pattern was quite simple: after a Bible reading by the lector in charge, all rose, made the sign of the cross and said the *Our Father* with arms extended, then once again made the sign of the cross and made a full prostration to the ground; at the signal, they stood up, crossing themselves, and prayed silently until the signal to be seated again was given, and a new reading could start.[24] The services obviously evolved with time and grew richer, but no liturgical manuscript earlier than the sixth century has reached us and it is only with the ninth century that more abundant, though scattered, documentation becomes available that can suffice to reconstruct parts of the services.

2. General Survey of the Daily Services in the White Monastery

If we start with the description of Vespers, as liturgical books often do, we see that the monks gathered at evening for the common prayer, most probably now in the church, since services were more complicated and required a different environment. In the Hamuli monastery during the last years of the ninth century, and probably at that time in the White Monastery, too, the service began with an invitatory. There were readings from Holy Scripture, prayers said at times with the assembly prostrate on the ground and at other times in the standing position, and some hymns. Fr. Hans Quecke supposed that in the ninth century the hour of Compline—not mentioned in his manuscript—must have existed already, but joined to Vespers.[25] Afterward the monks retired for the night.

The night prayer began probably for an extended period 'at cockcrow,' that is, at the beginning of the fourth vigil of the night, about 3 a.m. by modern reckoning. Again, since his manuscript mentioned an hour of 'Prime,' Fr. Quecke supposed that by the end of the ninth century the night prayer actually began in the middle of the night, and that 'Prime' was, like today's Matins, said just before dawn.[26] I am not able to say at what time these services in fact began, or if they followed immediately one upon the other. As far as I know, liturgical manuscripts give no hint to that.

Both services together certainly lasted quite long, some two to three hours. They might have included the biblical odes and canticles of M 574 and some other pieces, such as the antiphons of M 575 (at least for some days), but they certainly included above all readings, *hermeniai,* and responsories, as mentioned in the *typika.*[27]

On some days Mass was celebrated after the morning service: it is usually called "the synaxis hour," in Coptic *p-nau n-synage.* Several proper chants were used for Mass: the *trisaghion,* hymns for the gospel, for the kiss of peace and several other hymns. Of course, there were readings and an *anaphora,* the latter being in the *Missal* (see A. 1 above).

We know nearly nothing about other hours of prayer: they probably had an invitatory taken from the Bible,[28] and then, perhaps, some psalms, or a reading from Scripture recited by heart.

3. Psalms

Psalms are found everywhere in the liturgy of Upper Egypt:[29] they are used in any service as constituent parts of hymns, to be sung as responsories or to accompany a meditation. But was the Psalter systematically read in the White Monastery, from beginning to end or in any other way (for example, with prescribed series, such as in the modern Coptic *Agbeyya*)? As far as I know, there is no mention of that at all.

Indeed, the famous tradition of the 'Angel's Rule' concerns only Lower Egypt, and in any case it talks about "twelve prayers," not "twelve psalms."[30] The information given by Abu-l Barakat Ibn Kabar about the monastery of St. George in Sadamant, where the whole Psalter was read every day according to a rather complicated system,[31] does not seem to have been known in the White Monastery—otherwise at least some traces of it should have been found. Thus, I have come to think that, in the White Monastery and possibly in all Pachomian monasteries, at least for some time, the divine service was organized *without* current psalmody, with only biblical readings and responsories, together with hymns; for the main part, hymns and responsories were composed of a blend of psalm verses. Since liturgical documents give no evidence about this point, I hope other scholars will be able to help to collect information in literary texts or elsewhere.[32]

4. Biblical and Patristic Readings

In the White Monastery, as in all Pachomian monasteries, the Bible (Old and New Testaments) was read at the main services, in the evening and the morning: the lives of Pachomius and of Shenoute bear witness to that.[33] Besides, the liturgical fragments, mainly from the *typika*, show that there were also readings of extracts from Shenoute and other authors during the vigils. In the first centuries, these readings were probably often done by heart,[34] but in the course of time lectionaries came to be composed. The matter is long and complicated: I shall return to it in a specialized paper.

5. Different Kinds of Hymns, Based on Scripture

Next to the readings, the services included different kinds of hymns, most of which were composed of psalm verses. Because of space limitation, I will introduce them only briefly and return to this matter later on.

The *hermeniai* were certainly one of the most distinctive features of the White Monastery liturgy, and they probably built up the framework of the services. Fr. Quecke gave some information about them in 1970, and came back to this topic more than once.[35] Their basic principle was rather simple: you collect psalm verses containing the same keywords, such as, "king," "priest," "sky," and you sing them one after the other, thus creating a rhapsody of psalm verses. These 'rhapsodies,' however, implied further complications, mixing the *hermenia* with responsories, and so on, so that it is far from easy to tell exactly how they functioned. Abu-l-Barakat alludes to them too, but gives us no further useful information.[36] Besides, M 574 has also 'lesser *hermeniai*' that have not yet been studied.[37]

The rubrics regularly mention *shto* and *ekhmoos*. While the second obviously means "while you are sitting," the former probably means "prostration," as Crum rightly guessed.[38] They must be related to the way the service was conducted in Pachomian monasteries, as said above (B.1), including prostrations on the ground and a return to the sitting position after each reading. In time, it came to be considered natural to develop chants to emphasize these strong moments.

There were also other responsories: *ouôhm*, *lexis*, and *tagma*. They may have been said by the people, or by a second choir, as an answer to a hymn sung by the cantors.

The term *hymnos* is also frequently met in the *typika*. Fr. Quecke devoted to it an article containing nearly all that is known about it;[39] he showed that there were lists of psalm verses from which the cantors chose what they were to sing (according to principles that we do not know), and that the rubric *hymnos* referred to these lists.[40] The *hymnos* could be 'pure' or specialized for given times of the Mass, such as the gospel, the kiss of peace, or the communion.

A hymn, also made of psalm verses and abbreviated as '*alph*' in the rubrics of the *typika*, was complementary to the *hymnos*, but how it functioned is still an enigma.[41] Something more could probably be said, but the question needs further research.

6. Ecclesiastical Poetry

While the Coptic Church does not use the same amount of ecclesiastical poetry as the Byzantine rite, it has a number of pieces that have been in use for many centuries. There were acrostic hymns, with twenty-four stances for the twenty-four letters of the Greek alphabet,[42] like those of M 574;[43] today's psalis seem to be their offspring[44]. Similar compositions regularly appear, often incomplete, in the papyri.[45]

Next to them is the Antiphonary found in M 575,[46] somehow the ancestor of today's *Difnar*. No such composition has yet been found in the White Monastery, but I have been able to identify something like that in the published documents, to which I shall return later on.

One often meets the word *poièkon*; Fr. Quecke suggested (but did not publish his reflections on the subject) that it stands for *poiètikon*.[47] It is a rather short piece, like the Byzantine *troparion*, but much research has still to be done about it, as emphasized recently.[48]

Last but not least, Mass as well as processions and other services abundantly used the 'developed *Trisaghion*.' In the modern Coptic liturgy, the *Trisaghion* is sung with the Christological additions: (Christ, you) *who were born of the Virgin . . . who were crucified for our sake . . . who rose from the dead and ascended into heaven . . .*; in Upper Egypt, there were full sets of hymns, starting with *Haghios ho Theos*, but continuing with other invocations, either Christological or (more often) not.[49] The *Trisaghion* could also be used as a responsory to psalm verses sung by the cantors, or to other chants.[50]

7. Liturgical Calendar

The ecclesiastical year has a fixed part, which follows the order of the year (in that case, from 1st Tut to 5th or 6th Epagomens), and a movable part, which is bound to the paschal cycle. We know the liturgical calendar of Lower Egypt quite well, but that of Upper Egypt has not yet been studied in detail: the material is there, but still lacks specialized studies.

Conclusion

Although much more could be said, it is already possible to give a general idea about how liturgy functioned in the White Monastery. More details will appear later, in a much longer paper. However, a call should be made to all scholars working with White Monastery material—archaeologists, art historians, philologists, "Shenoutologists" (if I may coin a new expression)— . . . to be kind enough to point out any detail they might happen to find in their own research that could be of some help to understand how the liturgical services really functioned 'on the ground,' since liturgical documents are usually silent on that point.

Notes

1. Since the length of this paper is limited, I am offering here only a general overview of the question. A detailed study will appear later in the *Bulletin de la Société d'Archéologie copte*.
2. Brakmann 2004: 138.
3. Cf. Orlandi 2002: 227ff (who however has no interest in liturgical manuscripts).
4. Cf. Zanetti 1992.
5. The edition of this text is currently being prepared by Dr. Youhanna Nessim Youssef and myself. Cf. Youssef 1998; Youssef 2003, etc.
6. Cf. Youssef 1997, Muyser 1935.
7. Zanetti 1994.
8. Lanne 1958.
9. Brakmann 2004: 155ff, about Henner 2000.
10. Brakmann 2004: 157–58 and n. 180.
11. Zanetti 1985.
12. Zanetti 1996.
13. Schüssler 1995–2004 and Schüssler 2002.
14. Depuydt 1993.
15. Zanetti 1985: 14–21.

16. Most recently by Brakmann 2004: 150ff.

17. Burmester 1933–1934. Cf. Zanetti 1994: 767 and *passim*; Schüssler 2002: lectionaries "sa 105L" and "sa 108L" (the latter is R$_4$ of Burmester 1933–1934). Cf. also Atanassova 2004.

18. Quecke 1983.

19. Zanetti 1995. Three other sheets should be added to the five published in 1994: Paris, BN copte 120 (20), fol. 163 and fol. 165, as well as a sheet preserved in the Victoria and Albert Museum in London.

20. Pleyte and Boeser 1897, Crum 1905 and 1909, as well as Wessely 1901–1923.

21. Taft 1986: 57–73 gives an excellent survey together with the reference to sources.

22. Quecke 1970: 346 points out that the service described in M 574 can have been only of local use. But up to now little else has been done about old Sahidic liturgy!

23. Veilleux 1968: 296 and 300, n.108.

24. Veilleux 1968: 307ff.

25. Quecke 1970: 146.

26. Quecke 1970: 184–90.

27. Cf. Quecke 1983.

28. As in Quecke 1970: 424ff and 108ff (Hamuli monastery), where the invitatories were Ps 11: 8 for Terce, Ps 64: 6ab for Sext and Ps. 137: 8bc for None.

29. "Coptic liturgy makes use of psalms and parts of psalms in an amount that is quite unique in the Christian East. Much of this (material), which in the meantime has fallen out of use and is preserved only in fragmentary witnesses, is still lying in profound darkness" (Quecke 1995: 114).

30. Veilleux 1968: 324–39.

31. Cf. Zanetti 1990: 360. Although this paper concerns Lower Egypt, it can help give an idea of the several systems which were in use in Egypt in the past, as well as describe today's system.

32. It might also be true that the 'little hours,' which were fashioned later and are mentioned neither in lectionaries nor in *typika*, included a current psalmody (under foreign influence?), and that only the main and 'older' services of *lychnikon* (Vespers) and of the night preserved the old usage. The material found up to now does not allow one to draw any conclusions.

33. Veilleux 1968: 307–15.

34. Veilleux 1968: 311. Is this the reason for which the readings in the White Monastery were always short (usually some ten verses)?

35. Quecke 1970: 97–100; Quecke 1983; Quecke 1995. One should not forget that the word *hermeneia* can also mean 'commentaries,' or rather 'paraphrases,' of biblical texts (Urbaniak-Walczak 2004: 652).

36. Cf. Villecourt 1925: 271 ff.

37. Quecke 1970: 99.

38. Crum 1939: 792b; Urbaniak-Walczak 2004: 651.

39. Quecke 1995.

40. However, not all the verses are taken from the psalms: there were some exceptions. Quecke gives an example from Dan 3:86a, and another case that is non-biblical.

41. Cf. Quecke 1995: 113ff.— Although the natural way to solve this abbreviation is 'alphabeta,' the question is probably less simple than it seems (Quecke 1970: 101).

42. Just as there are acrostic psalms (for example, Ps. 118). In Bohairic, hymns based on the thirty-one letters of the Coptic alphabet (or thirty-two when one includes the 'sti,' which stands for number six) are rarer (Quecke 1970: 101 and n. 15).

43. Kuhn and Tait 1996.

44. Abd al-Masîn 1958.

45. Brashear and Satzinger 1990.

46. Krause 2003.

47. Cf. Henner 2000: 121 and n. 108.

48. Brakmann 2004: 142–46.

49. Cf. Brakmann 2004: 142.

50. Cf. McCoull 2004: 94 and 102.

19 Akhmim as a Source of Textiles

Cäcilia Fluck

History of Textile Production in Akhmim

According to the historian Strabo (*Geography* XVII, 41), Akhmim/Panopolis was a well-known production center of linen fabrics from pharaonic times. Up to now there is little literary evidence of textile manufacture in the town throughout the first millennium, the period to which most of the textile-finds belong. However, some documents confirm that various textile specialists worked in Panopolis during the fourth century A.D.[1] Written sources regarding local textile production in the following centuries are yet to be published. However, with regard to the continuity in the town under Muslim rule a fragment of a rug decorated with an Arab inscription, today in the Textile Museum, Washington (inv. T.M.73.726), is of particular importance. The inscription confirms that Akhmim remained a center of textile production in Islamic times: it tells us that the rug was made in an Akhmim factory in the year A.H. 203 (A.D. 818/9). The Arab author Ya'qubi (A.D. 891) recorded in his geographical work that 'cut rugs'—a special type of fabrics with a pile of cut weft loops—were produced in this town. The existence of a *tiraz*[2] of Akhmim is also certified by Mas'udi (A.D. 956).[3]

Discovery and Primary Research

It was in the eighteenth century that European travelers first took notice of the scant ruins of ancient Akhmim/Panopolis. Because former structures were overbuilt and used as quarries for the buildings of following generations, hardly any architectural remains survived. The site was continuously settled from pre-dynastic times onward and is supposed to have been one of the most important cities in Egypt until the fifteenth century. Belonging to it are extended necrop-olises from where thousands of textiles of almost all periods originate.[4]

First excavations in the three major cemeteries were conducted in the years 1884–1888 by the team of the French Egyptologist Gaston Maspero (1846–1916). As we learn from the letters of his fellow-traveler, Charles E. Wilbour (1833–1896), "Maspero had an idea of stopping at Ekhmeem, not to find the famous tombs . . . but some graves where there are said to be fine mummy cloths."[5] Maspero himself gives an important description of the 'Byzantine and Coptic mummies.'[6] The discovery of the cemeteries attracted not only scholars but above all robbers and dealers, who plun-dered and demolished the site. The disastrous result is soberly described by Klaus P. Kuhlmann as 'the beginning of the end for a unique archaeological situation.'[7] Although the archaeological context is irretrievably lost today, Akhmim is considered one of the major find-spots for textiles of the first millennium A.D. There is no doubt that most of the textiles circulating in

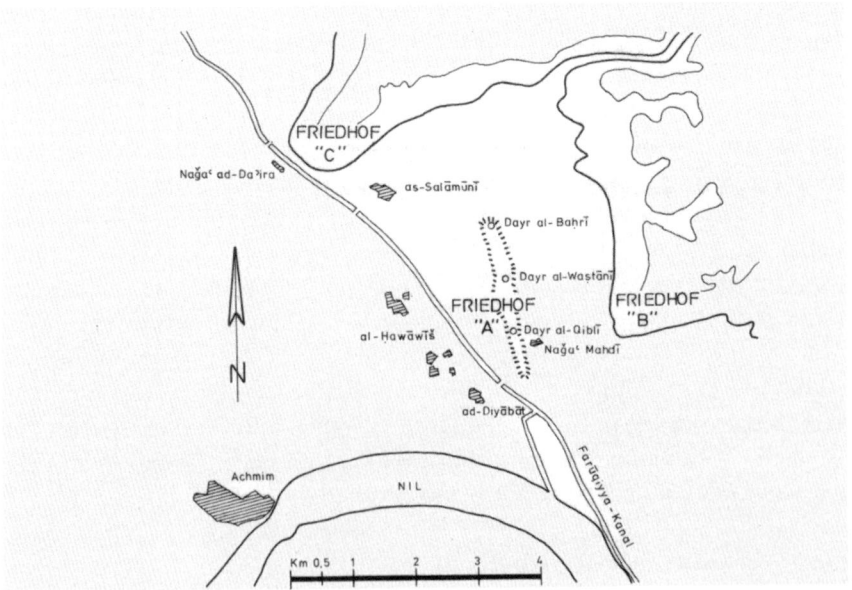

Fig. 19.1: Map of the necropolises of Akhmim; after Kuhlmann 1983: 53, fig. 14.

the years 1885–1886 came from there; nevertheless, the true provenance of each single fabric always has to be questioned. The necropolis which delivered most of the material of this era is situated to the northeast of the town and called al-Hawawis.

During the 1885/1886 season Maspero discovered a cemetery with burials of late antique to medieval times in this area between the Dayr al-Wastani and the Dayr al-Qibli.[8] In all probability, the bulk of textiles from Akhmim brought to Europe came from this site. In fact, it seems to be the source for the large collection acquired by Franz Bock (1823–1899), a German clergyman and textile historian from Aix-la-Chapelle who stayed in Egypt in 1886, although the location is not explicitly mentioned in his publications.[9] It cannot be excluded that further textiles of the first centuries A.D. originate from an urban cemetery that seems to have been used in Greco-Roman and Christian times.[10] Masses of textiles of an earlier date were also recorded in the tombs of the most northern cemetery, al-Salamuni ('Friedhof C' on the map Fig. 19.1), which was in use during the Old Kingdom and again only in the Late Kingdom and during the Greco-Roman period.[11]

Inspired by Maspero's finds and Bock's acquisitions other scholars and collectors like Vladimir G. de Bock (1850–1899), Theodor Graf (1840–1903),[12] Carl Schmidt (1868–1938), and in particular Robert Forrer (1866–1947) visited the site of Akhmim for further research and not least to purchase textiles and other objects, which were subsequently sold or donated to museums and collections worldwide. It was common practice among the dealers of their time to cut out the decorative elements of large fabrics like garments, hangings, or any other kind of cloth to be sold piece by piece in order to obtain as much profit as possible. This explains why nowadays fragments from one and the same cloth are distributed over various museums and private collections. It is one of the aims of scholars today to reassemble the formerly separated pieces and to reconstruct their original context.[13]

Robert Forrer's Research on Akhmim[14]

When Forrer arrived at Akhmim in the spring of 1894 he already owned a considerable collection of more than 2,000 textiles. According to his own words he bought them on the antiquities market in Cairo, which was supplied through agents who acquired the textiles from the local finders.[15] Although it seems probable that the greater part of Forrer's collection originates from Akhmim, the real provenance of the textiles he assembled before his own excavations is questionable. The only information concerning their origin is given to us through dealers, and we cannot be sure whether the material from Akhmim was not mixed with that from other sites in their stores. In fact, several museum textiles today show the name of the town Akhmim stitched or written on them in modern times, and we tend to believe this reference.[16]

It is curious to note that the first comprehensive studies on the Akhmim finds were written by Forrer in the years *prior* to his arrival, and on the basis of objects only said to locate from there.[17] Nevertheless, his publications are one of the few with a scientific standard at that time. However, the most reliable and critical source remains the letters he wrote during his stay to Dr. Gustav Müller, the director of the journal *Antiquitäten-Zeitschrift*. All these letters were collected in a small illustrated volume which was published in 1895. In his fourth letter he minutely described the disastrous situation he was confronted with on his arrival in Akhmim: "Everywhere—as far as the eye could see—one notices black holes in the hills, where graves have been opened and, while approaching, other black points can be identified as corpses of opened and unwrapped mummies, which have carelessly been put down, decomposing very slowly."[18] Furthermore, Forrer's notes leave no doubt that the al-Hawawis cemetery was the place of his excavations.[19] He informed us about tombs of "Byzantine times" around the al-Qibli monastery, where splendid silk weavings had been found and probably priests were buried.

Forrer mentions another burial place, from Roman and Christian times, further to the north, which seems to have been the focal point of his excavations, and, according to Kuhlmann, must be located in the neighborhood of the al-Wastani Monastery[20] on the site of a prehistoric cemetery. The

Fig. 19.2: Cemetery A (al-Hawawis) from northwest. B = Dayr al-Wastani, C = Dayr al Qibli; after Kuhlmann 1983: pl. 19 b).

common type of grave used in the late Roman and Christian period is classified by Forrer as flat graves, orientated in a west–east direction, consisting of a pit 2 m long, 0.80 cm wide, and 1.30–1.50 m deep. The walls are partly faced with mud bricks.[21] It is worth noting that Forrer clearly distinguished between burials of different social classes. The mummy bundles of privileged people were much larger than those of the less well-off. They were fitted out with a considerable number of decorated dresses and cloths and then fastened to a wooden board on the back, while the poorer people were only wrapped in a few layers of mostly undecorated cloth.[22] Fortunately, in one of his letters Forrer also described the unwrapping of one of his more elaborate mummy-finds in detail.[23] The outer wrappings were coverings with purple stripes. Beneath he found a layer of bandages followed by eleven layers of linen under which another layer of bandages came to light. Pieces of crumpled linen were used to fill the angles between the shoulder and the head. Below these the corpse was wrapped in a mantle with blue cross-bands and star ornaments in tapestry woven in the middle of the cloth. Now a wooden board on which the corpse was laid became visible. Having raised the mantle Forrer observed more layers of cloth and a lump of resin in the area of the stomach that could be identified as incense. Again two cloths with purple stripes appeared, and finally six alternating coverings and bandages followed by another cloth directly on the body and a rolled up cloth round the neck. Further rags of partly decorated fabrics, among which Forrer found a damaged tunic, were used as a sort of padding for the body of the deceased, who was a man about forty to fifty years old and 1.85 m tall.[24]

Forrer's description gives an idea of the enormous quantity of cloth which was necessary for only one burial. That is why it is nowadays impossible even approximately to estimate the total amount of textiles deriving from the cemeteries of Akhmim.

The most important items of Forrer's former textile collection are today stored at the Museum für Byzantinische Kunst in Berlin, the Musée royaux d'art et d'histoire in Brussels, the Museum of Fine Arts in Budapest (Szépmüvészeti Múzeum Közleményei), the Museum im Andreasstift in Worms, and at the Martin von Wagner-Museum in Würzburg.[25]

Samples of Typical Akhmim Textiles

It is only accidental that textiles themselves tell us about their provenance, like the rug fragment in Washington already mentioned. Another sample might be a late antique square tapestry kept in the Victoria and Albert Museum in London (inv. 2137 – 1900). In the center a *tyche*, the personification of a city, is depicted. She is fitted out with typical attributes such as a cornucopia filled with flowers and fruits and an ear of corn. Her head is crowned with the symbol of a town wall.[26] Above it the letters ΠΑΝΟΣ can be read, a version of the town's name, Panopolis, known from Greek and Coptic documents.[27] There is good reason to presume that this tapestry was woven in one of the town's textile factories.

Usually we have to believe the information given by the finders and collectors about the object's provenance. As mentioned before, the most reliable source concerning the Akhmim textiles are the publications written by Robert Forrer. However, one has to keep in mind that even if the find spot of an artifact is guaranteed this does not necessarily mean that it was produced in the same place. Textiles belong to the type of movable objects ranking as popular trade-goods throughout history, implying that imported pieces occur side by side with samples of local production. However, if we compare the textiles documented by Forrer with other lots said to originate from Akhmim, a certain conformity cannot be denied in several cases. From our present knowledge it is possible to classify special groups of fabrics with particular stylistic and technical features or with characteristic patterns that allow us to attribute them to workshops in Akhmim.[28] The most characteristic is a group of silk weavings.[29] Fortunately, a unique sample of a nearly undamaged linen tunic with a complete set of silk decoration survived.[30] The trimmings consist of shoulder bands, roundels at the height of the knees, and sleeve panels that are doubtlessly woven to shape. They definitely do not belong to the numerous recycled silk weavings cut out from discarded cloths to be used as decorative elements later. All trimmings on the tunic show a homogenous, symmetrically arranged pattern of emblematic palmettes or rosettes and other floral motifs framed by tendrils. The sleeve panels also contain a pair of armed horsemen attacked by a soldier with a lance in the outer compartments. Above the horsemen's head the Greek name ZAXAPIOY can be read. This name and that of Joseph appear quite often on related silk weavings from Akhmim in connection with horsemen. The meaning of these names has been controversial. Some take them for the names of the horsemen, others for the owners. This is not convincing because silks inscribed with these names are quite numerous and also appear on silks with a purely floral pattern. It is more convincing to understand them as names of weavers or workshops.[31]

Generally the Akhmim silks show only little variation in motif, which always appear bichrome, that is bright on either a green, red, or violet background. Apart from the afore mentioned motifs, human figures—warriors or dancers, single or in pairs—and busts, as well as birds, are occasionally found. There also exists a female pendant of the hunting or fighting horsemen interpreted as Amazons.[32]

Silks with narrative scenes such as those on the famous so-called Mary Silk depicting episodes of the life of the Mother of Jesus in the Abegg-Stiftung at Riggisberg (inv. 3100b) are exceptional so far. This silk is dated between the fourth and fifth centuries A.D.,[33] while the typical Akhmim silks are attributed to the seventh to tenth centuries. This has recently been confirmed by radiocarbon analyses. The results of the analyses prove that two stylistic groups of silks with a central palmette motif occurring either in an organic or in a stylized version existed almost contemporaneously. This refutes the former thesis, according to which stylized motifs were produced in a later period than those of a more naturalistic manner.[34] Another group of textiles distinctive to the Akhmim region seem to be cushions or coverings with a long pile decorated with relatively large squares with identical structural features: all show a central circle with one or two heraldic figural motifs (a hunter or mythological figures)

Fig. 19.3: Fragment of silk weaving with amazons. © Gustav-Lübcke Museum, Hamm, inv. 1341–1342.

inside, framed by a band of smaller circles containing erotes or various animals, leaves, and blossoms. The corners or the middle of the sides are often emphasized by multicolored baskets of fruit, which contrast with the otherwise

Fig. 19.4: Square tapestry with hunter set within a piled linen fabric. © Katoen Natie Collection, Antwerp, inv. 533 / DM 53.

monochrome pattern of dark red color, imitating true purple on a bright background. Sporadically, some tiny details are also accented in vivid colors.

Furthermore, a particular series of tapestries decorated with scenes from the life of the patriarch Joseph and other biblical subjects is connected with the town of Akhmim.[35] Some peculiar features suggest that they were made in specialized workshops. The group is commonly dated from between the seventh and tenth centuries and is characterized by an intensive red background on which scenes from the Bible are illustrated. The acting figures appear very compact and are drawn with dark outlines. They are depicted with oversized eyes in simplified faces and stylized, but colorful garments. They are all executed in a high quality. About seventy of these pieces have now been identified, telling the story of the Old Testament patriarch Joseph (Genesis 37).

Fig. 19.5: Tapestry roundel with scenes from the life of the patriarch Joseph. © Katoen Natie Collection, Antwerp, inv. 625 / DM 144.

The most prominent and complex samples are large roundels presenting a cycle of nine scenes from the first part of the story ending with Joseph's arrival in Egypt. They are arranged either clockwise or anti-clockwise around a central circle with a depiction of the dreaming Joseph. A few samples also comprise scenes from the second part of the story taking place in Egypt. Apart from this, there exist smaller roundels and sleeve bands with an abbreviated version of the narrative on which only selected scenes are shown.[36]

Corresponding to the silks, the Joseph tapestries, and the decorations of pile fabrics mentioned above are carried out in different stylistic versions whereas the structural scheme principally remains the same. It is still an open question whether special stylistic features speak for different workshops—as is occasionally postulated—or not. To summarize, it seems that stylized motifs are woven in a less careful manner and often with coarser materials than equal motifs woven in a more naturalistic and elaborate way. However, this does not automatically mean that they were woven in different factories. One could also imagine that high-quality fabrics were produced side by side with less valuable ones in the same workshop. Further research is necessary before more precise results can be obtained.[37]

Fig. 19.6: Quilted cap from Mamluk times. © Stiftung Moritzburg, Halle, inv. T 129, Photograph: Gabriele Schrade (FH Köln).

In conclusion, the inexhaustible number of textiles attributed to Akhmim and spread out over collections worldwide affirms that the al-Hawawis necropolis from which the majority of the pieces derived must have been in use from Roman times onward, at least throughout the first millennium.

A special kind of quilted cap, of which several samples—all located to Akhmim—exist, doubtless belongs to the Mamluk period.

It is not certain in which cemetery they were discovered. Perhaps they belong to the finds Forrer made in an urban cemetery during his stay in Akhmim.[38] So far later samples have not been found, which corresponds perfectly to Kuhlmann's report that the town's importance waned in the fifteenth century.[39] Interestingly, Akhmim is the only one of all the ancient weaving towns that has preserved its reputation as a textile production center up to the present day.[40]

Notes

1. Wipzycka 1991: 2220.
2. The term *tiraz* is of Persian origin and means 'embroidery.' It became a term for a state textile factory in Islamic times.
3. Kühnel 1960: 1–2.
4. For an extensive study of the literary sources and archaeological remains of Akhmim see Kuhlmann 1983. After having finished this paper, I came to know about an article by Maya Müller, "From the History of Archaelogy: The Destruction of the Late Antiquity Necropolises in Egypt Reconsidered," in *BAR International Series* 1448 (2005), 43–48, dealing among other things with the discovery and exploitation of the cemeteries of Akhmim at the end of the nineteenth century.
5. Capart 1936: 244.
6. Maspero 1886: 210–12.
7. Kuhlmann 1983: 2, 50–52.
8. Maspero 1886: 210; Kuhlmann 1983: 55.
9. Bock 1886; Borkopp 1989: 20. Bock only hinted generally at cemeteries in Upper Egypt: Bock 1886: 2–3, 10, 14–15, 17.
10. Forrer 1901: 71–72; Kuhlmann 1983: 49, 53.
11. Kuhlmann 1983: 71–86. Cf. Kuhlmann 1983: 71: "der Abhang ist übersät mit den Überresten der aus ihren Gräbern herausgerissenen und zerfledderten Mumien; in den zerschlagenen Kammern liegt, z. T. noch ballenweise, zerwühlt, feiner Achmimer Stoff, ehemals und noch heute berühmtes Produkt der einheimischen Webereien . . . , das man den Toten in reichlichem Maße beigegeben hatte."
12. There is some uncertainty concerning the accession year of the Akhmim textiles given to the Museum für Angewandte Kunst in Vienna by Theodor Graf. According to the catalogue edited by Noever (2005): *passim*, the Akhmim textiles were acquired in 1883, i. e. before Maspero excavated the site, which diverges from Riegl (1889:

VII–VIII), who wrote: "Diesem Leichenfelde sollen namentlich die zahlreichen von Dr. Bock nach Europa in den Handel gebrachten Stücke entstammen, was nicht hinderte, dass auch H. Graf daselbst noch reiche Beute machen konnte . . . . " If my interpretation of Riegl's utterance is correct, Graf visited Akhmim after Bock had been there, which was not before 1886. It seems to me that the group of Akhmim textiles in the Museum für Angewandte Kunst was by mistake mixed with a collection of textiles acquired in 1883 from Theodor Graf.

13. Several samples are listed in Renner 1974: 3–4; Renner-Volbach 2002: 30.

14. For Robert Forrer, his textile collection, and his researches in Egypt see Schnitzler 1999: 48–56 and Preiß 2007: 66–77.

15. Forrer 1891a: 10.

16. This is not limited solely to Forrer's textiles but includes those from other previous owners as well.

17. Forrer 1889; Forrer 1891a; Forrer 1891b; Forrer 1893.

18. Forrer 1895: 31.

19. Forrer 1895: 30, 32, 34; Kuhlmann 1983: 59–60.

20. Kuhlmann 1983: 60.

21. Forrer 1895: 38–41; Kuhlmann 1983: 62.

22. Forrer 1895: 43–44.

23. Forrer 1895: 44–48.

24. Forrer 1895: 44–48; Kendrick 1920: 15–16; Horak 1995: 41–42. For further descriptions of mummies from Akhmim cf. Horak 1995: 46–48.

25. Wulff and Volbach 1926: 159; Errera 1916: 207; Török 1993: 13, 91; Renner-Volbach 2002: 11–12; Renner 1974: 1.

26. Kendrick 1920: 62–63, no. 51, pl. XII; Rutschowscaya 1990: 36–37; Horak 2001: 44.

27. Karig 1975: 54.

28. Renner 1974: 1–9; Renner-Volbach 2002: 12–14; Desrosiers 2004: 16–17, 19–20.

29. Falke 1913: 43–48.

30. Victoria and Albert Museum, London, inv. 820–1903: Kendrick 1922: 75–76, no. 794, frontispiece; Desrosier 2004: 19, fig. 7.

31. Fluck 2006: 160–61 with further references.

32. Stauffer 1992: 45–52.

33. Cf. Schrenk 2004: 185–88, no. 62 with further references. The silk fragments belong to the same funerary context as the large wall hanging of the Abegg-Stiftung (inv. 3100a) showing Dionysos and his followers, cf. Schrenk 2004: 26–34, no. 1. The provenance and date depend on comparable textiles.

34. De Moor, Schrenk, and Verhecken-Lammens 2006: 85–94.

35. Renner-Volbach 2002: 13.

36. Fluck 2001: 9–31 with further references.

37. For more samples and details of typical Akhmim textiles see Renner-Volbach 2002: 12–14.

38. Forrer 1901: 71–72.

39. Kuhlmann 1983: 1, 14, 32–33.

40. Ammoun 1991: 28–31. I am very grateful to Antoine De Moor, Anja Preiß, and Ellen Schwinzer for the permission to publish photos and plans of the archives of the Stiftung Moritzburg in Halle, the Katoen Natie Collection in Antwerp, and the Gustav-Lübcke Museum in Hamm. Special thanks are owed to Gebbe List-Petersen, Anja Preiß, Klaus Ohlhafer, and Sofia Schaten for revising the text and for offering valuable insights.

20 Snapshots on the Sculptural Heritage of the White Monastery at Sohag
The Wall Niches

Suzana Hodak

THE SCULPTURAL REMAINS of both monastic churches in the Sohag region, the so-called Red and White Monasteries (Dayr al-Ahmar and Dayr al-Abyad)[1], is of great importance with regard to our absolutely insufficient knowledge of Coptic architectural sculpture in general.[2]

It is primarily the White Monastery, but also the Red Monastery, that provides a first-rate sculptural heritage in the truest sense of the word. Although both churches contain a mixture of spolia besides the pieces originally made for the building, and both churches suffered much destruction (and these destructions, especially the following repairs, may falsify in some cases the original outlook of the sculptural composition), enough of the original sculpture of the mid- to late-fifth century survived *in situ* (that is, in its original functional context, if not at its original place), thus allowing to build up an important chronological specification for the sculptural production of the fifth century. Moreover, it is possible to analyze the sculpture within a given architectural context.

In the following we will concentrate mainly on the White Monastery, because in the Red Monastery by far the most of the 'sculptural' decoration were painted as a substitute for carved decoration. Even the relatively few carved architectural members, as, for example, the column or pilaster capitals, the pediments of the wall niches or the supraports, were enriched by a layer of polychrome color—this, however, might have been the rule rather than the exception not only in the classical Greek and Roman world, but also in Egypt from the pharaonic period on to late antiquity.[3] Thanks to the extraordinary well-preserved condition of the interior of the triconch sanctuary in the Red Monastery, we have a vivid impression of this. However, even in the White Monastery, as we will refer to in the following, we can find traces of painting both as substitute for and as additional adornment of carved decoration.[4]

State of Research on the Sculptural Decoration of the White Monastery

Besides the former more general and almost incidental references to the sculptural decoration in what is until today the major study of the two church buildings, made by Monneret de Villard in 1925–1926,[5] and the questionable, at least, value of the attempt undertaken by Philipp Akermann in 1976,[6] one should primarily refer to the contributions of Hans-Georg Severin.[7] However, his research is in its initial state. We are still lacking the substantial basis for a systematic research of the sculptural program. We have neither a systematic and complete photographical[8] nor an analytical documentation of the church building itself or of its sculptural decoration.

The aim of the present contribution can neither be to propose a complete, distinctive discussion of the sculptural program, nor to repeat sketchy overviews of the different sculptural members.[9] On the contrary, the focus will be on one part of the original architectural conception of the mid-fifth century—the wall niches—whose significance is not only attested by its role within the architectural plan; thanks to the preservation of their rich sculptural decoration, the wall niches become a 'talking witness' of the sculptural heritage of the White Monastery.[10]

It is important to note that the following statements present only an intermediate status of work—they are first *snapshots* of the material.

The Architecture

In order to obtain a concrete idea about the 'architectural' significance of the wall niches on the one hand, but also their actual status quo, it is necessary to refer first of all to the building itself, namely a comparison of its original architectural conception and its actual appearance (Fig. 20.1).[11] In its original architectural conception the church was of primarily basilical character, with three aisles and a return aisle on the west side with upper galleries and an elaborated triconch sanctuary at its east end surrounded by several annex rooms, among them an octagonal baptistery. At the western end of the church a narthex with columned exedrae at its lateral ends was built, and along the south side of the church a long, narrow hall with an absidial end on its western side was attached—the so-called 'south narthex.' At its eastern end a door still leads to a square room (the former library), whereas at its western end there was once a rectangular room.

As already mentioned, the church suffered several periods of destruction and repair, the first collapse as early as between the sixth and eighth centuries. After the collapse of the wooden roof of the naos at some time in the Middle Ages, it most probably remained unroofed and lost its function. The rebuilt church was reduced almost to the size of the former sanctuary with the addition of an area in front of it. The remaining part of the former naos was later occupied by several civilian structures that were removed in 1984.[12] In the southwest part of the church the wall between the nave and the south narthex collapsed and the western absidial end of the south narthex disappeared almost completely. Finally, the former rectangular room in the southwest corner of the church was totally rebuilt to a square-domed structure in the beginning of the nineteenth century.

Concerning the original architectural conception, we can clearly state the continuous increase of complexity from west to east. In spite of the later reconstructions and repairs one could state a parallel increase also in the complexity and richness of the sculptural decoration with its climax in the triconch sanctuary with its two-storied columned architecture separated by broad entablature zones (in the upper story supporting the semidome), and niches arranged in the intercolumnar sections of the wall behind. However, the wall niches as architectural feature are not restricted to the triconch sanctuary. We can already clearly state from the ground plan that they dominate all the main parts of the church except to the square room at the east end of the south narthex.

The Wall Niches
Number
According to Grossmann's reconstruction, there are seventy-seven wall niches. The numeration in Fig. 20.1 is based on those made by Akermann (Nos. 1–56) and is supplemented by those niches that Akermann did not count (Nos. 60–65, 67–69) respectively that have been reconstructed by Grossmann (Nos. 57–59, 66, 70–77).

The seventy-seven niches are distributed in the building as follows:

- Triconch sanctuary: thirty niches (Nos. 1–30): Each conch contains ten niches, arranged in two superimposed rows.
- Baptistery: six niches (Nos. 35–40).
- Nave: eighteen niches (Nos. 31–34, 41, 42, 50, 51, 58–67): Niches 59 and 60 have disappeared completely; niche 58 figures only in a small rest of the lower part of the semicircular niche back, and of niche 33 only a small fragment of the niche head is still visible. Niches 51 and 31 are each almost half hidden behind later constructions.
- West narthex: seven niches (Nos. 43–49).
- South narthex: sixteen niches (Nos. 52, 53–56 [each time two niches one upon the other], 57, 68–77); niche 57 is not preserved. Concerning niches 70–77, those within the columned[13] exedra (Nos. 72–76) have disappeared, whereas the status quo of niches 70, 71, and 77 cannot yet be verified.[14]

Appearance

In the White Monastery we can number at least four different variations of niches (Fig. 20.2). To be exact, we can distinguish on the basis of two principal niche types—the barrel-vaulted rectangular niche and the hemispherical-vaulted semicircular niche[15]—between three realizations of the niche crowning:[16]

1. Hemispherical-vaulted semicircular niche crowned by an archivolt (see Fig. 20.2a)

    Owing to the state of preservation of the wall niches and the lack of research in this area, it is difficult to decide whether or not a niche belongs to this first group—this problem occurs also with the following groups (for example, see in this context niches 62, 36, 38 or 39; more certainty perhaps concerning niches 35 and 52). The archivolt of the niche 25, however, may belong to a later 'repair.'

2. Barrel-vaulted rectangular or hemispherical-vaulted semicircular niches with a broken niche pediment: The broken niche pediment is attached to the niche itself (see Figs. 20.2b–c)

    Strictly speaking, a broken niche pediment is a composite pediment, combining the triangular (for example, niches 8, 10, 28, 30, 32, 47, 48, 53–56) or curved (for example, niche 9) center of the pediment above the niche itself with its two lateral broken ends, the latter resting on supports flanking the niche.

As a rule, one can state for the White Monastery that the choice of the supports depends on the type of niche, that is, the broken niche pediment of a barrel-vaulted rectangular niche rests on half pilasters with half capitals of Corinthian order (see Fig. 20.2b), whereas in the case of a hemispherical-vaulted semicircular niche half columns, also with half capitals of Corinthian order, are chosen (see Fig. 20.2c).[17] The complete pediment is framed by a cornice. Both niches are further accentuated by a cornice running along the inner surface of the niches forming the lower limitation of the niche head. Beneath this cornice one can notice in few cases a horizontal frieze with a painted decor or at least traces of paint on it—perhaps a substitute for carved decoration.[18]

The broken niche pediment is a distinctive Egyptian architectural feature deriving from Ptolemaic tradition.[19] Concerning the question of its continuation throughout the Roman period until the fourth century A.D., the discussion is still in progress.[20]

3. Barrel-vaulted rectangular or hemispherical-vaulted semicircular niches with a broken niche pediment: The broken niche pediment with a triangular center is separated from the niche as an autonomous member resting on supports, whereas the niche is crowned by an archivolt (see Fig. 20.2d).

As far as one can state owing to the problems already mentioned, the niches of this third group constitute the exception in the White Monastery (for example, see niches 45, 46 and 50; problematic are niches 63 and 49). By contrast, in the Red Monastery all the niches in the upper story of the conchs in the triconch sanctuary belong to this third group as further niches at the elaborated entrance front into the sanctuary. Also regarding these niches, the choice of the supports of the niche pediment obviously depends on the type of niche.

System

The two niche types are arranged, as Grossmann stated, in a strong system of alternating square and semicircular niches both in the horizontal and in the vertical order, also comprising the window and door openings as substitute for square or semicircular niches. Such a system of alternating semicircular and square niches is well known from Roman architecture back to the first century B.C.[21]

State of Preservation (Fig. 20.3)

Although the niches belong to the original architectural concept of the fifth century and were made of limestone, as were all other parts of the original architectural sculpture (whereas the pieces of granite and marble belong to later repairs or were reused spolia), in different respects they also represent the several periods of destruction and repair. The range of preservation includes the following niches: (1) Remarkably well-preserved niches (for example, niches 9 (see in Fig. 20.2b), 10, 28); (2) Niches with essential damage, as in the broken niche pediment and its lateral supports (for example, niches 7, 8, 41, 42, 61); in some cases only the contours of the broken niche pediment remain visible (for example, niches 6, 11, 12, 15, 17–19, 22); or (3) Niches whose original substance seems to be reduced to almost the fragmentary rest of the niche head inserted into a rebuilt (?) niche structure (niches 1–5, 21, 23, 64) or to be found without context in the debris.

The repairs and reconstructions of the niches 'create' further problems such as the strange, hybrid appearance of some niches (niches 49, 50 or 63) or the obvious mistakes (see niches 54, 56 and 25 with hemispherical-vaulted niche heads inserted in a false way into rectangular niches).

Because of these and other manipulations of the original material and the lack of analytical research there is no methodical basis for attempts such as that undertaken by Laszlo Török to create by means of the decoration of the niche heads a theological and/or liturgical concept.[22]

Sculptural Decoration[23]

a) *Niche head*

At least fifty-three niches present a niche head with sculptured decoration. The repertoire of motifs comprises the following six topical groups (Fig. 20.4):

- Vegetal patterns (tendrils and branches of various plants): ten niches (1, 3, 5, 7, 9, 16, 27, 29,[24] 37, 39)
- Shells: seventeen niches (4,[25] 6, 11, 15,[26] 25, 30 (with a central cross)), 34, 35, 38, 47, 48, 50, 52, 53, 55, 65 and the separate fragment of a niche head)[27]
- Vases with growing vine tendrils: eleven niches (10, 14, 17, 22, 24, 28,[28] 31, 36, 40, 51, 56)

- Animals:[29] eight or nine niches (eagle: 32 (with peacocks), 66; peacock: 42, 61, 67; gazelle/antelope: 12, 18, 41; see also 33)
- Wreathed crosses:[30] three or four niches (2,[31] 8, 26; see also 33[32])
- Interlace (looped) surface patterns: three niches (13, 19, 54)

It appears to be striking that there seem to be no counterparts, despite of the topic they have in common, especially with regard to a relatively homogeneous motif, like the shell, for example.[33]

b) *Cornice beneath the niche head*
- Modillion:[34] niches 34, 35, 36, 41, 42, 45, 46, 49, 51(?), 52, 65, 66, 67
- Band of acanthus leaves: niche 56[35]
- Zigzag band: niches 9, 10 (?)[36]
- (Undulating) vine tendril: niches 63, 38[37]
- Row of tangent circles formed of four spindels:[38] niche 62
- Two-strand guilloche:[39] niche 37

c) *Intrados of the hemispherical-vaulted niche*[40]
- Two rows of looped circles with floral filling motifs:[41] niche 66
- Surface pattern: diagonal grid with filling motifs:[42] niche 41
- Two-strand guilloche of vine tendrils: niche 39
- Surface pattern: tangent octagons forming squares with filling motifs:[43] niches 9, 37
- Acanthus scroll enclosing rosettes: niche 61

d) *Center of the broken niche pediment (Fig. 20.5)*
- Variations of tendrils/branches of different plants (sometimes flanking a central cross): niches 10 (vine tendril), 27, 31, 41, 53, 54(?), 61, 66(?)
- Two-strand tendril forming circular medallions filled with rosettes: niche 67
- Looped guilloche:[44] niche 28
- Two-strand guilloche with an alternation of closed and opened loops, the latter forming circular medallions filled with rosettes:[45] niche 65
- Two-strand guilloche with opened loops, forming circular medallions filled with floral motifs:[46] niche 9
- Central cross flanked by a two strand guilloche with opened loops, forming five circular medallions with different vegetal and ornamental filling motifs: niche 55

- Two-strand guilloche with opened loops, forming lozenges with floral, trefoil and quatrefoil filling: niches 2, 56
- Looped zigzag band: separate niche fragment found in the debris
- Row of tangent squares and lozenges with trefoil and quatrefoil filling: niche 47
- Two peacocks drinking from a central vessel: niches 26,[47] 42
- Two gazelles/antelopes (?)[48] flanking a plant (tree?): niche 32

e) Archivolt
- Row of tangent rectangles with inscribed lozenges and squares in alternation, both with further filling motifs: niche 50
- Two-strand guilloche: niche 35[49]
- Central cross flanked by vases with growing vine tendrils: niche 52

f) Cornice of the broken niche pediment or the archivolt
- Two zones: modillion and astragal/bead and reel: for example, niches 9, 10, 34, 42, 47, 48, 50, 53, 54, 55, 56[50]
- Zigzag band with trefoil filling: niches 2, 30
- Two zones: astragal and two-strand guilloche: niche 32

g) Supports of the broken niche pediment
- Half columns: The preserved examples (for example, niches 8, 10, 26, 28) are decorated with half vertical and diagonal fluting.
- Half pilasters: The preserved examples (niches 9, 27) are decorated with an elaborated motif consisting of a pair of tangent opposed undulating bands/tendrils forming oval medallions filled with floral motifs.
- Half capitals: The preserved examples are of Corinthian order.

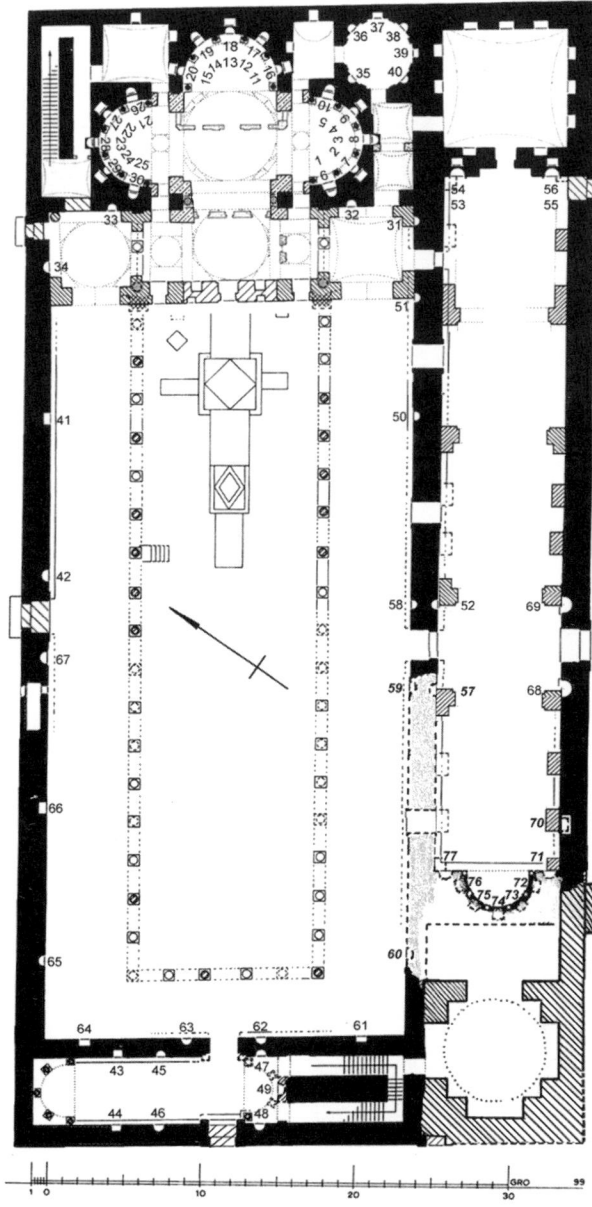

Fig. 20.1: Reconstruction of the ground plan of the White Monastery (Reconstruction: Suzana Hodak on the basis of following plans: Grossmann 2002a: fig.150; ibid. 1982: 116, fig. 48A; and Akermann 1976).

Fig. 20.2: The repertoire of niches in the White Monastery: a [niche 52], b [niche 9], c [niche 26], d [niche 45]. Photograph: Suzana Hodak and Siegfried G. Richter.

Fig. 20.3: Examples of the different states of preservation of the wall niches: see (in horizontal direction from left to right) niches 42, 64, 6 (detail) and the separate fragment of a niche head. Photograph: Suzana Hodak and Siegfried G. Richter.

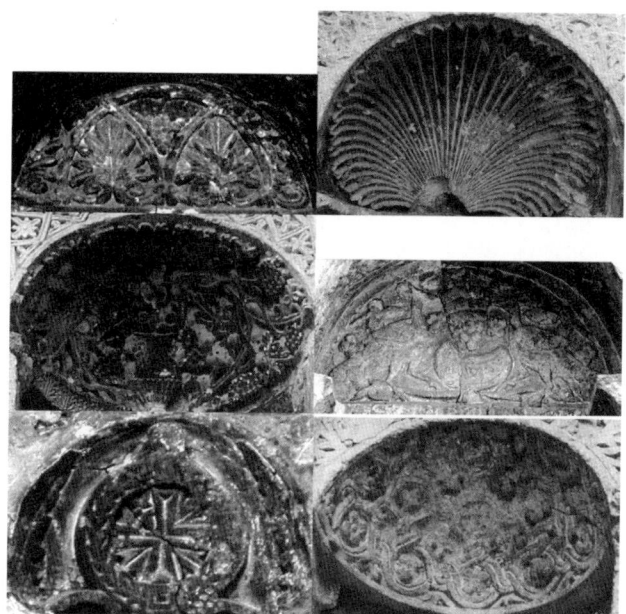

Fig. 20.4: The repertoire of motifs of the sculptured niche heads: see (in horizontal direction from left to right) niches 37, 52, 56, 61, 8 and 54. Photograph: Suzana Hodak and Siegfried G. Richter.

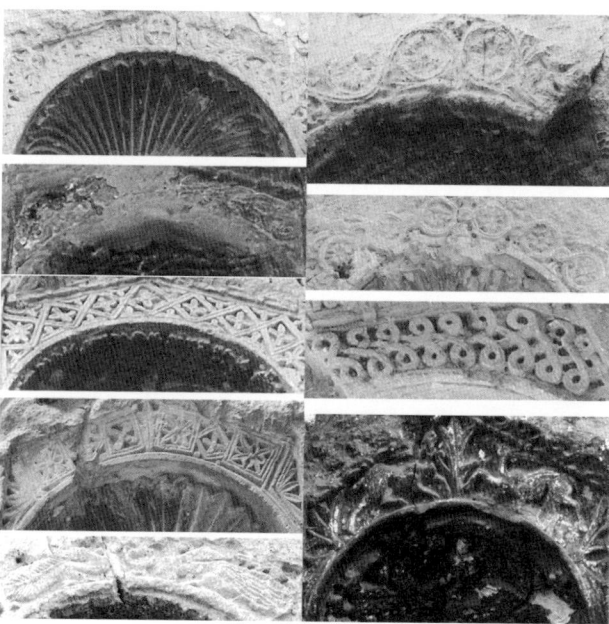

Fig. 20.5: Examples of the repertoire of motifs of the sculptured center of the broken niche pediments: see (in horizontal direction from left to right) niches 53, 67, 28, 65, 56, separate fragment of a niche head, 47, 32 and 42. Photograph: Suzana Hodak and Siegfried G. Richter.

Notes

1. Although it is well known that these two buildings are indeed *only* the churches of the former monasteries of Anba Shinuda and Anba Bishoi, their popular names will be used in the following; see Grossmann 2002b: 528.

2. Concerning the situation of Coptic sculpture, see with additional bibliographical references for example, Severin 1977: 243–53; 1981: 315–36; 1991a: 2112–17; 1993: 63–85; 1998: 295–338; Török 1970: 437–84; Thomas 1989: 54–64; Krumeich 2003: *passim*.

3. For the "Coptic" period, see for example, Thomas 1989: 54–64 *(passim)*; Thomas 2000: *passim* (cf. Index), esp. pp. 26–27. For some examples of painted sculpture in limestone or wood, see Török 2005a: 180, 187–88, 207–208, 238.

4. See in note 18.

5. See Monneret de Villard 1925–1926, vol. 2: 121–31.

6. Akermann 1976. He tried to present a catalogue of the preserved and/or visible wall niches with carved decoration and the friezes and cornices of the triconch sanctuary. See the review of Severin 1980: 100–101.

7. See cited titles in note 2.

8. Our major source for pictures is still Monneret de Villard's study of the two churches. See in addition to this few published pictures of the courtesy of H.-G. Severin (cf. in Krumeich 2003, vol. 1: figs. 3–5, 26, 31, 32, 43, 44, 47, 50, 52, 54) and the project of a photographical documentation excluding the sanctuary, which was undertaken by E. Bolman (see Bolman 2004a: 381–82).

9. See for example, Severin 1991b: 769–70; Grossmann 2002b: 126–28.

10. I would especially like to thank Prof. Dr. Siegfried Richter for his immense support in taking the photographs. Except Fig. 20.1 (see note 11), the other figures are based on photographs taken by him or the author.

11. Fig. 20.1 attempts to present an *approximate* idea of the present-day state of preservation of the church with focus on the wall niches. The plan is based on the reconstruction of the original ground plan and a detailed plan of the actual appearance of the sanctuary, both prepared by Grossmann (see Grossmann 2002a: 528–36, fig.150 and Grossmann 1982: 116, fig. 48A) and for the southwestern part of the church on the ground plan published by Akermann 1976.

12. See Grossmann 1991a: 768.

13. See still some column shafts in situ in a picture published by Monneret de Villard 1925–1926, vol. 1: fig.23. Today the exedra is completely 'cleaned.'

14. The reconstruction of the niches 70 and 72–76 is relatively 'up to date' (see Grossmann 2002a: fig.150 dated to 1999) as they are lacking in the previous publications of the reconstructed ground plan of the church (see for example, Grossmann 1984–1985: 71, fig.1; Grossmann 1991a: 768 and Grossmann 1998:

233, fig.13). This important fact is obviously not recognized by Török (2005b: fig.28) as he refers to the obsolete ground plan of 1998.

15. For the different type of niches, see Hornbostel-Hüttner 1979: 17.

16. Cf. Severin 1993: 63–85 and Krumeich 2003, vol. 1: 125–32.

17. The form of the center of the pediment seems not to depend on the type of the niche.

18. See especially the niche 65 with a red-colored zigzag band with outline in brown-red color, framed by orange bands; see perhaps also the niches 8 and 51. Compare the possible traces of paint on the horizontal zone beneath the cornice on the wall in the southeast corner of the south narthex. Further traces of paint are also visible on other architectural members of the niches, so on the cornice beneath the niche head (for example, niches 9, 10, 45, 61, 65); the broken niche pediment (for example, niche 10) and the supports of the broken niche pediment (for example, niche 10).

19. Concerning the genesis of the broken pediment, see Bergmann 1988: 59–77, esp. 68–70. Concerning its characteristic in the White Monastery, see Krumeich 2003, vol. 1: 130.

20. See contrary to the negative position of for example, Severin (1993: 70–71) on the base of new finds Török (2005b: 119–20); cf. also McKenzie 1996: 116.

21. See Grossmann 2002b: 118–20.

22. See Török 2005b: 159–62. Török refers only to the niches, which figure in Akermann's work, ignoring those niches in the nave which were "uncovered" in the meantime; cf. also note 14.

23. The documentation of the sculptural decoration remains incomplete, because several niches cannot yet be studied. Because of the apparent problems of an adequate nomenclature for ornamental motifs (see Hodak 2004: 53), a reference is, whenever possible, made to a comparable motif in the catalogue of Balmelle and Prudhomme 1985.

24. According to Akermann (1976: 5 note 3) this niche is without sculptural decoration and was never sculptured as also the niches 15, 20, and 49.

25. The interpretation of this motif is difficult; see Akermann 1976: 25.

26. See note 24.

27. Concerning the etymology of the Greek word for 'conch' from the shell decoration itself, see Hornbostel-Hüttner 1979: 3–4, 20; for the shell motif, see 195–99.

28. According to Akermann 1976: 72–73; actually hidden behind a modern icon placed in the niche.

29. For the range of animal motifs, see Krumeich 2003, vol. 1: 152–55.

30. See Krumeich 2003, vol. 1: 143–48. According to Török (2005b: 161–62) it is a triumphal (jeweled) crown held in God's hand.

31. According to Akermann (1976: 20–21) this niche should be decorated with a shell motif.

32. According to Akermann (1976: 84–85) the center of the decoration is a wreathed cross.

33. See on the contrary Akermann (1976: 22–23), who pretends that the niches 3 and 5 present an almost identical decoration.

34. See Krumeich 2003, vol. 1: 115–22.

35. Cf. Krumeich 2003, vol. 2: 79–80; Krumeich 2003, vol. 1: pl. 47; the cornice was not noted by Akermann 1976: 130–31.

36. See note 18.

37. Concerning this motif in general, see Krumeich 2003, vol. 1: 80–96.

38. Cf. Balmelle and Prudhomme 1985: 94, pl. 46a–b.

39. Cf. ibid.: 120–21, pls.70c–j, 71a–e.

40. It was not yet possible to verify the intrados of the niches 1, 3, 5, 12, 14, 21, 23, 27, and 29.

41. Cf. ibid.: 368, pl. 235a.d.

42. Cf. ibid.: 188–89, pl. 124a–c.

43. Cf. ibid.: 251, pl.163b.

44. Cf. ibid.: 124–25, pls. 74e.h, 75a.

45. Cf. ibid.: 119, pl. 69f–g.

46. Cf. ibid.: 119, pl. 69a–b.

47. Not noted by Akermann 1976: 68–69.

48. According to Török (2005b: 161) these animals represent 'harts.'

49. Not noted by Akermann 1976: 94–95.

50. The modillion zone is not noted by Akermann 1976: 130–31.

21 The Triconch Sanctuaries of Sohag

Dale Kinney

LE PROBLÈME DE *l'abside tréflée, de son origine, de son développement, l'histoire enfin de ce type de structure, a eté dans ces dernières années l'argument de bien de travaux; mais, malgré cela, je crois que l'étude peut donner encore quelque résultat si on voudra profiter d'une documentation bien précise et abandonner toutes les théories aprioristiques."*[1] Published in 1925, these words still describe the situation nearly a century later: despite much recent discussion about the origin and history of the triconch sanctuary ('abside tréflée'), there is still much we do not know, and new research continues to challenge old theories and assumptions. This paper will review the course of scholarship since Ugo Monneret de Villard wrote those sentences, especially as it pertains to the churches of the monasteries of St. Shenoute and St. Bishoi.

The triconch—trichorum or τρίκογχος—was an established building type in late antiquity. Its name describes its defining feature, three semi-circular exedrae or apses. The basic idea was realized in many variations, large and small, roofed and unroofed, free-standing and embedded, centralized and longitudinal; and it was used for many purposes, public and private, secular and religious. Most often the three exedrae are aligned on cruciform axes, as at Sohag, but the axes are not always of equal length; one may be elongated, isolating the central conch in a focal position, and the apses are not always of the same size. In the class of triconches the Sohag examples stand out for their monumentality and relatively good state of preservation. Its triconch

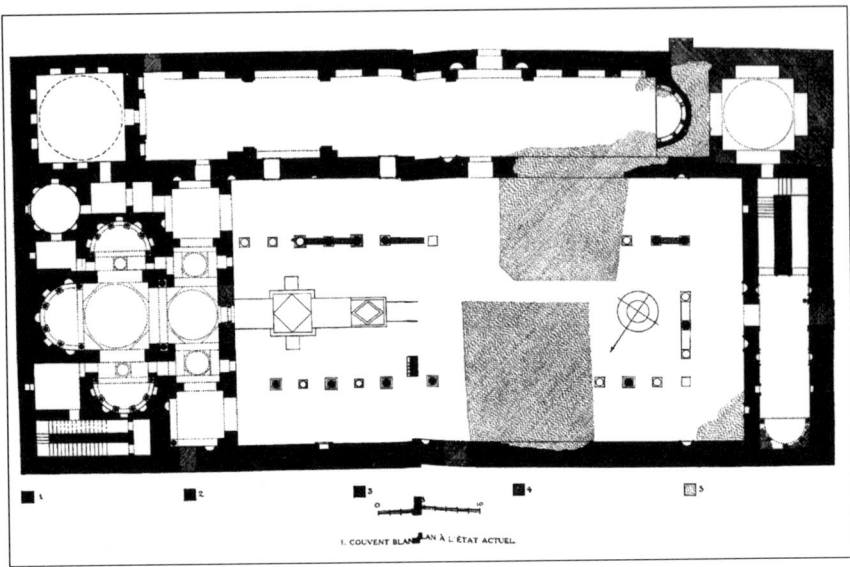

Fig. 21.1: Plan of the church of St. Shenoute (Monneret de Villard 1925–1926, vol. 1: pl. 1).

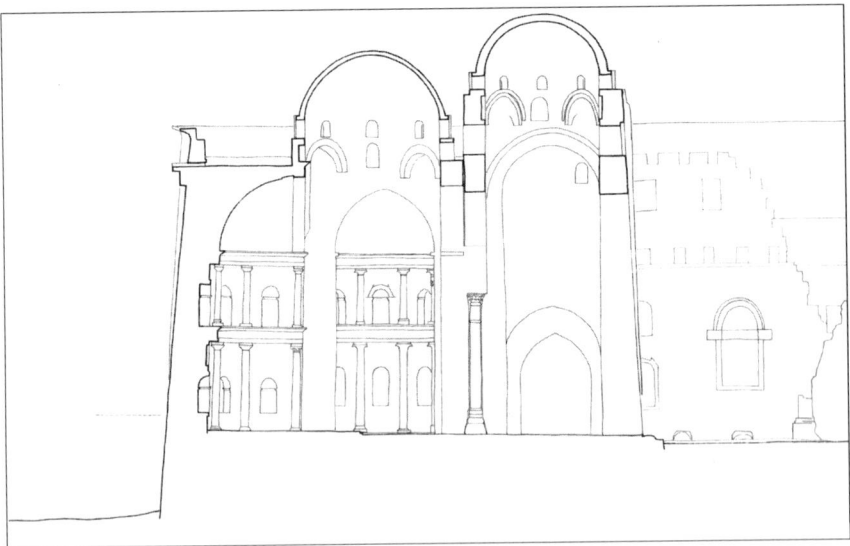

Fig. 21.2: Church of St. Shenoute, north–south section through triconch, Technische Hochschule Darmstadt, 1962.

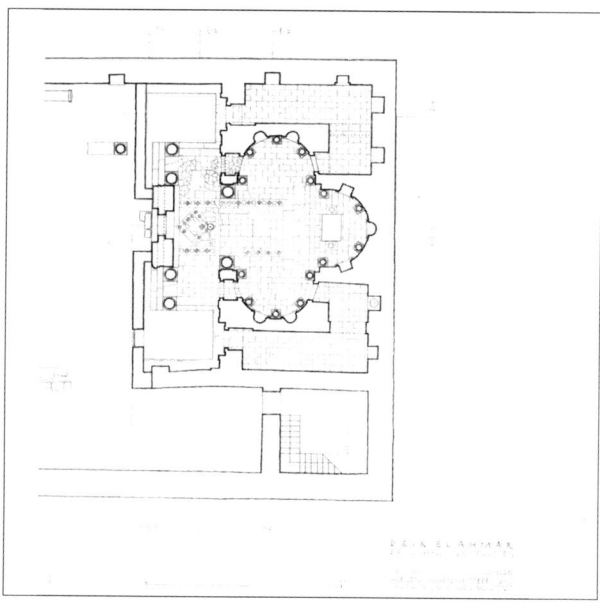

Fig. 21.3: Church of the Monastery of St. Bishoi, plan of triconch, Technische Hochschule Darmstadt, 1962.

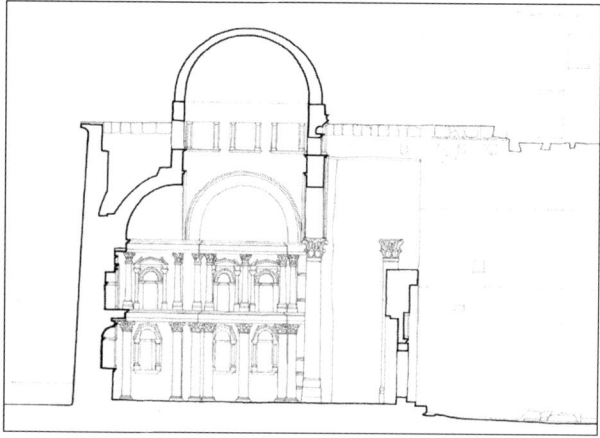

Fig. 21.4: Church of the Monastery of St. Bishoi, east–west section through triconch, Technische Hochschule Darmstadt, 1962.

sanctuary makes the Church of St. Shenoute, in particular, a major monument of early Christian architecture, and places Sohag in an international nexus of ambitious and innovative church designs as well as at the source of a significant regional tradition.[2]

Some details of the design of both of the Sohag triconches are unknown or speculative due to damage and restorations. The triconch of the Church of St. Bishoi (the Red Monastery) is closer to its original state than the triconch of St. Shenoute (the White Monastery), which seems to have burned and partially collapsed at an early date.[3] Both triconches were closed off from their respective naves to become independent buildings in the Middle Ages, and both are now still hidden behind tall north–south walls with small doors, as shown in the plan of the Church of St. Shenoute published by Monneret de Villard as the "*état actuel*" of 1925 (Fig. 21.1). Plans and sections made by students at the Technische Hochschule Darmstadt in 1962

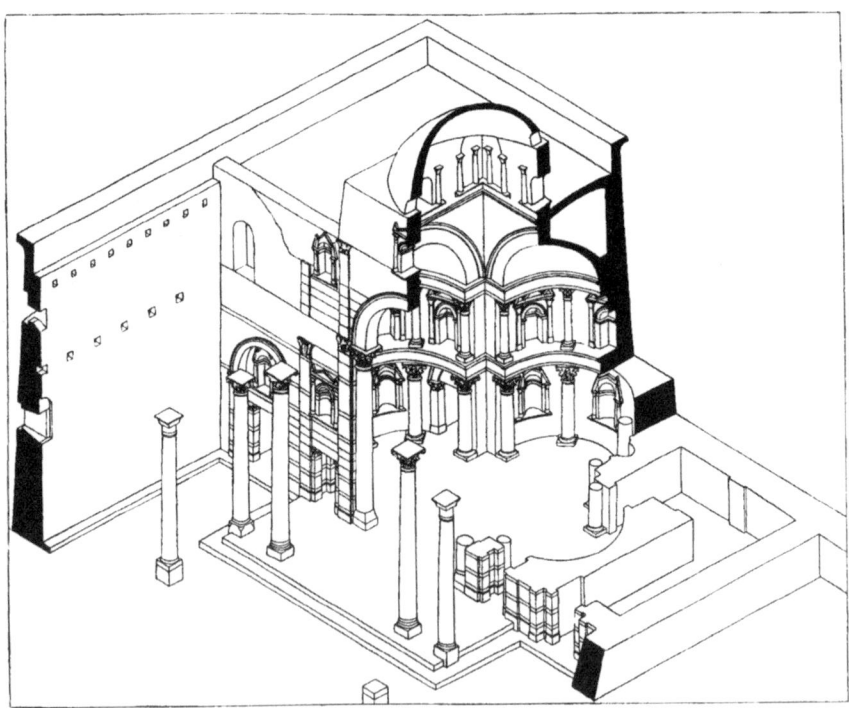

Fig. 21.5: Triconch of the Monastery of St. Bishoi, axonometric elevation (Monneret de Villard 1925–1926, vol. 2: fig. 123).

(Figs. 21.2 and 21.4) show both triconches in essentially their present form, although some features have changed in the intervening forty-five years.[4] Monneret's axonometric rendering of the triconch of St. Bishoi (Fig. 21.5) intimates the grandeur of conception that can still be sensed in both buildings, despite all of their trials and deformations. The impact is easier to grasp today at the Red Monastery thanks to the efforts of the conservators and other experts coordinated by Elizabeth Bolman.

Both triconches feature semi-circular exedrae opening off a square space. Passageways through the lateral apses lead east into rooms tucked into the spaces between the outer curves of the exedrae and the straight walls that frame the building externally, and west into transverse spaces between the triconch and the nave. The three apses are all of the same size and height, and all are similarly articulated with two rows of framed niches. In their present state, both triconches have domes over the central space and semi-domes over the apses. The semi-domes in the triconch of St. Bishoi are original and convey the intended appearance. The domes of both triconches, however, are replacements for a superstructure of a different kind. Somers Clarke, who studied these buildings before Monneret de Villard and the restorations promoted by the Comité de Conservation des Monuments de l'Art Arabe, opined that because of the relative thinness of its walls the triconch of St. Shenoute must have been covered originally by a wooden roof, an opinion shared today by Peter Grossmann. The triconch of St. Bishoi, smaller and later than that of the White Monastery, may have been vaulted but probably was not domed.[5]

Another significant difference between the triconches occurs in the relation of the exedrae to the central space. In the church of St. Shenoute's monastery, the east apse opens directly off the central square but the north and south apses are separated from it by two broad arches, the second of which currently is higher and carries a small cupola. The effect is to elongate the square and to push the lateral apses outward into near alignment with the aisles of the basilica; in other words, to make the triconch occupy more of the width of the east end. The triconch at the Red Monastery is more compact, with all three exedrae opening directly from the center; consequently, its width is not much greater than that of the nave. The compact design requires that the passageways to the peripheral spaces go through the walls of the north and south apses, rather than through piers under intermediate arches as in the Church of St. Shenoute. The passageways in turn alter the pattern of the wall niches, as they replace two of them at ground level in each apse (Fig. 21.2). Thus while the eastern apse has three niches, two square and one rounded, the lateral apses each have two rounded niches flanking a column. By contrast, the design of the triconch of the White Monastery church permits all three apses to be identical, with five alternately rectangular and semi-circular niches in each. The alternation is ingeniously managed so that a semi-circular niche falls in the center of the east apse and rectangular ones in the centers of the side apses.

The fourth side of both triconches was open to the west under an arch supported by tall columns. Clarke noted that the north–south brick wall that divides the triconch of St. Shenoute from its basilica must coincide with an original division of the church, because the pavement between it and the triconch—"formed of sundry slabs of red granite, bearing traces of hieroglyphs and patterns, terribly broken up"—was uniformly 38 cm higher than the pavement of the nave.[6] Not much more could be said about the western facade, however, because this zone of St. Shenoute's church has been so thoroughly rebuilt. Clarke turned to the triconch of the Red Monastery church, where there was also a transverse wall (later removed) in which he could see four columns, a shorter pair aligned with the columns of the aisles of the basilica and a taller, inner pair that framed the opening into the triconch (Fig. 21.5). The central columns are thought to have supported what Peter Grossmann later termed a "forward trium-phal arch." Clarke also found original paving in this area, "consist[ing] of small squares of dark granite and basalt, inlaid upon bands of white marble." These fragments were evidently still in situ in 1962 (Fig. 21.2) but are not there today. As at the Church of St. Shenoute, there was a change of level between the space in front of the triconch and the nave, which was lower.[7]

Literary and epigraphical evidence indicates that the Church of St. Shenoute, including the triconch, was built and dedicated just before 450 with the participation of "the most illustrious Count Caesarius, son of Candidianus," who is referred to as "founder" in an inscription over the door into the south aisle.[8] Recent attempts to date the Red Monastery tri-conch place it a century later, in the fourth or fifth decades of the sixth century.[9] There is some reason to think that the later triconch was origi-nally free-standing; in any case it seems to have been built and decorated by more skilled workmen than the basilica.[10] Clearly, the purpose of the Red Monastery triconch was to reproduce—duplicate or 'copy'—the triconch of St. Shenoute's church, for reasons that are still uncertain. The design

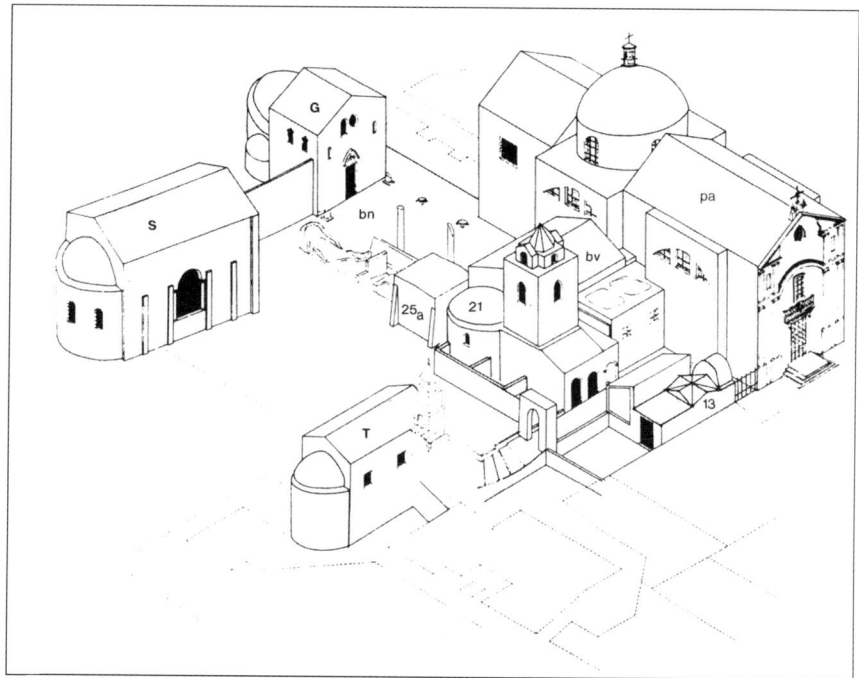

Fig. 21.6: Monastery of St. Paulinus, Nola, axonometric elevation (Lehmann 2004: fig. 1a).

was given by St. Shenoute's triconch, and the genesis of the design must be sought in the context of the fifth century, historical and typological.

Monneret de Villard sought to answer the question of origins taxonomically, by sorting all of the triconch basilicas known in his day into three types: (A) aisled basilicas with a trefoil structure enclosed at the east end; (B) a simplified version in which the trefoil is appended to a single nave; (C), the type of the Church of St. Paulinus at Nola in Campania (Fig. 21.6, G), which "according to texts" was an aisled basilica with a trichorum. "A" is the type of the Sohag churches and the church in the precinct of the Hathor Temple at Dendera (now dated by Grossmann to the sixth century), as well as the monastery Church of St. Theodosius (Dayr Dosi) in Palestine and the ceremonial hall in the Umayyad palace at Mschatta in Syria.[11] Monneret believed that the "A" group constituted an "Egypto-Palestinian" type that was the source of the "B" group, and

"C" was a parallel invention. He argued that the type originated in Syria, or with a Syrian architect, because other aspects of the triconches also showed Syrian connections. The triconch form itself and the elevation of the Sohag apses, with superimposed rows of niches, were a Roman inheritance; Monneret de Villard pointed in particular to the nymphaeum at Gerasa in modern Jordan.[12] Triconches were widespread in Roman architecture and Monneret de Villard found that they were most common in baths and palaces. Although he did not make much of it, Monneret de Villard implied that it was through palace architecture that the trefoil form entered churches.[13]

Twenty years later, André Grabar published the groundbreaking first volume of *Martyrium*, which offered a comprehensive explanation not only of the triconch but of all centralized forms in Christian architecture on the basis of what he called a "functional" approach: "the same religious functions call forth the same types of buildings and images."[14] To account for the many examples of *cellae trichorae* found in Christian cemeteries in Rome, North Africa, Gaul, Pannonia, and Palestine, Grabar looked for pagan buildings of like form and function. Although the archaeological record is weak, an inscription found in Tolentino commemorating a funerary *panteum cum tricoro* (also cited by Monneret de Villard) bolstered his case that Christian triconch chapels originated in the architectural typology of pagan tombs. Grabar's overarching theory was that Christians deliberately adopted the forms of pagan funerary architecture for *martyria*—buildings marking the tombs of martyrs as well as "theophanic" sites in Palestine—because of their functional associations. Thence these forms came into use for nonfunerary purposes, as at Sohag.[15] An additional factor specific to Sohag, in his view, was Shenoute's intention to establish new pilgrimage centers in Upper Egypt, "to invite [Egyptian] Christians . . . to replace pilgrimage to the Holy Land with pious visits to the churches of their own country. Shenoute . . . urged his countrymen to consider the grand monasteries that he founded at Sohag as Jerusalem, as sacred as the ancient city in Palestine." This suggested that the triconch had become a signifier of ongoing theophany rather than of particular historic manifestations of the deity.[16]

Grabar later observed that his theory of meaningful typologies resembles the linguistic concept of "semantic families."[17] Irving Lavin evoked a similar connection with his term "associative architecture" in an influential article of 1962, which sought to modify Grabar's theory by allowing for the prominence of triconch rooms in palaces from late antiquity onward.

"The triconch . . . appears as a kind of test case in the evolution of medieval 'associative' architecture . . . . Largely as a result of its associations, a Roman architectural tradition was transferred to Byzantium, there to play a role [in the typology of Byzantine palaces] that has no real parallel in the west."[18] Extending his argument to ceremonial *triclinia* of all shapes, Lavin endorsed the long-standing belief that the aulic associations of centralized forms made them seem suitable for churches. "With the establishment of Christianity as the state religion, many of its official aspects were conceived in terms of the imperial cult . . . . The heavens are 'imperial domiciles,' and the eternal city a palace . . . . The church is also described in the same terms as the royal palace."[19] To signify the "house of the Lord," church buildings were built to look like the grand rooms where earthly rulers received their guests.

Lavin did not apply the analogy of palace *triclinia* explicitly to triconch basilicas, but Peter Grossmann did so thirty years later. Grossmann proposed that there could have been a metonymic transfer from ceremonial triclinia of the type seen at Piazza Armerina to the site of the Christian eucharist ("since the holy communion in a church is in a way understandable as a kind of meal"), not directly, but via cemetery triconches where the eucharist was also celebrated.[20] Subsequently he qualified this argument to account for the possibility that the idea for the triconch design came from Shenoute or his monks, not an architect. This might make a derivation from funerary triconches seem more likely; yet "it cannot be excluded that the triconch was viewed as an exceptionally rich spatial form, and for that reason was used in an ambitious church building . . . ; in that case only correspondingly shaped palace spaces would have come up as models, which takes us again back to dining rooms."[21]

Grossmann was responding to a challenge to the existence of such associative typologies raised by Tomas Lehmann, whose archaeological study of the buildings erected and described by St. Paulinus of Nola at Cimitile, northeast of Naples (Fig. 21.6), led him to reconsider the origin of the triconch basilica. Following a number of German scholars more or less militantly skeptical of the idea that antique architectural forms were or could be '*Bedeutungsträger*,' Lehmann insisted that "like nearly every spatial form in Roman architecture, the centralized building was not tied to any purpose, nor was it in the early Christian period, when one finds centralized spaces in various forms as baptisteries, memorial buildings, and episcopal and community churches."[22] Insisting further that the historical study of triconches should be based on modern taxonomic criteria rather than the imprecise vocabulary of ancient sources, Lehmann demonstrated that the building that St. Paulinus himself called *absidem trichoram*—the sanctuary space of his new basilica in the cemetery of St. Felix—is not a triconch, because the lateral "apses" are smaller and lower than the eastern one and do not, therefore, fit the model of "three, usually semi-circular conches or apses of equal size, which are added in the manner of a cloverleaf to a central crossing that is often a square" (Fig. 21.6, G).[23] Since Paulinus's Basilica Nova was dedicated in 403, the effect of eliminating it from the category of triconch basilicas was to reopen the question of when and where the type originated; Egypt (Sohag), Crete, and North Africa are all contenders.

Applying an equally formalist approach, Iris Stollmayer argued that triconch basilicas were not a type *(Baukonzept)*, so Lehmann's exclusion of St. Paulinus's trefoil-ended basilica is unfounded; this "supposedly homogenous class of buildings disintegrates into a variety of particular forms," including the one at Cimitile.[24] Stollmayer effectively takes us back to Monneret de Villard, positing three formally defined categories: freestanding triconches *(Zentralbauten)*, single-naved triconch basilicas, and triconch basilicas with nave and aisles. But unlike Monneret, however, she denied that these categories reveal any filiations or genealogy; on the contrary, they break down into discrete regional groups: Egyptian, Lycian, Armenian, Croatian. Only buildings within regions show direct interrelationships, with one church often serving as the model for the rest, as the Sohag churches were prototypical for Egypt. Stollmayer also denied any functional connotations of the triconch; according to her, because the form was employed in many contexts, including villas, baths, and cemeteries, it had no fixed associations. The possibility of "semantic families" of buildings or of "associative architecture" is ruled out, at least for triconches. "The buildings cited are not related to one another by a standardized form, nor demonstrably by function or symbolism, nor can any common origin or genesis be discerned. Late antique triconch churches have in common a 'theme,' which . . . was varied at will . . . ."[25]

The result of these latest interventions is to leave us with the proverbial elephant in the room: an imposing triconch basilica whose presence cannot be explained. It is not at all obvious that the monastery church of a desert father in Upper Egypt would be the first datable instance of this "theme," as well as its most ambitious realization. If the idea was Shenoute's, one feels compelled to ask where he got it, why it seemed appropriate, and how he communicated it to the workmen charged to construct it.

The last question points to the difficulty with Stollmayer's position that the triconch basilica was not a *Baukonzept*. That the triconch, at least, was indeed an architectural concept is indicated by the existence of a word for it, *trichorum*. The triconch existed in discourse, like the basilica, and discourse was one means of its dissemination. Another was non-verbal representation in plans and models. Donors carry models of their buildings in early Christian mosaics (for example, in the apse of San Vitale at Ravenna), and the use of plans is attested for a building exactly contemporary with St. Paulinus's constructions at Nola, the cathedral at Gaza erected in 402–407. According to the fifth-century biographer of the cathedral's founding bishop, as the people of Gaza were arguing about what form the new church should take, whether that of the destroyed temple of Zeus Marnas, which it replaced, or a totally different one, a letter arrived from the Empress Eudoxia:

> Enclosed in the letter was the plan (σκάριφος) of the holy church in the form of a cross . . . and the letter contained instructions that the holy church be built according to this plan. . . . Furthermore, the letter announced the dispatch of costly columns and marbles.[26]

Following these instructions,

> The holy Bishop [Porphyry] ... engaged the architect Rufinus from Antioch, a dependable and expert man, and it was he who completed the entire construction. He took some chalk and marked the outline (θέσις) of the holy church according to the form of the plan (σχῆμα τοῦ σκαρίφου) that had been sent by the most pious Eudoxia.[27]

A triconch plan etched into the pavement of the temple court at Dendera is in 1:1 scale to the triconch that actually was built there, so it is certain that the drawings were a factor in the spread of ecclesiastical triconches in Egypt.[28]

The likelihood that other aspects of the Gaza scenario were reenacted at Sohag—the intervention of an important, if not imperial, secular patron and the participation of an architect from a major metropolis—supports the reconstruction of the process proposed by Monneret de Villard, although the architect did not necessarily come from Syria. The monumental niched triconch in the court of the Peirene Fountain in Corinth, recently redated from the second century to the second half of the fourth, suggests the possibility of late antique prototypes in the eastern Mediterranean, and, as has often been suggested, Alexandria may be a more likely source of the Sohag design.[29] Betsey Ann Robinson traced the Peirene triconch to the *triclinia* first studied by Lavin, and explained it as the deliberate appropriation of a building type from "domestic architecture of the most opulent sort," a transferral to the public sphere of "an architecture of convivium" that would have been very familiar to members of the social class that governed Corinth in late antiquity.[30]

That class was a frequent presence at Sohag. According to Heike Behlmer, "the number and high rank of the government officials Shenoute reports to have been intimate with is quite astonishing," and included governors, counts, and military commanders. "From Shenoute's own works one obtains the impression of a secular aristocracy disposed to travel . . . in style, accompanied by their families, clerks and servants . . . . They would come freely to the local holy man . . . and discuss theological questions among equals. . . ."[31] Among them was the comes Caesarius, who came often, at least once with the hegemon Taurinus and their entourages, to discuss problems in the church at Alexandria. If the "Magnificent Count Caesarius" commemorated as founder on the lintel in St. Shenoute's basilica was not this Count Caesarius but another (which seems unlikely), he was in any case of the same social stratum. To such men, the grandiose form of the triconch would have seemed as appropriate as it did to the ruling class in Corinth—appropriate on one plane to their own status as patrons, and on another, allegorical plane to the Lord whose theophany was ongoing in the Christian liturgy that would be performed there.

It is possible to agree with Tomas Lehmann and Iris Stollmayer that the triconch had no fixed or exclusive associations without entirely rejecting the idea that triconches were a form of "associative architecture." Peter Grossmann cautioned that similarities among buildings must be judged in three dimensions—in mass and height, kind and quality of decoration, "the quality of space"—rather than in the "calligraphy" of the ground plan.[32] It is from elevations that associations—we might think of them as social memories—arise. In elevation the Sohag triconches evoke certain public buildings—the fountains in Corinth and Gerasa. A different elevation might have recalled other kinds of triconches and therefore, a different set of associations. In plan or concept, however, all triconches represent the number three. St. Paulinus made this obvious by decorating the main apse of his triconch with an image of the Trinity, accompanied by verses that are preserved in a letter to his friend Sulpicius Severus: "In full mystery sparkles the Trinity . . . . The holy unity of the Trinity meets in Christ, who likewise has His insignia in threefold . . . ."[33] Paulinus described his triconch in the same terms, as a unity of three: "an undulating apse *(absis sinuata)* unfold[ing] itself with two recesses, one to the right and one to the left."[34] The symbolism of three was latent in every triconch, whether or not the patron recognized or exploited it. Whatever the associative meanings of the triconch's material realization, it was the symbolic potential of the concept that evidently appealed to St. Paulinus, and arguably to St. Shenoute as well.[35]

Notes

1. Monneret de Villard 1925–1926: vol. 2: 48.
2. Krautheimer 1986: 113–17.
3. Grossmann 2002a: 533–34 dates the fire that partially destroyed the triconch to the Persian invasion in 619.
4. Peter Grossmann kindly shared these drawings with Nicholas Warner, project architect at the Red Monastery, who in turn shared them with me.
5. Clarke 1912: 153; Grossmann 2006: 45.
6. Clarke 1912: 153.
7. Ibid.: 169.
8. Lefebvre 1920a: cols. 471–75; Emmel 1998: 93–95.
9. Severin (forthcoming).
10. Grossmann 2002a: 538.
11. For the church at Dendera see Grossmann 2002a: 443–46. For Dayr Dosi: Stollmayer 1999: 134 and 148 Nr. 30.
12. Monneret de Villard 1925–1926, vol. 2: 129–30. For the nymphaeum: MacDonald 1986: 200 and Fig. 105 (p. 106).
13. Monneret de Villard 1925–1926, vol. 1: 47–64.
14. Grabar 1946, vol. 1: iii.
15. Ibid.: 102–19.
16. Ibid.: 328.
17. Ibid.: iii.
18. Lavin 1962: 12.
19. Ibid.: 16.
20. Grossmann 1992: 190.
21. Grossmann 2002b: 124.

22. Lehmann 1996: 320–21.

23. Ibid.: 323, 354.

24. Stollmayer 1999: 140.

25. Ibid.: 141.

26. Mark the Deacon, Life of Porphyry 76; trans. Mango 1972: 31; ed. Gregoire and Kugener 1930: 60.

27. Mark the Deacon, Life of Porphyry 78; trans. Mango 1972: 31; ed. Gregoire and Kugener 1930: 62.

28. Grossmann 2002a: 445.

29. Robinson 2001: 118–31. I am grateful to Sarah Lepinski for directing me to this study.

30. Ibid.: 134–39.

31. Behlmer 1998: 346–51.

32. Grossmann 1992: 188.

33. Paulinus of Nola, Epistula 32, 10.8–15: trans. Goldschmidt 1940: 38–39.

34. Paulinus of Nola, Epistula 32, 13.14: trans. Goldschmidt 1940: 40–41.

35. This study of the Sohag triconches was carried out under the auspices of the Red Monastery Project in collaboration with the Egyptian Supreme Council of Antiquities and the Coptic Church. I am grateful to Zahi Hawass, Abdallah Kamel, Magdi al-Ghandour, Abdallah Attar, and Muhammad Abd al-Rahim of the SCA, as well as to His Holiness Pope Shenouda III, Bishop Yohannes, Father Wissa, and Father Antonius for their generous hospitality and support. Work is being funded and administered by USAID and ARCE, under the Egyptian Antiquities Conservation Project (EAC) Agreement No. 263–A-00-04-00018-00. Thanks to Michael Jones, Red Monastery Project Manager for EAP/ARCE, and EAC Director for his assistance and on-site advice. I also thank Dr. Elizabeth Bolman for the priceless opportunity to be part of the Red Monastery team.

22 Two Witnesses of Christian Life in the Area of Balyana

The Church of the Virgin and the Monastery of Anba Moses[1]

Ashraf Alexandre Sadek

THE TOWN OF Balyana stands on the west bank of the Nile in the Sohag governorate. I have had many opportunities to be in touch with Christian life in this area of Upper Egypt through my acquaintance with the local bishop, Anba Wissa. In this study I shall deal mainly with two buildings that have played an important part in the lives of Christians here: the old church of the Virgin, which has not yet been studied sufficiently, and the Monastery of Anba Moses of Abydos, two kilometers north of the famous temple of Pharaoh Seti I. We will describe their present state and give a catalogue of the icons kept there.

In his general study, Stefan Timm sums up the known points of the history of Balyana as follows:[2]

> Balyana is attested as an episcopal center as early as in the eleventh century, because of a controversy in which the Bishop of Balyana opposed the Patriarch Shenoute I (850–880). This event is reported in both the *Synaxarium* and *History of the Patriarchs*.

From the tenth century we have two inscriptions on gravestones mentioning Balyana and quoted in the *Coptic Encyclopedia*: from the year 932 comes the tombstone of Kyra Susinne, whose father Psate was from Balyana;[3] the second tombstone, dated 939, is that of Apa Theodorarus, son of Moses, a presbyter from Balyana.[4] This is also witness to the fact that the name 'Moses' was still used in the area of Balyana in the tenth century, probably as it had been famous in previous centuries because of Moses of Abydos. It is presumed to have derived from the ancient suffix 'messes,' which was added to create, for example, the name 'Ra-messes.' Another inscription, undated, mentions a deacon from Balyana.[5]

In the eleventh century Bishop Mark of Balyana (who died in 1092) took part in an attempt to dismiss the patriarch Christodoulos (1047–1077); the plot had been organized by John, Bishop of Sakha (west of the Delta). We also know that said Bishop of Balyana was an elector of Christodoulos's successor, and that at the synod held in Old Cairo in 1086 he was himself elected dean of Egyptian bishops.

The *History of the Patriarchs* also mentions that the Patriarch Christodoulos ordained Poimen, who was originally from Balyana, as Bishop of Armant.

In the twelfth century a man from Balyana became bishop of his home city. After that we have no mention of Balyana as a bishopric until the beginning of the twentieth century.

Stefan Timm mentions two other modern churches in Balyana and concludes by stressing the fact that the church of the Virgin was never studied. However, Bishop Samuel published in 1990, among many other plans, the plan of this church,[6] as well as that of the Dayr Anba Moses.

The two monuments we present here are of interest both for their architecture and history, as they bear witness to Christianity past and present in this area. We visited them several times, the last time being in November 2005, and we shall try to give as detailed an account as possible of their present state.

The Church of the Virgin in Balyana
Mentions of the Church by Travelers

The church of the Virgin in Balyana is mentioned by several travelers :

- In 1668, the French priests Protais and Charles-François visited the city and the church "under the earth." "*Le jour n'y entre que par la porte et encore peu, d'autant que la cour est toute ombragée d'un arbre, qui la couvre fort proprement.*"[7]
- Wansleben also mentions the church.
- Claude Sicard, travelling at the beginning of the eighteenth century, mentioned this city, which in his time was famous for its date palms. He says, "We visited in this burg a very deep church, called Our Virgin, which the Nile invades and floods for two or three months

each year. The nave is encumbered by a *sidr* or *nabqa*, very old and full of branches."[8]

Description of the Church

The church is situated within the precinct of the parish of the Virgin, which also includes a modern church.

A flight of about fifteen steps leads down to the church that was excavated in the rock at about three meters below ground level, which explains why it is flooded for part of the year. The steps have been modernized. The entrance is through a heavy, carved wooden door situated on the left side of the stairs on the northwest corner of the church.

From the entrance, the church appears to be lying on the right-hand side for a length of 20 meters and 13 meters in depth; it is composed of two naves separated by pillars and a sanctuary separated from the second nave by wooden panels. The church is covered by nine rounded domes; the dome at the center of the second nave is of wood, from which a light is hanging. The highest point of the vaults is six meters; the height of the roof is four meters. The church is in quite a good state of conservation, and was not modified by remodeling. The plaster of the walls and vaults is falling apart in some places, and floods have damaged the sanctuary.

Fig. 22.1: The First Nave. Photograph: A.A. Sadek.

Fig. 22.2: The tunnel entrance door.
Photograph: A.A. Sadek.

The first nave is separated from the second by four enormous pillars; which have square angles in the first nave and are rounded in the second nave. The circumference of each pillar is 4.70 meters, and they are 1.35 meters thick. The pillars are separated by carved wooden panels.

On the west wall are three large niches, each 1.30 meters deep. They end with arches about half a meter deep, enclosed by a wall. Ancient icons are stored within the two first niches, some of them documented by the Supreme Council of Antiquities (SCA) and bearing a file number (see appendix). The third niche contains old, abandoned *corsi* with icons dating from the twentieth century.

A beautiful old wooden lectern is stored at the south end of this nave. On the north wall is an old niche of about one square meter, with small columns on each side. On the north wall of the second nave is a small, deep niche.

On the wall in the northeast angle a small door about 60 cm above the ground opens on to a grotto that is accessible through a tunnel about one meter high. This tunnel, which is beautifully dressed in raw brick, runs behind the sanctuary toward the east.

According to tradition, this was where the liturgical vessels were hidden in case of attack. We suggest it may have been a storing place during the inundation. In any case, there is no doubt this was a hiding place where even a man could take refuge.

Fig. 22.3: The tunnel. Photograph: A.A. Sadek.

Fig. 22.4: The second nave and altars. Photograph: A.A. Sadek.

Three domes crown this second nave, the central spire of which is of carved wood. This nave opens onto four altars. The sanctuary is composed of four altar chapels, all of them arched and vaulted. The left altar is dedicated to St. Michael.

The central altar is dedicated to the Holy Virgin. This is the largest chapel; its wall juts into the adjacent street and we were told that it floods each time a water pipe in the street bursts, which happens often enough.

The third altar is dedicated to St. George, and the one on the right-hand side to St. Bishoi. This altar is situated in the wooden part of the church.

After this fourth altar is a wall in which is carved the font, a round bowl 53 cm in diameter and 60 cm deep.

Fig. 22.5: The spire. Photograph: A.A. Sadek.

Fig. 22.6: The priest Abuna Bola sitting on the steps leading to the main altar. Photograph: A.A. Sadek.

Catalogue of the Icons

Eight icons are kept in this church, and one in the modern church above. Seven icons have been registered by the SCA, two of which bear the signature of Astasi al-Rumi.

> 1- The Entry into Jerusalem
> File No./159/2000
> Dated: 1912
> Dimensions: H: 0.93 m/W: 0.85 m
> Conservation: very good
> Style: Syrian
> Inscriptions in Arabic:
> - "Hosanna, blessed is he who comes in the name of the Lord."
> -"The Mount of Olives."
> -"City of Jerusalem."
> -"Remember, O Lord, your servant Thomas Abdel-Malik, who offered you this icon."

2- St. George
File No.3/159/2000
No signature
No date
Dimensions: H: 0.70 m/W: 0.50 m
Conservation: very poor
Style: Coptic

3- Virgin of Perpetual Help (Italian icon type)
File No.8/159/2000
No signature
No date
Dimensions: H: 0.92 m/W: 0.70 m
Conservation: good
Style: Italian

4- Crowned Virgin (with John the Baptist as a child kissing the feet
of Jesus)
File No.4/159/200
Signed: Astasi al-Rumi
Date: 1580
Dimensions: H: 1.10 m/W: 0.60 m
Conservation: good
Style: Coptic
Inscription in Arabic: "Reward, O Lord, in the Kingdom of Heaven he
who works."

5- Large Virgin with Child
No number
No signature
Dimensions: H: 1.25 m/W: 1.05 m
Painted on gazelle skin
Conservation: good
Style: Italian
Inscriptions in Arabic: Jesus Christ/Our Lady Mary the Virgin/(right:)
the Sun—the Angel Gabriel/(left:) the Moon—the Angel Michael.
"Reward, O Lord, in the Kingdom of Heaven he who works"

6- Nativity (with scenes of Jesus's life: the Adoration of the Magi, the killing of the Innocents, the Flight to Egypt.)
No number
No signature
No date
Dimensions: H: 0.95 m/W: 0.68 m
Conservation: very good
Style: Greek (compare with an eighteenth-century Greek icon in Beirut, in *Icônes arabes*, p. A 35, n 6.)

7- Diptych: Right panel: an archangel; left panel: a mosque (the rest is damaged)
No number
No signature
No date
Dimensions of the right panel: H: 0.90 m/W: 0.64 m
Dimensions of left panel: H: 0.90 m/W: 0.44 m
Conservation: badly damaged
Style: Unknown

8- St. Demiana
No number
No signature
No date
Dimensions: H: 0.90 m/W: 0.60 m
Conservation: Very poor, broken in two parts
Style: Coptic

9- Triptych of the Passion of Christ (this icon is in the new church)
File No.5/159/2002
Signed: Astasi al-Rumi
No date
Dimensions: H: 0.80 m/W: (central panel) 0.40 m; (left and right panels) 0.20 m
Conservation: good; this is the masterpiece of the collection
(Compare with the icon of the same type in the Museum für Spätantike und Byzantinische Kunst, Berlin, published in Géorgiennes, éd., *Icônes arabes, art Chrétien du Levant*," Méolans-Revel, 2003, A. 74, N 43)

The Monastery of Anba Moses (or Mosios)
Moses of Abydos

The life of Moses of Abydos is well known through various documents, The *Synaxarium* mentions him only on 7 Barmudah (in the Coptic calendar) as "Moses of Balyana" and spiritual father of St. Macrobius.[9] In the White Monastery his feast is celebrated on 25 Abib as "Moses, archimandrite of Ebot (Abydos or Afud)." Fragments have been preserved of three codices detailing his life and of an encomium published in part by E. Amélineau, W. Till, and H. Munier.[10] He is also mentioned in the *Life* of his disciple Macrobius, founder of a community at Lycopolis to the south of Assiut, preserved in a Coptic fragment in the Museum of Antiquities in Leiden and in an Arabic version, and in the *Life* of Abraham of Farshout, archimandrite of Pbow, who was deposed by Justinian.[11]

The life of Moses has been studied by both R-G. Coquin in 1986[12] and Peter Grossman in 1999.[13] They point out a few elements worth mentioning in this study. First, Moses of Abydos was born a short time after Shenoute's death in 466 and lived through the first half of the sixth century. Second, there is an important link between St. Shenoute and Moses of Abydos: Shenoute, before his death, had a vision of the birth of Moses, and he knew that Moses would destroy the temples and contribute to the conversion of pagans. Fourth, it is attested that Moses founded a monastery for men and one for women. The latter is located in the temple of Seti I as is shown by the graffiti in one of the chapels. Many elements prove that the monastery of Abydos was of the Pachomian style, organized in 'houses.' In his letters, Moses often quotes Shenoute. Indeed, Moses was involved in various struggles with the temples. Moses also played a part in the discussions with Justinian about monophysitism and it seems that Severius of Antioch took refuge for some time in the monastery Abydos.

The Monastery of Moses of Abydos

The monastery at Abydos was famous, since it was mentioned in several records including this thirteenth-century reference by Abu al-Makarim:[14]

> City of Bulyana. This lies to the west bank of the Nile, in Upper Egypt. Here is the monastery known as the Monastery of Bâni Mûsâ, which was restored at the expense of As-Safi, who was his Abbot; it lies to the west of the city and its correct name with that of his church is said to be St. Moses.[15]

The construction plan of this monastery is unlike any that can be seen else-where. It is enclosed within a wall. Its gate is plated with iron and studded with nails. It contains a water-wheel, which irrigates a plot of vegetables. The pure body (of the saint) is buried in the monastery. The biography of Anbâ Christodoulos, the sixty-sixth patriarch, relates that the pillars of this monastery all transpired, until the drops ran down like water . . . .

The fifteenth-century Arab historian al-Maqrizi also mentions this mon-astery, as does Claude Sicard, who refers to the monastery of St. Moses, which he visited in 1718: "an old monastery of Moses the Abbot, made of bad bricks, situated at the west of the village at the foot of mount Afodos." Here again, the notes made by Serge Sauneron and Maurice Martin mention some confusion concerning St. Moses, whom they thought was different from Moses of Balyana.[16]

The monastery is situated eleven kilometers west of Balyana, two kilo-meters after the temples of Seti I in Abydos. The road runs to the right of the temple and climbs a hill; on the left can be seen the temple of Ramesses II. Then the road goes on through desert belonging to the Supreme Council of Antiquities and arrives at the small village of Bani-Mansur (formerly Arrabah al-Madfuna).

On the left hand side lies a Christian cemetery in which the bishopric is building a new church.

The village is surrounded by the remains of the ancient wall made of bricks. We enter the precinct through a first door, then a second. The residents lived in this first precinct in small houses. We are told that the monastery accommodated about a million monks in the fifth century.

Church Entrance

The western wall of the monastery church has been renewed by the local church team of the bishopric. The wall is covered with brown limestone. A small door (1.70 m/0.90 m) of carved wood opens in this wall; it is enclosed within a decoration made of red and black bricks placed in geo-metrical patterns.

The wall is 5.30 m high. About 4 meters above the ground it is pierced by four ogive-shaped windows, each about 0.80 cm high.

At the left angle of the wall an old baptistery is lying upside down on the ground. Its shape is slightly conical.

Dimensions:

0.85 m high; 0.45 m diameter in its lowest part ; 0.65 m diameter at its highest part.

On the left of this wall, in the yard, is the wall of the nave precinct, with a small door equally decorated with colored bricks in geometrical patterns.

On entering through the main door, one finds oneself in a church whose shape is very similar to that of St. Mary's Church at Balyana, only much bigger. However, this church is being restored, which is not the case the old church of the Virgin in Balyana.

The priest, Abuna Bola, says that until the sixteenth century there was not one but two churches placed side by side. The one on the left was dedicated to St. Moses; the one on the right to St. Demiana. According to archaeological reports, this church is older than the other.[17] Bishop Samuel noticed a similarity between the seven altars of the nearby temple of Seti and the seven altars of the church of the monastery. The two churches are currently separated by an enormous pillar.

St. Moses's Church measures 18 meters and St. Demiana's 14 meters in length, so the church now appears to measure 32 meters in length.

Like St. Mary's, this church is composed of two naves and a sanctuary, separated from one another by carved wooden panels and each measuring 4.50 meters in width.

On both the northwest and the southwest sides rooms function as 'prenaves.' The font was probably in one of these. The naves and the sanctuary are covered by domes. Arches and niches are scattered throughout.

We are told that the old haikal was destroyed by insects. During the restoration, a new iconostasis was made from the remains of the St. Shenoute's Church in Balyana, which has been totally destroyed. Thus the wooden panels of the church date back to the Middle Ages, except for the panel introduced into the main sanctuary of St. Moses, which is original.

There are altogether seven panels for the iconostasis.

Catalogue of Icons

Only one icon is kept in the church; it represents Moses holding Macrobius. It has been repainted and offers no interest except for the identification of Moses of Abydos with Moses of Balyana, the spiritual father of Macrobius, as told in the *Synaxarium*.

The remaining icons are kept in a room high up in a building near the enclosure wall. None of these icons has a file number, but one is signed by Astasi al-Rumi. Two more icons represent St. Moses and St. Macrobius.

Moses holding Macrobius

One icon is of the same type as the one kept in the church; St. Moses holding St. Macrobius, who is represented as a very small figure.
Dimensions : 0.80m/0.52

Crowned Moses and Macrobius

The second is different: St. Moses is crowned while St. Macrobius is standing by himself as a small child.

No signature
No date
Dimensions: W: 0.82 m/W: 0.60 m
Style: unknown
Conservation: good
Inscription in Arabic: St. Mosios

Two icons represent St. Demiana:

Demiana Seated

The first is a badly restored icon showing Demiana seated, her head bent, and surrounded by the forty virgins.

No signature
No date
Dimensions: H: 0.78 m/W: 0.55 m
Conservation: badly repainted
Style: unknown

Demiana/George/Abu Sayfayn

The second is a beautiful triptych showing Demiana in the center, Abu Sayfayn on the right, and St. George on the left.

Signature: Astasi al-Rumi
Date: 1581 of the era of Martyrs
Dimensions: H: 1 m/W: 1.4 m
Conservation: very good
Style: Coptic
Inscriptions: St. George the Martyr/Abu Sayfayn the Martyr/The Great Saint and Martyr Demiana

Crucifixion
No signature
No date
Dimensions: H: 0.82 m/W: 0.70 m
Conservation: badly repainted
Style: originally Coptic
Inscriptions in Arabic: "Christ's Cross/Lord have mercy on your servant Aoud Tadros . . . . Reward, O Lord, in your Kingdom, he who has worked."

Deposition of Christ
No signature
No date
Dimensions: H: 0.38 m/W: 0.55 m
Conservation: probably, and unfortunately, repainted.
Style: unknown

Resurrection
No signature
No date
Dimensions: H: 0.70 m/W: 0.4 2m
Conservation: badly repainted
Style: originally Coptic

Archangel Michael "psychopump"
No signature
No date
Dimensions: H: 1.0 m/W: 0.75 m
Conservation: good
Style: naive; Italian background

Conclusions

Concerning the two monuments described here, I would like to draw attention to two points. First, renovation is necessary, both for the old church of Balyana, which still suffers from flooding in spite of the fact that the flow of the Nile is now stabilized, and for some icons that are unprotected or stored in dirty or unsafe places; some are not even registered by the SCA; these icons bear witness to Coptic art and quite a few are very valuable and deserve to be protected. It is essential to provide local people with the means to have them restored and kept in a safe place.

Second, uncontrolled restoration is still in process; at least seven icons we have seen have been repainted by unskilled people; the restoration of the pieces also should be performed under the control of competent people to avoid new paints or varnishes as can be seen in St. Moses's Monastery, or the destruction of valuable objects such as haikals.

Some concluding remarks about Christianity in the region of Balyana: The Balyana area is deeply marked by Christian monasticism, and it is clear that the history of the monastery of Abydos was influenced both by the proximity of the ancient Egyptian temples of Abydos and by the proximity of the White Monastery about fifty kilometers away.

There is currently evidence of increasing activity. The monastery of Abydos is being restored and renewed, and a very active Christian population is living within its precincts. We admired the nursery school located at the entrance, the new church building in the cemetery, and other facilities.

Christian life in Balyana has received a boost; the bishopric is creating schools for Christian children who find no place in public schools. Strolling through the streets of Balyana with a priest, we noticed how respectful toward him the people, both Christian and Muslim, seemed to be.

The Coptic Orthodox Diocese of Balyana currently has twenty-nine churches, sixty-three priests and one bishop.

The present situation, however, presents difficulties for church members. The memories of the terrible events of al-Kosheh in 1998 and 2000 are still vivid, and our last pictures reveal the way we felt, when looking from the small church precinct toward the street, about the church being surrounded by enormous mosques—a feeling of insecurity, or of the confrontation between David and Goliath.

Notes

1. I wish to thank my colleague and friend Adel Sidarus who encouraged me to do this study, and Rami Sawiris for helping with the computer.
2. Timm 1984–1992: 312–15.
3. Stern 1878: 9–28, esp. 26ff.
4. Crum 1904: 38–43.
5. Ibid.
6. Al-Suriani and Habib 1990: 65–66.

7. Quoted in Timm 1984–1992.

8. Sicard 1982: 97–98.

9. *Synaxarium*, 7 Barmudah.

10. All references can be found in the *Coptic Encyclopaedia*, 1679.

11. Ibid.

12. Coquin 1986: 1–14.

13. Grossman 1999: 51–64.

14. Abu Saleh the Armenian 1895, fol. 81: 231–32.

15. Here a footnote shows that this Moses was confused with Moses the Black; in fact, the *Synaxarium* mentions this St. Moses as being the abbot of this monastery and the spiritual father of St. Macrobius; however it is confirmed by iconography, and this Moses is certainly not Moses the Black.

16. Sicard 1982: 66–68.

17. Cf. al-Suriani and Habib 1990: 64.

23 Toward an Understanding of the 'Akhmim Style' Icons and Ciboria
The Indigenous and the Foreign[1]

Zuzana Skálová

THE LATE FOURTEENTH-century painting by Gherardo Starnina, *La Tebaide,* in the Galleria degli Uffizi in Florence, provides perhaps the last medieval visualized memory of the (ideal) Christian sacred landscape along the Nile in Upper Egypt, densely inhabited by hermits tending their blossoming gardens or praying in private caves and chapels on the edge of the desert.[2] From this glorious late antique and Coptic era in the Akhmim environs, next to two important monasteries built and decorated in the fifth century and beyond, Dayr Anba Shenoute (the White Monastery) and Dayr Anba Bishoi (the Red Monastery), numerous small monasteries also survived that were revitalized in the Ottoman period.

In 1717 the map of the *Déserts de la basse Thébaïde* was painted for the French Jesuit Père Claude Sicard (1676–1726), to be sent to Europe. Considering that Father Sicard came together with an Armenian Catholic artist, Michel, to Egypt in 1712 from Aleppo in Syria, we may wonder if they could know the enigmatic Mattary in Cairo.[3] Indeed, certain data coincide. In this map a cameo is inserted depicting an elderly pilgrim walking across the Western Desert to the Red Sea monasteries who is identified by Sicard as a "'*Religieux Copte*' *de la basse Thébaïde.*"[4] Wearing the blue turban and red shoes required by Ottoman rulers, and leaning on a stick, this spirited Christian carries before him a rosary (a symbol of Catholic piety) with a pendant Orthodox cross, arguably, an attribute of an Orthodox convert to Unia (Fig. 23.1).[5]

Fig. 23.1: Map of *Déserts de la Basse Thébaïde*, 1717, watercolor. Detail. BN Paris: RC.C.7626 (original). After Skálová and Gabra 2003, ill. 42.

At this time Latin missionaries were beginning successfully to convert Copts. Significantly, on some Akhmim icons and ciboria eligible for this preliminary survey, even Christ, the Virgin Mary, and saints hold the rosary while the style in which they are painted can be associated with the Mattary school, but are less accomplished. The illuminator and painter Mattary, believed to be an Armenian from eastern Syria, painted in Egypt icons on paper in an oriental style imported along the Silk Road. This overall stylistic language of the Beylik–Mamluk era would dominate Coptic religious art until the 1730s, when a Copt, Ibrahim al-Nasih, started a new workshop in Cairo, but might have lingered in the province.

After 1517 Egypt was reduced by the new rulers in far Istanbul to a regional status. The remaining Circassian Mamluks became part of larger Turcophone military cavalry elite, their ranks strengthened by Turkish beys. These so-called 'Beylik Mamluks' of quite diverse ethnicity became increasingly independent from the Sublime Porte administration, amassing wealth and thus able to sponsor charities and the arts. With the new rule came new techniques, materials, and styles, first applied to Islamic art, but also adopted by Christian artisans.

For example, illustrations in the Coptic–Arabic *Maimar*, kept in the Coptic Museum in Cairo and dated to 1687, already hint at a symbiosis of different cultures coexisting in the Middle East: the acculturation of two visual languages, Islamic and Christian, Orthodox as well as Western.[6]

Arabicized Copts were needed as administrators and translators of these new lords. Among the scribal class, close to the Coptic Patriarchate in Cairo, and their relatives in Upper Egypt, we should look for the rich benefactors who sponsored widespread reconstruction of ancient churches and their refurbishments, first in the capital and abandoned major desert monasteries, and later in the provinces. Dr. Magdi Guirguis, specialist in Ottoman

Coptic–Arabic archival documents (permits for rebuilding of old churches were needed from the Muslim authorities!), confirms the Coptic notables' affluence and favorable circumstances in this period, as they lived in 'un esprit d'harmonie' with Muslims. [7]

The transformation of the Ottoman Empire influenced the circumstances of the Christians identified as *'Ahl al-dhimma'*, or 'people under (Muslim) protection,' considerably.[8] Only when the Turks granted certain commercial privileges, diplomatic immunity and, importantly, religious leniency, the so-called Capitulations (from 1535) to Western powers, did European consuls, merchants, and missionaries begin to settle in the main cities of the Middle East. In 1690 missionaries obtained the right to teach and 'convert' members of the Eastern-rite Churches to Roman Catholicism, the Unia. The Uniate movement did not require Orthodox converts to give up their language and traditions—or their icons. Easily portable Roman Catholic and Greek Orthodox as well as Uniate religious prints circulated widely and were used not only as potent tools of evangelization, but also as models.[9]

The initial (unofficial) Catholic religious missions to the legendary Thebaide coincided with the spiritual awakening of Coptic society, and they found a cooperative clergy. First came the Jesuits in the sixteenth century. Franciscans established a hospice in Akhmim and a mission in Girga in 1664. It would seem that through their travels the Latin missionaries again linked the Coptic Mother Church and the Ethiopic Church. Akhmim's strategic position for departure to distant Ethiopia was of importance.[10] Carrying printed sacred pictures, the proselytizers provided models for both Ethiopian and Coptic icon painters; hence a certain superficial 'ecumenical' affinity, iconographical and stylistic, modified by each country's different traditions and political situation.

The sources of a new Christological iconography for Eastern Christians were multiple. Claire Bosc-Tiessé researched the most influential illustrated books the Portuguese Catholic fathers carried with them into sixteenth-century Ethiopia: These were *Evangelicae Historiae Imagines*, printed in many editions since 1593 in Antwerp (a collection of 153 gospel illustrations, engraved by Flemish masters after Italian drawings), and St. Ignatius of Loyola's *Spiritual Exercises*.[11]

Popular among Arabophone Christians, however, must have been the *Evangeliarum Arabicum*, printed in Rome in 1590–1591 for the Middle East.[12]

To these sources should be added the illustrated *Piscator Bible* and the first Armenian Bible with Dutch woodcuts, printed in Amsterdam in 1666, which became the pattern books for the Armenian lay craftsmen *(naqqash)*, organized in guilds *(hamker)*, who also painted icons in Egypt (in the phase preceding Mattary).[13]

As it is evident that the aforementioned Western 'tools of evangelization' also reached Copts and influenced their art, research in the archives and libraries of the Catholic seminaries in Cairo and in Europe is needed. Father Sicard's missionary visits to Upper Egypt were of lasting influence. He became friendly with the local hierarchy and was able in 1718 to establish the first Coptic Catholic seminary in Akhmim.[14] His convert, Rufail al-Tuki (1703–1787) from Girga, went to study in Rome, and in 1735 became the first Orthodox Copt ordained as a Coptic Catholic priest, A year later Youstus al-Maraghi was ordained in Akhmim.[15] From that time the province was, so to say, in direct contact with the nascent 'Rome on the Nile,' Cairo, with its multiplying Latin seminaries, and the Vatican.[16]

Akhmim Architecture, Arts, and Crafts[17]

While in Cairo there has been a successive series of renewals of ancient patriarchal churches from the early-eighteenth century until today, the Christian monuments in Akhmim province preserved their (arguably) first Ottoman-era refurbishment until the 1980s. On the basis of old photographs and a recent visit to the church of St. Mercurius Abu Sayfayn in Akhmim and five small monasteries—Dayr Anba Thomas, Dayr al-Adra Hawawish, Dayr Mari Guirguis al-Hadidi, Dayr al-Malak, and Dayr al-Shohada, scattered along the Nile in the surrounding area—it appears that not only icons and ciboria but also murals were painted, manuscripts illustrated, textiles embroidered, and woodwork fabricated: screens, partitions, icon frames *(maqsurat)*, and reliquaries were made for the embellishment of ancient edifices, rebuilt in the same 'Beylik–Mamluk' style.

In the last two decades, however, these compounds have been enlarged to suit the current renaissance of monasticism and pilgrimages, their furbishing 'revitalized' and modernized. For an art historian this progress means that little-known and charming Coptic Ottoman visual culture, almost erased in Cairo, is vanishing before it has been properly documented and studied. The reader is referred to publications in color illustrating these ongoing changes: the *Guide to Ancient Coptic Churches and Monasteries in Upper Egypt* by Samuel al-Suriany and Badie Habib,[18] books by Nabil Atalla, who photographed icons and ciboria in the Akhmim province prior to their restoration,[19] and a recent survey by Adeline Jeudy reproducing ciboria described below in post-restoration state.[20]

Architecture

The renewal of Christian monuments in Akhmim and its surroundings manifested itself in the reduction of the old triconchal churches, into a new shape with a transept. Their original size was most probably respected. Some small desert monasteries, for example, Dayr al-Hadidi and Dayr al-Besada, still have late antique stone walls, portals, and reused fragments. Abstract patterns, executed skillfully in cheap clay bricks (often hidden today under modern paints), which seem at first glance to derive from Islamic architecture, could appear in more detailed study to echo the chromatography and ornamentation of the aforementioned White Monastery (carved in stone) and the Red Monastery (imitating in illusionist style the luxurious carved patterns of the former).[21] Looking at the old

Figure 23.2: Brick- and woodwork of Dayr Mari Guirguis al-Hadidi. Photograph: Sami Sabri Shaker, 1970s.

photographs of these small monasteries and their churches, we realize that their Ottoman-era brickwork was perhaps modest but attractive workmanship, emphasizing Christianity by crosses of different shapes, and symbolic numbers, in imitation of antique usage (figure 2).[22]

Screens

The *hijab* of this period was made inexpensively: simple rectilinear designs, mainly crosses, were fashioned from pieces of locally available wood and painted with pastel-tinted curvilinear floral motifs. A few screens preserved their cresting, for example in Dayr al-Shohada. In Cairo we see such (painted) cresting on the icon of St. George in the Chapel of Mar Jacoub in the northern gallery of the church of St. Mercurius, Dayr Abu Sayfayn, ascribed to Mattary.[23] His workshop also provided the screen for the same chapel, topped by an epistyle with the *Twelve Apostles* and a ciborium, the last of their kind.[24]

Ciboria

The eighteenth-century wooden painted ciboria in the Akhmim area survived, perhaps worn-out but complete. They were crafted from thin planks of local wood, probably eucalyptus *(athel)*, cut by a saw, some embellished with Islamic decorative elements—stalactites *(mukarnas)* or abstract star dishes *(tabak negmi)* in combination with shells. Shells were placed into squinches and/or in the center of the inner dome, adding parochial intimacy as these were familiar from surviving late antique caves and early Christian buildings, their symbolism alluding to salvation and rebirth further enhanced by the figurative decoration.

Two kinds of ciboria were produced:

First, a more traditional type follows the ancient form of columned canopy standing over the altar. A sole Fatimid example, carved and painted on its outer side with floral ornamentation, is in the Coptic Museum. From an early Ottoman period three wooden ciboria remain in the sanctuaries of the church of the Holy Virgin, al-Mu'allaqa, in Old Cairo, the central ciborium now cleaned and appearing to have been painted in the middle or second half of the fifteenth century by the itinerant artist who also decorated the apse of the St. James Chapel in the catholicon of the Greek Orthodox Monastery of St. Catherine, Mount Sinai (cleaned in 1963). His art echoes Middle Byzantine Sinai icons.[25]

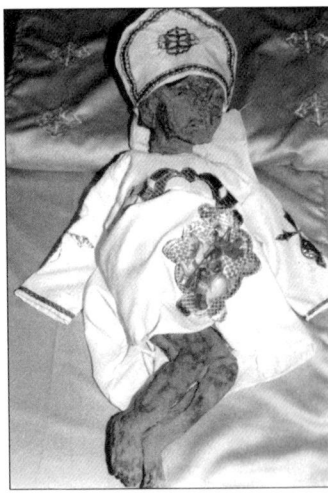

Fig. 23.3: Canopy ciborium in Dayr Anba Thomas. Photograph: Atalla 1989: 121.

Fig. 23.4: Mummy of a martyred child. Pamphlet of Dayr al-Shohada, 2006.

Dayr Anba Thomas has such a canopy ciborium with innovative inner decoration possibly illustrating a liturgical source.[26] Unusually, in its dome float angels dressed in short tunics. Their legs are awkwardly distorted (Fig. 23. 3). These angels could simply represent sparsely dressed cherubim from Western prints as rendered by a chaste Copt working in Mattary's style. More close to home would be the wish to commemorate children murdered in the Era of the Martyrs, during the memorable Akhmim massacre. In Dayr al-Shohada, in a special room, a corpse of a toddler, dressed in baptismal garb leaving its broken legs exposed to the gaze of pilgrims, could have stirred the artist (Fig. 23.4). A Latin belief that unbaptized innocents dwell as angels in heaven would go a long way to forge a link allowing that this holy relic was in the monastery in the eighteenth century, similarly dressed.

A second type of a ciborium, a so-called 'Cairene dome,' derives from Islamic architecture (see, for example, the Qalamun Mosque in Cairo). Its shallow dome rests on horizontal wooden beams, being part of a wooden ceiling decorated with *tabak negmi*. Inside, heaven with Christian saints is revealed. The church of St. Mercurius Abu Sayfayn in Akhmim has three such ciboria.[27] In the monastic churches in Dayr al-Shohada or Dayr Barsoum and Dalosham are smaller ciboria with reduced decoration (Fig. 23.5).[28]

The blue color of the inner dome represents the heavenly realm where Christ and the Virgin are seated on 'baroque' thrones placed on an Arabic-looking dais.[29] The staring eyes and crossed position of hands of the barefoot saints are familiar from sacred pictures attributed to the lesser works of Mattary's workshop; here in Akhmim they were painted even more incompetently, directly on wood with coarsely ground local pigments mixed with

gum Arabic. The local, probably untrained artists simplified their technique by using primary colors without modeling of schematic clothing. Many finer details and ornamental motifs are, however, often lost by overcleaning.

Two features are new: the rosary and the head cover. Christ, angels, and male saints wear red scull caps, the bishops black ones, and in the

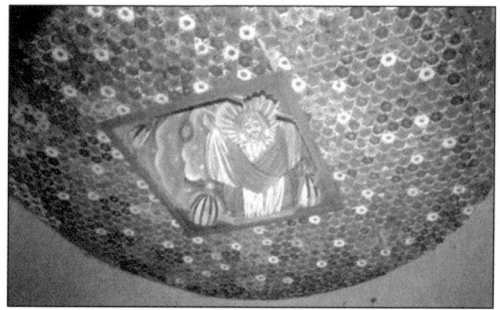

Fig. 23.5: *Tabak negmi* ciborium in Dayr al-Shohada (over-painted). Photograph: Sami Sabri Shaker, 1980s.

aforementioned Coptic–Arabic *Maimar* from 1687 a yellow scull cap is part of the officiating priest's sacerdotal attire.[30] The Virgin and female saints wear loose veils, sometimes dotted, in reminiscence of clouds on more refined Greek engravings (Fig. 23.7).

Icons

The workshops that produced ciboria issued icons based on the same miscellaneous models. These are painted in an identical technique on thin plain panels, which are sometimes embellished with carved columns and arches to frame the principal saints; we note that these votive icons belong to a category of Byzantine *proskynitarion*. We note, too, that there are no extant icons portraying solely Christ. Votive icons of the Virgin and Christ Child, the angels and local saints and martyrs, Pachomius and his sister Dalusham,[31] and Anba Thomas, were numerous.[32]

For example, the ultimate model for the locally popular image of *The Archangel Michael* with large striped wings seems to be a Cretan black-and-white woodcut (circa 1706), printed in the Monastery of St. Catherine, Mount Sinai, which was turned into an emblem by the skillful use of brilliant colors applied into the lines (Fig. 23.6).[33] Once created, the angel was dully replicated.

On the titular icon painted for the monastery bearing his name, *Anba Thomas* (+ 453) stands barefoot, his head covered with a thrice-blessed black

Figs. 23.6a–c: *From left*. The Archangel Michael, woodcut, 43 x 34 cm; the carved block is dated 1706, inscribed "The Archon Michael," and signed "Matthios Hieromonk." The impression (center) is a recent one (1977), Monastery of Saint Catherine, at Mount Sinai. After Papastratos 1990: vol. 1. fig. 194. On the right is one of many Akhmim icons based on this Greek print (Dayr al-Salamun). Photograph: Sami Sabri Shaker, 1970s.

cap, wearing a striped homespun coat and foreign-looking megalos-chema (see Fig. 24.7). He is blessing the beholder with a beneficiary cross and displays the rosary. The refined, earlier icon of the venerable Anba Shenoute the Archimandrite (without the rosary) in the church of St. Shenoute, Deir Abu Sayfayn, Old Cairo, might have been a prototype, this visual connection pointing to local veneration of both saints.[34]

Narrative icons depicting biblical stories in the eighteenth century are less numerous. Scenes of the Flight into Egypt, the Passion, and the Ascension had Western models, but this would not help to date unsigned icons as the prototypes were reduced to the most rudimental and they were perpetuated even through the nineteenth century. They neverthe-

Figure 23.7: Icon of the Virgin Mary and Child. Akhmim area provenance. Photograph courtesy of Gawdat Gabra.

less attest to changing Christological perceptions. The ancient iconographic details of these local works, however, continue to surprise us. For example, on the naive Crucifixion icon in the Coptic Museum, signed by Abuna Abd al-Shahid and dated A.M. 1584/A.D. 1868, the Virgin and John acknowledge Christ's triumph over death with a pinkish-red garland bound with ribbons resembling a 'lucky knot' or 'lock of fertility', carried by the deceased in pre-Christian funeral or mummy portraits (see Fig. 24.9).[35] Possibly such artifacts were fabricated until recently in rural Upper Egypt.

Another ancient iconographical detail is the Christ Child's gesture of blessing with all the fingers of the hand extended and the hand held up palm out, which is particularly interesting for this volume as it can be traced back to wall paintings from the eighth century in the ancient Coptic Red Monastery, rediscovered two years ago by professional cleaning.[36] It is probable that some images were still visible in the eighteenth and even the nineteenth century (see Figs. 23.7 and 25.5).

Conclusion

The Akhmim ciboria and icons with saints displaying rosaries fit into the period between the inimitable Mattary and the sophisticated Ibrahim al-Nasih, who worked between the 1740s and 1780. It is art of a theological and artistic revival, of ecumenism but also of provincial restraint, and lacking major artists. Without documents, with which Dr. Guirguis works so persuasively, this attribution remains preliminary. New discoveries in the illustrated and dated Coptic-Arabic manuscripts from the Akhmim region, presented by Father Bigoul al-Suriany in this volume, will expand our knowledge. The meaning of the rosary as the symbol of the Coptic Catholic faith or as a sign of modernity has to be further researched.

Christians in Upper Egypt cling to their traditions. Perhaps the most interesting feature of the modest Akhmim figurative art from the Beylik–Mamluk and missionary eras are those details that are loaned from late antique and early Coptic art in the Thebaide. Used more than a millennium later on hybrid Coptic-Arabic icons, these local attributes and gestures again demonstrate the remarkable survival of indigenous iconography.

Notes

1. I thank Dr. Gawdat Gabra for inviting me to the Sohag Symposium and for suggesting this subject of research and two architects, Sameh Adli and Prof. Dr. Sami Sabri Shaker, who generously shared with me their expert knowledge and documentation.

2. Del Francia Barocas 1998: ill. III.

3. Van Moorsel *et al.* 1994: 47–48, cat. no. 51; Skálová, "Icons from the Ottoman Era (1517-1798)", 120-136, ills. 59-59a, in: Skálová and Gabra 2003: ill. 59a, for Mattary's signature on the triptych with *Four Desert Fathers* in the Monastery of the Syrians spotted by Abuna Bigoul al-Suryani and 132–6, ills. 42, 55, 56. 58, 60, cat. nos. 24–27, for his technique and style.

4. For the full map see Skálová and Gabra 2003: 120–1, ill. 42.

5. The rosary is a Latin device employed in prayer and the accretion of a series of words by repetition to induce a meditative state.

6. Arabic *Maimar* no. 477, fol. 12, Coptic Museum, Cairo, dated A.M. 1403/A.D. 1687. See Skálová and Gabra 2003: 131, ill. 53.

7. Guirguis 2004: 943–45; Guirguis 2005.

8. For the Turkish administration of non-Chalcedonian Christians, see Cragg 1992: 117.

9. Papastratos 1990.

10. See Elli 2003: 2, 265–66, 273; Meurice 2004: 956–57.

11. This short relation ended in 1605. In 1660 followed the *auto-da-fé* of Frankish books. See Bosc-Tiessé's fine study (1999) and bibliography.

12. Bosc-Tiessé (1999: 86, n. 25) quoting Jules Leroy, '*L'évangéliaire éthiopien illustré du British Museum* (Orient. 510) et ses sources iconographique.'

13. See Skálová and Gabra 2003: 124–29, ills. 44–52.

14. Sicard was the superior of the Jesuit Seminary in Cairo. See Meurice 2004: 955–56 (quoting Sicard 1982, vol. 1: 108 and vol. 2: 52).

15. Elli 2003: vol. 3, appendix B, 36–51, and Bibliography.

16. See Anthony O'Mahony (Heythrop College, University of London) who used the term 'Rome on the Nile' in his paper for the Symposium "New Faith in Ancient Lands: Dynamics of Western Missions in the Middle East (1800–1914)." This symposium was organized by H. Murre-van den Berg and C. van der Leest, 27–29 January 2005, Leiden University, Faculty of Theology, Department History of Christianity. To be published under the title *The Catholic Church, the Vicar Maximus Giuaid (1821–1831), the Propaganda Fide and the Franciscans in Early Nineteenth-Century Egypt* (forthcoming).

17. For the term 'Akhmim style' see Van Moorsel *et al.* 1994: 60–62, cat. nos. 51 (pl. 14a), 52 (pl. F1).

18. Al-Suryani and Habib 1990. Their original photos were not available for research.

19. Atalla 1996, 1998, 2002.

20. Jeudy 2004.

21. See contributions by Elizabeth S. Bolman and Suzana Hodak in this volume.

22. Restorer of monastic architecture Sameh Adli explains how these bricks were made: when burned in the traditional way (three days on platforms above a charcoal fire), different shades are produced according to their proximity to the heat: the nearby ones became black (*chorfush*), while others made of yellow clay look golden.

23. For this icon, re-restored by the author and her trainees in 1992 under the aegis of the Egyptian-Netherlands Coptic Icons Conservation Project (1989–1996), see Skálová and Gabra 2003: 226, cat. no. 27.

24. These fragile paintings were over-restored in 1989. Jeudy attributes the ciborium to Mattary, publishing it in its post-restoration state, when plain timber replaced the original fabric in need of patient conservation. The same methods were used later in Akhmim, again demonstrating the influence of the capital on the province (compare Jeudy 2004: 68–69, pls. 1–3 and 16).

25. For the photographs see Jeudy 2004: pls. 18–20. The attribution of inner paintings in al-Mu'allaqa southern ciborium, re-restored competently by the Russian team in 2004, to a painter who also worked in Sinai, is mine. For the recent photographs see Drandakis 1990: figs. 20–25.

26. For original state see Atalla 1986: 95, 97; for description see Jeudy 2004: 76–78, pl. 14.

27. Unpublished here for lack of space.

28. Atalla 2002: fig. on p. 19.

29. For example, the large *Virgin and Christ Child Enthroned*, painted on paper, in al-Mu'allaqa, in Old Cairo, re-restored in 1990s by Mona Hossein.

30. See note 6.

31. Atalla 1998, vol. 1: fig. on p. 65, whose photograph shows the richness of detail when the icon was still in original state of preservation.

32. Vansleb (1677) mentions the existence of icons in Coptic churches, their main subjects, Christ, his Mother, saints and angels, their didactic function, and their miraculous powers reflected in popular beliefs, but also how the sacred pictures were venerated with burning lamps placed too close and finally disposed of as fuel needed for preparation of holy oil, *Myron*.

33. For the print in the Greek Orthodox Monastery of St. Catherine at Mount Sinai, see Papastratos 1990, vol. 1: 192, fig. 194. The monastery had its own printing press and therefore preserved many matrices.

34 Skálová and Gabra 2003: 220–21, cat. no. 24.

35. For the icon see Van Moorsel *et al*. 1994: 60–61, no. 68 and pl. H1, Atalla 1998: 67; for the 'lucky knot' Corcoran 1995: 171–80, pl. 19. See also Kamil 2002.

36. Bolman 2004b: fig. 1.

24 Coptic Art during the Ottoman Period

Documentation of the Akhmimic Style

Fr. Bigoul al-Suriany

History of the Akhmimic Style

In the course of the seventeenth century, during the Ottoman period, significant innovations were introduced into Coptic art, which has led some scholars to speak of the 'Akhmimic style.' In order to study this style we need first to take into account the difficult situation of the Christians in Egypt during this time resulting from changes in political, social, cultural, and religious life. These changes played an important role in the interaction between the East and the West.[1]

Throughout the medieval centuries, the Coptic Orthodox Church had suffered from several waves of intervention by either the Islamic rulers or European Catholic ideologies, which threatened the survival of Coptic Christian identity.[2]

In the fourteenth century, under the Mamluk sultans, only nineteen churches were recorded for the whole area of Lower Egypt, including the Delta and Alexandria.[3] The rest of the churches had been demolished or damaged by the Muslims, with or without the support of the rulers. Permission for reconstruction or restoration was never given.[4] On the other hand, the Vatican was increasingly attentive to the development of Christian Orthodox thought in the Middle East, particularly in Christian Egypt.[5]

The history of Coptic Egypt may help us to understand why Coptic art almost disappeared in the period from the tenth to the late sixteenth century. In this chapter, I will address the question of how, following that period, innovations in Coptic art came about and developed.

According to the art historians, it is very hard to investigate the factors that contributed to the emergence of the so-called Akhmimic style and the circumstances under which this happened.

The Christian kings and emperors from the West and the North (Europe, the Vatican, and Russia) acted as protectors of the Christians and of the Christian monuments and sites within the Ottoman Empire, in particular in the Holy Land and the surrounding provinces.[6] Their influence resulted in greater flexibility on the part of the Ottomans in giving permissions for restoration and renovations of the old and damaged churches and Christian sites.[7] Subsequently, during the second half of the seventeenth century, the Copts were allowed to restore their churches.[8] At the same time, there were increasing efforts from the Vatican to attract and accommodate the Coptic Orthodox Church.[9] Then, by A.D. 1674, Catholic monks established their first mission in Upper Egypt. From then onward there was a deliberate attempt to spread the Catholic faith among the Copts.[10]

The Catholic missionaries, therefore, were eager to use the opportunity to help and support the poor areas of Upper Egypt in the renovation and restoration of their churches. They also assisted them in copying illuminated manuscripts of liturgical and biblical content, and they offered their Christian decorations and paintings for use inside the churches. This explains why products of this style were valueless in comparison with the pure or undiluted Coptic art of the pre-tenth century.

Dating

The first evidence of this style is found in manuscript illumination. The earliest examples are in the four Gospels manuscripts dated A.M. 1379 (A.D. 1663).[11] There are a considerable number of manuscript illuminations from different places dated to the late seventeenth century. Then, in St. Paul's Monastery near the Red Sea, we can see the same style in the wall paintings and in the icons of the iconostasis of the main church, which were painted and decorated by A.D. 1732.[12]

The style continued with the same characteristics until the end of the nineteenth century. Some interesting developments took place later, and there were some local variations. Father Abd al-Shahid from Akhmim signed an icon with his name in A.M. 1584 (A.D. 1868).[13]

Although it is clear that the style existed from A.D. 1663, P. van Moorsel saw the second half of the eighteenth century as the beginning of this type of work, arguing that it continued throughout the nineteenth century.[14] Z. Skálová said that it started around A.D. 1700, which in fact is closer to the truth.[15]

Descriptions and Definitions

Initially, because of its varied sources of inspiration and its originally imitative nature, neither the technique nor the iconography was considered purely Coptic. The style consisted of elements from different areas, especially from Islamic lands.[16]

Zuzana Skálová suggested that certain elements were transferred from workshops in the Holy Land. In addition, she pointed to the influence of the first printed Armenian Bible (Amsterdam, 1666), suggesting that this and other European illustrated printed Bibles became the new pattern books for eastern artists.[17] This means this style originates from religious Armenian art, based on sixteenth- and seventeenth-century Italian and Flemish models. Van Moorsel also suggested that the artists were of Armenian origin and that many of the characteristics of this new style must be regarded as Armenian.[18]

In my opinion, the main inspiration for this style were the illuminations in the manuscript of Beatus of Liebana, a monk who lived in Liebana, Austrica, in northern Spain in the late eighth century.[19] This manuscript, which contained a commentary on the Apocalypse, was highly appreciated in the monastic community over the centuries. Moreover, it was made famous by a number of copies after the ninth century. These were used by the Catholic missions in Africa and Middle East. The style of painting in the Beatus manuscript is known as Mozarabic, because it was of Arabic inspiration.[20]

The Catholic missionaries in Upper Egypt, in their attempt to find suitable decoration for the illumination of Coptic manuscripts, to a certain extent imitated the illuminations and ornaments of the Beatus manuscript. Accordingly, many of the illuminations incorporated Catholic concepts. The style then developed within the Coptic churches in some areas of Egypt. Several theological and doctrinal problems appeared in paintings of this style, because it incorporated different elements from the Byzantine, the Greek, and Roman Catholic artistic traditions. As a result, this led to problems in defining iconographical aspects and the identity of the artists.

The style existed in book illuminations, in wall paintings, and in icons over more than two centuries (1663–1890). It becomes clear, therefore, that we are not just dealing with a single workshop or an artist! In addition, we have no evidence for one artist producing paintings on all kinds of materials. In general, this was a phase in the religious politics of the Vatican toward the Coptic Orthodox Church. The specific details of the procedures in every kind of painting show some defects in the way of preparation and the treatments of colors.

In particular, in the field of icon painting, there were three different kinds of substrates: canvas, paper, and over prints. In all cases, the wooden supports for the icons were set at an angle, rag papers (which were cheap) were used as a substrate instead of gesso, and gelatin was used as the binding medium. As a result, the colors became opaque and after some time the icons became dark.

This technique for painting icons—the use of glue tempera[21]—was not used in Coptic painting before this time. The colors and pigments are pale and opaque owing to poor quality and impurity. All icons of this technique are without varnish, which results in the quick deterioration of the uncovered paintings. The colors, which no longer followed traditional Coptic symbolism, were selected at random. The painter used flat colors, which made the themes unreadable.

In this style, the ornaments sometimes become main subjects. The inscriptions are illegible, with very random locations. After long practice, the workshop or its painters started to add some shadow to the solid colors.

The hand of this style shows a very strange canon of human figures. It also presents the paintings in two dimensions with a flat background in almost one solid color. In many cases, plants and/or geometric ornaments were used in the design. The explanatory inscriptions are in two languages, Coptic and its Arabic translation. The features of the faces are very strange, and often distinguished by almond eyes, mustaches on men, and straight noses.[22]

The same ornaments that were used in the wall paintings and in the icons, consisting of geometric and flower motifs, were subsequently applied in the illuminations of the manuscripts. A number of illuminations of this style are known, while some specific developments may be discerned that may be attributed to different hands in the same manuscript. This means that there was a scriptorium with different styles. The images in the manuscripts show the influence of the Catholic mission in Egypt during the seventeenth to the nineteenth centuries, which is very clear from the ms. Coptic Museum,

no. 28, bibl. 99, and ms. Coptic Patriarchate, no. 50, bibl. 204, both dated
A.M. 1405 (A.D. 1688/9).[23]

The Artists of this Style

Unsigned wall paintings found both near Akhmim and in St. Paul's
Monastery near the Red Sea are by the same hand. This painter was
identified only in 1990, when his name, Mattary, was found on a triptych in
the Museum of the Monastery of the Syrians in Wadi al-Natrun.[24] Mattary
painted icons, triptychs, and ciboria.

There are many paintings of the same style, which is now known as
Mattary's style, in different areas: in Old Cairo in St. Barbara's Church, in
St. Mercurius's Church, and in the nunnery of St. Mary in Harat Zuwayla,
Cairo, as well as in Wadi al-Natrun, in the Monastery of St. Bishoi, and
in the Monastery of the Syrians. In Akhmim there are many works in this
style in several churches and monasteries. Some damaged works can be
found in the Red Sea monasteries. Although there are several works by
Mattary in the churches of Old Cairo, there is only one ciborium there.
The rest of the ciboria produced or painted by him must have been made
for Akhmim, as three of his ciboria can be located in the monasteries of
this area.[25] In addition, we can identify the same hand in the illuminations
of some manuscripts.

The other icon painter was Father Abd al-Shahid from Akhmim.[26] The
particular development that the new style underwent in the hands of Father
Abd al-Shahid was very limited. He applied the new style only in icons
on wooden panels, for which he used slightly different materials. He was
working in one site only, the Akhmim area. He painted one triptych for the
church of St. Cyriacus and Jullieta in Tahta. Father Abd al-Shahid signed
one icon in Akhmim, but most of his works were collected from the neighboring churches and can now be found in the Coptic Museum in Cairo.
We have no evidence either that his works were transferred to Cairo, or
that his workshop was based in Cairo.

The deacon Yuhanna from Harat al-Rum, Cairo illuminated some
manuscripts.[27] Deacon Yuhanna should obviously be distinguished from
Yuhanna al-Armani, as the deacon was only a scribe and book illuminator
who became a priest.

Unfortunately, we have no information about these painters. Some
scholars, however, identified Mattary as an Armenian[28] who came to Egypt
through the Holy Land. This is far from certain, however.

The Locations of this Style

It thus becomes clear that the Catholic missionaries in the Akhmim area of Upper Egypt established the style, and that it spread from there to certain other places. Most of this art is in the Red Sea monasteries, in particular St. Paul's Monastery, where the style is found on the wall paintings, the domes, and the iconostasis of the Cave Church as well as in some manuscript illuminations in the library.[29] Other examples are in the churches of Old Cairo, Abu Sayfan and St. Barbara, in the Coptic Museum, in the Coptic Patriarchate Library, and in the monasteries of Wadi al-Natrun: the Syrian Monastery, St. Bishoi's Monastery, and St. Macarius's Monastery.

The following pages provide some tables for the classification of most of the paintings of this style.

Wall paintings

Place	Subject	Paintings	Colors	Date
1. Red Sea: St. Paul's Monastery	Dome of the Martyrs	Equestrians, martyrs, geometric decoration with Coptic and Arabic inscriptions	Brown, yellow, green, white, red, and black	A.D. 1713
	Dome of the Twenty-four Elders of the Apocalypse	Christ on the throne in mandorla, with the Cherubim and the Twenty-four Elders standing around the throne	Red, yellow, green, white, and black	A.D. 1713
	There are more than thirty paintings on the walls of the church, of archangels, the seven angels with trumpets, and several martyrs and fathers of monasticism; all are in the same style and by the same hands			
2. Akhmim area: al-Shuhada's Monastery	The vault of the Sanctuary	Angels within vegetal decorations and colors	Red, black, white, yellow, and blue	Without

Icons (ciboria, triptychs, and flat icons)
Ciboria: all the ciboria found only in the area of Akhmim[30]

Place	Subject	Paintings	Colors	Date
1. St. Thomas the Hermit	Pantokrator	Christ in mandorla surrounded by cherubim with the Crowned Virgin and saints on the opposite side; blue background	Red, black, yellow, green, blue, and white	Without
2. St. Mercurius's Church (three ciboria)	Pantokrator	Christ in mandorla surrounded by cherubim and the Crowned Virgin on the opposite side; yellow background	White, red, yellow, green, and black	Without
3. al-Malak's Monastery	Pantokrator	Christ in mandorla surrounded by cherubim and the Crowned Virgin on the opposite side; blue background	Red, white, green, blue, black, and yellow	Without
4. St. Bakhum's Monastery	Pantokrator	The Christ in mandorla surrounded by cherubim and the Crowned Virgin on the opposite side; yellow background	Red, yellow, green, black	Without

Triptychs

Works by Mattary

Place	Subject	Paintings	Colors	Date
1. The Monastery of the Syrians, Wadi al-Natrun	Four desert fathers	St. Antony the Great and St. Macarius the Great, with two disciples	Red, blue, green, yellow, white, and black	Without
	St. Pasti and St. Ghalinikos (one shutter is missing)	Bishops St. Psati and St. Ghalinikos are standing frontally, unknown monk on one shutter	Red, blue, green, yellow, white, and black	Without
2. St. Macarius's Monastery, Wadi al-Natrun	Crucifixion. (covered with printed icon on paper)	Christ crucified in the center flanked by the three women and St. John; the two robbers crucified on the two shutters	White, red, blue, yellow, and black	Without
	Virgin with Child, and St. George and St. Mercurius	Virgin in the center carrying Christ, and St. George, St. Mercurius on the two shutters	White, red, blue, green, yellow, brown, and black	Without
3. St. Bakhum and his sister Dalusham the martyrs, Akhmim	Holy Family and two Archangels	St. Mary carrying the Child and standing next to St. Joseph, the Holy Spirit as a dove over them	Red, blue, yellow, white, and black	Without

4. St. Thomas the Hermit, Akhmim	Holy Family and two Archangels	St. Mary carrying the Child and standing next to St. Joseph; two Archangels on the two shutters	Red, blue, yellow, green, white, and black	Without
5. St. Barbara's Church, Old Cairo	Four Martyrs	St. Aba Kyr and John with St. Barbara and St. Juliana	White, red, yellow, green, and black	Without
6. al-Mu'allaqa Church, Old Cairo	Virgin with Child	The Virgin carries Christ in the front; two Saints on the two sides	White, red, green, brown, and black	Without
7. St. Mary's Nunnery, Harat Zuwayla, Cairo	Archangel Michael and four other Saints	Archangel Michael in the center panel; each shutter has two different themes: the first has the Annunciation and St. George; the other has St. Mercurius and another martyr (?)	Yellow, brown, blue, orange, and black	Without
	St. Victor the Martyr	One Shutter of a triptych represents St. Victor the Martyr	Red, blue, yellow, green, white, and black	Without

8. St. Anthony's Monastery, Red Sea	Virgin with Child, and two Archangels in the two shutters	Virgin carrying Christ in the middle, two Archangels on the two sides	White, red, green, and black	Without

Works by Father Abd al-Shahid

1. Church of St. Cyriacus and St. Jullieta, Tahta	Archangel Michael and three martyrs, and the Annunciation	Archangel Michael in the center; on the two shutters three martyrs, and the Annunciation	Red, yellow, green, brown, and black	Without
	Crucifixion	Christ crucified in the center, flanked by the three women and St. John; the two robbers crucified on the two shutters	White, red, green, yellow, brown, and black	Without

Flat Icons

Works by Mattary

Place	Subject	Paintings	Colors	Substrate	Date
1. Monastery of St. Bakhum and his sister Dalusham, Akhmim	St. Bakhum and his sister Dalusham	The two Saints are standing frontally, holding crosses in their right hands	White, red, blue, yellow, green, and black	Canvas on wood	Without

2. Dayr al-Naghamish, Akhmim	Crucifixion	Christ crucified in the center with three women and St. John standing under the Cross	White, red, green, orange, and black	Canvas on wood	Without
	Holy Family	The Virgin carrying Christ and standing next to St. Joseph frontally; reddish background	Red, blue, white, green, yellow, and black	Canvas on wood	Without
3. Church of St. Cyprian and St. Justin, al-Maragha, Tahta	Virgin with Child	Virgin enthroned with Child, two angels are crowning her and two angels standing beside the throne; green background	Red, white, green, and black	Canvas on wood	Without
	Two Archangels	Archangel Michael holding a cross-staff and Archangel Gabriel holding a scroll standing frontally in the background	White black, green, and orange	Canvas on wood	Without

4. Church of St. Mary, Juhajna, Tahta	Crucifixion	Christ crucified between the two robbers, the three women and St. John standing below; green background	Yellow, green, red, white, and black	Canvas on wood	Without
	Archangel Michael	The Archangel Michael standing frontally with the devil under his legs; reddish background	Red, white, green, and black	Canvas on wood	Without
5. Monastery of St. Thomas the Hermit, Akhmim	St. Thomas the Hermit	The Hermit standing frontally, holding the Catholic rosary and wearing the Coptic Schema; reddish background	Yellow, white, red, blue, and black	Canvas on wood	Without

6. St. Paul's Monastery, Red Sea	Iconostasis of the Sanctuary of St. John the Baptist	Baptism of Christ in the center; three icons to the right and the left represent the twelve Apostles; reddish background	White, red, blue, yellow, green, brown, and black	Paper, canvas on wood	A.D. 1732
	Iconostasis of the sanctuary of Archangel Michael	The Virgin with Child in the center; the three icons to the right and the left represent the twelve Apostles; reddish background	White, red, blue, yellow, green, brown, and black	Paper, canvas on wood	A.D. 1732
7. al-Mu'allaqa church, Cairo	The Virgin with the Child	The Virgin standing frontally and carrying Christ; the holy spirit as a dove coming from above; yellow background	Yellow, red, blue, white, brown, and black	Canvas on wood	Without

8. Coptic Museum, Cairo	Holy Family	Virgin carrying Christ and standing frontally beside St. Joseph; reddish background	White, blue, red, green, brown, black	Canvas on wood	Without
	Twenty-four Elders	The Twenty-four Priests seated on chairs, holding censers in their right hands; yellow background	Yellow, brown, white, and black	Paper, canvas on wood	Without
	St. Anthony and two disciples	Three monks standing frontally, with two lions below in the left and right corners; brown background	White, red brown, green, gold, and black	Canvas on wood	Without
9. St. Mercurius's Church, Old Cairo	Twelve Apostles (Iconostasis)	Twelve Apostles each one in separate icon, standing frontally; brown background	White, red, blue, yellow, green, brown, and black	Paper, canvas on wood	Without
	Crucifixion	Three crosses, Christ in the center, with men and women surrounding the crosses	Red, green, yellow, white, and black	Paper, canvas on wood	Without

	Three Hebrews in the Fiery Furnace	The three Hebrews standing frontally with the archangel under a large arch, with two small men on the right side	White, red, blue, yellow, brown, and black	Paper, canvas on wood	Without
	Virgin with Child and angels	The Virgin carrying the Christ the archangels	White, yellow, red, blue, brown, and black	Paper, canvas on wood	Without
	St. George	The Saint on horseback frontally, holding a cross staff in his right hand and killing the dragon	White, red, blue, brown, yellow, and black	Paper, canvas on wood	Without
	St. Mercurius Abu Sayfayn	The Saint on horseback in the foreground, holding a sword in each hand and killing the dragon (man)	White, red, brown, yellow, green, and black	Paper, canvas on wood	Without
10. St. Bishoi's Monastery, Wadi al-Natrun	The three Anba Makarys	The three saints are standing all together in the front; brown background	White, red, blue, brown, and black	Paper, canvas on wood	Without

11. The Monastery of the Syrians, Wadi al-Natrun	Crucifixion	Christ crucified between the two robbers, the three women and St. John standing below; green background	Yellow, red white, green, and black	Paper, canvas on wood	Without
	Vision of St. Yuhanna Kama	The Virgin gives St. Yuhanna the three coins, with St. Athanasius the Great at the back; gold background	Gold, yellow, green, white, red, and black	Paper, canvas on wood	Without
	Virgin with Child	The Virgin standing frontally, carrying Christ; green background	Red, white, green, brown, and black	Paper, canvas on wood, covered with print paper	Without
	Ascension of the Virgin	The Virgin ascends to heaven surrounded by angels. Printed Latin inscription on the printed canvas	Dark printed Catholic icon, majority in black	Over printed paper, on wooden support	Without
	St. John the Baptist	The Saint standing in the foreground	Red, yellow	Over print paper, on wooden support	Without

	St. Tekla Haymanot	The Saint standing in the foreground	White and black	Over print paper, on wooden support	Without

Works by Father Abd al-Shahid

1. St. Mary's Church, Banga, Tahta	Embalmment of Christ	St. Joseph and St. Nikodimos embalming Christ frontally, with the Virgin standing between the two Marys in the upper zone; reddish Background	White, red, blue, yellow, green, brown, and black	Canvas on wood	Without
	Resurrection of Christ	Christ rises from his tomb with a red flag in his left hand, with a small angel standing in the left corner below Christ, and the guardians with their swords standing below beside the angel; green and orange background	White, red, green, orange, yellow, and black	Canvas on wood	Without

2. Coptic Museum, Old Cairo	Crucifixion	Christ crucified between two robbers on smaller crosses, with the three women, and St. John standing under the Cross; orange background	White, red, green, blue, brown, yellow, and black	Canvas on wood	(A.M. 1584) A.D. 1868
	Double-sided icon: the Crucifixion and the Entry into Jerusalem	Christ crucified in the center between two small crosses, with the three women standing frontally below beside St. John. Christ on horseback in the center, surrounded by people; below Coptic inscription in frame	White, red blue, brown, yellow, and black

White, red, blue, green, and black | Canvas on wood | (A.M. 1614) A.D. 1898 |

	Crowned Hodegetria	The crowned Virgin standing in the foreground and carrying Christ, with four Angels surrounding her	White, red, brown, green, and black	Canvas on wood	Without
	Crucifixion	Christ crucified in the center between two robbers who are crucified on smaller crosses, with the three women and St. John standing under the cross	White, red, green, blue, brown, yellow, and black	Canvas on wood	Without

Conclusion

Some conclusions can be drawn from the study of the Akhmimic style, both the contents and the characteristics. This style, initiated by Mattary, was prevalent in Egypt during the second half of the seventeenth century until the end of the nineteenth century. The Akhmimic style is a worldwide Catholic contribution, which is comparable to the Mozarabic style. Like the Mozarabic style it consisted of different cultural characteristics and styles, helping to spread the Catholic faith throughout the Middle East and Africa. Some scholars have considered two different styles in two separate periods, but from this study it appears that it was one style with two sequential stages, from about the year A.D. 1663 to about the year A.D. 1890.

Fig. 24.1: Wall painting, Dome of the Martyrs, St. Paul's Monastery. Photograph: Atalla 2002.

Fig. 24.2: Illumination of St. Mark the Evangelist, Coptic Museum Library. Photograph: Atalla 2002.

Fig. 24.3: Iiumination of the Revelation, Book of Beatus of Libana. Photograph: Grubb 1997.

Fig. 24.4: Painting of the Pantokrator, ciborium, Akhmim. Photograph: Fr. Bigoul al-Suriany.

Fig. 24.5: Illumination of Archangel St. Michael, Coptic Museum Library. ciborium, Akhmim. Photograph: Fr. Bigoul al-Suriany.

Fig. 24.6: Painting of the Holy Family, triptych, Akhmim. Photograph: Atalla 2002.

Fig. 24.7: Painting of St. Thomas the Hermit, Akhmim. Photograph: Atalla 2002.

Fig. 24.8: Painting of St. John the Baptist, the Monastery of the Syrians. Photograph: Fr. Bigoul al-Suriany.

Fig. 24.9: Painting of the Crucifixion, Father Abd al-Shahid. Photograph: Atalla 2002.

Notes

1. Nakhla 2001: 12–13.
2. Ibid.: 46–47, 51, 54, 58, 82.
3. Al-Maqrizi 1998: 404–406.
4. Bahr 1999: 281–82.
5. Fawzy 1967: 171–77.
6. Nakhla 2001: 110–13.
7. Lane-Poole 1901: 253, 278.
8. Nakhla 2001: 15.
9. Ghattas 1967: 16–17.
10. Nakhla 2001: 29–42.
11. Atalla 2000: 149.
12. Lyster 1999: 46–49.
13. Atalla 2000: 60–69.
14. Van Moorsel *et al.* 1994: 254–55.
15. Skálová 2003: 120–140.
16. Most of these Islamic characters came from central northern Asia and the Ottoman Empire, in particular, present Turkey and Syria.
17. Skálová 2003: 122.
18. Van Moorsel 1994: 47–48.
19. Grubb 1997: 14.
20. Grubb 1997: 15; Nordenfalk 1988: 86–93; Huyghe 1981: 79–81, 113.
21. Skálová 2003: 125.
22. Van Moorsel 1994: 60.
23. Atalla 2000: 118–19.
24. Van Moorsel 2000: 254–55.
25. Jeudy 2004: 67–88.
26. Van Moorsel 1994: 62–64.
27. Atalla 1998: 154–163.
28. Laferrière 1990.
29. Lyster 1999: 49.
30. Jeudy 2004: 85.

25 The Red Monastery Conservation Project, 2006 and 2007 Campaigns
Contributing to the Corpus of Late Antique Art

Elizabeth S. Bolman

THE MASSIVE WALL painting conservation project now underway in the church at the Red Monastery near Sohag is contributing substantially to the known corpus of late antique art. Obscured under layers of soot, dust and varnish for centuries, even most specialists of Coptic art had little familiarity with these paintings.[1] The newly cleaned figural images and non-figural architectural polychromy are of great significance, and even in advance of their publication have drawn considerable interest not only from Coptologists but also from specialists in Late Antiquity and the Byzantine world.[2] The results of early campaigns of conservation work are now in press, and in this article I will introduce the monument and present previously unpublished findings from work in 2006 and early 2007.[3]

The appellation "Red Monastery" is a colloquial name for the Monastery of Anba Pishay or Bishay, in the Sahidic dialect. Scholars have traditionally called it the Monastery of St. Bishoi, but the inscription in the recently revealed painting of this saint in the Red Monastery church spells it with the Sahidic ending, as does the current abbot. This monumental church was the heart of a sizeable community, which was itself part of a larger "federation" of monasteries, centered at the so-called White Monastery of St. Shenoute.[4] The even larger church at the White Monastery, a few kilometers away, was commissioned in the fifth century by one of the greatest early monastic leaders of Egypt, Shenoute of Atripe (346–465). While the two churches are the best surviving structures from this federation, these once extensive monastic communities have left important material traces, mostly unstudied as yet, and an exceptional body of texts. The existence in the outskirts of Sohag of archaeological remains from one of the formative locations of Christian monasticism, coupled with monumental architecture, high-quality sculpture and rare wall paintings, is extraordinary enough. What makes this site very likely unique in the Mediterranean region is the combination of this wide range of material evidence and a substantial body of textual sources from the site. The conjunction of physical and written data furnishes a remarkable opportunity to learn more about late antique monasticism by crossing disciplinary boundaries. The project to conserve the wall paintings in the Red Monastery church is one component of a much larger project, designed to study monasticism in this area.[5]

The White and Red Monastery churches follow the same basic design with different primary building materials. Shenoute's fifth-century church, built in white limestone, is understood to have been the model for the somewhat later Red Monastery church, principally constructed of brick. According to a recent reevaluation of the sculpture by Hans-Georg Severin, the Red Monastery church most probably dates to circa 525.[6] Both churches are enclosed by tall perimeter walls, angled slightly inward, and topped by a cavetto cornice in the manner of pharaonic architecture. The majority of the interior space in both buildings consists of a long, rectangular nave terminating in a trilobed eastern end. The trefoil space functioned originally as the sanctuary. The naves now lack roofs, while the sanctuaries are enclosed, and the easternmost lobes have been screened off and function as the current sanctuaries of the churches.

The ancient sanctuary of the Red Monastery church is much better preserved than that at the White Monastery. This complex space rises in two registers of niches, embellished with columns, pilasters and pediments. A semidome completes each of the three lobes, above which is a clerestory topped by a modern dome. Severin has observed that "the architectural sculpture of the Red Monastery church—at least in the sanctuary and its western facade—is preserved to a unique degree. Nowhere else in Egypt do we know a monument of the late antique and early Byzantine period whose architectural sculpture is *in situ* up to the highest level of the building and can reliably be examined and estimated."[7] This interior space is aesthetically remarkable, with sweeping lines and dramatic contrasts of depth and mass. Almost all of the surfaces in the trilobed sanctuary and the preceding façade wall are painted with patterns and motifs belonging to the classical tradition. In contrast, the only paintings in the White Monastery church sanctuary that have survived in more than fragmentary form are medieval.

From the commencement of the project in 2002 and continuing into 2006, we focused primarily on the northern lobe of the triconch. In the autumn of 2006, we completed the conservation of this area and began work on the southern lobe, on which we concentrated in early 2007. The conservators have also recently completed test cleanings on the façade wall in front of the triconch and in the small chamber to the northeast of the tre-foil space, with remarkable results. All conservation and supporting scholarly and technical studies at the Red Monastery church have been funded by the United States Agency for International Development and administered by the American Research Center in Egypt.[8] The Coptic Church has provided expansive hospitality throughout the work. We are undertaking this project in collaboration with the Egyptian Supreme Council of Antiquities. I am the overall project director, and Luigi De Cesaris directs the challenging specialized work of conservation with the assistance of Alberto Sucato.[9]

De Cesaris and his team of conservators have carefully studied the paint and plaster layers, discerning in the northern apse four phases of painting.[10] Each phase was painted on plaster using tempera or, in some cases, encaustic (a wax-based paint). When later paintings were added, the artist or his assis-tants first prepared a new plaster layer that covered the earlier phases, with the exception of the fourth stage when two coats of whitewash were applied instead of the usual plaster preparation. In areas where later layers of plaster and paint have fallen off, it is possible to observe something of the character of the earlier paintings. To date, we have a very good idea of the appearance of the first, third and fourth paint layers. While evidence of a second layer clearly exists, it is very limited.

We have found evidence of the first layer on the arches framing the three semi-domes of the triconch, within the vault of the northern semi-dome and on the northern end of the façade wall. The northern half-dome seems to have initially been colored all or mostly red. Elsewhere, the earli-est paintings consist of very loosely applied pastel colors creating geometric patterns or generally vegetal motifs (Fig. 25.1). This kind of simple decora-tion would not have taken a long time to apply, in contrast to that of the later paint layers. Presumably, it was done immediately upon completion of the church in order to provide the interior of the sanctuary with a basic decorative scheme.

Fig. 25.1: First level of painted decoration, showing vegetal motifs against a white background, surrounded by paintings belonging to the fourth layer. Red Monastery church, border framing the eastern semidome, northern side. Photograph: E.S. Bolman. © ARCE.

Fig. 25.2: Second level of painted decoration, showing part of an eye, nostril and mouth revealed where part of the later painting of a cross (fourth layer) has fallen off. Photograph: E.S. Bolman. © ARCE.

Based on our work to date, the second layer of painted plaster is only apparent in the northern semi-dome. Part of an eye, a nostril, and a mouth are visible in an area where the third and fourth layers of painting have fallen off (Fig. 25.2). The second phase of painting evidently consisted of figural subjects that may have been restricted to this half dome. It is possible that this phase extended into the other domes as well, but it is definitely not found on the walls below or above the semi-domes.

The third phase of decoration in the church was extensive, and included painting in all regions of the triconch and the enclosing façade wall. It is characterized by bright pink and green encaustic paint, and also a strong orpiment yellow. As part of this work, the team of painters covered all columns, capitals, niches, walls, and half-domes with architectural polychromy. These decorative motifs have close ties to paintings found in the late antique monasteries of Apa Apollo and Apa Jeremiah that are typically dated to circa the sixth to seventh century.[11] This means that if the building was completed and first painted circa 525, then two more phases of work were undertaken in the church within a very short period of time. Similar geometric panels and curtains were found in a small triconch funerary chapel at the White Monastery, which was excavated by the SCA in 2002.[12] The non-figural paintings in the Red Monastery sanctuary often imitate other media, depicting for example, green-veined marble columns and multi-colored braids. The density of contrasting pattern and color creates variety, expressing essential components used to construct beauty in the late antique Roman world.[13]

The artists of the third phase also painted figural subjects on the backs of the niches found in the two tiers of each lobe, in the semi-domes, and on the walls above them. Many of these figures are visible because the whitewash of the later, fourth phase that originally covered them has flaked off due to its poor adhesion to the wax-based pinks and greens, or the destructive character of the orpiment. The recently conserved figure of the Patriarch Cyril, on the ground floor level of the northern lobe, demonstrates this point. As part of the third phase of painting, the artist depicted a full figure of the saint standing, with a black inscription stating his name and title. During the

Fig. 25.3: Patriarch Cyril, framed by a niche covered with architectural polychromy. The wall below the niche is enlivened with a painted geometric panel. North lobe, western niche. Photograph: E.S. Bolman. © ARCE.

fourth phase this composition was covered by a bust-length figure, again of Cyril, that now survives primarily as an outline (Fig. 25.3). Today, one can discern both figures at the same time. Remnants of two books can be seen, one smaller, higher up and held by the standing representation of the third phase, and a bigger one lower down, held by the larger scale portrait of the fourth and final phase of work. Besides the flaking of the whitewash and the resulting loss of pigment, this area has also suffered considerable additional damage because it is much more accessible than the paintings in the higher zones of the triconch, where paintings from the fourth phase survive in better condition.

The two levels of niches in the northern lobe demonstrate the construction of an Egyptian identity, established first during the third phase of work in the church, and repeated again in the fourth. The middle register includes four monastic saints, three of whom can be readily identified by inscriptions. At the furthest left (west) is Besa, followed by Shenoute, an unknown saint, and Pishay, at the far right. These three, and presumably their colleague, all helped shape monasticism in the immediate area.[14] The ground-floor level, as mentioned above, includes portraits of Athanasios, Cyril, and Theophilos, all patriarchs of the Egyptian Church. They broaden the scope of the statement to include the papacy, and with it the country of Egypt.

Prior to the 2006 campaign, we could discern something of the iconography of the third phase of painting under the fourth layer owing to the thinness of the whitewash upon which it was applied. We were not, however, confident that we could distinguish the stylistic features of this third period. After conservation we now have two figural paintings clearly visible on the third plaster layer, and they are in very different styles. The apostle or evangelist in the region of the clerestory on the northern side of the church, which was uncovered in November of 2004, is consistent with other works of art dated to the sixth century in the Mediterranean region.[15] He fills the frame between two windows, staring out at us in a frontal position, and holds a gemmed codex in his covered left hand. The artist has used soft brushstrokes, and rendered a well-modeled, bulky figure with a very large halo. While the hand and wrist are outlined, otherwise the painter has not employed lines or other schematic devices, preferring a primarily illusionistic rendering.

Painted on the same (third) plaster layer, above the eastern side of the southern semi-dome, is a newly uncovered figure presented in a very different style. Facing west, an angel holds a tray with a vessel filled with a red liquid, presumably wine, and a spoon for giving it to the faithful during the eucharist (Fig. 25.4).[16] The artist created the figure using both outlines and some passages of modeling. The dark lines around the angel's body and dress create a dynamic stylized pattern, and are far removed from the impression of naturalistic solidity of the clerestory figure on the opposite wall. Lines and not contrasts of light and shadow are the dominant tools used to make the figure recognizable. While both paintings include purple, white, gray, and brown, and what is perhaps a similar red, the depiction of the angel does not, at least in its current condition, have the green and golden orange-yellow used in the clerestory figure. The yellow employed for the halos is different as well, the angel having a harsher, brighter hue. Both images have remnants of the fourth phase's geometric motifs painted over them, making it very clear that neither was created during the last phase of work. We do not know if the stylistic differences between the apostle and the angel exist because the same

Fig. 25.4: Angel holding a tray with elements for the Eucharist. Eastern end of the wall above the southern semidome. Photograph: E.S. Bolman. © ARCE.

team had one or more artists working in different modes, or if they were executed at different times. All we can say with certainty is that both images are painted on the third phase of plaster. Additional figures on either side of the northern and southern semi-domes, while much less well preserved, demonstrate that the dominant figural style of the third phase of painting, at least in this area, is that of the angel and not the apostle in the clerestory.

The artist or artists of the fourth phase, as stated above, did not apply the typical preparatory layer of plaster, but instead used whitewash. They concentrated their attention on the semi-domes and the backs of the niches. In addition, precise geometric patterns were used to cover the figural subjects on the walls framing the semi-domes that belong to the third period of work. These designs were executed with precise, dark outlines. Much of the non-figural architectural decoration of the third phase was left undisturbed, while in some areas it was lightly retouched, generally in white. This means that the viewer today sees primarily figural subjects from the last period, and architectural polychromy belonging to the third phase of work.

The northern semi-dome depicts a monumental, enthroned nursing Virgin Mary (the *Galaktotrophousa*), flanked by standing prophets holding open scrolls, in a complex, but shallow, architectural space. This composition was conserved between 2002 and 2004. Balancing the monumental Virgin and Christ Child, the southern apse includes an even larger Christ seated on a jeweled throne set against a similar two-tiered arcade hung with numerous lamps and censers (Fig. 25.5). Whereas the Virgin's head is well below the central arch of the lower arcade, Christ's obscures it and rises above it. The figure of Christ is not as well preserved as that of the Virgin, and may have been somewhat repainted. He holds a huge closed codex in his left hand and raises his right hand in a gesture of blessing. Two angels lean out from behind the arcade, with one hand raised, palm facing outward, and the other holding a bunch of fabric from their robes. The four evangelists flank him, two on either side, each holding a closed codex. The halo now visible around the head of Christ actually belongs to the third phase of painting, which apparently included the same subject, but positioned slightly higher. The pigment of the halo of the Christ belonging to the fourth phase has fallen off, once again owing to problems created by the thinness of the whitewash and the corrosive character of the orpiment

Figure 25.5: Christ Enthroned between Evangelists, south semi-dome. View showing Christ and the right half of the apse only. Photograph: E.S. Bolman. © ARCE.

used by the third painter. What appears to be the remains of a crown on top of Christ's head is actually a capital. Considerable evidence exists in both semi-domes that the artist of the fourth phase painted the architectural framework, lamps, censers, and furniture before adding the figures. When the pigment of the figural subjects falls off, the architecture and other elements are revealed. In March of 2007, the cleaning and conservation of the southern apse was completed.

The subjects of the two semi-domes interact with each other. The Old Testament prophets presenting their scrolls to the Virgin Mary demonstrate that they foretold the incarnation of Christ, establishing what is a standard typological relationship between the Old and New Testaments. The authors of the four Gospels appear opposite, with the massive adult Christ, balancing the depiction of Christ as a child with his appearance in heaven, and including the dominance of his new Word, the Gospels, in the form of the books that all of them hold. These two half-domes constitute only two of the three monumental compositions, the most important of which is the central, eastern semi-dome. This area has not yet been conserved, and so will not be discussed here.

The style of the fourth and final phase of painting in the triconch has ties to paintings uncovered at Saqqara and generally dated to the sixth or seventh century, and also to a painted panel found at Edfu and now in the Musée du Louvre, from the first half of the seventh century.[17] Strong, dark outlining and also the restrained use of modeling characterize these paintings. The outlines are sharper, more saturated, and often wider than those of the third-period angel. The palette is different, with lavender, apricot, burgundy, pale brownish-orange and mauve predominating. The yellow is the warmer color of an egg yolk, less golden than the halo of the clerestory figure, and not as harsh as that used by the painters of the third phase. Precisely defined patterns cover textiles and architectural elements, in a manner not seen earlier.

Paul van Moorsel dated these paintings, when obscured by dirt, soot and varnish, to 1301, based on an inscription elsewhere in the church.[18] In earlier publications, I attributed this phase to circa the eighth century, a slightly later date than the stylistic comparanda warranted. At present, I would suggest a span of the seventh to eighth century, although we know so little of the chronology of Egyptian Christian art in this period that this is still only a guess.

The paintings in the trilobed area of the eastern end itself all date to Late Antiquity. Test cleanings in the small room to the northeast of the trefoil show at least two layers of paint, the uppermost of which was painted as part of the fourth phase of work in the church, and so is also part of this early period. Additional test cleanings on the façade wall in front of the trefoil indicate that most of these paintings belong to the third phase of work, although one small fragment of a medieval figure's head has survived.[19] The extent of this phase of medieval painting, and its fate, are unknown to us at present, but after conservation of the façade wall has been completed, we hope to have more information.[20]

The northern end of the church wall, closest to the façade wall in front of the sanctuary, includes a faint but legible painting of a medieval equestrian saint (Fig. 25.6). Paul Dilley has demonstrated that its long donor inscription credits the work to Paul the Deacon, the son of the blessed Klate, and identifies the saint as an obscure martyr named Aganistos. Dilley

does not believe that the painter, Mercurios, is the same artist as the Mercurios who wrote his name with a date corresponding to A.D. 1301 in the Red Monastery, but has observed that the handwriting has closer ties to the Armenian inscription in the White Monastery eastern semi-dome, dated to A.D. 1124 Dilley is still working on deciphering the fragmentary date written at the end of Paul the Deacon's dedicatory inscription next to the figure of Aganistos.[21] The test cleaning of the inscription and the horse's head show that this painting will be impressive again, after conservation.

By the end of 2007, almost half of the paintings in the enclosed eastern end of the church will be cleaned and conserved. The results to date demonstrate that this church includes the most complete

Figure 25.6. Donor inscription belonging to the painting of the equestrian martyr Aganistos. Test cleaning. Photograph: E.S. Bolman. © ARCE.

example of non-figural painted architectural polychromy dating to Late Antiquity anywhere in Egypt, and very likely the Mediterranean region. While the marbles and mosaics of Istanbul and Ravenna convey the taste for variety and color, in the Red Monastery church sanctuary we see what must have been a common medium for its production, paint. The four phases of painting were undertaken within a short period of time—perhaps not much more than a century. These endeavors almost certainly required more than one artist for at least the first, third, and fourth phases, as well as a large amount of scaffolding, plaster, and pigments. The size of the task, and the fact it was carried out repeatedly, attest to the wealth and energy of the monastery in this period.[22] While the full magnitude of the iconographic program of the fourth, and to some extent also the third, phase of work will not be apparent until the end of conservation, we can already discern something of its complexity.

Notes

1. As recently as 1970, one of the most prolific writers about Coptic art and culture could, mystifyingly, write the following: "For obvious reasons, however, the White Monastery has attracted considerably more ecclesiastical and scholarly attention than its sister monastery, the Red Monastery, which is situated three kilometers north of it" (Meinardus 1969–1970: 111–17). For a demonstration of preference for the White Monastery over the Red, compare the attention paid to the two in the *Coptic Encyclopedia*. Five pages are devoted to the Red Monastery, and ten to the White Monastery. Atiya 1991a: 736–40, 761–70. The endeavor to document and publish both churches as part of the *Peinture murale chez les Coptes* would certainly have raised the profile of the Red Monastery church even without conservation, but I doubt it would have attracted attention outside of the relatively small community of Coptologists. Karel Inneméé has taken over the publication of this project from Paul van Moorsel.

2. I base this assertion on the enthusiastic reactions of numerous Byzantinists and scholars of Late Antiquity who have attended my presentations of this monument.

3. Bolman 2006: 1–24; Bolman 2007; Bolman 2004b: cover–9.

4. Layton 2002: 25–55.

5. This larger work is the project of a multi-disciplinary "Consortium for Research and Conservation in the Monasteries of the Sohag Region." See: http://egypt.cla.umn.edu/consortium.html.

6. Severin 2004. Severin (forthcoming).

7. Severin 2004.

8. Conservation of almost all of the north lobe was funded by USAID through EAP/ ARCE, under USAID Grant No. 263-G-00-93-00089-00 (formerly 263-0000-G-00-3089-00), and ongoing work is being funded and administered by the same institutions, under the Egyptian Antiquities Conservation Project (EAC) Cycle Two Subproject, USAID Agreement No. 263-A-00-04-00018-00. Copyright for all Red Monastery research, photography, studies, and documentation carried out during this period belongs to the American Research Center in Egypt, also the repository of the project's reports, and photographic and graphic documentation. The members of the Red Monastery Project thank USAID and ARCE for their exceptional support and assistance, particularly Gerry D.Scott, III, Robert K.Vincent, Jr., Janie Abd al-Aziz, Lara Shawky, and Madame Amira. Very special thanks goes to Michael Jones, EAC Director, for his consistent help and engagement with the project. Other project members are: Father Maximous al-Anthony, P. Dilley, P. Godeau, K. Innemée, D. Kinney, C. Meurice, H.-G. Severin, N. Warner, and U. Zanetti.

9. We began this project in 2002 with the master conservator Adriano Luzi, who sadly passed away in 2003. Assistant conservators who have worked on the project between 2002 and March 2007 are: E. Abrusca, E. Albanese, E. Antonelli, C. Arrighi, I. Bigiaretti, C. Compostella, I. De Martinis, L. De Prezzo, C. Di Marco, A.Meschini, D. Pistone, E. Ricchi, G. Russo, G. Tancioni, and M.C. Tomassetti.

10. De Cesaris, in collaboration with Sucato, 2003. All reference to paint and plaster layers is based on the work of De Cesaris and Sucato.

11. Bolman 2006: 15–16.

12. Bolman et al. 2007.

13. For a much more extensive coverage of these points, see Bolman 2006.

14. For more on these four monastic saints and their ties to Shenoute's federation, see Bolman 2007.

15. For a discussion of his style and comparative material, see Bolman 2007.

16. A third element is on the tray, which looks like a sort of stand. It may be an early form of the ark which holds the chavice, now typically made out of wood and enclosed.

17. Busts of Angelic Virtues, Cell 709. Quibell 1909: pl. IX. Henne 1924: 10, 35–36, pls. XIX, XX. Paris, Musée du Louvre, inv. no. AF 10878-AF 10879. Rutschowscaya 1992: 60–62, cat. no. 40.

18. Van Moorsel's dating of the painting was published in a dissertation: Langener 1996: 163. For the inscription, see: Monneret de Villard 1925–1926, vol. 2: fig. 221. In a brief description of the paintings, written for the general public, Van Moorsel and Innemée refer to two dates, ca. 1000 and 1301, without explicitly tying either to the

final phase of painting in the Red Monastery sanctuary. Van Moorsel and Innemée 1997: 70–71.

19. My thanks to Innemée for drawing to my attention the fragment on the eastern transverse wall (north side), prior to the trefoil.

20. Additional information about the medieval paintings may be forthcoming from Meurice's examinations of archival photographs of the Red Monastery church.

21. Dilley 2007.

22. For more on the subject of the financial state of Shenoute's federation during his lifetime and afterward, and its relationship to the Red Monastery paintings, see Bolman (forthcoming).

Abbreviations

BIFAO	*Bulletin de l'Institut Français d'Archéologie Orientale du Caire*
BSAC	*Bulletin de la Société d'Archéologie Copte*
CopticaJ Coptica	Journal of the St. Mark Foundation and St. Shenouda Archimandrite Coptic Society
CSCO	Corpus Scriptorum Christianorum Orientalium
DOP	*Dumbarton Oaks Papers*
IFAO	Institut français d'archéologie orientale du Caire
RT	*Recueil de Travaux Relatifs a la Philologie et a l'Archéologie Égyptiennes*
ZÄS	*Zeitschrift für ägyptische Sprache und Altertumskunde*

Bibliography

'Abd al-Masîh, Y. 1938. "Doxologies in the Coptic Church." *BSAC* 4, pp. 97–113.

———. 1942. "Unedited Bohairic Doxologies. I (Tût – Kyahk)." *BSAC* 8, pp. 31–61.

———. 1946–1947. "Unedited Bohairic Doxologies. II (Tûbah – an-Nasî)." *BSAC* 11, pp. 95–158.

———. 1958. "A Greco-Arabic Psali." *Bulletin de l'Institut des Études Coptes* 1, pp. 75–100.

Abû Sâlih the Armenian. 1895. *Churches and Monasteries of Egypt*, ed. B.T.A. Evetts. Oxford: Clarendon Press.

Akermann, P. 1976. "Le décor sculpté du Couvent blanc. Niches et frises." *Bibliothèque d'études coptes* 14.

Amélineau, É.C. 1884. "Fragments coptes du Nouveau Testament dans le dialecte thébaine." *RT* 5, pp. 105–39.

———. 1886–1888a. "Fragments de la version thébaine de l'écriture (Ancien Testament)." *RT* 7, pp. 197–217; 8, pp. 10–62; 9, pp. 101–130; 10, pp. 67–96, 169–81.

———. 1886–1888b. "Fragments thébains inédits du Nouveau Testament." *ZÄS* 24, pp. 41–56, 103–14; 25, pp. 47–57, 100–110, 125–35; 26, pp. 96–105.

———. 1888–1895. *Monuments pour servir à l'histoire de l'Égypte chrétienne au IVe et Ve siècle*. 2 fascicles. Mémoires publiés par les membres de la mission archéologique française au Caire 4. Paris: Ernest Leroux.

———. 1889. *Monuments pour servir à l'histoire de l'Égypte chrétienne au IVe siècle. Histoire de saint Pakhôme et de ses communautés*. Annales du Musée Guimet 17. Paris: Ernest Leroux.

———. 1907–1914. *Oeuvres de Schenoudi*. Texte copte et traduction française. 2 vols. Paris: Ernest Leroux.

Ammoun, D. 1991. *Crafts of Egypt*. Cairo: The American University in Cairo Press.

Anonymous. 1983. *al-Usra al-masihiya wa-l-qira'at al-kanasiya*. Cairo: The Church of the Virgin Mary, Maadi.

Atalla, N.S. 1986. *Coptic Icons*. Cairo: Lehnert and Landrock.

———. 1989. *Coptic Art*. Vol. 1: *Wall Paintings*. Cairo: Lehnert and Landrock.

———. 1996. *Icons in Egypt*. Cairo: Lehnert and Landrock.

———. 1998. *Coptic Icons*. 2 vols. Cairo: Lehnert and Landrock.

———. 2000. *Illustrations from Coptic Manuscripts*. Cairo: Lehnert and Landrock.

———. 2002. *Coptic Icons*. Cairo: Lehnert and Landrock.

Atanassova, D. 2004. "Zu den sahidischen Pascha-Lektionaren." In *Coptic Studies on the Threshold of a New Millennium: Proceedings of the Seventh International Congress of Coptic Studies, Leiden, 27 August–2 September 2000*, eds. M. Immerzeel and J. van der Vliet, vol.1, pp. 607–620. Leuven: Uitgeverij Peeters en Dep. Oosterse Studies.

Atiya, A.S., ed. 1991a. *The Coptic Encyclopedia*. 8 vols. New York, N.Y.: Macmillan.

———. 1991b. "The List of Saints." In *The Coptic Encyclopedia*, ed. Atiya, vol. 7, pp. 2173–90. New York, N.Y.: Macmillan.

Bagnall, R.S., and K.A. Worp. 2004. *Chronological Systems of Byzantine Egypt*, 2nd. ed. Leiden and Boston: E.J. Brill.

Bahr, M. 1999. *al-Qira'a al-masriya fi-'ahd al-salatin al-mamalik*. Cairo: General Egyptian Book Organization.

Balestri, J.P. 1904. *Sacrorum Bibliorum fragmenta Copto-Sahidica Musei Borgiani*. Vol. 3: *Novum Testamentum*. Rome: Sacra Congregatio de Propaganda Fide.

Balmelle, C., and R. Prudhomme. 1985. *Le décor géometrique de la mosaïque romaine. Répertoire graphique et descriptif des compositions linéaires et isotropes*. Paris: Picard.

Barnard, L.W. 1997. "Athanasius and the Pachomians." *Studia Patristica* 32, pp. 3–11.

Barns, J. 1964. "Shenoute as a Historical Source." In *Actes du Xe congrès international de papyrologues: Varsovie-Cracovie, 3–9 Septembre, 1961*, ed. Jøzef Wolski, pp. 151–59. Wroclaw, Warsaw, and Krakow: Zakład Narodowy imienia Ossolin skich Wydawnictwo Polskiej Akademii Nauk.

Basilios, Archbishop. 1991. "Ambo." In *The Coptic Encyclopedia*, ed. Aziz S. Atiya, vol. 1, pp. 111a–112a. New York, N.Y.: Macmillan.

Basset, R., ed. 1916. *Le synaxaire arabe jacobite (rédaction copte: Vol. III, Les mois de toubeh et d'amchir*. Patrologia Orientalis 11(5). Paris: Firmin-Didot. Reprinted Turnhout: Brepols, 1973.

Bauer, A., and J. Strzygowski. 1905. *Eine alexandrinische Weltchronik. Text und Miniaturen eines griechischen Papyrus der Sammlung W. Goleniščev*. Denkschriften der kaiserlichen Akademie der Wissenschaften, philosophisch-historische Klasse 51, 2. Vienna: Gerold.

Baumeister, T. 1972. *Martyr Invictus. Der Martyrer als Sinnbild der Erlösung in der Legende und im Kult der frühen koptischen Kirche: Zur Kontinuität des ägyptischen Denkens*. Forschungen zur Volkskunde 46. Münster: Regensberg.

Behlmer, H. 1996. *Schenute von Atripe: De Iudicio (Torino, Museo Egizio, Cat. 63000, Cod. IV)*. Turin: Ministero per i Beni Culturali e Ambientali.

————. 1998. "Visitors to Shenoute's Monastery." In *Pilgrimage and Holy Space in Late Antique Egypt*, Religions in the Graeco-Roman World 134, ed. David Frankfurter, pp. 341–71. Leiden: E.J. Brill

————. 2000. "Koptische Quellen zu (männlicher) Homosexualität." *Studien zur Altägyptischen Kultur* 28, pp. 27–53.

————. 2004. "The Recovery of the Coptic Sources for the Study of Gender in Late Antiquity." *Orientalia* n.s. 73, pp. 255–69.

————. Forthcoming. *Heilige Schriften als rhetorische Waffe*. Autoritative Texte und ihre literarische Verarbeitung im Werk des ägyptischen Klostervorstehers Besa.

Bell, D.N. 1983. *Besa: The Life of Shenoute*. Cistercian Studies 73. Kalamazoo, Mich.: Cistercian Publications.

Bénazeth, D., and A. Boud'hors. 2003. "Les clés de Sohag: somptueux emblèmes d'une austère reclusion." In *Études coptes VIII: Dixième journée d'études, Lille 14–16 juin 2001*, Cahiers de la bibliothèque copte 13, ed. Chr. Cannuyer, pp. 19–36. Lille and Paris: Association francophone de coptologie.

Bergmann, M. 1988. "Perspektivische Malerei in Stein. Einige alexandrinische Architekturmotive." In *Bathron, Beiträge zur Architektur und verwandten Künsten. Für H. Drerup zu seinem 80. Geburtstag*, Saarbrüker Studien zur Archäologie und Alten Geschichte 3, eds. H. Büssing and F. Hiller, pp. 59–77. Saarbrüken: Saarländische Druckerei und Verlag.

Bilaniuk, 1991. "Coptic Relations with Rome," In *The Coptic Encyclopedia*, ed. Aziz S. Atiya, vol. 2, 609–11. New York, N.Y.: Macmillan.

Bingen, J. 1999. "L'épigraphie grecque de l'Égypte post-constantinienne." In *XI Congresso internazionale di epigrafia greca e latina, Roma, 18–24 settembre 1997: Atti*, vol. 2, pp. 613–24. Rome: Edizioni Quasar.

Bock, F. 1886. *Kunstgeschichtliche Beiträge über die vielfarbigen Gobelin-Wirkereien und Purpurstickereien der spätrömischen und frühbyzantinischen Kunstepoche (III.–VIII. Jh.) aufgefunden in alt-koptischen Begräbnisstätten Oberägyptens im Frühjahr und Sommer 1886*. Hannover.

de Bock, W. 1901. *Matériaux pour servir à l'archéologie de l'Égypte chrétienne*. St. Petersburg: E. Thiele.

Bolman, E.S. 2004a. "Appendix. Documentary Photography at the Monasteries of Anba Shinuda and Anba Bishoi, Sohag." *DOP* 58, pp. 381–82.

————. 2004b. "Chromatic Brilliance at the Red Monastery Church." *Bulletin of the American Research Center in Egypt*, Fall 2004, pp. 1–9.

————. 2006. "Late Antique Aesthetics, *Chromophobia*, and the Red Monastery, Sohag, Egypt." *Eastern Christian Art* 3, pp. 1–24.

————. 2007. "The Red Monastery Conservation Project, 2004 Campaign: New Contributions to the Corpus of Late Antique Art." In *Interactions: Artistic Interchange Between the Eastern and Western Worlds in the Medieval Period*, ed. C. Hourihane, pp. 260–281. Princeton: Index of Christian Art.

————., L. Blanke, D. Brooks Hedstrom, M. Khalifa, C. Meurice, S. Muhammad, G. Pyke, and P. Sheehen. 2007. "Late Antique and Medieval Painted Decoration at the White Monastery (Dayr al-Abiad), Sohag." *Bulletin of the American Research Center in Egypt* 192, pp. 5–11.

Boon, A. 1932. *Pachomiana Latina: Règle et épitres de S. Pachome, épitre de S. Théodore et "Liber" de S. Orsiesius*. Louvain: Bureaux de la Revue.

Borkopp, B. 1989. "Franz Bock und Wilhelm Rautenstrauch. Zur Geschichte der koptischen Sammlung in Trier." In *Die koptischen Textilien der Sammlung Wilhelm Rautenstrauch im Städtischen Museum Simeonstift Trier*, ed. C. Nauerth, pp. 16–25. Trier: Selbstverlag des Städtischen Museums Simeonstift.

Bosc-Tiessé, C. 2004. "The Use of Occidental Engravings in Ethiopian Painting in the 17th and 18th Centuries." In *The Indigenous and the Foreign in Christian Ethiopian Art. On Portuguese–Ethiopian Contacts in the 16th–17th Centuries*, ed. M. João Ramos with Isabel Boavida, pp. 83–102. Aldershot: Ashgate.

Boud'hors, A. 1987. *Catalogue des fragments coptes*. Vol.1: *Fragments bibliques nouvellement identifiés*. Paris: Bibliothèque nationale.

———. 1998. *Catalogue des fragments coptes de la Bibliothèque nationale et universitaire de Strasbourg*. Leuven: Peeters.

———. and R. Boutros. 2001. *L'Homélie sur l'église du Rocher attribuée à Timothée Ælure*. Patrologia Orientalis 49, fasc. 1 = no. 217. Turnhout: Brepols.

———., C. Nakano, and P. Werner. 1996. "Fragments coptes de l'Ancien Testament au Musée du Louvre." *Le Muséon* 109, pp. 17–58.

Bouriant, U. 1887. "Fragment d'un livre de médicine en copte thébain." *Académie des inscriptions et belles-lettres. Comptes rendus* ser. 4/15, pp. 319–20.

———. 1889. "Fragments Bachmouriques." *Mémoires de l'institut égyptien* 2, pp. 567–604.

Brakke, D. 1998. *Athanasius and Asceticism*. Baltimore, Md. and London: The Johns Hopkins University Press.

———. 2006. *Demons and the Making of the Monk: Spiritual Combat in Early Christianity*. Cambridge, Mass. and London: Harvard University Press.

Brakmann, H. 2004. "Fragmenta Graeco-Copto-Thebaica. Zu Jutta Henners Veröffentlichung alter und neuer Dokumente südägyptischer Liturgie." *Oriens Christianus* 88, pp. 117–72.

Brashear, W., and H. Satzinger. 1990. "Ein akrostichischer griechischer Hymnus mit koptischer Übersetzung (Wagner-Museum K 1003)." *Journal of Coptic Studies* 1, pp. 37–58.

Brooks Hedstrom, D.L. 2005. "An Archaeological Mission for the White Monastery." *Coptica* 4, pp. 1–26.

Brown, 2003. "Stations of the Cross." In *New Catholic Encyclopedia*, 2nd ed., vol. 13, pp. 499–501. Washington, D.C.: Catholic University of America.

Bumazhnov, D. 2006. *Der Mensch als Gottes Bild im christlichen Ägypten. Studien zu Gen 1,26 in zwei koptischen Quellen des 4.–5. Jahrhunderts*, Studien und Texte zu Antike und Christentum 34. Tübingen: Mohr Siebeck.

Burmester, O.H.E. 1933–1934. *Le lectionnaire de la semaine Sainte*. Patrologia Orientalis 24, pp. 169–294; 25, pp. 175–485. Turnhout: Brepols.

———. 1967. *The Egyptian or Coptic Church, a Detailed Description of Her Liturgical Services and the Rites and Ceremonies Observed in the Administration of Her Sacraments.* Cairo: Publications de la Société d'Archéologie Copte.

Campagnano, A. 1978. "Monaci egiziani fra V e VI secolo." *Vetera Christianorum* 5, pp. 223–246.

———. 1985a. *Preliminary Editions of Coptic Codices: Monb. GB: Life of Manasses–Encomium of Moses–Encomium of Abraham.* Corpus dei Manoscritti Copti Letterari. Rome: Centro Italiano Microfisches.

———. 1985b. *Preliminary Editions of Coptic Codices: Monb. GC: Life of Abraham–Encomium of Abraham.* Corpus dei Manoscritti Copti Letterari. Rome: Centro Italiano Microfisches.

Capart, J., ed. 1936. *Travels in Egypt (December 1880 to May 1891). Letters of Charles Edwin Wilbour.* Brooklyn, N.Y.: Brooklyn Museum.

de Cesaris, L., in collaboration with A. Sucato. 2003. "Red Monastery–Monastery of St. Bishoi, Conservation of the Wall Paintings. Technical Report, Third Mission, 10/04/2003–11/10/2003." Unpublished report submitted to the Egyptian Antiquities Project of the American Research Center in Egypt.

Chadwick, H. 2001. *The Church in Ancient Society: From Galilee to Gregory the Great.* Oxford History of the Christian Church. Oxford: Oxford University Press.

Chaine, M. 1905. "Fragments sahidiques inédits du Nouveau Testament." *Bessarione* 17, ser. 2, 8, pp. 276–80.

Champollion, J.F. 1818. "Observations sur les fragments coptes (en dialect bachmourique) de l'Ancien et du Nouveau Testament, publies par. M.W.F. Engelbrecht, à Copenhague." In *Annales encyclopédiques*, pp. 350–61.

Charles, R.H. 1981. *The Chronicle of John (c. A.D. 690) Coptic Bishop of Nikiu.* Text and Translation Society Series 3, London 1916. Reprinted Amsterdam: Philo Press.

Chassinat, É. 1902. "Fragments de manuscrits coptes en dialecte fayoumique." *BIFAO* 2, pp. 171–206.

———. 1911. *Le quatrième livre des entretiens et épîtres de Shenouti.* Mémoires publiés par les members de l'IFAO 23. Cairo: IFAO.

——. 1921. *Un papyrus médical copte.* Mémoires publiés par les members de l'IFAO 23. Cairo: IFAO.

Cherix, P. 1979. *Étude de lexicographie copte: Chenouté, Le discours en présence de Flavien (les noms et les verbes).* Paris: J. Gabalda.

Chiovard, F. 2003. "Relics." In *New Catholic Encyclopedia*, 2nd ed., vol. 12, pp. 50–56. Washington, D.C.: Catholic University of America.

Chitty, D.J. 1957. "A Note on the Chronology of the Pachomian Foundations." *Studia Patristica 2 = Texte und Untersuchungen* 64, pp. 379–85.

Ciasca, A. 1885–1889. *Sacrorum Bibliorum fragmenta Copto-Sahidica Musei Borgiani.* 2 vols. Rome: Sacra Congregatio de Propaganda Fide.

Clark, E.A. 1992. *The Origenist Controversy: The Cultural Construction of an Early Christian Debate.* Princeton, N.J.: Princeton University Press.

———. 1999. *Reading Renunciation. Asceticism and Scripture in Early Christianity.* Princeton: Princeton University Press.

Clarke, S. 1912. *Christian Antiquities in the Nile Valley. A Contribution Towards the Study of the Ancient Churches.* Oxford: Clarendon Press.

Colin, G. 1982. *La Version Éthiopienne de la Vie de Schenoudi.* CSCO 444, 445; Scriptores Aethiopici 75, 76. Leuven: Peeters.

Coquin, R.-G. 1975. "Les inscriptions pariétales des monastères d'Esna: Dayr al-Šuhadâ – Dayr al-Fahûrî." *BIFAO* 75, pp. 241–84.

———. 1986. "Moïse d'Abydos." *Cahier de la Bibliothèque copte* 3, pp. 1–14.

———. 1991a. "Akhmim: Monasteries." In *The Coptic Encyclopedia*, ed. A.S. Atiya, vol. 1, pp. 78. New York, N.Y.: Macmillan.

———. 1991b. "Church of Abu Sayfayn." *In The Coptic Encyclopedia, ed. Aziz S. Atiya, vol. 2, pp. 549–52. New York, N.Y.: Macmillan.*

———. 1991c. "Pbow: History." In *The Coptic Encyclopedia*, ed. A.S. Atiya, vol. 6, pp. 1926–1927. New York, N.Y.: Macmillan.

———. 1991d. "Saint Victor of Tabennese." In *The Coptic Encyclopedia*, ed. A.S. Atiya, vol. 7, p. 2308. New York, N.Y.: Macmillan.

———. and M. Martin. 1991. "Dayr Anbâ Shinûdah: History." In *The Coptic Encyclopedia*, ed. A.S. Atiya, vol. 3, pp. 761–66. New York, N.Y.: Macmillan.

Corcoran, L.H. 1995. *Portrait Mummies from Roman Egypt (I–IV Centuries A.D.) With a Catalogue of Portrait Mummies in the Egyptian Museum.* Chicago, Ill.: Oriental Institute of the University of Chicago.

Cragg, K. 1992. *The Arab Christian: A History in the Middle East.* London: Mowbray.

Cramer, M. 1955. *Das altägyptische Lebenszeichen im christlichen (koptischen) Ägypten,* 3rd ed. Wiesbaden: Harrassowitz.

———. 1957. *Archäologische und epigraphische Klassifikation koptischer Denkmäler des Metropolitan Museum of Art, New York, und des Museum of Fine Arts, Boston, Mass.* Wiesbaden: Harrassowitz.

———. 1969. *Koptische Hymnologie in deutscher Übersetzung.* Wiesbaden: Harrassowitz.

———. 1981. "Zum Aufbau der koptischen Theotokie und des Difnars: Bemerkungen zur Hymnologie." In *Probleme der koptischen Literatur*, ed. P. Nagel, pp. 197–223. Halle-Wittenberg: Martin-Luther-Universität.

Criscuolo, L. 2002. "A Textual Survey of Greek Inscriptions from Panopolis and the Panopolite." In *Perspectives on Panopolis. An Egyptian Town From Alexander the Great to the Arab Conquest. Acts from an International Symposium Held in Leiden on 16, 17 and 18 December 1998*, Papyrologica Lugduno-Batava 31, eds. A. Egberts, B. Muhs, and J. van der Vliet, pp. 55–59. Leiden: E.J. Brill.

Crislip, Andrew T. 2005. *From Monastery to Hospital: Christian Monasticism and the Transformation of Health Care in Late Antiquity.* Ann Arbor, Mich.: University of Michigan Press.

———. 2006a. "'I Have Chosen Sickness': The Controversial Function of Sickness in Christian Ascetic Practice." In *Asceticism and its Critics*, ed. Oliver Freiberger (New York: Oxford University Press, 2006), pp. 179–209.

———. 2006b. "A Coptic Request for Materia Medica." *Zeitschrift für Papyrologie und Epigraphik* 157, pp. 165–68.

Crum, W.E. 1902. *Coptic Monuments*. Catalogue général des antiquités égyptiennes du Musée du Caire, nos. 8001–8741. Cairo: Service des Antiquités. Reprinted Osnabrück: Otto Zeller, 1975.

———. 1904a. "A Study in the History of Egyptian Monasticism" (review of Leipoldt, *Shenoute*). *Journal of Theological Studies* 5, pp. 129–33.

———. 1904b. "Coptic Graffiti, etc." In *Osireion at Abydos, Publications of the British School of Archaeology in Egypt 9*, ed., M.A. Murray, pp. 38–43.

———. 1904c. "Inscriptions from Shenoute's Monastery." *Journal of Theological Studies* 5, pp. 552–69.

———. 1905. *Catalogue of the Coptic Manuscripts in the British Museum*. London: British Museum.

———. 1909. *Catalogue of the Coptic Manuscripts in the Collection of the John Rylands Library*. Manchester: University Press.

———. 1939. *A Coptic Dictionary*. Oxford: Clarendon Press.

———. 1992. *The Monastery of Epiphanius at Thebes*, Pt. 2. New York: Metropolitan Museum.

Cuegney, C. 1880. "Quelques fragments coptes-thébains inedits de la Bibliothèque nationale." *RT* 4, pp. 94–105.

Cureton, W., and C. Rieu. 1846–1871. *Catalogus codicum manuscriptorum orientalium qui in Museo Britannico asservantur, Pars secunda: Codices arabicos amplectens*. London: British Museum.

David, É., ed. 2003. *Gaston Maspero, lettres d'Égypte. Correspondance avec Louise Maspero [1883–1914]*. Paris: Seuil.

David, J. 1910. "Fragments de l'Evangile selon Saint Matthieu en dialecte moyen-égyptien." *Revue biblique* n.s. 7, pp. 80–92.

Dechow, J. 1988. *Dogma and Mysticism in Early Christianity: Epiphanius of Cyprus and the Legacy of Origen*. North American Patristic Society, Patristic Monograph Series 13. Macon: Mercer University Press.

Delaporte, L.J. 1905. "Fragments thébains du Nouveau Testament." *Revue biblique* 2, pp. 337–97, 557–63.

———. 1906. *Fragments sahidiques du Nouveau Testament: Apocalypse*. Paris: Geuthner.

———. 1908. *Fragments sahidiques du Nouveau Testament: Evangile de Saint Jean*. Paris: Geuthner.

Del Francia Barocas, L. 1998. *Antinoë cent'anni dopo: catalogo della mostra, Firenze, Palazzo Medici Riccardi, 10 luglio-10 novembre 1998*. Firenze: Istituto papiro-logico "G. Vitelli."

De Moor, A., S. Schrenk, and C. Verhecken-Lammens. 2006. "New Research on the So-called Akhmīm Silks." In *Textiles in situ. Their Find Spots in Egypt and Neighbouring Countries in the First Millennium C.E.*, Riggisberger Berichte 13, ed. S. Schrenk, pp. 85–94. Riggisberg: Abegg-Stiftung.

Depuydt, L. 1993. *Catalogue of the Coptic Manuscripts in the Pierpont Morgan Library*. Corpus of Illuminated Manuscripts 5. Leuven: Peeters.

Desrosiers, S. 2004. *Soieries et autres textiles de l'antiquité au XVIe siècle*. Musée national du moyen âge–Thermes de Cluny. Paris: Réunion des musées nationaux.

Dilley, P. 2007. "Report for 2006 Red Monastery Project Season." Unpublished report submitted to the Egyptian Antiquities Project of the American Research Center in Egypt.

Drandakis, N.B. 1990. "Post-Byzantine Icons (Cretan School)." In *Sinai: Treasures of the Monastery of Saint Catherine*, ed. K.A. Manafis. Athens: Ekdotike Athenon S.A.

Drescher, J. 1970. *The Coptic (Sahidic) Version of Kings I, II (Samuel I, II)*. CSCO 313; Scriptores Coptici 35 (text). Leuven: Secrétariat du CSCO.

Egberts, A., B. Muhs, and J. van der Vliet, eds. 2002. *Perspectives on Panopolis. An Egyptian Town From Alexander the Great to the Arab Conquest. Acts from an International Symposium Held in Leiden on 16, 17 and 18 December 1998*. Papyrologica Lugduno-Batava 31. Leiden: E.J. Brill.

Elanskaya, A. 1969. "Coptic Manuscripts of the M. E. Saltykov-Schedrin State Public Library." *Palestinskii Sbornik* 20, pp. 3–150.

―――. 1994. *The Literary Coptic Manuscripts in the A.S. Pushkin State Fine Arts Museum in Moscow*. Supplements to Vigiliae Christianae 18. Leiden: E.J. Brill.

Elli, A. 2003. *Storia della Chiesa Copta: Vol. 2, L'Egitto Arabo e Musulmano. Il miracolo di una sopravvivenza Christiana interra d'Islam*. Studia Orientalia Christiana 13. Cairo: Franciscan Centre of Christian Oriental Studies.

Elm, S. 1994. *"Virgins of God:" The Making of Asceticism in Late Antiquity*. Oxford: Oxford University Press.

Emmel, S. 1995. "Theophilus's Festal Letter of 401 as Quoted by Shenute." In *Divitiae Aegypti. Koptologische und verwandte Studien zu Ehren von Martin Krause*, eds. C. Fluck *et al.*, pp. 93–98. Wiesbaden: L. Reichert.

―――. 1998. "The Historical Circumstances of Shenute's Sermon *God Is Blessed*." In *ΘΕΜΕΛΙΑ: Spätantike und koptologische Studien, Peter Grossmann zum 65. Geburtstag*, Sprachen und Kulturen des Christlichen Orients 3, eds. Martin Krause and Sofia Schaten, pp. 81–96. Wiesbaden: L. Reichert.

―――. 2002. "From the Other Side of the Nile: Shenute and Panopolis." In *Perspectives on Panopolis. An Egyptian Town from Alexander the Great to the Arab Conquest. Acts from an International Symposium Held in Leiden on 16, 17 and 18 December 1998*, Papyrologica Lugduno-Batava 31, eds. A. Egberts, B. Muhs, and J. van der Vliet, pp. 95–113. Leiden: E.J. Brill.

―――. 2004a. "Shenoute the Monk: The Early Monastic Career of Shenoute the Archimandrite." In *Il monachesimo tra eredità e aperture: atti del Simposio "Testi e temi nella tradizione del monachesimo cristiano" per il 50° anniversario dell'Istituto Monastico di Sant'Anselmo. Roma, 28 maggio–1 giugno 2002*, Analecta Monastica 8 = Studia Anselmiana 140, eds. M. Bielawski and D. Hombergen, pp. 151–74. Rome: Centro Studi Sant' Anselmo.

―――. 2004b. *Shenoute's Literary Corpus*. 2 vols. CSCO 599–600; Subsidia 111–112. Leuven: Peeters.

―――. 2005. "Shenoute." In *Encyclopedia of Religion*, 2nd ed., ed. L. Jones, vol. 12, pp. 8318–20. Detroit and London: Macmillan Reference USA.

————. 2006–2007. "Al-'Anba Shinuda ra'is il-mutawahhidin: Hay'atuhu wa ta'limuhu," trans. Noss-hy Abdel-Shahid Botros. *Dirasat aba'iya wa lahutiya* 18, pp. 45–50; 19, pp. 40–46.

————. 2007. "Coptic Literature in the Byzantine and Early Islamic World." In *Egypt in the Byzantine World, 300–700*, ed. R.S. Bagnall, pp. 83–102. Cambridge: Cambridge University Press.

————. Forthcoming. "Shenoute of Atripe and the Christian Destruction of Temples in Egypt: Rhetoric and Reality." In *From Temple to Church: Destruction and Renewal of Local Cultic Topography in Late Antiquity*, Religions in the Graeco-Roman World 163, eds. J. Hahn, S. Emmel, and U. Gotter. Leiden: E.J. Brill.

Engelbreth, W.F. 1811. *Fragmenta basmurico-coptica Veteris et Novi Testamenti, quae in Museo Borgiano Velitris asservantur.* Hauniae: Popp.

Errera, I. 1916. *Collection d'anciennes étoffes égyptiennes.* Brussels: Goossens.

van Esbroeck, M. 1998. "La légende d'Apa Jeremias et Apa Johannes et les fragments Chester Beatty Copte 829." *Orientalia* 67, pp. 1–63.

Evelyn-White, H.G. 1973. *The Monasteries of the Wadi 'n Natrun.* 3 vols. Publications of the Metropolitan Museum of Art Egyptian Expedition 2, 7, 8. New York, N.Y.: Metropolitan Museum of Art, 1926–1933. Reprinted New York, N.Y.: Arno Press.

Falke, O. von 1913. *Kunstgeschichte der Seidenweberei*, vol. 1. Berlin: Wassmuth.

Fawzy, Fr. B. 1967. "Masa'i al-ittihad bayn al-kanisa al-kathulikiya wa-l qanisa al-qubtiya al-urthuduksiya," in *al-Kana'is al-sharqiya al-kathulikiya*, edited by Aba Subhi Hamawi al-Yasu'i. Vol. 2 of *Dalil ila qira'at tarikh al-kanisa*, chapter 3. Beirut: Dar al-Mashriq.

Feder, F., ed. 2002. *Biblia Sahidica: Ieremias, Lamentationes (Threni), Epistula Ieremiae et Baruch.* Texte und Untersuchungen zur Geschichte der altchristlichen Literatur 147. Berlin and New York, N.Y.: de Gruyter.

Fluck, C. 2001. "Vestimenta Josephi Berolinensia. Gedanken zur Josefsgeschichte auf Wirkereien des Museums für Byzantinische Kunst in Berlin." In *Realia Coptica: Festgabe zum 60. Geburtstag von Hermann Harrauer*, ed. U. Horak, pp. 9–31. Vienna: Holzhausen.

————. 2006. "'Denkt liebevoll an mich …'. Textilien mit Inschriften im Museum für Byzantinische Kunst, Berlin." In *Textile Messages. Inscribed Fabrics from Roman to Abbasid Egypt*, eds. C. Fluck and G. Helmecke, pp. 151–71. Leiden: E.J. Brill.

Forget, J., ed. 1906. *Synaxarium Alexandrinum.* CSCO 48; Scriptores Arabici, ser. 3, vol. 18 (text). Beryti: E Typographeo catholico.

————., ed. 1921. *Synaxarium Alexandrinum.* CSCO 78; Scriptores Arabici, ser. 3, vol. 1 (translation), pp. 401–405. Rome: Karolus de Luigi.

Forrer, R. 1889. *Versuch einer Classification der antik-koptischen Textilfunde.* Antiqua 7, pp. 57–86, 91–92.

————. 1891a. *Die Gräber- und Textilfunde von Achmim-Panopolis.* Basel: Birkhäuser.

————. 1891b. *Römische und Byzantinische Seiden-Textilien aus dem Gräberfelde von Achmim-Panopolis.* Basel: Birkhäuser.

————. 1893. *Die frühchristlichen Alterthümer aus dem Gräberfelde von Achmim-Panopolis*. Zurich: Lohbauer.

————. 1895. *Mein Besuch in el-Achmim. Reisebriefe aus Ägypten*. Strasbourg: Schlesier.

————. 1901. *Über Steinzeit-Hockergräber zu Achmim, Naqada etc. in Oberägypten und über europäische Parallelfunde*. Achmim Studien I. Strasbourg.

Förster, H. 2002. *Wörterbuch der griechischen Wörter in den koptischen dokumentarischen Texten*. Berlin: de Gruyter.

Frandsen, P. J. and E. Richter-Aeroe. 1981. "Shenoute: A Bibliography." In *Studies Presented to Hans Jakob Polotsky*, ed. D.W. Young, pp. 147–76. East Gloucester, Mass.: Pirtle and Polson.

Funk, W.-P. 1990. "Zur Faksimileausgabe der koptischen Manichaica in der Chester-Beatty-Sammlung, I." *Orientalia* 59, pp. 524–41.

Gabra, G. 1989. "Bemerkungen zum Text des Difnars über Pesyntheus, Bischof von Koptos." *Le Muséon* 102, pp. 5–18.

————. 1993. "Bemerkungen zum Text des Difnars über Moses, Bischof von Awsim ca. 740–70." *BSAC* 32, pp. 63–71.

————. 1996. "Untersuchungen zum Difnar der Koptischen Kirche: I, Quellenlage, Forschungsgeschichte und künftige Aufgaben." *BSAC* 35, pp. 37–52.

————. 1998. "Untersuchungen zum Difnar der Koptischen Kirche: II, Zur Kompilation." *BSAC* 37, pp. 49–86.

Galtier, E. 1905. "Contribution à l'étude de la littérature arabe-copte: I, Fragment de la Vie arabe de Schnoudi." *BIFAO* 4, pp. 105–12.

Garrett, S.R. 1995. "Paul's Thorn and Cultural Models of Affliction." In *The Social World of the First Christians: Essays in Honor of Wayne A. Meeks*, eds. L. Michael White and O. Larry Yarbrough, pp. 91–94. Minneapolis: Fortress Press.

Gascou, J. 1991. "The Monastery of Metanoia." In *The Coptic Encyclopedia*, ed. A.S. Atiya, vol. 5, pp. 1608–11. New York, N.Y.: Macmillan.

Ghattas, S. 1967. "Masirat al-kanisa al-qubtiya al-kathulikiya ma' al-nuwwab wa-l mudabirin al-rasuliyin," in *al-Kana'is al-sharqiya al-kathulikiya*, edited by Aba Subhi Hamawi al-Yasu'i. Vol. 2 of *Dalil ila qira'at tarikh al-kanisa*, chapter 4. Beirut: Dar al-Mashriq.

————. 2004. "Une stèle funéraire panopolite du Musée archéologique de Strasbourg." In *Cahiers alsaciens d'archéologie, d'art et d'histoire* 47, pp. 7–10.

Ghica, V. 2001. "Sermon arabe pour le troisième dimanche du Carême, attribué à Chenouté (ms. *Par. ar.* 4761)." *Annales Islamologiques* 35, pp. 143–58.

Giorgi, A. 1789. *Fragmentum Evangelii S. Iohannis Graeco-Copto-Thebaicum Saeculi IV*. Rome: Antonio Fulgoni.

Godron, G. 1970. *Textes coptes relatifs à Saint Claude d'Antioche*. Patrologia Orientalis 35(4), no. 166. Turnhout: Brepols.

Goehring, J.E. 1986a. "New Frontiers in Pachomian Studies." In *The Roots of Egyptian Christianity*, eds. B.A. Pearson and J.E. Goehring, pp. 236–57. Philadelphia, Pa.: Fortress Press. Reprinted with addendum in Goehring 1999a, pp. 162–86.

———. 1986b. *The Letter of Ammon and Pachomian Monasticism.* Patristische Texte und Studien 27. Berlin: de Gruyter.

———. 1989. *Chalcedonian Power Politics and the Demise of Pachomian Monasticism.* Occasional Papers 15. Claremont, Calif.: Institute for Antiquity and Christianity. Reprinted in Goehring 1999a, pp. 241–61.

——— 1992. "The Origins of Monasticism." In *Eusebius, Christianity, and Judaism,* eds. H.W. Attridge and G. Hata, pp. 235–55. Detroit, Mich.: Wayne State University Press. Reprinted in Goehring 1999a, pp. 13–35.

———. 1996. "Withdrawing from the Desert: Pachomius and the Development of Village Monasticism in Upper Egypt." In *Harvard Theological Review* 89, pp. 267–85. Reprinted in Goehring 1999a, pp. 89–109.

———. 1999a. *Ascetics, Society, and the Desert: Studies in Early Egyptian Monasticism.* Harrisburg, Pa.: Trinity Press International.

———. 1999b. "The Fourth Letter of Horsiesius and the Situation in the Pachomian Community Following the Death of Theodore." In Goehring 1999a: 221–40.

———. 2006. "Remembering Abraham of Farshut: History, Hagiography, and the Fate of the Pachomian Tradition." In *Journal of Early Christian Studies* 14, pp. 1–26.

Goldhill, S. 1993. "The Sirens' Song: Authorship, Authority and Citation." In *What is an Author,* eds. M. Biriotti and N. Miller, pp. 137–54. Manchester and New York, N.Y.: Manchester University Press.

Goldschmidt, R.C. 1940. *Paulinus' Churches at Nola. Texts, Translations and Commentary.* Amsterdam: Noord-Hollandsche Uitgevers Maatschappij.

Grabar, A. 1946. *Martyrium. Recherches sur le culte des reliques et l'art chrétien antique.* Vol. 1: *Architecture.* Paris: Collège de France. Reprinted London: Variorum, 1972.

Graf, G. 1944–1953a. *Geschichte der christlichen arabischen Literatur (GCAL): I, Die Übersetzungen.* Studi e Testi 118. Vatican City: Biblioteca Apostolica Vaticana.

———. 1944–1953b. *Geschichte der christlichen arabischen Literatur (GCAL): II, Die Schriftsteller bis zur Mitte des 15. Jahrhunderts.* Studi e Testi 133. Vatican City: Biblioteca Apostolica Vaticana.

———. 1944–1953c. *Geschichte der christlichen arabischen Literatur (GCAL): V, Register.* Studi e Testi 172. Vatican City: Biblioteca Apostolica Vaticana.

Gregoire, H. and M.-A Kugener, ed. and French trans. 1930. Marc le Diacre, *Vie de Porphyre.* Paris: Société d'édition "Les Belles lettres."

Grillmeier, A. 1979– 2002. *Jesus der Christus im Glauben der Kirche.* 5 vols. Freiburg: Herder.

Grohmann, A. 1913. "Die im Äthiopischen erhaltenen Visionen Apa Schenoute's von Atripe: I, im Äthiopischen erhaltenen Visionen." *Zeitschrift der deutschen morgenländischen Gesellschaft* 67, pp. 187–267.

———. 1914. "Die im Äthiopischen, Arabischen und Koptischen erhaltenen Visionen Apa Schenoute's von Atripe: II, Die arabische Homilie des Cyrillus." *Zeitschrift der deutschen morgenländischen Gesellschaft* 68, pp. 1–45.

Grossmann, P. 1982. *Mittelalterliche Langhauskuppelkirchen und verwandte Typen in Oberägypten: eine Studie zum mittelalterlichen Kirchenbau in Ägypten.* Abhandlungen des Deutschen Archäologischen Instituts Kairo, Koptische Reihe 3. Glückstadt: J.J. Augustin.

————. 1984–1985. "New Observations in the Church and Sanctuary of Dayr Anbā Šinūda – The so-called White Monastery – at Suhāg." *Annales du Service des Antiquités de l' Égypte* 70, pp. 69–73.

————. 1991a. "Church Architecture in Egypt." In *The Coptic Encyclopedia, ed. Aziz S. Atiya*, vol. 2, pp. 552a–555a. New York, N.Y.: Macmillan.

————. 1991b. "Cross in Square." In *The Coptic Encyclopedia*, ed. Aziz S. Atiya, vol. x, pp. 660b–661b. New York, N.Y.: Macmillan.

————. 1991c. "Dayr Apa Jeremiah: Archeology." In *The Coptic Encyclopedia*, ed. Aziz S.Ataya, vol. x, pp. 773–74. New York, N.Y.: Macmillan.

————. 1991d. "Dayr Anbā Shinūdah: Architecture." In *The Coptic Encyclopedia*, ed. A.S. Atiya, vol. 3, pp. 766–69. New York, N.Y.: Macmillan.

Grossmann, P. 1991e. "Pbow: Archeology." In *The Coptic Encyclopedia*, ed. A.S. Atiya, vol. 6, pp. 1927–1929. New York, N.Y.: Macmillan.

————. 1992. "The Triconchoi in Early Christian Churches of Egypt and their Origins in the Architecture of Classical Rome." In *Roma e l'Egitto nell'Antichità classica. Cairo, 6–9 febbraio 1989: atti del I Congresso internazionale italo-egiziano*, pp. 181–190. Rome: Istituto poligrafico e Zecca dello Stato, Libreria dello Stato.

————. 1998. "Koptische Architektur." In *Ägypten in spätantik-christlicher Zeit: Einführung in die koptische Kultur*, Sprachen und Kulturen des christlichen Orients 4, ed. M. Krause, pp. 209–93. Wiesbaden: L. Reichert.

————.1999. "Zu Moses of Abydos und die Bischöfe seiner zeit." *BSAC* 38, pp. 51–64.

————. 2002a. *Christliche Architektur in Ägypten*. Handbook of Oriental Studies I.62. Leiden: E.J. Brill.

————. 2002b. "Die klassischen Wurzeln in Architektur und Dekorsystem der grossen Kirche des Schenuteklosters bei Suhāğ." In *Perspectives on Panopolis. An Egyptian Town from Alexander the Great to the Arab Conquest. Acts from an International Symposium Held in Leiden on 16, 17 and 18 December 1998*, Papyrologica Lugduno-Batava 31, eds. A. Egberts, B. Muhs, and J. van der Vliet, pp. 115–31, pls. 3–5. Leiden: E.J. Brill.

————. 2004. "Zum Grab des Shenute." *Journal of Coptic Studies* 6, pp. 85–105.

————. 2006. "Zum Dach über dem Ostumgang der Kirche des Bishuyklosters bei Suhag." *Eastern Christian Art* 3, pp. 37–46.

————, D.L. Brooks Hedstrom, and M. Abdal-Rassul. 2004. "The Excavation in the Monastery of Apa Shenute (Dayr Anba Shinuda) at Suhag." *DOP* 58, pp. 371–82 (with figs. A–E and pls. 1–20 between pp. 372 and 373).

Grubb, Nancy. 1997. *Revelations, Art of the Apocalypse*. London: Abbeville Press.

Guidi, I. 1889. *Le traduzioni dal copto*. Nachrichten von der Königlichen Gesellschaft der Wissenschaften und der Georg-Augusts-Universität zu Göttingen 3, pp. 49–56. Berlin: Weidmann.

Guirguis, M. 2000. "Atar al-arhina 'ala awda' al-Qibt fi l-qarn al-Tamin 'ashar." *Annales Islamologiques* 34, pp. 23–44.

————. 2004. "Ibrahim al-Nasih et la culture copte au XVIIIe siècle." In *Coptic Studies on the Threshold of a New Millennium: Proceedings of the Seventh International Congress of Coptic Studies, Leiden, 27 August–2 September 2000*, eds. M. Immerzeel and J. van der Vliet, vol. 2, pp. 939–52. Leuven: Uitgeverij Peeters en Dep. Oosterse Studies.

————. 2005. "Organization of the Coptic Community in the Ottoman Period." In *Society and Economy in Egypt and the Eastern Mediterranean, 1600–1900*, eds. N. Hanna and R. Abbas, pp. 201–16. Cairo: The American University in Cairo Press.

van Haelst, J. 1976. *Catalogue des papyrus littéraires juifs et chrétiens*. Paris: Sorbonne.

Hahn, J. 2004. *Gewalt und religiöser Konflikt. Studien zu den Auseinandersetzungen zwischen Christen, Heiden und Juden im Osten des Römischen Reiches (von Konstantin bis Theodosius II)*. Klio F. 8. Berlin: Akademie.

Hanna, A., and H. Takla. 1994–1997. "St Shenouda's Writings." In *St. Shenouda Coptic Newsletter* 1(1), p. 1; 1(2), p. 2; 1(4), pp. 4–6; 2(3), p. 1; 2(4), pp. 1–2; 3(1), pp. 7–8; 3(2), pp. 4–5; 3(3), pp. 3–4; 4(1), pp. 2–5.

Hebbelynck, A. 1911–1912 "Les manuscrits coptes-sahidiques du Monastère Blanc. Recherches sur les fragments complémentaires de la collection Borgia." *Le Muséon* 12, pp. 91–154; 13, pp. 275–362.

————. 1913. "Fragments inédits de la version copte sahidique d'Isaïe: 1, Fragments de la Bibliothèque nationale de Paris." *Le Muséon* 14, pp. 177–227.

————. 1922a. "Fragment Borgia de l'Épître aux Romains en copte sahidique." *Le Muséon* 35, pp. 193–210.

————. 1922b. "Fragment fayoumique de la première Épître aux Corinthiens." *Le Muséon* 35, pp. 3–16.

Hebel, U.J. 1991. "Towards a Descriptive Poetics of Allusion." In *Intertextuality. Research in Text Theory*, Untersuchungen zur Texttheorie 15, ed. Heinrich F. Plett, pp. 135–64. Berlin and New York: de Gruyter.

Helman, G. 1994. *Culture, Health and Illness: An Introduction for Health Professionals*, 3rd ed. Oxford: Butterworth-Heinemann.

Henne, H. 1924. *Rapport sur les fouilles de Tell Edfou (1921–1922)*. Cairo: IFAO.

Henner, J. 2000. *Fragmenta Liturgica Coptica: Editionen und Kommentar liturgischer Texte der Koptischen Kirche des ersten Jahrtausends*. Studien und Texte zu Antike und Christentum 5. Tübingen: Mohr Siebeck.

Heussi, K. 1936. *Der Ursprung des Mönchtums*. Tübingen: Mohr.

Hodak, S. 2004. "The Ornamental Repertoire in the Wall-paintings of Wadi al-Natrun: Remarks on a Methodical Approach." *Coptica* 3, pp. 43–68.

Holthuis, S. 1993. *Intertextualität: Aspekte einer rezeptionsorientierten Konzeption*. Stauffenburg Colloquium 28. Tübingen: Stauffenburg.

Horak, U. 1995. "Koptische 'Mumien.' Der koptische Tote in Grabungsberichten, Funden und literarischen Nachrichten." In *Biblos. Beiträge zu Buch, Bibliothek und Schrift*, Österreichische Nationalbibliothek 44.1, pp. 39–71. Vienna: Phoibos.

————. 2001. "Von Alexandria bis Panopolis – Stadtpersonifikationen auf spätantiken Stoffen aus Ägypten." In *Realia Coptica: Festgabe zum 60. Geburtstag von Hermann Harrauer*, ed. U. Horak, pp. 37–52. Vienna: Holzhausen.

Horn, J. 1986. *Studien zu den Märtyrern des nördlichen Oberägypten*. Vol 1: *Märtyr-erverehrung und Märtyrerlegende im Werk des Schenute. Beiträge zur ältesten ägyptischen Märtyrerüberlieferung*. Göttinger Orientforschungen 4; Ägypten, 15, 1. Wiesbaden: Harrassowitz.

Hornbostel-Hüttner, G. 1979. *Studien zur römischen Nischenarchitektur*. Studies of the Dutch Archaeological and Historical Society 9. Leiden: E.J. Brill.

Horner, G. 1911–1924. *The Coptic Version of the New Testament in the Southern Dialect otherwise called Sahidic and Thebaic*. 7 vols. Oxford: Clarendon Press.

Hussey, J.M. 1966. *The Cambridge Medieval History*. Vol. 4: *The Byzantine Empire: Part 1, Byzantium and Its Neighbours*. Cambridge: Cambridge University Press.

Huyghe, R. 1981. *Larousse Encyclopedia of Byzantine and Medieval Art*. London: Hamlyn.

Hyvernat, H. 1886. *Les actes des martyrs d'Egypte*. Paris: Ernest Leroux.

———. 1896. "Étude sur les versions coptes de la Bible." *Revue biblique* 5, pp. 427–33, 540–69.

Ishaq, E. M. 1991. "Difnar." In *The Coptic Encyclopedia*, ed. A.S. Atiya, vol. 3, pp. 900–901. New York, N.Y.: Macmillan.

Jansma, N.S.H. 1973. *Ornements des manuscrits coptes du Monastère blanc*. Scripta Archaeologica Groningana 5. Groningen: Wolters-Noordhoff.

Jeudy, A. 2004. "Icônes et ciboria: relation entre les ateliers coptes de peinture d'icônes et l'iconographie du mobilier liturgique en bois." In *Eastern Christian Art in its Late Antique and Islamic Contexts*, vol. 1, pp. 67–87. Leuven: Peeters.

Johnson, D.W. 1976. "Further Fragments of a Coptic History of the Church: Cambridge OR. 1699R." *Enchoria* 6, pp. 7–17.

———., ed. 1980. *A Panegyric on Macarius Bishop of Tkôw attributed to Dioscorus of Alexandria*. CSCO 415, 416; Scriptores Coptici 41 (text), 42 (translation). Leuven: Secrétriat du CSCO.

———. 1987. "Coptic Reactions to Gnosticism and Manichaeism." *Le Muséon* 100, pp. 199–209.

Jördens, A. 2004. "Reliquien des Schenute in Frauenkonvent." In *Paramone*, Archiv für Papyrusforschung 16, eds. J. Cowey and B. Kramer, pp. 142–56. Munich and Leipzig: K.G. Saur.

Junker, H. 1977. *Koptische Poesie des 10. Jahrhunderts*. Hildesheim and New York: Georg Olms.

Kamal, Sabri Kolta. 1991. "Medicine, Coptic." In *The Coptic Encyclopedia*, ed. Aziz S. Ataya, vol. x, pp. 1578–82. New York, N.Y.: Macmillan.

Kamil, J. 2002. *Christianity in the Land of the Pharaohs*. London: Routledge.

Kamil, M. 1942. "Letters to Ethiopia from the Coptic Patriarchs, Yo'annas XVIII (1770–1796) and Morqos VIII (1796–1809)." *BSAC* 8, pp. 89–143.

Kapoïan-Kouymjian, A. 1988. *L'Égypte vue par des arméniens (XIe–XVIIe siècles)*. Paris: Fondation Singer-Polignac.

Kapur, R. 1999. "The Two Faces of Secularism and Women's Rights in India." In *Religious Fundamentalisms and the Human Rights of Women*, ed. C.W. Howland, pp. 143–53. New York: Palgrave.

Karig, J.S. 1975. "Achmim." In *Lexikon der Ägyptologie* I, eds. W. Helck and E. Otto, pp. 54–55. Wiesbaden: Harrassowitz.

Keil, V. 1978. "Zur Form der Regel des Schenute." In *Göttinger Miszellen* 30, pp. 39–44.

Kendrick, A.F. 1920, 1922. *Catalogue of Textiles from Burying-grounds in Egypt, Victoria and Albert Museum Department of Textiles.* Vols. 1, 3. London: HMSO.

Khalil, Samir, "Bar Hebreaus" In *The Coptic Encyclopedia*, ed. Aziz S. Atiya, vol. 2, pp. 345–46. New York, N.Y.: Macmillan.

———. 1991. "Yusab," In *The Coptic Encyclopedia*, ed. Aziz S. Atiya, vol. 7, pp. 2360a–2362a. New York, N.Y.: Macmillan.

Khater, A., and O.H.E. Burmester. 1970. *History of the Patriarchs of the Egyptian Church.* Textes et documents 13. Cairo: Société d'Archéologie Copte.

Khosroyev, A.L. 1995. *Die Bibliothek von Nag Hammadi. Einige Probleme des Christentums in Ägypten während der ersten Jahrhunderte.* Altenberge: Oros.

———. 2003. "Aus der Lektüre der koptischen Mönche in arabischer Zeit." In *Die koptische Kirche in den ersten drei islamischen Jahrhunderten*, Hallesche Beiträge zur Orientwissenschaft 36, ed. W. Beltz, pp. 121–29. Halle-Wittenberg: Martin-Luther-Universität, Institut für Orientalistik.

King, K.L. 2003. *What is Gnosticism?* Cambridge, Mass., and London: Belknap.

Klein, W. 1992. "Ein koptisches Antimanichaikon von Schenute von Atripe." In *Studia Manichaica 2. Internationaler Kongreß zum Manichäismus. 6–10. August 1989, St. Augustin/Bonn*, eds. G. Wießner and H.-J. Klimkeit, pp. 367–79. Wiesbaden: Harrassowitz.

Koenen, L. 1983. "Manichäische Mission und Klöster in Ägypten." In *Das Römisch-Byzantinische Ägypten. Akten des internationalen Symposions 26–30. September 1978 in Trier*, Aegyptiaca Treverensia 2, eds. G. Grimm, H. Heinen, and E. Winter, pp. 93–108. Mainz: Philipp von Zabern.

Kohlbacher, M. 1999. "Minor Texts for a History of Asceticism: Editions in Progress." In *Ägypten und Nubien in spätantiker und christlicher Zeit*, ed. S. Emmel, vol. 2, pp. 144–54. Wiesbaden: L. Reichert.

Kraatz, W. 1904. *Koptische Akten zum Ephesinischen Konzil vom Jahre 431.* Texte und Untersuchungen zur Geschichte der altchristlichen Literatur, Neue Folge 11, 2. Leipzig: J.C. Hinrichs.

Krall, J. 1887. "Aus einer koptischen Klosterbibliothek." In *Mitteilungen aus der Papyrus Erzherzog. Rainer* 1, pp. 62–72; 2–3, pp. 43–73.

Krause, M. 1981. "Das christliche Alexandrien und seine Beziehungen zum koptischen Ägypten." In *Alexandrien. Kulturbegegnung dreier Jahrtausende im Schmelztiegel einer mediterranen Großstadt*, Aegyptiaca Treverensia 1, ed. N. Hinske, pp. 53–62. Mainz: Philipp von Zabern.

———. 1991a. "Inscriptions." In *The Coptic Encyclopedia*, ed. A.S. Atiya, vol. 4, pp. 1290–99. New York, N.Y.: Macmillan.

———. 1991b. "Papyri, Coptic Medical." In *The Coptic Encyclopedia*, ed. A.S. Atiya, vol. x, pp. 1886–88. New York, N.Y.: Macmillan.

————. 2003. "Das koptische Antiphonar aus dem Handschriftenfund von Hamuli." In *Ägypten-Münster. Kulturwissenschaftliche Studien zu Ägypten, dem Vorderen Orient und verwandten Gebieten. Festschrift E. Graefe*, eds. A.I. Blöbaum, J. Kahl, and S.D. Schweitzer, pp. 167–85. Wiesbaden: Harrassowitz.

Krautheimer, R. 1986. *Early Christian and Byzantine Architecture*, 4th ed., rev. with S. Ćurčić. Harmondsworth, U.K.: Penguin.

Krawiec, R. 1998. "Space, Distance and Gender: Authority and the Separation of Communities in the White Monastery." *Bulletin of the American Society of Papyrologists* 35, pp. 45–63.

————. 2002. *Shenoute and the Women of the White Monastery: Female Monasticism in Late Antique Egypt*. Oxford: Oxford University Press.

————. 2003. "From the Womb of the Church: Monastic Families." *Journal of Early Christian Studies* 11, pp. 283–307.

Krumeich, K. 2003. *Spätantike Bauskulptur aus Oxyrhynchos. Lokale Produktion – äußere Einflüsse*. 2 vols. Wiesbaden: L. Reichert.

Kugener, M.-A. 1904. "Sévère, patriarche d'Antioche (512–518): deuxième partie, Vie de Sévère par Jean, supérieur du monastère de Beith-Aphthonia." Patrologia Orientalis 2(3), no. 8. Paris: Firmin-Didot.

Kuhlmann, K.P. 1983. *Materialien zur Archäologie und Geschichte des Raumes von Achmim*. Deutsches Archäologisches Institut Abteilung Kairo, Sonderschrift 11. Mainz: Philipp von Zabern.

Kuhn, K.H., 1956. *Letters and Sermons of Besa*. CSCO 157, 158; Scriptores Coptici 21 (text), 22 (translation). Leuven: Secrétariat du CSCO.

————. 1966. *A Panegyric on John the Baptist Attributed to Theodosius Archbishop of Alexandria*. CSCO 268, 269; Scriptores Coptici 33 (text), 34 (translation). Leuven: Secrétariat du CSCO.

————. 1978. *Panegyric on Apollo Archimandrite of the Monastery of Isaac by Stephen Bishop of Heracleopolis Magna*. CSCO 394, 395; Scriptores Coptici 39 (text), 40 (translation). Leuven: Secrétariat du CSCO.

————. and W.J. Tait. 1996. *Thirteen Coptic Acrostic Hymns from manuscript M574 of the Pierpont Morgan Library*. Oxford: Griffith Institute.

Kühnel, E. 1960. "The rug tirāz of Akhmīm." In *The Textile Museum Workshop Notes* 22, pp. 1–2, pls. I–IV.

Lacau, P. 1901. "Textes de l'Ancien Testament en copte sahidique." *RT* 23, pp. 103–24.

Ladeuze, P. 1898. *Étude sur le cénobitisme pakhomien pendant le IVe siècle et la première moitié du Ve*. Louvain: J. van Linthout. Reprinted Frankfurt-am-Main: Minerva, 1961.

Laferrière, P. 1990. "Mattari, Peintre d'icônes en Egypte, XVIIIe siècle," n.p.

Łajtar, A. 1993. "Zu einer christlichen Inschrift mit dem Gebet an den heiligen Georgios aus Wadi Bir el-Ain, Ägypten." *Zeitschrift für Papyrologie und Epigraphik* 98, pp. 243–44.

————. and A. Twardecki. 2003. *Catalogue des inscriptions grecques du Musée national de Varsovie*. Journal of Juristic Papyrology, Supplement II. Warsaw: Warsaw University.

Lane-Poole, S. 1901, *History of Egypt*. London: Methuen and Co.

Langener, L. 1996. *Isis lactans – Maria lactans: Untersuchungen zur koptischen Ikonographie*. Arbeiten zum spätantiken und koptischen Ägypten 9. Altenberge: Oros.

Lanne, E. 1958. "Le grand eucharologe du Monastère Blanc." *Patrologia Orientalis* 28(2). Paris: Firmin-Didot.

van Lantschoot, A. 1929. *Recueil des colophons des manuscrits chrétiens d'Égypte*. Bibliothèque du Muséon 1. Louvain: J.-B. Istas.

Lavin, I. 1962. "The House of the Lord. Aspects of the Role of Palace Triclinia in the Architecture of Late Antiquity and the Early Middle Ages." *Art Bulletin* 44, pp. 1–27.

Layton, B. 1986. *Catalogue of the Literary Manuscripts in the British Library Acquired after 1906*. London: British Library.

————. 1995. "Prolegomena to the Study of Ancient Gnosticism." In *The Social World of the First Christians. Essays in Honor of Wayne A. Meeks*, eds. L.M. White and O.L. Yarbrough, pp. 334–50. Minneapolis: Fortress Press.

————. 2002. "Social Structure and Food Consumption in an Early Christian Monastery: The Evidence of Shenoute's *Canons* and the White Monastery Federation A.D. 385–465." *Le Muséon* 115, pp. 25–55.

————. 2003. "Monastic Order in Shenoute's White Monastery Federation." Unpublished paper read at the conference "Living for Eternity," Minneapolis.

————. 2006. "Nouvelles recherches sur la vie au monastère de Chenouté." In *Études coptes IX, Onzième journée d'études*, Cahiers de la bibliothèque copte 14, eds. A. Boud'hors, J. Gascou, and D. Vaillancourt, pp. 233–37. Paris: de Boccard.

————. 2007. "Rules, Patterns, and the Exercise of Power in Shenoute's Monastery: The Problem of World Replacement and Identity Maintenance." *Journal of Early Christian Studies* 15, pp. 45–73.

————. Forthcoming. "The Monastic Rules of Shenoute." In *The Administration of Monastic Estates in late antique and Early Islamic Egypt: In memory of Sarah Clackson*, Supplements to the Bulletin of the American Society of Papyrologists, eds. A. Boud'hors, J. Clackson, and P. Sijpestein. Oakville, Conn.: American Society of Papyrologists.

Lease, G. 1991. *Traces of Early Egyptian Monasticism: The Faw Qibli Excavations*. Occasional Papers 22. Claremont, Calif.: Institute for Antiquity and Christianity.

Leclercq, H. 1921. "Égypte." In *Dictionnaire d'archéologie chrétienne et de liturgie*, ed. F. Cabrol, vol. 4(2), pp. 2401–571. Paris: Letouzey et Ané.

Lefebvre, G. 1907. *Recueil des inscriptions grecques-chrétiennes d'Égypte*. Cairo: Service des Antiquités de l'Égypte. Reprinted Chicago: Ares, 1978.

————. 1910. "Égypte chrétienne. II." *Annales du Service des Antiquités de l'Égypte* 10, pp. 50–65.

————. 1911. "Égypte chrétienne. IV." *Annales du Service des Antiquités de l'Égypte* 11, pp. 238–50.

————. 1920a. "Deir-el-Abiad." In *Dictionnaire d'archéologie chrétienne et de liturgie*, ed. F. Cabrol, vol. 4(1), cols. 459–502. Paris: Letouzey et Ané.

————. 1920b. "Inscription grecque du Deir-el-Abiad." *Annales du Service des Antiquités de l'Égypte* 20, p. 250.

————. 1925. "Hymnes." In *Dictionnaire d'archéologie chrétienne et de liturgie*, ed. F. Cabrol, vol. 6(2), pp. 2826–928. Paris: Letouzey et Ané.

Lefort, L.T. 1929. "Anhang." In *Türkische Turfan-Texte II*, Sitzungsberichte der Preussischen Akademie der Wissenschaften, philosophisch-historische Klasse, eds. W. Bang and A. von Gabain, pp. 429–30. Berlin: Akademie.

————. 1935. "Athanase, Ambroise et Chenoute 'Sur la virginité'." *Le Muséon* 48, pp. 55–73.

————. 1935. "Un passage obscur des hymnes à Chenoute." *Orientalia* 4, pp. 411–15.

————. 1939. "Les premiers monastères pachômiens: Exploration topographique." *Le Muséon* 52, pp. 379–407.

————. 1955. "Catéchèse christologique de Chenoute." *ZÄS* 80, pp. 40–45.

Lehmann, T. 1996. "Zur Genese der Trikonchosbasiliken." In *Innovation in der Spätantike. Kolloquium Basel 6. und 7. Mai 1994*, ed. B. Brenk, pp. 317–57. Wiesbaden: L. Reichert.

————. 2004. "'(Unum) ex tribus sacris universi orbis Coemeteriis.' Kurzführer zu den spätantiken Bauten des Pilgerheiligtums des hl. Felix in Cimitile/Nola." In *Cimitile di Nola/Cimitile bei Nola. Inizii dell'arte cristiana e tradizioni locali. Anfänge der christlichen Kunst und lokale Überlieferungen*, ed. Mario de Matteis and Antonio Trinchese. Oberhausen: Athena, 2004.

Leipoldt, J. 1903. *Schenute von Atripe und die Entstehung des national ägyptischen Christentums*. Texte und Untersuchungen zur Geschichte der altchristlichen Literatur 25.1 (neue Folge 10.1). Leipzig: J.C. Hinrichs.

————. 1906–1913. *Sinuthii Archimandritae Vita et Opera Omnia*. 3 vols. (numbered 1, 3, 4). CSCO 41, 42, 73; Scriptores Coptici 1, 2, 5. Paris: Imprimerie nationale.

————. 1964. "Ein Kloster lindert Kriegsnot. Schenutes Bericht über die Tätigkeit des Weißen Klosters bei Sohag während der Einfälle der Kuschiten." In . . . *und fragten nach Jesus. Beiträge aus Theologie, Kirche und Geschichte, Festschrift für E Barnikol zum 70. Geburtstag*, eds. U. Meckert, G. Ott, and B. Satlow, pp. 52–56. Berlin: Evangelische Verlagsanstalt.

Lemm, O. von. 1885a. *Bruchstücke der sahidischen Bibelübersetzung nach handschriften der K. Öffenlichen bibliothek zu St. Petersburg*. Leipzig: J.C. Hinrichs.

————. 1885b. "Sieben sahidische Bibelfragmente." *ZÄS* 23, pp. 19–22.

————. 1890–1892. "Sahidische Bibelfragmente." In *Akademia nauk. Leningrad. Mélanges asiatiques* 10, pp. 5–16, 79–97.

————. 1890–1906. "Sahidische Bibelfragmente." In *Bulletin Akademia nauk. S.S.S.R. Leningrad* ser 4, 1, pp. 257–68; 373–91; ser 5, 25, pp. 093–0137.

————. 1912. "Part of the Epistle of Apostle James in Coptic. The W.S. Golenischev Collection." In *Monuments of Emperor Alexander III Fine Arts Museum in Moscow* 1–2, p. 59, pl. X (in Russian).

van Lent, J. 1999. "An Unedited Copto-Arabic Apocalypse of Shenute from the Fourteenth Century: Prophecy and History." In *Ägypten und Nubien in spätantiker und christlicher Zeit: Akten des 6. Internationalen Koptologen-kongresses, Münster, 20 – 26. Juli 1996*, eds. S. Emmel, M. Krause, S.G. Richter, and S. Schaten, pp. 155–68. Wiesbaden: L. Reichert.

Logan, A.H.B. 2006. *The Gnostics. Identifying an Early Christian Cult.* London: T. and T. Clark.

Louis, C. 2005. "Catalogue raisonné des manuscrits littéraires coptes conservés à l'IFAO du Caire. Contribution à la reconstitution de la bibliothèque du monastère Blanc." Ph.D. dissertation, École Pratique des Hautes Études, Paris.

———. 2007. "Nouveaux documents concernant l'affaire des parchemins coptes du monastère Blanc." In *Actes du VIIIe congrès international d'études coptes (Paris, juin 2004)*, eds. N. Bosson and A. Boud'hors, vol. 1, pp. 99–114. Leuven-Paris-Dudley: Peeters.

Lubomierksi, N. 2007. *Die Vita Sinuthii: Form- und Überlieferungsgeschichte der hagiographischen Texte über Schenute den Archimandriten.* Studien und Texte zu Antike und Christentum 45. Tübingen: Mohr Siebeck.

Lucchesi, E. 2000. "Un nouveau témoin copte du *Sermon sur la conduite chrétienne* du Pseudo-Chenouté." *Orientalia Christiana Periodica* 66, pp. 419–22.

Lyster, W. 1999. *Monastery of St. Paul, Egypt.* Cairo: American Research Center in Egypt.

MacCoull, L. 2004. "Greek Paschal Troparia in Ms Paris copte 120." *Le Muséon* 117, pp. 93–106.

MacDonald, W.L. 1986. *The Architecture of the Roman Empire.* Vol. 2: *An Urban Appraisal.* New Haven, Conn. and London: Yale University Press.

MacMullen, R. 1984. *Christianizing the Roman Empire (A.D. 100–400).* New Haven, Conn. and London: Yale University Press.

Malak, H., 1964. "Les livres liturgiques de l'Église copte." In *Mélanges Eugène Tisserant: Vol. 3, Orient chrétien*, Studi e Testi 233, pp. 1–35. Vatican City: Biblioteca apostolica vaticana.

Mango, C. 1972. *The Art of the Byzantine Empire 312–1453: Sources and Documents.* Englewood Cliffs, N.J.: Prentice-Hall.

al-Maqari, F. and M. Girgis. 1913. *Kitab al-Absaliyat wa-l-Turuhat al-Watos wa-l-Adam* Cairo.

al-Maqrizi. 1998. *Kitab al-mawa'idh wa-l-i'tibar.* Beirut: Dar al-Kutub al-Alamiya.

Marjanen, A., ed. 2005. *Was There a Gnostic Religion?* Publications of the Finnish Exegetical Society 87. Helsinki: Finnish Exegetical Society; Göttingen: Vandenhoeck & Ruprecht.

Martin, M. 1982. "Note sur la communaute copte entre 1650 et 1850." *Annales Islamologiques* 18, pp. 193–215.

Martin, J. 2001. *Spätantike und Völkerwanderung.* Oldenbourg Grundriss der Geschichte 4. 4th ed. Munich: Oldenbourg.

Martindale, J.R. 1980. *The Prosopography of the Later Roman Empire:* Vol. 2, A.D. 395–527, Cambridge: Cambridge University Press.

Martinez, F.J. 1990. "The King of Rum and the King of Ethiopia in Medieval Apocalyptic Texts from Egypt." In *Coptic Studies, Acts of the Third International Congress of Coptic Studies Warsaw, 20–25 August 1984*, ed. W. Godlewski, pp. 247–59. Varsovie: PWN-Editions Scientifiques de Pologne.

Maspero, G. 1886. "Rapport à l'Institut Égyptien sur les fouilles et travaux exécutés en Égypte pendant l'hiver de 1885–1886." *Bulletin de l'Institut Égyptien* 7, pp. 196–251.

———. 1889. "Fragment de l'Évangile selon St. Matthieu en dialecte bachmourique." *RT* 11, p. 116.

———. 1892. *Fragments de la version thébaine de l'Ancien Testament*. Mémoires publiés par les membres de la mission archéologique française au Caire 6. Paris: Ernest Leroux.

———. 1907. "Compte rendu de 'J.B. Chabot, "Inventaire sommaire des manuscrits coptes de la Bibliothèque nationale," *Revue des bibliothèques* 16, 1906, pp. 351–67'." In *Revue critique* 43, pp. 322–23.

Matteaus, B. 1985. *al-Difnar: Qubti-'Arabi*. Beni Sueif: Anba Ruweis Druckerei.

Matteaus, B., Bishop Samuel, G. Sarkis, and M. Morcos. 1995. *al-Absaliyat al-Watos wa-l Adam*. Vol. 2. Beni Sueif: Diocese of Beni Suief.

McEnerney, J. 1987. *St. Cyril of Alexandria: Letters 1–50*. The Fathers of the Church 76. Washington, D.C.: Catholic University of America Press.

McKenzie, J. 1996. "Alexandria and the Origins of Baroque Architecture." In *Alexandria and Alexandrianism. Papers Delivered at a Symposium Organized by The J. Paul Getty Museum and The Getty Center for the History of Art and the Humanities and Held at the Museum, April 22–25, 1993*, pp. 109–125. Malibu, Calif.: J. Paul Getty Museum.

McNally, S., and I.D. Schrunk. 1993. *Excavations in Akhmîm, Egypt: Continuity and Change in City Life from Late Antiquity to the Present*. British Archaeological Reports, International Series 590. Oxford: Tempus Reparatum.

McVey, K.E., ed. and trans. 1993. *A Homily on Blessed Mar Severus, Patriarch of Antioch, by George, Bishop of the Arabs*. CSCO 531; Scriptores Syri 217. Leuven: Peeters.

Meinardus, O.F.A. 1965. *Christian Egypt*. Cahiers d'histoire égyptienne. Cairo: IFAO.

———. 1969–1970. "Some Lesser Known Wall-Paintings in the Red Monastery at Sohag." *BSAC* 20, pp. 111–17.

———. 1977. *Christian Egypt Ancient and Modern*, 2nd rev. ed. Cairo: The American University in Cairo Press.

———. 1991. "Dayr Anba Antuniyus." In *The Coptic Encyclopedia*, ed. Aziz S. Atiya, vol. 10, pp. 719b–729a. New York, N.Y.: Macmillan.

Mertens, M. "Alchemy, Hermetism and Gnosticism at Panopolis *c.* 300 A.D.: The Evidence of Zosimus." In *Perspectives on Panopolis. An Egyptian Town From Alexander the Great to the Arab Conquest. Acts from an International Symposium Held in Leiden on 16, 17 and 18 December 1998*, Papyrologica Lugduno-Batava 31, eds. A. Egberts, B. Muhs, and J. van der Vliet, pp. 165–75. Leiden: E.J. Brill.

Meurice, C. 2004."Voyageurs, missionnaires et consuls dans la région de Tahta (Moyenne-Égypte), de la deuxième moitié du XVIIe au début du XXe siècle." In *Coptic Studies on the Threshold of a New Millennium: Proceedings of the Seventh International Congress of Coptic Studies, Leiden, 27 August–2 September 2000*, eds. M. Immerzeel and J. van der Vliet, vol. 2 pp. 953–1058. Leuven: Uitgeverij Peeters en Dep. Oosterse Studies.

Miller, B. 1998. *Weisung der Väter. Apophthegmata patrum, auch Gerontikon oder Alphabeticum genannt*. Sophia 6. Trier: Paulinus.

Mina, T., ed. 1937. *Le martyre d'Apa Epima*. Cairo: Service des Antiquités de l'Égypte.

Mingarelli, G.L. 1785. *Aegyptiorum Codicum Reliquiae Venetiis in Bibliotheca Naniana Asservatae*. 2 vols. Bologna: Laelius a Vulpe.

van Minnen, P. 2002. "The Letter (and Other Papers) of Ammon: Panopolis in the Fourth Century A.D.." *Perspectives on Panopolis. An Egyptian Town From Alexander the Great to the Arab Conquest. Acts from an International Symposium Held in Leiden on 16, 17 and 18 December 1998*, Papyrologica Lugduno-Batava 31, eds. A. Egberts, B. Muhs, and J. van der Vliet, pp. 177–99. Leiden: E.J. Brill.

Moftah, R. et al. 1991. "Music, Coptic: Description of the Corpus and Present Musical Practise." In *The Coptic Encyclopedia*, ed. A.S. Atiya, vol. 6, pp. 1715–28. New York, N.Y.: Macmillan.

Monneret de Villard, U. 1923. "La fondazione del Deyr el-Abiad (*SB* III 6311)." *Aegyptus* 4, pp. 156–62.

———. 1925–1926. *Les Couvents près de Sohâg (Deyr el-Abiad et Deyr el-Ahmar)*, vols. 1–2. Milan: Tipografia Pontificia Arcivescovile S. Giuseppe.

Montserrat, D. 1998. "Pilgrimage to the Shrine of SS Cyrus and John at Menouthis in Late Antiquity." In *Pilgrimage and Holy Space in Late Antique Egypt*, Religions in the Graeco-Roman World 134, ed. D. Frankfurter, pp. 257–79. Leiden: E.J. Brill.

van Moorsel, P. 2000. *Called to Egypt*. Collected Studies on Painting in Christian Egypt. Leiden: Nederlans Institut voor Het Nabije Oosten.

———. 2002. *Le monastère de Saint Paul, près de la mer Rouge*. Mémoires de l'IFAO 120. Cairo: IFAO.

———., M. Immerzeel, and L. Langen. 1994. *Catalogue général du musée copte: The Icons*. Cairo: Supreme Council of Antiquities Press.

———. and K. Innemée. 1997. "Brève histoire de la 'Mission des peintures coptes.'" In *Dossiers d'archéologie* 226, pp. 70–71.

Moussa, M. 1998–1999. "I Am Amazed: Shenoute of Atripe's Endorsement of Alexandrian Theology in the White Monastery." *Bulletin of Saint Shenouda the Archimandrite Coptic Society* 5, pp. 19–40.

Munier, H. 1914. "Sur deux passages de la Genèse en copte sahîdique." *Annales de Service des Antiquités* 13, pp. 187–92.

———. 1916. *Catalogue générale des antiquités égyptiennes du Musée du Caire nos. 9201–9304, Manuscrits coptes*. Cairo: IFAO.

———. 1916. "Recueil de manuscrits coptes de l'Ancien et du Nouveau Testament." *BIFAO* 12, pp. 243–57.

————. 1919–1923. "Mélanges de littérature copte." *Annales de Service des Antiquités* 19, pp. 225–41; 21, pp. 77–88; 23, pp. 210–28.

Münter, F.C. 1786. *Specimen versionum Danielis copticarum, nonum eius caput memphitice et sahidice exhibens*. Rome: Fulgonius.

Muyser, J. 1935. *Maria's heerlijheid in Egypte*. Een studie der Koptische Maria-literatuur, deel 1 (second part never published). Leuven and Utrecht: Sint-Alfonsusdrukkerij and De Gemeenschap.

————. 1944. "Contribution à l'étude des listes épiscopales de l'Eglise Copte." *BSAC* 10, pp. 116–76.

Nagel, P. 1983–1984. "Studien zur Textüberlieferung des sahidischen Alten Testamentes." *ZÄS* 110, pp. 51–74; 111, 138–64.

————. 1987. "Sahidische Pentateuchfragmente." *ZÄS* 114, pp. 134–66.

————. 1989a. "Editionen koptischer Bibeltexten seit Till 1960." *Archiv für Papyrusforschung* 35, pp. 43–100.

————. 1989b. "Fragmente eines Sahidischen Genesiskodex der Nationalbibliothek zu Paris (BN 1291 fol. 8V13)." *ZÄS* 116, pp. 71–90.

Nakhla, K.S. 2001. *The History of the Popes of Alexandria*, 2nd edn. Vol. 4. Cairo: The Syrian Monastery.

Nau, F. 1899–1900. "Une version syriaque inédite de la Vie de Schenoudi." In *Revue semitique d'epigraphie et d'histoire ancienne* 7, pp. 357–63; 8, pp. 153–67; 252–65.

Noever, P., ed. 2005. Verletzliche Beute. Spätantike und frühislamische Textilien aus Ägypten. Vienna: Hatje/Cantz, Ostfildern-Ruit.

Nordenfalk, C. 1988. *Book Illumination*. Geneva: Skira.

Nunn, J. 2002. *Ancient Egyptian Medicine*. London: British Museum Press; repr. Norman, Okla.: University of Oklahoma Press.

Nutton, V. 1984. "From Galen to Alexander: Aspects of Medicine and Medical Practice in Late Antiquity." *DOP* 38, pp. 1–14.

O'Leary, D.L. 1926–1930. *The Difnar (Antiphonarium) of the Coptic Church (First Four Months), from the Manuscript in the John Rylands Library, Manchester, with Fragments of a Difnar Recently Discovered at the Dēr Abū Makar in the Wādi n Natrūn*, I–III. London: Luzac.

Orlandi, T. 1974. *Constantini episcopi urbis Siout enconomia in Athanasium duo*, CSCO 349, Scriptores Coptice 37. Leuven: Peeters.

————. 1985. *Shenute contra Origenistas. Testo con introduzione e traduzione*. Rome: Centro Italiano Microfisches.

————. 2002. "The Library of the Monastery of Saint Shenute at Atripe." In *Perspectives on Panopolis. An Egyptian Town From Alexander the Great to the Arab Conquest. Acts from an International Symposium Held in Leiden on 16, 17 and 18 December 1998*, Papyrologica Lugduno-Batava 31, eds. A. Egberts, B. Muhs, and J. van der Vliet, pp. 211–31. Leiden: E.J. Brill.

————. 2003. *Corpus dei manoscritti copti letterari*. http://rmcisadu.let.uniroma1.it/cmcl/ammini/entrata.html. Casalini Libri.

————. 2004. "Clavis patrum copticorum." In *Corpus dei manoscritti copti letterari*. http://rmcisadu.let.uniroma1.it/cgi-bin/cmcl/chiamata.cgi.

Painchaud, L., and T. Janz. 1997. "The 'Kingless Generation' and the Polemical Rewriting of Certain Nag Hammadi Texts." In *The Nag Hammadi Library after Fifty Years*, Nag Hammadi and Manichaean Studies 44, eds. J. Turner and A. McGuire, pp. 439–60. Leiden: E.J. Brill.

Papastratos, D. 1990. *Paper Icons: Greek Orthodox Religious Engravings 1665–1899*, trans. John Leatham. 2 vols. Athens: Papastratos.

Pellegrini, A. 1907. "Stele funerarie copte del Museo archeologico di Firenze." In *Bessarione* 22, ser. 3, 3, pp. 20–43.

Pharr, C. 1952. *The Theodosian Code and Novels and the Sirmondian Constitutions*. Corpus Juris Romani 1. Princeton: Princeton University Press.

Plett, H. F. 1991. "Intertextualities." In *Intertextuality*, Research in Text Theory (Untersuchungen zur Textheorie) 15, ed. H.F. Plett, pp. 3–29. Berlin and New York: de Gruyter.

Pleyte, W., and P.A.A. Boeser. 1897. *Manuscrits coptes du musée d'antiquités des Pays-Bas à Leide*. Leiden: E.J. Brill.

Pococke, R. 1743, 1745. *A Description of the East and Some other Countries*. 2 vols. London: printed for the author.

Polotsky, H.-J. 1932. "Koptische Zitate aus den Acta Achelai." *Le Muséon* 45, pp. 18–20.

Preiß, A. 2007. "Robert Forrer und die Stoffe in der Stiftung Moritzburg." In *Verborgene Zierde–Spätantike und frühislamische Textilien in Halle*, eds. G. Brands and A. Preiß, pp. 66–77. Halle: Stiftung Moritzburg.

Quatremère, É. 1808. *Recherches critiques et historiques sur la langue et la litterature de l'Égypte*. Paris: Imprimerie imperiale.

Quecke, H. 1968. "Ein Pachomiuszitat bei Schenute." In *Probleme der koptischen Literatur*, ed. P. Nagel, pp. 155–71. Halle-Wittenberg: Martin-Luther Universität.

———. 1970. *Untersuchungen zum Stundengebet*. Louvain: Institut Orientaliste.

———. 1975. *Die Briefe Pachoms: Griechischer Text der Handschrift W. 145 der Chester Beatty Library*. Textus patristici et liturgici II. Regensburg: Friedrich Pustet.

———. 1983. "Zwei Blätter aus koptischen Hermeneia-Typika in der Papyrussammlung der Österreichischen Nationalbibliothek (P. Vindob. K 9725 und 9734)." In *Festschrift zum 100jährigen Bestehen der Papyrussammlung der Österreichischen Nationalbibliothek*, pp. 194–206; pls. 10, 11. Vienna: Hollinek.

———. 1995. "Psalmverse als 'Hymnen' in der koptischen Liturgie?" In *Christianisme d'Égypte*, Cahiers de la bibliothèque copte 9, pp. 101–14. Paris and Louvain: Peeters.

Quibell, J. 1909. *Excavations at Saqqara 1907–1908*, vol. 3. Cairo: IFAO.

Ranke-Heinemann, U. 1964. *Das frühe Mönchtum. Seine Motive nach den Selbstzeugnissen*. Essen: Hans Driewer.

Renner, D. 1974. *Die koptischen Stoffe im Martin von Wagner Museum der Universität Würzburg*. Wiesbaden: Harrassowitz.

Renner-Volbach, D. 2002. *Die sogenannten koptischen Textilien im Museum Andreasstift der Stadt Worms*. Wiesbaden: L. Reichert.

Reymond, E.A.E., and J.W.B. Barns 1973. *Four Martyrdoms from the Pierpont Morgan Coptic Codices*. Oxford: Clarendon Press.

Richter, S.G. 1997. *Die Aufstiegspsalmen des Herakleides*. *Untersuchungen zum Seelenaufstieg und zur Seelenmesse bei den Manichäern*. Sprachen und Kulturen des christlichen Orients 1. Wiesbaden: L. Reichert.

———. 2000. "Ein manichäischer Sonnenhymnus." In *Studia Manichaica 2. Internationaler Kongreß zum Manichäismus, Berlin, 14–18. July, 1997*, Berichte und Abhandlungen Berlin-Brandenburgische Akademie der Wissenschaften, Sonderband 4, eds. R.E. Emmerick, W. Sundermann, and P. Zieme, pp. 482–93. Berlin: Akademie.

Riegl, A. 1889. Die ägyptischen Textilfunde im K.K. österreichischen Museum, Vienna: Waldheim.

Rieu, C. 1894. *Supplement to the Catalogue of the Arabic Manuscripts in the British Museum*. London: Trustees of the British Museum.

Robinson, B.A. 2001. "Fountains and the Culture of Water at Roman Corinth." Ph.D. dissertation, University of Pennsylvania.

Rossi, C. 2006. *The Treasures of the Monastery of Saint Catherine*. Cairo: The American University in Cairo Press.

Rousseau, P. 2007. "The Successors of Pachomius and the Nag Hammadi Codices: Exegetical Themes and Literary Structures." In *The World of Early Egyptian Christianity. Language, Literature and Social Context. Essays in Honor of David. W. Johnson*, eds. J.E. Goehring and J.A. Timbie, pp. 140–57. Washington, D.C.: Catholic University of America Press.

Rutschowscaya, M.-H. 1990. *Coptic Fabric*. Paris: Adam Biro.

———. 1992. *La peinture copte*. Paris: Réunion des musées nationaux.

SB = Sammelbuch griechischer Urkunden aus Ägypten. Strasbourg: Truebner (presently, Wiesbaden: Harrrassowitz), 1915– .

SB Kopt = Koptisches Sammelbuch. Mitteilungen aus der Papyrussammlung der Österreichischen Nationalbibliothek, n.s. vol. 23, 1 ss., ed. M.R.M. Hasitzka, Vienna: Hollinek, 1993– .

Schaff, P., and H. Wace. 1994. *A Selection of Nicene and Post-Nicene Fathers*. 2nd series, 38 vols. Peabody, Mass.: Hendrickson.

Scheidel, W. 2001. *Death on the Nile: Disease and the Demography of Roman Egypt*. Mnemosyne Supplements 228. Leiden: E.J. Brill.

Schenke, H.-M. 2001. "Das Evangelium nach Philippus (NHC II, 3)." In *Nag Hammadi Deutsch*. Vol. 1: *NHC I,1–V,1*, eds. H.-M. Schenke, H.-G. Bethge, and U.U. Kaiser, pp. 183–213. Berlin: de Grutyer.

Schläpfer, L. 1966. *Das Leben des heiligen Johannes Chrysostomus. Heilige der ungeteilten Christenheit*. Düsseldorf: Patmos.

Schleifer, J. 1909–1914. *Sahidische Bibel-fragmente aus dem British Museum zu London*. 3 vols. Vienna: Hölder.

———. 1912. *Bruchstücke der sahidischen Bibel-übersetzung*. Vienna: Hölder.

Schmitz, F.-J. 2003. *Das Verhältnis der Koptischen zur griechischen Überlieferung des Neues Testaments. Dokumentation und Auswertung der Gesamtmaterialien beider*

Traditionen zum Jakobusbrief und den beiden Petrusbriefen. Berlin and New York: de Gruyter.

————. and G. Mink. 1986–1991. *Die Sahidischen Handschriften der Evangelien. Liste der Koptischen Hanschriften des Neuen Testaments.* Vols. 1, 2.1, 2.2. Berlin and New York: de Gruyter.

Schnitzler, B. 1999. *Robert Forrer (1866–1947). Archéologue, écrivain et antiquaire.* Collection "Recherches et documents" 65. Strasbourg: Publications de la société savante d'Alsace en coédition avec les musées de Strasbourg.

Schrenk, S. 2004. *Textilien des Mittelmeerraumes aus spätantiker bis frühislamischer Zeit.* Riggisberg: Abegg-Stiftung.

Schroeder, C.T. 2002. "Disciplining the Monastic Body: Asceticism, Ideology, and Gender in the Egyptian Monastery of Shenoute of Atripe." Ph.D. dissertation, Duke University. (Later published as *Monastic Bodies: Discipline and Salvation in Shenoute of Atripe.* See Schroeder 2007).

————. 2004. "'A Suitable Abode for Christ': The Church Building as Symbol of Ascetic Renunciation in Early Monasticism." *Church History: Studies in Christianity and Culture* 73, pp. 472–521.

————. 2006. "Prophecy and *Porneia* in Shenoute's Letters: The Rhetoric of Sexuality in a Late Antique Egyptian Monastery." *Journal of Near Eastern Studies* 65, pp. 81–97.

————. 2007. *Monastic Bodies: Discipline and Salvation in Shenoute of Atripe.* Philadelphia, Pa.: University of Pennsylvania Press.

Schüssler, K. 1974–1975. "Die Koptische Überlieferung des Alten und Neuen Testaments." *Enchoria* 4, pp. 31–60; 5, pp. 25–43.

————. 1995–2004. *Biblia Coptica – Das Sahidische Alte und Neue Testament.* 1.1, pp. 1–20; 1.3, pp. 21–48, 49–92; 1.4, pp. 93–120; 3.1, pp. 500–20; 3.2, pp. 521–40; 3.3, pp. 541–60. Wiesbaden: Harrassowitz.

————. 2002. "Analyse der Lektionarhandschrift sa 530." *Journal of Coptic Studies* 4, pp. 133–66.

SEG = Supplementum Epigraphicum Graecum, Leyden: A.W. Sijthoff (continued, Amsterdam: J.C. Gieben; Leiden: Brill), 1923– .

Severin, H.-G. 1977. "Frühchristliche Skulptur und Malerei in Ägypten." In *Spätantike und frühes Christentum,* Propyläen Kunstgeschichte Supplementband 1, ed. B. Brenk, pp. 243–53. Berlin: Propyläen.

————. 1980. Review of "Ph. Akermann, Le décor sculpté du couvent Blanc. Niches et Frises." *Byzantinische Zeitschrift* 73, pp. 101–102.

————. 1981. "Problemi di scultura tardoantica in Egitto." *Corso di cultura sull'arte ravennate e bizantina* 28, pp. 315–336.

————. 1991a. "Sculpture in Stone, Coptic." In *The Coptic Encyclopedia,* ed. A.S. Atiya, vol. 7, pp. 2112–17. New York, N.Y.: Macmillan.

————. 1991b. "Dayr Anbā Shinūdah: Architectural Sculpture." In *The Coptic Encyclopedia,* ed. A.S. Atiya, vol. 3, pp. 769–70. New York, N.Y.: Macmillan.

————. 1993. "Zum Dekor der Nischenbekrönungen aus spätantiken Grabbauten Ägypten." *Riggisberger Berichte* 1, pp. 63–85.

————. 1998. "Zur Skulptur und Malerei der spätantiken und frühmittelalterlichen Zeit in Ägypten." In *Ägypten in spätantik-christlicher Zeit: Einführung in die koptische Kultur*, Sprachen und Kulturen des christlichen Orients 4, ed. M. Krause, pp. 295–338. Wiesbaden: L. Reichert.

————. 2004. "Notes on the Architectural Sculpture of Dayr Anbā Bišūy ('Red Monastery') near Sūhāǧ." Prepared for The Red Monastery Project Final Report.

————. Forthcoming. "On the Architectural Decoration and Dating of the Church of Dayr Anbā Bišūy ('Red Monastery') near Sūhāǧ in Upper Egypt." *DOP*.

Seybold, C. 1912. *Severus ibn al Muqaffaʿ, alexandrinische Patriarchengeschichte von S. Marcus bis Michael I 61–767 nach der ältesten 1266 geschriebenen Hamburger Handschrift*. Veröffentlichungen aus der Hamburger Stadtbibliothek 3. Hamburg: Lucas Gräfe.

Shore, A.F. 1979. "Extracts of Besa's Life of Shenoute in Sahidic." *Journal of Egyptian Archaeology* 65, pp. 134–39, pls. 24, 25.

Shoucri, MARK VIII. 1991. In *The Coptic Encyclopedia*, ed. Aziz S. Atiya, vol. x, pp. 1538b–1539a. New York, N.Y.: Macmillan.

Sicard, C. 1982. *Oeuvres* I–III. Edited by M. Martin, Bibliothèque d'étude, 83–85. Cairo: IFAO.

Skálová, Z., and G. Gabra. 2003, 2006. *The Icons of the Nile Valley*. Cairo: Longman.

Stauffer, A. 1992. "Une soierie 'aux amazones' du Musée Gustav Lübcke à Hamm: À propos de la diffusion des cartons pour la production des soies figurées aux VIIe/Xe siècles." *Bulletin du centre international d'études de textiles anciens* 70, pp. 45–52.

Stern, L. 1878. "Sahidische Inschriften an alten denmälern." *Zeitschrift für ägyptische Sprache und Altertumskunde* 16, 1878: 9–28, esp. 26ff.

Stollmayer, I. 1999. "Spätantike Trikonchoskirchen – Ein Baukonzept?." *Jahrbuch für Antike und Christentum* 42, pp. 116–57.

al-Suryani, S. 1986. *Tartib al-biʿa ʿan makhtutat al-batriarkyia bi-Misr wa-l-Askandariya wa makhtutat al-adyura wa-l-kanaʾis*. 3 vols. Cairo.

————. and B. Habib. 1990. *Guide to Ancient Coptic Churches and Monasteries in Upper Egypt*. Cairo: Institute of Coptic Studies.

Swanson, M. 2005. "St. Shenoute in Seventeenth-Century Dress: Arabic Christian Preaching in *Paris, BN ar. 4761*." *Coptica* 4, pp. 27–42.

————. 2006. "Common Wisdom: Luqman the Wise in a Collection of Coptic Orthodox Homilies." *Currents in Theology and Mission* 33, pp. 246–52.

Taft, R. 1986. *The Liturgy of Hours in East and West*. Collegeville, Minn.: Liturgical Press.

Takla, H.N. 1996–1997. "The Sahidic Book of Tobit." *Bulletin of Saint Shenouda the Archimandrite Coptic Society* 3, pp. 1–25.

————. 2005. "The Library of the Monastery of St. Shenouda the Archimandrite." *Coptica* 4, pp. 43–51.

———. 2006. "Christianity in Sohag Symposium (January 31–February 5, 2006)." *St. Shenouda Coptic Quarterly* 2(3), pp. 3–30.

Thissen, H.-J. 1992–1993. "Zur Begegnung von Christentum und 'Heidentum'; Schenute und Gessios." *Enchoria* 19/20, pp. 155–64.

———. 2001. *Des Niloten Horapollon Hieroglyphenbuch: Vol. 1, Text und Übersetzung.* Archiv für Papyrusforschung und verwandte Gebiete 6. Munich: K.G. Saur.

Thomas, T.K. 1989. "An Introduction to the Sculpture of Late Roman and Early Byzantine Egypt." In *Beyond the Pharaohs: Egypt and the Copts in the Second to Seventh Centuries A.D*, ed. F.D. Friedman, pp. 54–64. Providence, R.I.: Museum of Art, Rhode Island School of Design.

———. 2000. *Late Antique Egyptian Funerary Sculpture: Images for this World and the Next.* Princeton, N.J.: Princeton University Press.

Thompson, H. 1922. "Dioscorus and Shenute." In *Receuil d'études égyptologiques dédiées à la mémoire de J.F. Champollion à l'occasion du centenaire de la lettre à M. Dacier relative à l'alphabet des hiéroglyphes phonétiques lue à l'Académie des inscriptions et belles-lettres le 27 septembre 1822*, pp. 367–76. Bibliothèque de l'École des hautes Études. Sciences historiques et philologiques 234. Paris: Librairie ancienne Honoré Champion, Édouard Champion.

Tidda, F. 2001. "Terminologia della luce e battesimo nelle iscrizioni greche cristiane." In *Vetera Christianorum* 38, pp. 103–24.

Till, W. C. 1933. "Ein Sahidisches Baruchfragment." *Le Muséon* 46, pp. 35–41.

———. 1934. *Koptische Pergamente Theologischen Inhalts.* Mitteilungen aus der Papyrussamlung Nationalbibliothek in Wien, n.s. 2, Vienna: Oesterreichische Staatsdruckerei.

———. 1935. *Koptische Heiligen und Martyrerlegenden.* Orientalia Christiana Analecta 102. Rome: Pontificium Institutum Orientalium Studiorum.

———. 1937. "Sahidische Fragmente des Alten Testaments." *Le Muséon* 50, pp. 175–237.

———. 1939. "Kleine Koptische Bibelfragmente." *Biblica* 20, pp. 241–63, 381–86.

———. 1951. *Die Arzneikunde der Kopten.* Berlin: Akademie.

Timbie, J. 1995. "The Relics of Apa Shenoute and the Use of qalassa in BN Copte 68." In *Studies in the Christian East in Memory of Mirrit Boutros Ghali,* Publications of the Society for Coptic Archaeology 1, ed. L.S.B. MacCoull, pp. 89–93. Washington, D.C.: Society for Coptic Archaeology.

———. 1998. "A Liturgical Procession in the Desert of Apa Shenoute." In *Pilgrimage and Holy Space in late antique Egypt*, Religions in the Graeco-Roman World 134, ed. David Frankfurter, pp. 415–41. Leiden: E.J. Brill.

———. 2005. "The State of Research on the Career of Shenoute in 2004." *CopticaJ* 4, pp. 52–74.

Timm, S. 1984–1992. *Das christlich-koptische Ägypten in arabischer Zeit.* 6 vols. Wiesbaden: L. Reichert.

Török, L. 1970. "Notes on the Chronology of late antique Stone Sculpture in Egypt." In *Coptic Studies, Acts of the Third International Congress of Coptic Studies*

Warsaw, 20–25 August 1984, ed. W. Godlewski, pp. 437–84. Varsovie: PWN-Editions Scientifiques de Pologne.

———. 1993. *Coptic Antiquities II*. Bibliotheca Archaeologica 12. Rome: "L'Erma" di Bretschneider.

———. 2005a. *After the Pharaohs. Treasures of Coptic Art from Egyptian Collections*. Budapest: Museum of Fine Arts.

———. 2005b. *Transfigurations of Hellenism. Aspects of Late Antique Art in Egypt A.D. 250–700*. Probleme der Ägyptologie 23. Leiden: E.J. Brill.

Troupeau, G. 1972–1974. *Catalogue des manuscrits arabes*. Première partie: *Manuscrits chrétiens*. 2 vols. Paris: Bibliothèque nationale.

Urbaniak-Walczak, K. 2004. "'Hermeneiai'-Fragmente oder den 'Hermeneiai' verwandte Texte aus Deir el-Naqlun (Faijum)." In *Coptic Studies on the Threshold of a New Millennium: Proceedings of the Seventh International Congress of Coptic Studies, Leiden, 27 August–2 September 2000*, eds. M. Immerzeel and J. van der Vliet, vol.1, pp. 647–63. Leuven: Uitgeverij Peeters en Dep. Oosterse Studies.

Vansleb [J.M. Wansleben]. 1677. *Nouvelle relation en forme de journal d'un voyage fait en Egypte . . . en 1672 & 1673*. Paris: Estienne Michallet.

———. 1677. *Histoire de l'Eglise d' Alexandria*. Paris.

Vaschalde, A. 1919–1933. "Ce qui a été publié des versions coptes de la Bible." *Revue biblique* 28, pp. 220–43, 513–31; 29, pp. 91–106, 241–58; 30, pp. 237–46; 31, pp. 81–88, 234–58; in *Le Muséon* 43, pp. 409–31; 45, pp. 117–56; 46, pp. 299–313.

Veilleux, A. 1968. *La liturgie dans le cénobitisme pachômien au quatrième siècle*. Studia Anselmiana 57. Rome: Herder.

———. 1980–1982. *Pachomian Koinonia*. 3 vols. Cistercian Studies Series 45–47. Kalamazoo, Mich.: Cistercian Publications.

Villecourt, L. 1925. "Les Observances liturgiques et la discipline du jeûne dans l'Église copte (Ch. xvi–xix de la Lampe des Ténèbres)." *Le Muséon* 38, pp. 261–320.

Vinzent, M. 1998. "Das 'heidnische' Ägypten im 5. Jahrhundert." In *Heiden und Christen im 5. Jahrhundert*, eds. J. van Oort and D. Wyrwa, pp. 32–65. Leuven: Peeters.

Vivian, T. 2005. "'Those Whom God Made Famous throughout the World': Holy Men from Middle and Lower Egypt in the Writings of Saint Shenoute the Great." *Coptica* 4, pp. 75–85.

van der Vliet, J. 1993. "Spätantikes Heidentum in Ägypten im Spiegel der koptischen Literatur." In *Begegnung von Heidentum und Christentum im spätantiken Ägypten*. Riggisberg: Riggisberger Berichte 1, 99–130.

———. Forthcoming. "Parerga: Notes on Christian Inscriptions from Egypt and Nubia." *Zeitschrift für Papyrologie und Epigraphik*.

Wagner, G. 1982. "Deux prières chrétiennes du Wadi Bir el-Aïn." *BIFAO* 82, pp. 349–54.

Weiss, H.F. 1969–1970. "Zur Christologie des Schenute von Atripe." *BSAC* 20, pp. 177–209.

Wessely, C. 1901–1923. *Studien zur Palaeographie und Papyruskunde*, 1–23. Leipzig: Avenarius.

———. 1908. *Sahidische-griechische Psalmenfragmente*. Vienna: Hölder

———. 1909–1917. *Griechische und koptische Texte theologischen Inhalts*. 5 vols. Studien zur Palaeographie und Papyruskunde 9, 11, 12, 15, 18. Leipzig: Verlag H. Haessel Nachfolger.

———. 1913. *Die Wiener handschrift der sahidische Acta Apostolorum*. Vienna: Hölder.

———. 1914. *Sahidische Papyrusfragmente der paulinischen briefe*. Vienna: Hölder.

Westendorf, W. 1999. *Handbuch der altägyptischen Medizin*. Handbuch der Orientalistick 36.1. Leiden: Brill.

Who Was Who. Vol 3: *1929–1940*. London: A. & C. Black, 1941 (reprinted 1947).

Wiesmann, H. 1952. *Sinuthii Archimandritae Vita et Opera Omnia*. CSCO 108; Scriptores Coptici 12. Louvain. Imprimerie Orientaliste, L. Durbecq.

Wietheger, C. 1992. *Das Jeremias-Kloster zu Saqqara unter besonderer Berücksichtigung der Inschriften*. Arbeiten zum spätantiken und koptischen Ägypten 1. Altenberge: Oros.

Wilfong, T.G. 2002. *Women of Jeme: Lives in a Coptic Town in late antique Egypt*. Ann Arbor, Mich.: University of Michigan Press.

Wipszycka, E. 1991. "Textiles, Coptic: Organization of Production." In *The Coptic Encyclopedia*, ed. A.S. Atiya, vol. 7, pp. 2218–21. New York, N.Y.: Macmillan.

Woide, C.G. 1799. *Appendix ad Editionem Novi Testamenti Graeci e Codice MS. Alexandrino a Carolo Godofredo Woide Descripti*, ed. Henry Ford. Oxford: Clarendon Press.

Worrell, W. 1931. *The Proverbs of Solomon in Sahidic Coptic, According to the Chicago Manuscript*. Oriental Institute Publications 12. Chicago, Ill.: University of Chicago Press.

Wulff, O., and F.W. Volbach. 1926. *Spätantike und koptische Stoffe aus ägyptischen Grabfunden in den Staatlichen Museen*. Berlin: Wasmuth.

Young, D.W. 1969. "'Precept': A Study in Coptic Terminology." *Orientalia* n.s. 38, pp. 505–19.

———. 1970. "The Milieu of Nag Hammadi: Some Historical Considerations." *Vigiliae Christianae* 24, pp. 127–37.

———. 1993. *Coptic Manuscripts from the White Monastery: Works of Shenute*. Mitteilungen aus der Papyrussammlung der Österreichischen Nationalbibliothek n.s. 22. Vienna: Hollinek.

Youssef, Y.N. 1994. "Nicodème auteur des psalies." *Orientalia Christiana Periodica* 60, pp. 625–33.

———. 1998. "Recherches d'hymnographie copte: Nicodème et Sarkis." *Orientalia Christiana Periodica* 64, pp. 383–402.

———. 1997. "Une relecture des théotokies coptes." *BSAC* 36, pp. 157–70.

———. 1998. "Les textes en dialecte sahidique du Ms. 106 Lit., Bibliothèque Patriarcale au Caire." *BSAC* 37, pp. 121–33.

———. 2003a. "Consecration of the Myron at Saint Macarius (MS 106 Lit.)." *Coptica* 2, pp. 106–21.

———. 2003b. "The Icon Writer Hanna al-Armani According to an Ottoman Legal Document." *Annales Islamologiques* 37, pp. 443–48.

Zanetti, U. 1984. "Premières recherches sur les lectionnaires coptes." *Ephemerides Liturgicae* 98, pp. 3–34.

————. 1985. *Les lectionnaires coptes annuels: Basse-Égypte.* Publications de l'Institut Orientaliste de Louvain 33. Louvain-la-Neuve: Institut Orientaliste.

————. 1990. "La distribution des psaumes dans l'horologion copte." *Orientalia Christiana Periodica* 56, pp. 323–69.

————. 1992. "Abû-l-Barakât et les lectionnaires de Haute-Égypte." In *Actes du IV*e *Congrès Copte. Louvain-la-Neuve, 5 – 10 septembre 1988.* Vol. 2: *De la linguistique au gnosticisme*, Publications de l'Institut Orientaliste de Louvain 41, eds. M. Rassart-Debergh and J. Ries, pp. 450–62. Louvain-la-Neuve: Institut Orientaliste.

————. 1994. "Is the Ethiopian Holy Week Service Translated from Sahidic? Towards a Study of the *Gebra Hemâmât.*" In *Proceedings of the Eleventh International Conference of Ethiopian Studies, Addis Ababa, 1–6 April 1991*, eds. B. Zewde, R. Pankhurst, and T. Beyene, vol. 1, pp. 765–83. Addis Ababa: Institute of Ethiopian Studies, Addis Ababa University.

————. 1995. "Un index liturgique du Monastère Blanc." In *Christianisme d'Égypte*, Cahiers de la bibliothèque copte 9, pp. 55–75. Paris and Louvain: Peeters.

————. 1996. "Les lectionnaires coptes," with appendix "Les lectionnaires arabes." In *La Lecture liturgique des Épîtres catholiques dans l'Église ancienne*, Histoire du texte biblique 1, eds. C.-B. Amphoux and J.-P. Bouhot, pp. 141–96. Lausanne: Éditions du Zèbre.

Zoega, G. 1810. *Catalogus codicum copticorum manu scriptorum qui in museo Borgiano velitris adservantur.* Rome: Sacra Congregatio de Propaganda Fide. Reprinted Leipzig: J. C. Hinrichs'sche Buchhandlung, 1903.

Zuntz, D. 1932. "Koptische Grabstelen: Ihre zeitliche und örtliche Einordnung." *Mitteilungen des Deutschen Instituts für Ägyptische Altertumskunde in Kairo* 2, pp. 22–38.